Birth of the Bill of Rights

Birth of the Bill of Rights

Encyclopedia of the Antifederalists

VOLUME TWO: MAJOR WRITINGS

Jon L. Wakelyn

GREENWOOD PRESS

Westport, Connecticut • London

Library of Congress Cataloging-in-Publication Data

Wakelyn, Jon L.
  Birth of the Bill of Rights : encyclopedia of the Antifederalists / Jon L. Wakelyn.
    p.   cm.
  Includes bibliographical references and index.
  ISBN 0–313–31739–9 (set : alk. paper) — ISBN 0–313–33194–4 (v.1 : alk. paper) —
  ISBN 0–313–33195–2 (v.2 : alk. paper)
  1. Statesmen—United States—Biography.   2. Politicians—United States—Biography.
3. Revolutionaries—United States—Biography.   4. United States—Politics and government—To
1775—Sources.   5. United States—Politics and government—1775–1783—Sources.   6. United
States—Politics and government—1783–1809—Sources.   7. Constitutional history—United
States—Sources.   8. Political science—United States—History—18th century—Sources.
9. Political science—United States—History—19th century—Sources.   10. Federal
government—United States—History—Sources.   I. Title.
  E302.5.W35   2004
  973.4'092'2—dc22   2004047546
  [B]

British Library Cataloguing in Publication Data is available.

Library of Congress Catalog Card Number: 2004047546
ISBN: 0–313–31739–9 (set)
      0–313–33194–4 (vol. 1)
      0–313–33195–2 (vol. 2)

First published in 2004

Greenwood Press, 88 Post Road West, Westport, CT 06881
An imprint of Greenwood Publishing Group, Inc.
www.greenwood.com

Printed in the United States of America

∞™

The paper used in this book complies with the
Permanent Paper Standard issued by the National
Information Standards Organization (Z39.48–1984).

10 9 8 7 6 5 4 3 2 1

Contents

Introduction

This is a companion volume to *Birth of the Bill of Rights: Biographies*. Those leaders' writings and speeches in the state ratification conventions and elsewhere (including pamphlets, private and public letters, newspaper accounts, and even notes in their personal papers) are integral to their reasons for opposing ratification of the federal Constitution proposed in the autumn of 1787. This separate volume should give the reader insight into their activities and arguments during the debates over ratification of the federal Constitution. Those works, which remain the best arguments against the Constitution, offered alternatives to the design of the early governmental system and attempted to protect by codification the rights of citizens. In addition, they reveal much about the foundations of governance, the political values, and the desire for protection of personal freedom in this country. Though any collection is only a partial rendering of the arguments of those leaders, this volume reproduces some of the best works of those leaders. It is the largest single-volume collection of their works.

A few words are necessary to set these efforts into the context of debate and writing in those times. As authors the Antifederalists did not sign their own names to much of their written work. This is because some literally feared for their safety when attacking the values and integrity of their opponents. Instead, they adopted the names of ancient Greek and Latin great political philosophers and leaders, such as Cato and Brutus, perhaps to lend dignity to their own utterances. This has caused some difficulty in identifying who exactly wrote the articles and pamphlets. For example, the famous *Letters of a Federal Farmer*, long thought to have been the work of the Virginian Richard Henry Lee, now is considered by some scholars to have been written by the New Yorker Melancton Smith. Exact proof, however, is lacking, so other efforts of Lee and Smith are included and the *Letters* is left out of this volume. In this book, the authors are identified, and their noms de plume are also included.

Many of those authors, of both written and spoken works, had excellent classical training, especially in political theory. Therefore, they often quoted from ancient writers of history and theory, the insights on human nature found in Shakespeare, and modern theorists like Montesquieu. (When pertinent I have left in their quotes and identified the sources. Because Montesquieu's idea

of a small republic dominated their works, it has not been considered necessary to note him again and again.) Antifederalists used the experiences of past
governments to argue their own positions and to warn about political mistakes
in the proposed Constitution. Also, as students of human nature, they drew
on those great works of early political theory that discussed personal motiva-
tion for power and the corruption of power to buttress their arguments against
the Constitution.

As to rhetorical devices and flourishes in oral discourse and debate, many of
the Antifederalists were masters at their craft. Some convention orators such as
George Clinton, Patrick Henry, and George Mason chose phrases that sound
a bit stilted to our modern ear. To their own followers their utterances were
deemed most persuasive. At times loquacious, they readily and wittily took advantage of Federalist mistakes. A number of Antifederalist debaters, especially
in North Carolina, used the rhetorical device of humility—maintaining a lack
of experience in public speaking—and then spoke eloquently. Perhaps the pose
of the small farmer against the rich merchant enhanced their sense of grievance. See Christopher Grasso's *A Speaking Aristocracy* on the importance of
the growth of a public audience that demanded to hear from people of their
own class as often as the educated elite. In their debate rhetoric and tactics,
Antifederalists used class bias (even though most of them were middle and
upper middle class). Their arguments also reached near pathological frenzy over
the right to free speech and a free press. Perhaps this was why, when so many
of their speeches also appeared in what few newspapers they controlled, the
Antifederalists also demanded a free and open press.

Despite overwhelming control of the newspapers by the Federalists, Antifederalist speeches and writings circulated in the public, thanks to the reprinting of speeches, letters, and pamphlets in their partisan press. They also wrote
to one another across state lines and sent papers and articles to their fellow debaters and writers. In this way, the very best of the Antifederalists' writings and
speeches were made available to their leaders and often appeared in the debates
and writings of others. (When possible I will share with the reader Saul Cornell's excellent analysis of the reprinting of major Antifederalist pamphlets and
addresses.) One sees, then, mutual influence as well as close political ties in the
repetition of their ideas and arguments against the proposed government. To
read again their efforts in the various states' debates is perhaps to understand
how desperate the Antifederalists were to stop the tide of Federalist ascendancy
against their perceived majority.

Works of the Antifederalists are available in the printed proceedings and
newspaper reports of the state convention debates. Unfortunately, not all of
the states printed the debates. Stephen Elliot in the 1830s collected many of
the debates, and future scholars are indebted to him. Also, the Library of Congress has an excellent collection of original pamphlets and other Antifederalist
writings. I thank again David Kelley for assisting me in negotiating the byzan-
tine conditions of the Library's Rare Book Room. The law library at the Library of Congress also has a major collection of Antifederalist works. Historians
have from time to time printed some of the best of their efforts. In older biographies, such as those on George Mason, Elbridge Gerry, Richard Henry
Lee, and Samuel Adams, many letters and speeches are reproduced. New Yorker

John Lamb's papers at the New York Historical Society contain many letters from leading Antifederalists throughout the nation and reveal the many contacts those leaders had in other states. For other correspondence, papers, and printings of their works, the curious reader should consult G. Thomas Tanselle (ed.), *Guide to the Study of United States Imprints.*

Recent major collections of the writings and speeches of the Antifederalists have assisted this work immensely. With the aid of those editions, one is able to make a clear comparison with the earliest published efforts. Herbert Storing, in his multivolume reprinting of major Antifederalist works, has also added to the identification of those leaders' writings and placed them into the context of those times. Likewise, Bernard Bailyn's *Debates on the Constitution* in two volumes reprint a number of important Antifederalist publications. The multivolume edition of the *Documentary History of the Ratification Conventions* has provided scholars the wherewithal to read much of what those leaders wrote and said. (The reader is referred to that collection for much annotated information on the settings for action and the various issues concerning the Antifederalists.) This collection of their works is indebted especially to that marvelous research housed at the University of Wisconsin. Without the pioneering modern efforts of Merrill Jensen and his multitude of students, there could be little further work on the Antifederalists' accomplishments.

The major early effort to collect the debates and proceedings of the state ratification conventions begins with Jonathan Elliot's five-volume effort from the 1830s. To supplement Elliot's work, there are many original printings of the proceedings, debates, and minutes (some incomplete) of the various state conventions. For Pennsylvania see Paul L. Ford, *The Origins, Purpose, and Result of the Harrisburg Convention* (1890); and John B. McMaster and Frederick D. Stone (eds.), *Pennsylvania and the Federal Constitution* (1888). For Delaware see James M. Tunnell, *Ratification of the Federal Constitution by the State of Delaware* (1944). For New Jersey see *Minutes of the Convention of the State of New Jersey* (1787). For Georgia see Julia M. Bland (ed.), *Georgia and the Federal Constitution: Proceedings of the State Constitutional Convention* (1937). For Connecticut see Charles J. Hoadley and Leonard W. Labaree, *Public Records of the State of Connecticut* (1894). For Massachusetts see *Debates, Resolutions, and Other Proceedings of the Convention of the Commonwealth of Massachusetts* (1788); and Bradford K. Peirce (ed.), *Debates and Proceedings in the Convention of the Commonwealth of Massachusetts, Held in the Year 1788* (1856). Valuable for New Hampshire, where no proceedings were preserved, is Joseph B. Walker, *A History of the New Hampshire Convention* (1888). Inadequate but useful for Rhode Island is Theodore Foster (ed.), *The Minutes of the Rhode Island Convention of 1790* (1828). Also incomplete are the minutes from the convention of South Carolina, but see R. Haswell (comp.), *Debates Which Arouse in the House of Representatives of South Carolina, on the Constitution* (1788). For Virginia see Worthington C. Ford (ed.), *The Federal Constitution in Virginia, 1787–88* (1903); and David Robertson (ed.), *Debates and Other Proceedings in the Convention of Virginia* (3 vols., 1805). Most useful among the many printings on New York is Francis Childs, *Debates and Proceedings of the Convention of the State of New York* (1788). And for North Carolina, see Robert Ferguson, *The Hillsborough Convention* (1789).

This volume of Antifederalist works is organized so as to guide the interested reader chronologically through the Antifederalists' public and private opinions on the Constitution. It is set up by each state according to the first date when its ratification convention met. (Rhode Island only held a convention in 1790, after the federal government had been set in motion. However, its state legislature voted not to hold a convention but to have a popular referendum on the Constitution, and that has determined its place in this volume.) Arguments in the form of letters, speeches, and newspaper printings began in each state shortly after the Philadelphia Convention had ended in September 1787 and the Continental Congress had directed each state to hold a ratification convention. Those first efforts included here preceded the major debates within each state. The debates of each of the original thirteen states (this includes the Maine region of Massachusetts, Kentuckians from Virginia, and Tennesseans from North Carolina) are covered in this book. Concerned leaders, within and outside of the convention, also used the newspaper press and pamphlets to influence the proceedings in their states and others. Letters and writings produced after each state's convention reflected on the outcome and attempted to influence the proceedings of other ongoing state conventions. Thus, the arrangement of these leaders' works by chronology of state conventions gives the reader a sequential development of their arguments. This volume concludes with some afterthoughts published some years later by Antifederalist leaders.

In order to assist the reader, short, descriptive endnotes and occasional footnotes are given for each of the works included. The reader will be referred to the essays in the *Biographies* to understand pertinent parts of the Antifederalists' life stories, including their practical and theoretical political training as well as their social and business activities. Also, there will be some brief comment on their concerns about the Constitution in the endnotes to each work included in this volume. (The reader is referred to the introduction to the *Biographies* for more information on the issues that concerned the Antifederalists and how they discussed them.)

With this volume of the Antifederalists' works, the reader should come to appreciate the enormous contribution those leaders made to the making of civil government, as well as to the legal protection of individual rights, to the formation of the United States of America.

NOTE

I have at times used the texts' earliest spelling, punctuation, and grammar. In his second edition of 1836 Jonathan Elliot modernized the spelling and lettering of a number of these texts, and I have followed his example. In all cases I have endeavored to find and use the original texts, and have compared them with many later printings. As with all who have worked on these texts, I am grateful to the spate of recent printings of them. Full acknowledgment has been given to those many reproductions of these texts. Editorial changes, updating of language, and clarity of expression, aside from the work of Elliot, are my own. I have not followed the editorial efforts of these many modern editions of these works, but instead have sought my own clarity on what the original authors desired to convey to their readers and auditors.

1
Pennsylvania

November 20, 1787–December 15, 1787

Ratification #2, December 12, 1787

In favor 46–23

David Redick, Letter to William Irvine, *September 24, 1787*

The new plan of government proposed by the convention has made a bustle in the city and its vicinity, all people, almost, are for Swallowing it down at once without examining its tendencies.

I have thought it unsafe within the wind of hurricane to utter a Sylable about it: but to you Sir I may venture to Say that in my opinion the day on which we adopt the present proposed plan of government, from that moment we may Justly date the loss of American liberty. perhaps my fears hath contributed principlely to this opinion. I will change the moment that I See better. My dear Sir why is not the liberty of the press provided for? why will the Congress have power to alter the plan or mode of chusing Representatives? why will they have power to lay direct Taxes? why will they have power to keep Standing Armies in time of peace? why will they have power to make laws in direct contradiction to the forms of government established in the Several States? why will they have power to collect by law ten Dollars for ever German or Irishman which may come to Settle in America? why is the Trial by Jury destroyed in Civil causes before Congress? and above all I cannot imagine why the people in this city are So verry anxious to have it adopted instantly before it can be digested or deliberatly considered. If you were only here to See and hear those people, to observe the means they are using to effect this purpose, to hear the tories declare they will draw their Sword in its defence, to See the quaquers runing about Signing declarations and Petitions in favor of it befor the have time to examine it, to See Gentlemen runing into the Country and neibouring towns haranguing the Rabble. I Say were you to See and hear these things as I do you would Say, with me that: the very Soul of confidence itself ought to change into distrust. If this government be a good one or even a tollorable one the Necessities and the good Sense of America will lead us to adopt it. if otherwise give us time and it will be amended and then adopted, but I think the measures pursued here is a Strong evidence that these people know it will not bear an examination and therefor wishes to adopt it first and consider it afterward. I hope Congress will be very deliberate and digest it thoroughly before they Send it recommended to the States. I Sincerely hope that Such Gentlemen as were Members of Convention, and who have Seats in Congress may not be considered as verry proper Judges of their own Works.

David Redick was a Philadelphia lawyer with some political experience (see David Redick entry in *Biographies*). His letter to Irvine is an early attack on the speed with which the Philadelphia convention concluded its deliberations, making for an unsystematic government. Redick also addressed the dangers of speaking out against the Federalist majority, and he called for an amendment to the proposed Constitution to protect free speech. He finished his remarks with worries over Federalist anti-democratic policies.

REFERENCES

Irvine Papers, Pennsylvania Historical Society; Merrill Jensen and John P. Kaminski (eds.), *The Documentary History of the Ratification of the Constitution* (Madison: State Historical Society of Wisconsin, 1976), vol. 2.

Samuel Bryan ("Centinel"), I,
October 5, 1787

TO THE FREEMEN OF PENNSYLVANIA

Friends, Countrymen and *Fellow Citizens*, Permit one of yourselves to put you in mind of certain *liberties* and *privileges* secured to you by the constitution of this commonwealth, and to beg your serious attention to his uninterested opinion upon the plan of federal government submitted to your consideration, before you surrender these great and valuable privileges up forever. Your present frame of government, secures you to a right to hold yourselves, houses, papers and possessions free from search and seizure, and therefore warrants granted without oaths or affirmations first made, affording sufficient foundation for them, whereby any officer or messenger may be commanded or required to search your houses or seize your persons or property, not particularly described in such warrant, shall not be granted. Your constitution further provides "that in controversies respecting property, and in suits between man and man, the parties have a right *to trial by jury, which ought to be held sacred.*" It also provides and declares, "*that the people have a right of* FREEDOM OF SPEECH, *and of* WRITING *and* PUBLISHING *their sentiments, therefore* THE FREEDOM OF THE PRESS OUGHT NOT TO BE RESTRAINED." The constitution of Pennsylvania is *yet* in existence, *as yet* you have the right to *freedom of speech*, and of *publishing your sentiments.* How long those rights will appertain to you, you yourselves are called upon to say, whether your *houses* shall continue to be your *castles*; whether your *papers*, your *persons* and your *property*, are to be held sacred and free from *general warrants*, you are now to determine. Whether the *trial by jury* is to continue as your birth-right, the freemen of Pennsylvania, nay, of all America, are now called upon to declare.

Without presuming upon my own judgement, I cannot think it an unwarrantable presumption to offer my private opinion, and call upon others for their's; and if I use my pen with the boldness of a freeman, it is because I know that *the liberty of the press yet remains unviolated*, and *juries yet are judges.*

The late Convention have submitted to your consideration a plan of a new federal government—The subject is highly interesting to your future welfare—Whether it be calculated to promote the great ends of civil society, *viz.* the happiness and prosperity of the community; it behoves you well to consider, uninfluenced by the authority of names. Instead of that frenzy of enthusiasm, that has actuated the citizens of Philadelphia, in their approbation of the proposed plan, before it was possible that it could be the result of a rational investigation into its principles; it ought to be dispassionately and deliberately examined, and its own intrinsic merit the only criterion of your patronage. If ever free and unbiassed discussion was proper or necessary, it is on such an occasion.—All the blessings of liberty and the dearest privileges of freemen, are now at stake and dependent on your present conduct. Those who are competent to the task of developing the principles of government, ought to be encouraged to come forward, and thereby the better enable the people to make a proper judgment; for the science of government is so abstruse, that few are able to judge for themselves; without such assistance the people are too apt to yield an implicit assent to the opinions of those characters, whose abilities are held in the highest esteem, and to those in whose integrity and patriotism they can confide; not considering that the love of domination is generally in proportion to talents, abilities, and superior acquirements; and that the men of the greatest purity of intention may be made instruments of despotism in the hands of the *artful and designing.* If it were not for the stability and attachment which time and habit gives to forms of government, it would be in the power of the enlightened and aspiring few, if they should combine, at any time to destroy the best establishments, and even make the people the instruments of their own subjugation.

The late revolution having effaced in a great measure all former habits, and the present institutions are so recent, that their exists not that great reluctance to innovation, so remarkable in old communities, and which accords with reason, for the most comprehensive mind cannot foresee the full operation of material changes on civil polity; it is the genius of the common law to resist innovation.

The wealthy and ambitious, who in every community think they have a right to lord it over their fellow creatures, have availed themselves, very successfully, of this favorable disposition; for the people thus unsettled in their sentiments, have been prepared to accede to any extreme of government; all the distresses and difficulties they experience, proceeding from various causes, have been ascribed to the impotency of the present confederation, and thence they have been led to expect full relief from the adoption of the proposed system of government; and in the other event, immediately ruin and annihilation as a nation. These characters flatter themselves that they have lulled all distrust and jealousy of their new plan, by gaining the concurrence of the two men in whom America has the highest confidence, and now triumphantly exult in the completion of their long meditated schemes of power and aggrandisement. I would be very far from insinuating that the two illustrious personages alluded to, have not the welfare of their country at heart; but that the unsuspecting goodness and zeal of the one, has been imposed on, in a subject of which he must be necessarily inexperienced, from his other arduous engagements; and that the weakness and indecision attendant on old age, has been practised on in the other.

I am fearful that the principles of government inculcated in Mr. Adams's treatise, and enforced in the numerous essays and paragraphs in the newspapers, have misled some well designing members of the late Convention.—But it will appear in the sequel, that the construction of the proposed plan of government is infinitely more extravagant.[1]

I have been anxiously expecting that some enlightened patriot would, ere this, have taken up the pen to expose the futility, and counteract the baneful tendency of such principles. Mr. Adams's *sine qua non* of a good government is three balancing powers, whose repelling qualities are to produce an equilibrium of interests, and thereby promote the happiness of the whole community. He asserts that the administrators of every government, will ever be actuated by views of private interest and ambition, to the prejudice of the public good; that therefore the only effectual method to secure the rights of the people and promote their welfare, is to create an opposition of interests between the members of two distinct bodies, in the exercise of the powers of government, and balanced by those of a third. This hypothesis supposes human wisdom competent to the task of instituting three co-equal orders in government, and a corresponding weight in the community to enable them respectively to exercise their several parts, and whose views and interests should be so distinct as to prevent a coalition of any two of them for the destruction of the third. Mr. Adams, although he has traced the constitution of every form of government that ever existed, as far as history affords materials, has not been able to adduce a single instance of such a government; he indeed says that the British constitution is such in theory, but this is rather a confirmation that his principles are chimerical and not to be reduced to practice. If such an organization of power were practicable, how long would it continue? not a day—for there is so great a disparity in the talents, wisdom and industry of mankind, that the scale would presently preponderate to one or the other body, and with every accession of power the means of further increase would be greatly extended. The state of society in England is much more favorable to such a scheme of government than that of America. There they have a powerful hereditary nobility, and real distinctions of rank and interests; but even there, for want of that perfect equallity of power and distinction of interests, in the three orders of government, they exist but in name; the only operative and efficient check, upon the conduct of administration, is the sense of the people at large.

Suppose a government could be formed and supported on such principles, would it answer the great purposes of civil society; If the administrators of every government are actuated by views of private interest and ambition, how is the welfare and happiness of the community to be the result of such jarring adverse interests?

Therefore, as different orders in government will not produce the good of the whole, we must recur to other principles. I believe it will be found that the form of government, which holds those entrusted with power, in the greatest responsibility to their constituents, the best calculated for freemen. A republican, or free government, can only exist where the body of the people are virtuous, and where property is pretty equally divided, in such a government the people are the sovereign and their sense or opinion is the criterion of every public measure; for when this ceases to be the case, the nature of the government is changed, and an aristocracy, monarchy or despotism will rise on its ruin. The highest responsibility is to be attained, in a simple struction of government, for the great body of the people never steadily attend to the operations of government, and for want of due information are liable to be imposed on.—If you complicate the plan by various orders, the people will be perplexed and divided in their sentiments about the source of abuses or misconduct, some will impute it to the senate, others to the house of representatives, and so on, that the interposition of the people may be rendered imperfect or perhaps wholly abortive. But if, imitating the constitution of Pennsylvania, you vest all the legislative power in one body of men (separating the executive and judicial) elected for a short period, and necessarily excluded by rotation from permanency, and guarded from precipitancy and surprise by delays imposed on its proceedings, you will create the most perfect responsibility, for then, whenever the people feel a grievance they cannot mistake the authors, and will apply the remedy with certainty and effect discarding them at the next election. This tie of responsibility will obviate all the dangers apprehended from a single legislature, and will the best secure the rights of the people.

Having premised thus much, I shall now proceed to the examination of the proposed plan of government, and I trust, shall make it appear to the meanest capacity, that it has none of the essential requisites of a free government; that it is neither founded on those balancing restraining powers, recommended by Mr. Adams and attempted in the British constitution, or possessed of that responsibility to its constituents, which, in my opinion, is the only effectual security for the liberties and happiness of the people; but on the contrary, that it is a most daring attempt to establish a despotic aristocracy among freemen, that the world has ever witnessed.

I shall previously consider the extent of the powers intended to be vested in Congress, before I examine the construction of the general government.

It will not be controverted that the legislative is the highest delegated power in government, and that all others are subordinate to it. The celebrated *Montesquieu* establishes it as a maxim, that legislation necessarily follows the power of taxation. By sect. 8, of the first article of the proposed plan of government, "the Congress are to have power to lay and collect taxes, duties, imposts and excises, to pay the debts and provide for the common defence and *general welfare* of the United States; but all duties, imposts and excises, shall be uniform throughout the United States." Now what can be more comprehensive than these words; not content by other sections of this plan, to grant all the great executive powers of a confederation, and a STANDING ARMY IN TIME OF PEACE, that grand engine of oppression, and moreover the absolute controul over the commerce of the United States and all external objects of revenue, such as unlimited imposts upon imports, &c.—they are to be vested with every species of *internal* taxation;—whatever taxes, duties and excises that they may deem requisite for the *general welfare*, may be imposed on the citizens of these states, levied by the officers of Congress, distributed through every district in America; and the collection would be enforced by the standing army, however grievous or improper they may be. The Congress may construe every purpose for which the state legislatures now lay taxes, to be for the *general welfare*, and thereby seize upon every object of revenue.

The judicial power by 1st sect. of article 3 "shall extend to all cases, in law and equity, arising under this constitution, the laws of the United States, and treaties made or which shall be made under their authority; to all cases affecting ambassadors, other public ministers and consuls; to all cases of admiralty and maritime jurisdiction, to controversies to which the United States shall be a party, to controversies between two or more states, between a state and citizens of another state, between citizens of different states, between citizens of the same state claiming lands under grants of different states, and between a state, or the citizens thereof, and foreign states, citizens or subjects."

The judicial power to be vested in one Supreme Court, and in such Inferior Courts as the Congress may from time to time ordain and establish.

The objects of jurisdiction recited above, are so numerous, and the shades of distinction between civil causes are often-times so slight, that it is more than probable that the state judicatories would be wholly superceded; for in contests about jurisdiction, the federal court, as the most powerful, would ever prevail. Every person acquainted with the history of the courts in England, knows by what ingenious sophisms they have, at different periods, extended the sphere of their jurisdiction over objects out of the line of their institution, and contrary to their very nature; courts of a criminal jurisdiction obtaining cognizance in civil causes.

To put the omnipotency of Congress over the state government and judicatories out of all doubt, the 6th article ordains that "this constitution and the laws of the United States which shall be made in pursuance thereof, and all treaties made, or which shall be made under the authority of the United States, shall be the *supreme law of the land*, and the judges in every state shall be bound thereby, any thing in the constitution or laws of any state to the contrary notwithstanding."

By these sections the all-prevailing power of taxation, and such extensive legislative and judicial powers are vested in the general government, as must in their operation, necessarily absorb the state legislatures and judicatories; and that such was in the contemplation of the framers of it, will appear from the provision made for such event, in another part of it; (but that, fearful of alarming the people by so great an innovation, they have suffered the forms of the separate governments to remain, as a blind.) By sect. 4th of the 1st article, "the times, places and manner of holding elections for senators and representatives, shall be prescribed in each state by the legislature thereof; *but the Congress may at any time, by law, make or alter such regulations, except as to the place of chusing senators.*" The plain construction of which is, that when the state legislatures drop out of sight, from the necessary operation of this government, then Congress are to provide for the election and appointment of representatives and senators.

If the foregoing be a just comment—if the United States are to be melted down into one empire, it becomes you to consider, whether such a government, however constructed, would be eligible in so extended a territory; and whether it would be practicable, consistent with freedom? It is the opinion of the greatest writers, that a very extensive country cannot be governed on democratical principles, on any other plan, than a confederation of a number of small republics, possessing all the powers of internal government, but united in the management of their foreign and general concerns.

It would not be difficult to prove, that any thing short of despotism, could not bind so great a country under one government; and that whatever plan you might, at the first setting out, establish, it would issue in a despotism.

If one general government could be instituted and maintained on principles of freedom, it would not be so competent to attend to the various local concerns and wants, of every particular district; as well as the peculiar governments, who are nearer the scene, and possessed of superior means of information, besides, if the business of the *whole* union is to be managed by one government, there would not be time. Do we not already see, that the inhabitants in a number of larger states, who are remote from the seat of government, are loudly complaining of the inconveniences and disadvantages they are subjected to on this account, and that, to enjoy the comforts of local government, they are separating into smaller divisions.

Having taken a review of the powers, I shall now examine the construction of the proposed general government.

Art. I. sect. I. "All legislative powers herein granted shall be vested in a Congress of the United States, which shall consist of a senate and house of representatives." By another section, the president (the principal executive officer) has a conditional controul over their proceedings.

Sect 2. "The house of representatives shall be composed of members chosen every second year, by the people of the several states. The number of representatives shall not exceed one for every 30,000 inhabitants."

The senate, the other constituent branch of the legislature, is formed by the legislature of each state appointing two senators, for the term of six years.

The executive power by Art. 2, Sec. 1. is to be vested in a president of the United States of America, elected for four years: Sec. 2. gives him "power, by and with the consent of the senate to make treaties, provided two thirds of the senators present concur; and he shall nominate, and by and with the advice and consent of the senate, shall appoint ambassadors, other public ministers and consuls, judges of the Supreme Court, and all other officers of the United States, whose appointments are not herein otherwise provided for, and which shall be established by law, &c." And by another section he has the absolute power of granting reprievs and pardons for treason and all other high crimes and misdemeanors, except in case of impeachment.

The foregoing are the outlines of the plan.

Thus we see, the house of representatives, are on the part of the people to balance the senate, who I suppose will be composed of the *better sort*, the *well born*, &c. The number of the representatives (being only one for every 30,000 inhabitants) appears to be too few, either to communicate the requisite information, of the wants, local circumstances and sentiments of so extensive an empire, or to prevent corruption and undue influence, in the exercise of such great powers; the term for which they are to be chosen, too long to preserve a due dependence and accountability to their constituents; and the mode and places of their election not sufficiently ascertained, for as Congress have the controul over both, they may govern the choice, by ordering the *representatives* of a *whole* state, to be *elected* in *one* place, and that too may be the most *inconvenient*.

The senate, the great efficient body in this plan of government, is constituted on the most unequal principles. The smallest state in the union has equal weight with the great states of Virginia, Massachusetts, or Pennsylvania.—The Senate, besides its legislative functions, has a very considerable share in the Executive; none of the principal appointments to office can be made without its advice and consent. The term and mode of its appointment, will lead to permanency; the members are chosen for six years, the mode is under the controul of Congress, and as there is no exclusion by rotation, they may be continued for life, which, from their extensive means of influence, would follow of course. The President, who would be a mere pageant of state, unless he coincides with the views of the Senate, would either become the head of the aristocratic junto in that body, or its minion; besides, their influence being the most predominant, could the best secure his re-election to office. And from his power of granting pardons, he might skreen from punishment the most treasonable attempts on the liberties of the people, when instigated by the Senate.

From this investigation into the organization of this government, it appears that it is devoid of all responsibility or accountability to the great body of the people, and that so far from being a regular balanced government, it would be in practice a *permanent* ARISTOCRACY.

The framers of it; actuated by the true spirit of such a government, which ever abominates and suppresses all free enquiry and discussion, have made no provision for the *liberty of the press*, that grand *palladium of freedom*, and *scourge of tyrants*; but observed a total silence on that head. It is the opinion of some great writers, that if the liberty of the press, by an institution of religion, or otherwise, could be rendered *sacred*, even in *Turkey*, that despotism would fly before it. And it is worthy of remark, that there is no declaration of personal rights, premised in most free constitutions; and that trial by *jury* in *civil* cases is taken away; for what other construction can be put on the following, viz. Article III. Sect. 2d. "In all cases affecting ambassadors, other public ministers and consuls, and those in which a State shall be party, the Supreme Court shall have *original* jurisdiction. In all the other cases above mentioned, the Supreme Court shall have *appellate* jurisdiction, both as to *law and fact?*" It would be a novelty in jurisprudence, as well as evidently improper to allow an appeal from the verdict of a jury, on the matter of fact; therefore, it implies and allows of a dismission of the jury in civil cases, and especially when it is considered, that jury trial in criminal cases is expressly stipulated for, but not in civil cases.

But our situation is represented to be so *critically* dreadful, that, however reprehensible and exceptionable the proposed plan of government may be, there is no alternative, between the adoption of it and absolute ruin.—My fellow citizens, things are not at that crisis, it is the argument of tyrants; the present distracted state of Europe secures us from injury on that quarter, and as to domestic dissentions, we have not so much to fear from them, as to precipitate us into this form of government, without it is a safe and a proper one. For remember, of all *possible* evils, that of *despotism* is the *worst* and the most to be *dreaded*.

Besides, it cannot be supposed, that the first essay on so difficult a subject, is so well digested, as it ought to be;—if the proposed plan, after a mature deliberation, should meet the approbation of the respective States, the matter will end; but if it should be found to be fraught with dangers and inconveniencies, a future general Convention being in possession of the objections, will be the better enabled to plan a suitable government.

Son of the influential merchant George Bryan, who perhaps assisted in writing "Centinel," Samuel Bryan was an early professional politician and publicist from Philadelphia who made major contributions to the Antifederalist cause (see Samuel Bryan entry in *Biographies*). In this first "Centinel," one of twelve published in the *Gazetteer* of Eleazor Oswald, Bryan began one of the best sustained dissections of the proposed Constitution. Reprinted and quite influential in other states' deliberations, in this first "Centinel" Bryan explained his fears that the Constitution would create an aristocratic leadership. Bryan also questioned John Adams's writings in defense of Constitutional government.

REFERENCES

Herbert Storing, *Complete Anti-Federalist* (Chicago: University of Chicago Press, 1981), vol. 2; *Independent Gazetteer*, October 5, 1787.

NOTE

1. Refers to John Adams, *Defense of the Government of the United States.*

George Bryan ("An Old Whig"), I,
October 12, 1787

I am one of those who have long wished for a federal government, which should have power to protect our trade and provide for the general security of the United States. Accordingly, when the constitution proposed by the late convention made its appearance, I was disposed to embrace it almost without examination; I was determined not to be offended with trifles or to scan it too critically. "We want something: let us try this; experience is the best teacher: if it does not answer our purpose we can alter it: at all events it will serve for a beginning." Such were my reasonings;—but, upon further reflection, I may say that I am shaken with very considerable doubts and scruples, I want a federal constitution; and yet I am afraid to concur in giving my consent to the establishment of that which is proposed. At the same time I really wish to have my doubts removed, if they are not well founded. I shall therefore take the liberty of laying some of them before the public, through the channel of your paper.

In the first place, it appears to me that I was mistaken in supposing that we could so very easily make trial of this constitution and again change it at our pleasure. The conventions of the several states cannot propose any alterations— they are only to give their *assent* and *ratification*. And after the constitution is once ratified, it must remain fixed until two thirds of both the houses of Congress shall deem it necessary to propose amendments; or the legislatures of two thirds of the several states shall make application to Congress for the calling a convention for proposing amendments, which amendments shall not be valid till they are ratified by the legislatures of three fourths of the several states, or by conventions in three fourths thereof, as one or the other mode of ratification may be proposed by Congress.—This appears to me to be only a cunning way of saying that no alteration shall ever be made; so that whether it is a good constitution or a bad constitution, it will remain forever unamended. Lycurgus, when he promulgated his laws to the Spartans, made them swear that they would make no alterations in them until he should return from a journey which he was then about to undertake:—He chose never to return, and therefore no alterations could be made in his laws. The people were made to believe that they could make trial of his laws for a few months or years, during his absence, and as soon as he returned they could continue to observe them or reject at pleasure. Thus this celebrated Republic was in reality established by a trick. In like manner the proposed constitution holds out a prospect of being subject to be changed if it be found necessary or convenient to change it; but the conditions upon which an alteration can take place, are such as in all probability will never exist. The consequence will be that, when the constitution is once established, it never can be altered or amended without some violent convulsion or civil war.

The conditions, I say, upon which any alterations can take place, appear to me to be such as never will exist—two thirds of both houses of Congress or the legislatures of two thirds of the states, must agree in desiring a convention to be called. This will probably never happen; but if it should happen, then the convention may agree to the amendments or not as they think right; and after all, three fourths of the states must ratify the amendments.—Before all this labyrinth can be traced to a conclusion, ages will revolve, and perhaps the great principles upon which our late glorious revolution was founded, will be totally forgotten. If the principles of liberty are not firmly fixed and established in the present constitution, in vain may we hope for retrieving them hereafter. People once possessed of power are always loth to part with it; and we shall never find two thirds of a Congress voting or proposing any thing which shall derogate from their own authority and importance, or agreeing to give back to the people any part of those privileges which they have once parted with—so far from it; that the greater occasion there may be for a reformation, the less likelihood will there be of accomplishing it. The greater the abuse of power, the more obstinately is it always persisted in. As to any expectation of two thirds of the legislatures concurring in such a request, it is if possible, still more remote. The legislatures of the states will be but forms and shadows, and it will be the height of arrogance and presumption in them, to turn their thoughts to such high subjects. After this constitution is once established, it is too evident that we shall be obliged to fill up the offices of assemblymen and councillors, as we do those of constables, by appointing men to serve whether they will or not, and fining them if they refuse. The members thus appointed, as soon as they can hurry through a law or two for repairing highways or impounding cattle, will conclude the business of their sessions as suddenly as possible; that they may return to their own business.—Their heads will not be perplexed with the great affairs of state—We need not expect two thirds of them ever to interfere in so momentous a question as that of calling a Continental convention.—The different legislatures will have no communication with one another from the time of the new constitution being ratified, to the end of the world. Congress will be the great focus of power as well as the great and only medium of communication from one state to another. The great, and the wise, and the mighty will be in possession of places and offices; they will oppose all changes in favor of liberty; they will steadily pursue the acquisition of more and more power to themselves and their adherents. The cause of liberty, if it be now forgotten, will be forgotten forever.—Even the press which has so long been employed in the cause of liberty, and to which perhaps the greatest part of the liberty which exists in the world is owing at this moment; the press may possibly be restrained of its freedom, and our children may possibly not be suffered to enjoy this most invaluable blessing of a free communication of each others sentiments on political subjects—Such at least appear to be some men's fears, and I cannot find in the proposed constitution any thing expressly calculated to obviate these fears; so that they may or may not be realized according to the principles and dispositions of the men who may happen to govern us hereafter. One thing however is calculated to alarm our fears on this head;—I mean the fashionable language which now prevails so much and is so frequent in the mouths of some who formerly held very different opinions;—THAT COMMON PEOPLE HAVE NO BUSINESS TO TROUBLE THEMSELVES ABOUT GOVERNMENT. If this principle is just the consequence is plain that the common people need no information on the subject of politics. Newspapers, pamphlets and essays are calculated only to mislead and inflame them by holding forth to them doctrines which they have no business or right to meddle with, which they ought to leave to their superiors. Should the freedom of the press be restrained on the subject of politics, there is no doubt it will soon after be restrained on all other subjects, religious as well as civil. And if the freedom of the press shall be restrained, it will be another reason to despair of any amendments being made in favor of liberty, after the proposed constitution shall be once established. Add to this, that under the proposed constitution, it will be in the power of the Congress to raise and maintain a standing army for their support, and when they are supported by an army, it will depend on themselves to say whether any amendments shall be made in favor of liberty.

If these reflections are just it becomes us to pause, and reflect previously before we establish a system of government which cannot be amended; which will entail happiness or misery on ourselves and our children. We ought I say to reflect carefully, we ought not by any means to be in haste; but rather to suffer a little temporary inconvenience, than by any precipitation to establish a constitution without knowing whether it is right or wrong, and which if wrong, no length of time will ever mend. Scarce any people ever deliberately gave up their liberties; but many instances occur in history of their losing them forever by a rash and sudden act, to avoid a pressing inconvenience or gratify some violent passion of revenge or fear. It was a celebrated observation of one of our Assemblies before the revolution, during their struggles with the proprietaries, that "those who would give up essential liberty to purchase a little temporary safety deserve neither liberty nor safety."

For the present I shall conclude with recommending to my countrymen not to be in haste, to consider carefully what we are doing. It is our own concern; it is our own business; let us give ourselves a little time at least to read the proposed constitution and know what it contains; for I fear that many, even of those who talk most about it have not even read it, and many others, who are as much concerned as any of us, have had no opportunity to read it. And it is certainly a suspicious circumstance that some people who are presumed to know most about the new constitution seem bent upon forcing it on their countrymen without giving them time to know what they are doing.

George Bryan's major objection to the Constitution was its lack of protection for free speech (see George Bryan entry in *Biographies*). Without free speech, he wrote, there would be no way for opponents to offer amendments to the Constitution. Bryan also opposed the unsystematic way in which the Constitution discussed protection of other individual rights.

REFERENCES

Independent Gazetteer, October 12, 1787; Storing, *Complete*, vol. 3.

William Findley ("An Officer of the Late Continental Army"), *November 6, 1787*

TO THE CITIZENS OF PHILADELPHIA.

Friends, Countrymen, Brethren and Fellow Citizens, The important day is drawing near when you are to elect delegates to represent you in a Convention, on the result of whose deliberations will depend, in a great measure, your future happiness.

This convention is to determine whether or not the commonwealth of Pennsylvania shall adopt the plan of government proposed by the late convention of delegates from the different states, which sat in this city.

With a heart full of anxiety for the preservation of your dearest rights, I presume to address you on this important occasion—In the name of sacred liberty, dearer to us than our property and our lives, I request your most earnest attention.

The proposed plan of continental government is now fully known to you. You have read it I trust with the attention it deserves—You have heard the objections that have been made to it—You have heard the answers to these objections.

If you have attended to the whole with candor and unbiassed minds, as becomes men that are possessed and deserving of freedom, you must have been alarmed at the result of your observations. Notwithstanding the splendor of names which has attended the publication of the new constitution, notwithstanding the sophistry and vain reasonings that have been urged to support its principles; alas! you must at least have concluded that great men are not always infallible, and that patriotism itself may be led into essential errors.

The objections that have been made to the new constitution, are these:

1. It is not merely (as it ought to be) a CONFEDERATION of STATES, but a GOVERNMENT of INDIVIDUALS.

2. The powers of Congress extend to the *lives*, the *liberties* and the *property* of every citizen.

3. The *sovereignty* of the different states is *ipso facto* destroyed in its most essential parts.

4. What remains of it will only tend to create violent dissentions between the state governments and the Congress, and terminate in the ruin of the one or the other.

5. The consequence must therefore be, either that the *union* of the states

will be destroyed by a violent struggle, or that their sovereignty will be swallowed up by silent encroachments into a universal aristocracy; because it is clear, that if two different *sovereign powers* have a co-equal command over the *purses* of the citizens, they will struggle for the spoils, and the weakest will be in the end obliged to yield to the efforts of the strongest.

6. Congress being possessed of these immense powers, the liberties of the states and of the people are not secured by a bill or DECLARATION OF RIGHTS.

7. The *sovereignty* of the states is not expressly reserved, the *form* only, and not the SUBSTANCE of their government, is guaranteed to them by express words.

8. TRIAL BY JURY, that sacred bulwark of liberty, is ABOLISHED IN CIVIL CASES, and Mr. Wilson,[1] one of the convention, has told you, that not being able to agree as to the FORM of establishing this point, they have left you deprived of the SUBSTANCE. Here are his own words—*The subject was involved in difficulties. The convention found the task* TOO DIFFICULT *for them, and left the business as it stands.*

9. THE LIBERTY OF THE PRESS is not secured, and the powers of the congress are fully adequate to its destruction, as they are to have the trial of *libels*, or *pretended libels* against the United States, and may by a cursed abominable STAMP ACT (as the *Bowdoin administration* has done in Massachusetts) preclude you effectually from all means of information. *Mr. Wilson has given you no answer to these arguments.*

10. Congress have the power of keeping up a STANDING ARMY in time of peace, and Mr. Wilson has told you THAT IT WAS NECESSARY.

11. The LEGISLATIVE and EXECUTIVE powers are not kept separate as every one of the American constitutions declares they ought to be; but they are mixed in a manner entirely novel and unknown, even to the constitution of Great Britain; because,

12. In England the king only, has a *nominal negative* over the proceedings of the legislature, which he has NEVER DARED TO EXERCISE since the days of *King William*, whereas by the new constitution, both the *president general* and the *senate* TWO EXECUTIVE BRANCHES OF GOVERNMENT, have that negative, and are intended to *support each other in the exercise of it.*

13. The representation of the lower house is too small, consisting only of 65 members.

14. That of the *senate* is so small that it renders its extensive powers extremely dangerous: it is to consist only of 26 members, two-thirds of whom must concur to conclude any *treaty or alliance* with foreign powers: Now we will suppose that five of them are absent, sick, dead, or unable to attend, *twenty-one* will remain, and eight of these (*one-third*, and *one* over) may prevent the conclusion of any treaty, even the most favorable to America. Here will be a fine field for the intrigues and even the *bribery* and *corruption* of European powers.

15. The most important branches of the EXECUTIVE DEPARTMENT are to be put into the hands of a *single magistrate*, who will be in fact an ELECTIVE KING. The MILITARY, the land and naval forces are to be entirely at his disposal, and therefore:

16. Should the *senate*, by the intrigues of foreign powers, become devoted

to foreign influence, as was the case of late in *Sweden*, the people will be obliged, as the *Swedes* have been, to seek their refuge in the arms of the *monarch* or PRESIDENT GENERAL.

17. ROTATION, that noble prerogative of liberty, is entirely excluded from the new system of government, and great men may and probably will be continued in office during their lives.

18. ANNUAL ELECTIONS are abolished, and the people are not to re-assume their rights until the expiration of *two, four* and *six* years.

19. Congress are to have the power of fixing the *time, place* and *manner* of holding elections, so as to keep them forever subjected to their influence.

20. The importation of slaves is not to be prohibited until the year 1808, and SLAVERY will probably resume its empire in Pennsylvania.

21. The MILITIA is to be under the immediate command of congress, and men *conscientiously scrupulous of bearing arms,* may be compelled to perform military duty.

22. The new government will be EXPENSIVE beyond any we have ever experienced, the *judicial* department alone, with its concomitant train of *judges, justices, chancellors, clerks, sheriffs, coroners, escheators, state attornies and solicitors, constables, &c.* in every state and in every country in each state, will be a burden beyond the utmost abilities of the people to bear, and upon the whole.

23. A government partaking of MONARCHY and aristocracy will be fully and firmly established, and liberty will be but a name to adorn the *short* historic page of the halcyon days of America.

These, my countrymen, are the objections that have been made to the new proposed system of government; and if you read the system itself with attention, you will find them all to be founded in truth. But what have you been told in answer?

I pass over the sophistry of Mr. Wilson, in his equivocal speech at the state house. His pretended arguments have been echoed and re-echoed by every retailer of politics, and *victoriously* refuted by several patriotic pens. Indeed if you read this famous speech in a cool dispassionate moment, you will find it to contain no more than a train of pitiful sophistry and evasions, unworthy of the man who spoke them. I have taken notice of some of them in stating the objections, and they must, I am sure, have excited your *pity* and *indignation.* Mr. Wilson is a man of sense, learning and extensive information, unfortunately for him he has never sought the more solid fame of *patriotism.* During the late war he narrowly escaped the effects of popular rage, and the people seldom arm themselves against a citizen in vain. The whole tenor of his political conduct has always been strongly tainted with the spirit of *high aristocracy*, he has never been known to join in a truly popular measure, and his talents have ever been devoted to the patrician interest. His lofty carriage indicates the lofty mind that animates him, a mind able to conceive and perform great things, but which unfortunately can see nothing great out of the pale of power and worldly grandeur; despising what he calls the inferior order of the people, popular liberty and popular assemblies offer to his exalted imagination an idea of meanness and contemptibility which he hardly seeks to conceal—He sees at a distance the pomp and pageantry of courts, he sighs after those stately palaces and that apparatus of human greatness which his vivid fancy has taught him to consider as the supreme good. Men of sublime minds, he conceives, were born a different race from the rest of the sons of men, to them, and them only, he imagines, high heaven intended to commit the reins of earthly government, the remaining part of mankind he sees below at an immense distance, they, he thinks were born to serve, to administer food to the ambition of their superiors, and become the footstool of their power—Such is Mr. Wilson, and fraught with these high ideas, it is no wonder that he should exert all his talents to support a form of government so admirably contrived to carry them into execution—But when the people, who possess collectively a mass of knowledge superior to his own, inquire into the principles of that government on the establishment or rejection of which depend their dearest concerns, when he is called upon by the voice of thousands to come and explain that favorite system which he holds forth as an object of their admiration, he comes—he attempts to support by reasoning what reason never dictated, and finding the attempt vain, his great mind, made for nobler purposes, is obliged to stoop to mean evasions and pitiful sophistry; himself not deceived, he strives to deceive the people, and the treasonable attempt delineates his true character, beyond the reach of the pencil of a *West* or *Peale*, or the pen of a *Valerius.*

And yet that speech, weak and insidious as it is, is the only attempt that has been made to support by argument that political monster THE PROPOSED CONSTITUTION. I have sought in vain amidst the immense heap of trash that has been published on the subject, an argument worthy of refutation, and I have not been able to find it. If you can bear the disgust which the reading of those pieces must naturally occasion, and which I have felt in the highest degree, read them, my fellow citizens, and say whether they contain the least shadow of logical reasoning, say (laying your hands upon your hearts) whether there is any thing in them that can impress unfeigned conviction upon your unprejudiced minds.

One of them only I shall take notice of, in which I find that argument is weakly attempted. This piece is signed "An American Citizen" and has appeared with great pomp in four succeeding numbers in several of our newspapers. But if you read it attentively, you will find that it does not tell us what the new constitution is, but what it is not, and extolls it on the sole ground that it does not contain all the principles of tyranny with which the European governments are disgraced.

But where argument entirely failed, nothing remained for the supporters of the new constitution but to endeavor to inflame your passions—The attempt has been made and I am sorry to find not entirely without effect. The great names of WASHINGTON and FRANKLIN, have been taken in vain and shockingly prostituted to effect the most infamous purposes. What! because our august chieftain has subscribed his name in his capacity of president of the convention to the plan offered by them to the states, and because the venerable sage of Pennsylvania, has *testified* by his signature that *the majority of the delegates of this state* assented to the same plan, will any one infer from this that it has met with their entire approbation, and that they consider it as the master piece of human wisdom? I am apt to think the contrary, and I have good reasons to ground my opinion on.

In the first place we have found by the publication of *Charles Cotesworth*

Pinckney, Esquire, one of the *signing* members of the convention, who has expressed the most pointed disapprobation of many important parts of the new plan of government, that all the members whose names appear at the bottom of this instrument of tyranny have not concurred in its adoption.[2] Many of them might conceive themselves bound by the opinion of the majority of their state, and leaving the people to their own judgment upon the form of government offered to them, might have conceived it impolitic by refusing to sign their names, to offer to the world the lamentable spectacle of the disunion of a body on the decisions of whom the people had rested all their hopes. We KNOW, and the long sitting of the convention tells us, that, (as it is endeavoured to persuade us) concord and unanimity did not reign exclusively among them. The thick veil of secrecy with which their proceedings have been covered, has left us entirely in the dark, as to the *debates* that took place, and the unaccountable SUPPRESSION OF THEIR JOURNALS, the highest insult that could be offered to the majesty of the people, shews clearly that the whole of the new plan was entirely the work of an *aristocratic majority.*

But let us suppose for a moment that the proposed government was the unanimous result of the deliberations of the convention—must it on that account preclude an investigation of its merits? Are the people to be dictated to without appeal by any set of men, however great, however dignified? Freedom spurns at the idea and rejects it with disdain—We appeal to the collective wisdom of a great nation, we appeal to their general sense which is easily to be obtained through the channel of a multitude of free presses, from the opinions of *thirty-nine* men, who secluded from the rest of the world, without the possibility of conferring with the rest of their fellow-citizens, have had no opportunity of rectifying the errors into which they may have been led by the *most designing* among them. We have seen names not less illustrious than those of the members of the late convention, subscribed to the present *reprobated* articles of confederation, and if those patriots have erred, there is no reason to suppose that a succeeding set should be more free from error. Nay the very men, who advocate so strongly the new plan of government, and support it with the infallibility of Doctor Franklin, affect to despise the present constitution of Pennsylvania, which was dictated and avowed by that venerable patriot—They are conscious that he does not entirely approve of the new plan, whose principles are so different from those he has established in our ever-glorious constitution, and there is no doubt that it is the reason that has induced them to leave his respected name out of the *ticket* for the approaching election.

Now then my fellow-citizens, my brethren, my friends; if the sacred flame of liberty be not extinguished in your breasts, if you have any regard for the happiness of yourselves, and your posterity, let me entreat you, earnestly entreat you by all that is dear and sacred to freemen, to consider well before you take an awful step which may involve in its consequences the ruin of millions yet unborn—You are on the brink of a dreadful precipice;—in the name therefore of holy liberty, for which I have fought and for which we have all suffered, I call upon you to make a solemn pause before you proceed. One step more, and perhaps the scene of freedom is closed forever in America. Let not a set of aspiring despots, *who make us* SLAVES *and tell us 'tis our* CHARTER, wrest from you those invaluable blessings, for which the most illustrious sons of America have bled and died—but exert yourselves, like men, like freemen and like Americans, to transmit unimpaired to your latest posterity those rights, those liberties, which have ever been so dear to you, and which it is yet in your power to preserve.

William Findley, a western farmer and political leader who served in the state ratification convention, later became an influential member of the United States House (see William Findley entry in *Biographies*). In this letter, Findley accused the major Federalist leader James Wilson of deceiving the people of Pennsylvania by claiming the Constitution favored state government over national government. Findley insisted that powerful leaders sought to intimidate the people into ignoring their concerns about the weakness of state government.

REFERENCES

Independent Gazetteer, November 6, 1787; Storing, *Complete*, vol. 3.

NOTES

1. The arch-Federalist James Wilson. For the sake of clarity Wilson's name has been added to the text.
2. Charles Cootsworth Pinckney, Federalist of South Carolina.

John Smilie, Speech in the Pennsylvania State Ratification Convention, *November 28, 1787*

I expected, Mr. President, that the honorable gentleman would have proceeded to a full and explicit investigation of the proposed system, and that he would have made some attempts to prove that it was calculated to promote the happiness, power, and general interests of the United States. I am sorry that I have been mistaken in this expectation, for surely the gentleman's talents and opportunities would have enabled him to furnish considerable information upon this important subject; but I shall proceed to make a few remarks upon those words in the preamble of this plan, which he has considered of so super-excellent a quality. Compare them, Sir, with the language used in forming the state constitution and however superior they may be to the terms of the great charter of England, still, in common candor, they must yield to the more sterling expressions employed in this act. Let these speak for themselves:

"That all men are born equally free and independent, and have certain natural, inherent and unalienable rights, amongst which are, the enjoying and defending life and liberty, acquiring, possessing and protecting property, and pursuing and obtaining happiness and safety.

"That the people of this state have the sole, exclusive and inherent right of governing and regulating the internal police of the same.

"That all power being originally inherent in, and consequently derived from the people; therefore all officers of government, whether legislative or executive, are their trustees and servants, and at all times accountable to them.

"That government is, or ought to be, instituted for the common benefit, protection and security of the people, nation or community; and not for the particular emolument or advantage of any single man, family, or set of men, who are a part only of that community: And that the community hath an indubitable, unalienable and indefeasible right to reform, alter or abolish government in such manner as shall be by that community judged most conducive to the public weal."

But the gentleman takes pride in the superiority of this short preamble when compared with magna charta;—why, Sir, I hope the rights of men are better understood at this day, than at the framing of that deed, and we must be convinced that civil liberty is capable of still greater improvement and extension, than is known even in its present cultivated state. True, Sir, the supreme authority naturally rests in the people, but does it follow, that therefore a declaration of rights would be superfluous? Because the people have a right to alter and abolish government, can it therefore be inferred that every step taken to secure that right would be superfluous and nugatory? The truth is, that unless some criterion is established by which it could be easily and constitutionally ascertained how far our governors may proceed, and by which it might appear when they transgress their jurisdiction, this idea of altering and abolishing government is a mere sound without substance. Let us recur to the memorable declaration of the 4th of July, 1776. Here it is said:

"When, in the course of human events, it becomes necessary for one people to dissolve the political bands which have connected them with another, and to assume among the powers of the earth, the separate and equal station to which the laws of nature's God entitle them, a decent respect to the opinions of mankind requires that they should declare the causes which impel them to the separation.

"We hold these truths to be self evident; that all men are created equal; that they are endowed by their Creator with certain unalienable rights; that among these are life, liberty, and the pursuit of happiness. That to secure these rights, governments are instituted among men, deriving their just powers from the consent of the governed; that whenever any form of government becomes destructive of these ends, it is the right of the people to alter or to abolish it, and to institute a new government, laying its foundation on such principles, and organizing its powers in such form, as to them shall seem most likely to effect their safety and happiness."

Now, Sir, if in the proposed plan, the gentleman can shew any similar security for the civil rights of the people I shall certainly be relieved from a weight of objection to its adoption, and I sincerely hope, that as he has gone so far, he will proceed to communicate some of the reasons (and undoubtedly they must have been powerful ones,) which induced the late federal convention to omit a bill of rights, so essential in the opinion of many citizens to a perfect form of government.

John Smilie, a western farmer and political official, later served in the United States House (see John Smilie entry in *Biographies*). In this speech, he declared a special concern for the need for a bill of rights. Smilie wanted amendments to the Constitution to include statements about personal rights and to restrict the powers of central government. His efforts often were reported in the local press.

REFERENCES

John Bach McMaster, *Pennsylvania and the Federal Constitution* (Philadelphia: Historical Society of Pennsylvania, 1888), vol. 1; *Pennsylvania Herald*, November 30, 1787.

Robert Whitehill, Speech in the Pennsylvania State Ratification Convention, *November 30, 1787*

After the full exercise of his eloquence and ingenuity, the honorable delegate to the late convention, has not removed those objections which I formerly submitted to your consideration, in hopes of striking indeed, from his superior talents and information, a ray of wisdom to illuminate the darkness of our doubts, and to guide us in the pursuit of political truth and happiness. If the learned gentleman, however, with all his opportunities of investigating this particular system, and with all his general knowledge in the science of government, has not been able to convert or convince us; far be it from me to impute this failure to the defects of his elocution, or the languor of his disposition. It is no impeachment of those abilities which have been eminently distinguished in the abstruse disquisitions of law, that they should fail in the insidious task of supporting, on popular principles, a government which originates in mystery, and must terminate in despotism. Neither can the want of success, Sir, be ascribed to the want of zeal; for, we have heard with our ears, and our eyes have seen, the indefatigable industry of the worthy member in advocating the cause which he has undertaken. But Mr. President, the defect is in the system itself,—there lies the evil which no argument can palliate, no sophistry can disguise. Permit me, therefore, Sir, again to call your attention to the principles which it contains, and for a moment to examine the ground upon which those principles are defended. I have said, and with encreasing confidence I repeat, that the proposed constitution must eventually annihilate the independent sovereignty of the several states. In answer to this, the forms of election for supplying the offices of the federal head have been recapitulated; it has been thence inferred that the connection between the individual and the general governments is of so indissoluble a nature, that they must necessarily stand or fall together, and, therefore, it has been finally declared to be impossible, that the framers of this constitution, could have a premeditated design to sow in the body of their work, the seeds of its own destruction. But, Sir, I think it may be clearly proved, that this system contains the seeds of self-preservation, independent of all the forms referred to;—seeds which will vegitate and strengthen in proportion to the decay of state authority, and which will ultimately spring up and overshadow the thirteen commonwealths of America, with a deadly shade. The honorable member from the city has indeed, observed that every government should possess the means of its own preservation; and this constitution is possibly the result of that proposition.

For, Sir, the first article comprises the grants of powers so superlative in their nature, and so unlimitted in their extent, that without the aid of any other branch of the system, a foundation rests upon this article alone, for the extension of the federal jurisdiction to the most extravagant degree of arbitrary sway. It will avail little to detect and deplore the encroachments of a government clothed in the plenitude of these powers; it will afford no consolation to reflect that we are not enslaved by the positive deriliction of our rights; but it will be well to remember, at this day, Sir, that, in effect, we rob the people of their liberties, when we establish a power, whose usurpations they will not be able to counteract or resist. It is not alone, however, the operative force of the powers expressly given to Congress that will accomplish their independence of the states, but we find an efficient auxiliary in the clause that authorizes that body "to make all laws which shall be necessary and proper for carrying into execution the foregoing powers, and all other powers vested by this constitution in this government of the United States, or in any department or office thereof." Hence, sir, if it should happen, as the honorable members from the city have presumed, that by the neglect or delinquency of the states, no place and manner, or an improper place and manner for conducting the elections should be appointed, will it not be said that the general government ought not for this reason to be destroyed? and will it not therefore be necessary for carrying the powers of this constitution into execution, that the Congress should provide for its elections in such manner as will prevent the federal business from being frustrated, by the listless or refractory disposition of the states individually? This event is in a great measure provided for, indeed, by the plan itself; for, "the Congress may (constitutionally) at any time by law make or alter such regulations (that is the times, places, and manner of holding elections prescribed in each state by the legislatures thereof) except as to the places of choosing senators." If the power here given was necessary to the preservation of the proposed government, as the honorable members have contended, does it not, at the same time, furnish the means to act independent of the connection, which has been so often represented, as the great security for the continuance of the state sovereignties? Under the sanction of this clause, the senators may hold their seats as long as they live, and there is no authority to dispossess them. The duration of the house of representatives may likewise be protracted to any period, since the time and place of election will always be adapted to the objects of the Congress, or its leading demagogues; and as that body will ultimately declare what shall constitute the qualification of its members, all the boasted advantages of representation must terminate in idle form and expensive parade. If the voice of complaint should not then be silenced by the dread of punishment, easy it is nevertheless to anticipate the fate of petitions or remonstrances presented by the trembling hand of the oppressed, to the irritated and ambitious oppressor. Solicitation will be answered by those statutes which are to be the supreme law of the land, and reproach will be overcome by the frown of insolent authority. This Mr. President, is but a slight view of the calamities that will be produced by the exercise of those powers, which the honorable members from the city have endeavored to persuade us, it is necessary to grant to the new government, in order to secure its own preservation, and to accomplish the objects of the union. But in considering, Sir, what was necessary to the safety and energy of the government, some attention ought surely to have been paid to the safety and freedom of the people. No satisfactory reason has yet been offered for the omission of a bill of rights; but, on the contrary, the honorable members are defeated in the only pretext which they have been able to assign, that every thing which is not given is excepted, for we have shewn that there are two articles expressly reserved, the writ of Habeas Corpus, and the trial by jury in criminal cases, and we have called upon them, in vain, to reconcile this reservation with the tenor of their favourite proposition. For, if there was danger in the attempt to enumerate the liberties of the people, lest it should prove imperfect and defective, how happens it, that in the instances I have mentioned, that danger has been incurred? Have the people no other rights worth their attention, or is it to be inferred, agreeably to the maxim of our opponents, that every other right is abandoned? Surely, Sir, our language was competent to declare the sentiments of the people, and to establish a bar against the intrusions of the general government, in other respects as well as these; and when we find some privileges stipulated, the argument of danger is effectually destroyed; and the argument of difficulty, which has been drawn from the attempt to enumerate every right, cannot now be urged against the enumeration of more rights than this instrument contains. In short, Mr. President, it is our duty to take care that the foundation of this system is so laid, that the superstructure, which is to be reared by other hands, may not cast a gloom upon the temple of freedom, the recent purchase of our toil and treasure. When, therefore, I consider it as the means of annihilating the constitutions of the several states, and, consequently, the liberties of the people, I should be wanting to my constituents, to myself, and to posterity, did I not exert every talent with which Heaven has endowed me, to counteract the measures that have been taken for its adoption. That it was the design of the late federal convention to absorb and abolish the individual sovereignty of the states, I seek no other evidence but this system; for as the honorable delegate to that body has recommended, I am also satisfied to judge of the tree by its fruit. When, therefore, I behold it thus systematically constructed for the accomplishment of that object,—when I recollect the talents of those who framed it, I cannot hesitate to impute to them an intention corresponding with the principles and operation of their own work. Finally, Sir, that the dissolution of our state constitutions will produce the ruin of civil liberty is a proposition easy to be maintained, and which, I am persuaded, in the course of these debates, will be incontrovertibly established in the mind of every member, whose judgment is open to conviction, and whose vote has not been conclusively pledged for the ratification of this constitution, before its merits were discussed.

Another western farmer and political leader, Robert Whitehill later served in the United States House (see Robert Whitehill entry in *Biographies*). An effective debater, he opposed excessive powers of the federal Congress, especially in its use of the habeas corpus clause. He also defended the right of free discourse and popular assembly, and he called for printing the dissenting comments at the state convention.

REFERENCES

Bailyn, *Debate*, vol. 1; McMaster, *Pennsylvania and the Federal Constitution*.

William Findley, Speech in the Pennsylvania State Ratification Convention, *December 1, 1787*

In the Preamble, it is said, *We the People*, and not *We the States*, which therefore is a compact between individuals entering into society, and not between separate States enjoying independent power, and delegating a portion of that power for their common benefit. 2dly, That in the legislature each member has a vote, whereas in a confederation, as we have hitherto practised it, and from the very nature of the thing, a state can only have one voice, and therefore all the delegates of any state can only give one vote. 3d, The powers given to the federal body for imposing internal taxation will necessarily destroy the state sovreignties for there cannot exist two independent sovereign taxing powers in the same community, and the strongest will, of course, annihilate the weaker. 4th, The power given to regulate and judge of elections is a proof of a consolidation, for there cannot be two powers employed at the same time in regulating the same elections, and if they were a confederated body, the individual states would judge of the elections, and the general Congress would judge of the credentials which proved the election of its members. 5th, The judiciary power, which is co-extensive with the legislative, is another evidence of a consolidation. 6th, The manner in which the wages of the members is paid, makes another proof, and *lastly* the oath of allegiance directed to be taken establishes it incontrovertibly, for would it not be absurd that the members of the legislative and executive branches of a sovereign state should take a test of allegiance to another sovereign or independent body?

On December 1, 1787, William Findley made specific charges against federal powers, claiming those powers would lead to national consolidation (see William Findley entry in *Biographies*). He stated that the proposed Constitution destroyed the rights of the states. Findley also believed that the Constitution created an aristocratic government when it allowed the national legislators to decide on the time and place of elections and to serve in office for many years.

REFERENCES

Jensen and Kaminski, *Documentary History* (Madison: State Historical Society, 1976), vol. 2; Summation of Speech in *Pennsylvania Herald*, December 5, 1787.

Robert Whitehill, Speech in the Pennsylvania State Ratification Convention, *December 12, 1787*

Mr. Whitehill then read, and offered as the ground of a motion for adjourning to some remote day, the consideration of the following articles, which he said, might either be taken, collectively, as a bill of rights, or, separately, as amendments to the general form of government proposed.

1. The rights of conscience shall be held inviolable, and neither the legislative, executive, nor judicial powers of the United States, shall have authority to alter, abrogate, or infringe any part of the constitutions of the several states, which provide for the preservation of liberty in matters of religion.

2. That in controversies respecting property, and in suits between man and man, trial by jury shall remain as heretofore, as well in the federal courts, as in those of the several states.

3. That in all capital and criminal prosecutions, a man has a right to demand the cause and nature of his accusation, as well in the federal courts, as in those of the several states; to be heard by himself or his council; to be confronted with the accusers and witnesses, to call for evidence in his favor, and a speedy trial, by an impartial jury of the vicinage, without whose unanimous consent, he cannot be found guilty, nor can he be compelled to give evidence against himself; that no man be deprived of his liberty, except by the law of the land or the judgment of his peers.

4. That excessive bail ought not to be required, nor excessive fines imposed, nor cruel or unusual punishments inflicted.

5. That warrants unsupported by evidence, whereby any officer or messenger may be commanded or required to search suspected places, or to seize any person or persons, his or their property, not particularly described, are grievous and oppressive, and shall not be granted either by the magistrates of the federal government or others.

6. That the people have a right to the freedom of speech, of writing, and of publishing their sentiments, therefore, the freedom of the press shall not be restrained by any law of the United States.

7. That the people have a right to bear arms for the defence of themselves and their own state, or the United States, or for the purpose of killing game; and no law shall be passed for disarming the people or any of them, unless for crimes committed, or real danger of public injury from individuals; and as standing armies in the time of peace are dangerous to liberty, they ought not

to be kept up: and that the military shall be kept under strict subordination to and be governed by the civil power.

8. The inhabitants of the several states shall have liberty to fowl and hunt in seasonable times, on the lands they hold, and on all other lands in the United States not inclosed, and in like manner to fish in all navigable waters, and others not private property, without being restrained therein by any laws to be passed by the legislature of the United States.

9. That no law shall be passed to restrain the legislatures of the several states, from enacting laws for imposing taxes, except imposts and duties on goods exported and imported, and that no taxes, except imposts and duties upon goods imported and exported, and postage on letters shall be levied by the authority of Congress.

10. That elections shall remain free, that the house of representatives be properly increased in number, and that the several states shall have power to regulate the elections for senators and representatives, without being controuled either directly or indirectly by any interference on the part of Congress, and that elections of representatives be annual.

11. That the power of organizing, arming and disciplining the militia, (the manner of disciplining the militia to be prescribed by Congress) remain with the individual states, and that Congress shall not have authority to call or march any of the militia out of their own state, without the consent of such state, and for such length of time only as such state shall agree.

12. That the legislative, executive, and judicial powers be kept separate, and to this end, that a constitutional council be appointed to advise and assist the President, who shall be responsible for the advice they give; (hereby, the senators would be relieved from almost constant attendance) and also that the judges be made compleatly independant.

13. That no treaties which shall be directly opposed to the existing laws of the United States in Congress assembled, shall be valid until such laws shall be repealed or made conformable to such treaty, neither shall any treaties be valid which are contradictory to the constitution of the United States, or the constitutions of the individual states.

14. That the judiciary power of the United States shall be confined to cases affecting ambassadors, other public ministers and consuls, to cases of admiralty and maratime jurisdiction, to controversies to which the United States shall be a party, to controversies between two or more states—between a state and citizens of different states—between citizens claiming lands under grants of different states, and between a state or the citizens thereof and foreign states, and in criminal cases, to such only as are expressly enumerated in the constitution, and that the United States in Congress assembled, shall not have power to enact laws, which shall alter the laws of descents and distributions of the effects of deceased persons, the title of lands or goods, or the regulation of contracts in the individual states.

15. That the sovereignty, freedom and independency of the several states shall be retained, and every power, jurisdiction and right which is not by this constitution expressly delegated to the United States in Congress assembled.

Some confusion arose on these articles being presented to the chair, objections were made by the majority to their being officially read, and, at last, Mr.

Wilson desired that the intended motion might be reduced to writing, in order to ascertain its nature and extent. Accordingly, Mr. Whitehill drew it up, and it was read from the chair in the following manner.

"That this Convention do adjourn to the   day of   next, then to meet in the city of Philadelphia, in order that the propositions for amending the proposed constitution may be considered by the people of this state; that we may have an opportunity of knowing what amendments or alterations may be proposed by other states, and that these propositions, together with such other amendments as may be proposed by other states, may be offered to Congress, and taken into consideration by the United States, before the proposed constitution shall be finally ratified."

Using material from Virginia's George Mason on the absence of a bill of rights in the Constitution, Robert Whitehill argued for amendments to the proposed Constitution before voting on it (see Robert Whitehill entry in *Biographies*). In this maneuver, Whitehill lost.

REFERENCES

Jensen and Kaminski, *Documentary History*, vol. 2; *Pennsylvania Herald*, December 15, 1787.

Smilie, Findley, Whitehill, "Address and Reasons for Dissent of the Minority," in the Pennsylvania State Ratification Convention, *December 18, 1787*

It was not until after the termination of the late glorious contest, which made the people of the United States an independent nation, that any defect was discovered in the present confederation. It was formed by some of the ablest patriots in America. It carried us successfully through the war; and the virtue and patriotism of the people, with their disposition to promote the common cause, supplied the want of power in Congress.

The requisition of Congress for the five *per cent.* impost was made before the peace, so early as the first of February, 1781, but was prevented taking effect by the refusal of one state; yet it is probable every state in the union would have agreed to this measure at that period, had it not been for the extravagant terms in which it was demanded. The requisition was new moulded in the year 1783, and accompanied with an additional demand of certain supplementary funds for 25 years. Peace had now taken place, and the United States found themselves labouring under a considerable foreign and domestic debt, incurred during the war. The requisition of 1783 was commensurate with the interest of the debt, as it was then calculated; but it has been more accurately ascertained since that time. The domestic debt has been found to fall several millions of dollars short of the calculation, and it has lately been considerably diminished by large sales of the western lands. The states have been called on by Congress annually for supplies until the general system of finance proposed in 1783 should take place.

It was at this time that the want of an efficient federal government was first complained of, and that the powers vested in Congress were found to be inadequate to the procuring of the benefits that should result from the union. The impost was granted by most of the states, but many refused the supplementary funds; the annual requisitions were set at nought by some of the states, while others complied with them by legislative acts, but were tardy in their payments, and Congress found themselves incapable of complying with their engagements, and supporting the federal government. It was found that our national character was sinking in the opinion of foreign nations. The Congress could make treaties of commerce, but could not enforce the observance of them. We were suffering from the restrictions of foreign nations, who had shackled our commerce, while we were unable to retaliate: and all now agreed that it would be advantageous to the union to enlarge the powers of Congress; that they should be enabled in the amplest manner to regulate commerce, and to lay and collect duties on the imports throughout the United States. With this view a convention was first proposed by Virginia, and finally recommended by Congress for the different states to appoint deputies to meet in convention, "for the purposes of revising and amending the present articles of confederation, so as to make them adequate to the exigencies of the union." This recommendation the legislatures of twelve states complied with so hastily as not to consult their constituents on the subject; and though the different legislatures had no authority from their constituents for the purpose, they probably apprehended the necessity would justify the measure; and none of them extended their ideas at that time further than "revising and amending the present articles of confederation." Pennsylvania by the act appointing deputies expressly confined their powers to this object; and though it is probable that some of the members of the assembly of this state had at that time in contemplation to annihilate the present confederation, as well as the constitution of Pennsylvania, yet the plan was not sufficiently matured to communicate it to the public.

The majority of the legislature of this commonwealth, were at that time under the influence of the members from the city of Philadelphia. They agreed that the deputies sent by them to convention should have no compensation for their services, which determination was calculated to prevent the election of any member who resided at a distance from the city. It was in vain for the minority to attempt electing delegates to the convention, who understood the circumstances, and the feelings of the people, and had a common interest with them. They found a disposition in the leaders of the majority of the house to chuse themselves and some of their dependants. The minority attempted to prevent this by agreeing to vote for some of the leading members, who they knew had influence enough to be appointed at any rate, in hopes of carrying with them some respectable citizens of Philadelphia, in whose principles and integrity they could have more confidence; but even in this they were disappointed, except in one member: the eighth member was added at a subsequent session of the assembly.

The Continental convention met in the city of Philadelphia at the time appointed. It was composed of some men of excellent characters; of others who were more remarkable for their ambition and cunning, than their patriotism; and of some who had been opponents to the independence of the United States. The delegates from Pennsylvania were, six of them, uniform and decided opponents to the constitution of this commonwealth. The convention sat upwards of four months. The doors were kept shut, and the members brought under the most solemn engagements of secrecy. Some of those who opposed their going so far beyond their powers, retired, hopeless, from the convention, others had the firmness to refuse signing the plan altogether; and many who did sign it, did it not as a system they wholly approved, but as the best that could be then obtained, and notwithstanding the time spent on this subject, it is agreed on all hands to be a work of haste and accommodation.

Whilst the gilded chains were forging in the secret conclave, the meaner instruments of despotism without, were busily employed in alarming the fears of the people with dangers which did not exist, and exciting their hopes of greater advantages from the expected plan than even the best government on earth could produce.

The proposed plan had not many hours issued forth from the womb of suspicious secrecy, until such as were prepared for the purpose, were carrying about petitions for people to sign, signifying their approbation of the system, and requesting the legislature to call a convention. While every measure was taken to intimidate the people against opposing it, the public papers teemed with the most violent threats against those who should dare to think for themselves, and *tar and feathers* were liberally promised to all those who would not immediately join in supporting the proposed government be it what it would. Under such circumstances petitions in favour of calling a convention were signed by great numbers in and about the city, before they had leisure to read and examine the system, many of whom, now they are better acquainted with it, and have had time to investigate its principles, are heartily opposed to it. The petitions were speedily handed into the legislature.

Affairs were in this situation when on the 28th of September last a resolution was proposed to the assembly by a member of the house who had been also a member of the federal convention, for calling a state convention, to be elected within *ten* days for the purpose of examining and adopting the proposed constitution of the United States, though at this time the house had not received it from Congress. This attempt was opposed by a minority, who after offering every argument in their power to prevent the precipitate measure, without effect, absented themselves from the house as the only alternative left them, to prevent the measure taking place previous to their constituents being acquainted with the business—That violence and outrage which had been so often threatened was now practised; some of the members were seized the next day by a mob collected for the purpose, and forcibly dragged to the house, and there detained by force whilst the quorum of the legislature, *so formed*, compleated their resolution. We shall dwell no longer on this subject, the people of Pennsylvania have been already acquainted therewith. We would only further observe that every member of the legislature, previously to taking his seat, by solemn oath or affirmation, declares, "that he will not do or consent to any act or thing whatever that shall have a tendency to lessen or abridge their rights and privileges, as declared in the constitution the state governments, and produce one consolidated government, that will eventually and speedily issue in the supremacy of despotism.

In this investigation, we have not confined our views to the interests or welfare of this state, in preference to the others. We have overlooked all local circumstances—we have considered this subject on the broad scale of the general good: we have asserted the cause of the present and future ages: the cause of liberty and mankind.

In the "Address and Reasons of the Dissent of the Minority," the westerners Smilie, Findley, and Whitehill summed up their opposition to the Constitution (see John Smilie, William Findley, and Robert Whitehill entries in *Biographies*). Their principal concerns were excessive central government and depriving the people of personal rights. They also pointed out that Philadelphia Federalists dominated the convention and hardly allowed the opposition to speak at all.

REFERENCES

Jensen and Kaminski, *Documentary History*, vol. 2; *Pennsylvania Packet*, December 20, 1787.

Benjamin Workman ("Philadelphiensis"), V, "Diabolical Plots and Secret Machinations," *December 19, 1787*

My Fellow Citizens, If the arbitrary proceedings of the convention of Pennsylvania do not rouse your attention to the rights of yourselves and your children, there is nothing that I can say will do it. If the contempt and obloquy with which that body (whose legality even may be questioned) has treated your petitions, can not bring you to think seriously, what then will? When a few Demagogues despising every sense of order and decency, have rejected the petitions of the people, and in the most supercilious manner, triumphed over the freemen of America, as if they were their slaves, and they themselves their lords and masters. I say that if such barefaced presumption and arrogance, such tyrannical proceedings of the men, who, if acting constitutionally, were the servants of the people, be not sufficient to awaken you to a sense of your duty and interest, nothing less than the goad and the whip can succeed: your condition must be like that of the careless and insecure sinner, whom neither the admonitions nor entreaties of his friends, nor even the threatenings of awaiting justice, could reclaim or convince of his error; his reformation is neglected until it is too late, when he finds himself in a state of unutterable and endless woe.

It may be asserted with confidence, that besides the petitions that Mr. Whitehill presented to the convention from Cumberland county against the adoption of the new constitution, there is not a county or town in the state that should not have followed the example, if a reasonable time had been allowed for the petitions to come in. Now if we consider but for a moment how contemptuously the people were treated on this occasion, we may form some idea of the way in which they are hereafter to be governed by their *well born masters.* "The petitions being read from the chair. Mr. M'Kean said he was sorry that at this stage of the business so *improper* an attempt should be made; he hoped, therefore that the petitions would not be *attended to.*"[1] Where is the freeman in America that can tamely suffer such an insult to his dignity to pass with impunity; where is that pusillanimous wretch who can submit to this contumely? Is not this the language of Britain, in the years 1775 and 1776, renewed. What said George the third and his pampered ministers, more than this, to the petitions of America? Is it improper for freemen to petition for their rights? If it be; then I say that the impropriety consisted only in their not *demanding* them. Propriety requires that the people should approach their representatives with a becoming humility; but the governors of a free people must ever be considered as their servants, and are therefore bound to observe decency towards them, and to act according to their instructions and agreeably to conscience. If the petitions of the freemen of America, couched in decent and respectful terms, will not be attended to; then be it known, that their *demands* must and will be granted: If no better will do, the ultima ratio regum must secure to the people their rights. God in his providence has crowned them with success once already on this head; and their is little doubt, with the same assistance, but a second attempt will terminate just as much in favor of liberty.

The indignity offered to the people and their petitions, by the haughty lordlings of the convention, proclaims the chains of despotism already firmly riveted; like a herald it cries aloud, hush ye slaves, how dare you interrupt your *mighty rulers*, who alone have a divine right to establish constitutions and governments calculated to promote their own agrandizement and honor. Ah my friends, the days of a cruel Nero approach fast; the language of a monster, of a Caligula, could not be more imperious. I challenge the whole continent, the *well born and their parasites*, to show an instance of greater insolence than this, on the part of the British tyrant and his infernal junto, to the people of America, before our glorious revolution. My fellow citizens, this is an awful crisis; your situation is alarming indeed; yourselves and your petitions are despised and trampled under the feet of self-important nabobs; whose diabolical plots and secret machinations have been carried on since the revolution, with a view to destroy your liberties, and reduce you to a state of slavery and dependence; and alas! I fear they have found you off your guard, and taken you by surprise: these aspiring men have seized the government, and secured all power, as they suppose, to themselves, now openly browbeat you with their insolence, and assume majesty; and even treat you like menial servants, your representatives as so many conquered slaves, that, they intend to make pass under the yoke, as soon as leisure from their gluttony and rioting on the industry of the poor, shall permit them to attend such a pleasing piece of sport.

But I trust, these petty tyrants will soon find to their confussion, that their own imprudent zeal has defeated their designs. Providence has ordered, that they should begin to carry their arbitrary schemes too soon into execution, that, their boundless ambition should precipitate their destruction, and that the glory of God should be made perfect in the salvation of the poor. Blessed be his name, "He hath shewed strength with his arm; he hath scattered the proud in the imagination of their hearts. He hath put down the mighty from their seat, and exalted them of low degree. He hath filled the hungry with good things, and the rich he hath sent empty away." As a villain, who, secreted to rob and murder in the silent hour of night, issues forth from his lurking place before the people have retired to sleep, and thus frustrates his infernal design by impatience; so in like manner the lust of dominion has urged these despots on to the adoption of measures that will inevitably, and, I hope, immediately unhinge every part of their conspiracy against the rights of their fellow-men, and bring on themselves infamy and disgrace.

Figure to yourselves, my brethren, a man with a plantation just sufficient to raise a competency for himself and his dear little children; but by reason of the immoderate revenue necessary to support the *emperor*, the illustrious *well born Congress, the standing army*, &c. &c. he necessarily fails in the payment of his *taxes*; then a hard-hearted federal officer seizes, and sells, his cows, his horses, and even the land itself must be disposed of to answer the demands of government: He pleads unfruitful seasons, his old age, and his numerous, and helpless family. But alas! these avail him nothing, his farm, his cattle, and his all are sold for less than half their value to his wealthy neighbour, already possessed of half the land in the county, to whom also himself and his children must become servants and slaves, or else perish with hunger and want. Do I exaggerate here? No truly. View the misery of the poor under the despotic governments of Europe and Asia, and then deny the truth of my position, if you can. It is a common saying among the poor of Indostan, that to lie is better than to stand, to sleep is better than to wake, but death is best of all; for it delivers them from the cruelty of their nabobs. Even in the freest country in Europe, a lady's lap-dog is more esteemed than the child of a poor man. O God, what a monster is man! that a dog should be nourished and pampered up by him with dainties; whilst a being, possessed of knowledge, reason, judgement, and an immortal soul, bought with no less a price than the blood of our divine Redeemer, should be driven from his door, without admitting him even for a moment to assuage his hunger with the crumbs that might fall from his table.

But the members of the Federal Convention were men who have been all tried in the field of action, say some; they have fought for American liberty: Then the more to their shame be it said; curse on the villain who protects virgin innocence only with a view that he may himself become the ravisher; so that if the assertion were true, it only turns to their disgrace; but as it happens it is not true, or at least only so in part: This was a scheme taken by the despots and their sycophants to biass the public mind in favor of the constitution; for the convention was composed of a variety of characters; ambitious men Jesuites, tories, lawyers, &c. formed the majority, whose similitude to each other, consisted only in their determination to lord it over their fellow citizens; like the rays that converging from every direction meet in a point, their sentiments and deliberations concentered in tyranny alone; they were unanimous in forming a government that should raise the fortunes and respectability of the *well born few*, and oppress the plebians.

Reprinted and circulated throughout the states, this was one of at least five articles by Benjamin Workman, an immigrant who taught at the University of Pennsylvania (see Benjamin Workman entry in *Biographies*). In the article, Workman accused the Pennsylvania Federalists of excessive ambition.

REFERENCES

Independent Gazetteer, December 19, 1787; Jensen and Kaminski, *Documentary History*, vol. 2.

NOTE

1. Thomas McKean, Philadelphia delegate to the State Ratification Convention.

William Petrikin, *The Scourge,*
January 23, 1788

The various and repeated defeats which that party who arrogates to themselves
the appellation of federalists has received from the friends of liberty in Carlisle
has almost tortured their souls to distraction; many schemes of revenge has been
devised which have proved unsuccessful—Immediately after their last attempt
to rejoice was baffled, they betook themselves to law for revenge; as this was
their native region (some of the principal partizans being attornies) they assured
themselves of an easy victory, and solaced their ravenous souls with an ample
and speedy glut of revenge; threats, menaces and awful denounciations was now
issued out; nothing less than gaols, dungeons, chains and fetters, were to be the
portion of their adversaries, but their bravadoes were all visionary, their dastardly
souls shrunk back into their own native cowardice, and their sanguinary hopes
of vengeance was again disappointed. They then betook themselves to scrib-
bling; here again they promised themselves the advantage, having the learned
professions on their side, and by the help of their invention they fabricated a
system of falshood and misrepresentations, and procured an old man whom they
before employed as a spy to father them, which they published in the Carlisle
Gazette; this provoked one of the people to draw forth the dagger of truth and
thrust it into their bellies, which had the very effect he expected, and which
naturally results from such causes, viz. the dirt came out. I don't undertake the
disagreeable task of wading through such heaps of putrid matter from any design to point forth their nauseous qualities to the public; to suppose they needed
this, would be an insult upon their understanding, but I am a pationate friend
to liberty which makes me delight in tormenting tyrants; I must therefore give
the dagger another thrust, for there is more dirt yet. The authors of the piece
signed, another of the people, conscious that reason and truth detested their
cause like the rest of their new federal brethren, betake themselves to personal
slander, defamation and detraction, in order to vent their spleen and emit their
disappointed malice: after a most virulent declamation by way of introduction
they exclaim that "their piece is not the work of an attorney," in this I grant
they have justly corrected one of the people, perhaps it is not the work of one
attorney, I will believe it employed the heads of all the attorneys then in town,
and all the auxillaries they could procure to compose it; and it certainly does
honour to their literary acquisitions. They may without presumption vie with a
Solon, a Lycurgus, a Montesquieu or an Adams; they add "nor of needy obscure and starving adventurers whose precarious freedom depends on the nod
of their numerous creditors;" it is evident this alludes to the new-incomers; large

quantities of dirt of the same kind is disgorged in other places—they say, that "they are men equally void of credit, character or understanding;" and again, that "the old man would scarcely wish to barter an unembarrassed situation for poverty." By all these dirty and malicious hints, it is evident that the old man and his party, envies the rising consequence of the new-incomers, notwithstanding they affect to deny it; for it is manifest that such of the new-incomers as is here pointed at, is in much better credit than many of their malicious adversaries, whose credit would not permit them to appear in Philadelphia this fall (Some of them has not gone down these nine, twelve and eighteen months, and some of their greatest nabobs these two years; we would despise mentioning such circumstances, were it not to contrast these unembarrassed characters with those whom they are pleased to represent as needy, starving adventurers, &c.) least they should have a disagreeable interview with some of their "numerous creditors." Who rose from a state of insignificancy and contempt to an appearance of affluence, at the expence of the public, and retains that appearance at the nod of "their numerous creditors." I wish the public to examine into the truth of these facts, and then say who has reason to boast of an unembarrassed situation. They further add, "nor of a man who lives in violation of every divine precept and moral duty;" perhaps the authors of the old man's adopted brat may be very pious men for ought I know, but if they are, they have certainly sworn to conceal it from the rest of mankind, but men differ in opinion about religious as well as civil matters, perhaps they account it divine precepts and moral duties, to print falsehoods, threaten the lives of their neighbours, go to church once or twice of a Sunday to hear a solemn lecture on politics, blended with geography and astronomy, and interspersed with a few religious hints, and spend the remainder of the day in sacrificing to Bacchus; but it is evident this pious parade is not so much intended to embellish their own character as it is to defame that of another man's, but as his character is established in Pennsylvania infinitely above the reach of their malicious insinuations, and as Cumberland county hath already given demonstration to the world that they esteem him a better man than any of their fraternity; I shall therefore leave the public indignation to be their scourge; and only observe, that it is evident the dagger has made a large orrifice when such large quantities of dirt comes out. Yet notwithstanding this great fluxion there is more dirt yet. The next passage that represents itself is of the same diabolical nature, they say, "nor of one who basely deserted a constitution which he approved by an uplifted hand in a town meeting, and who under the smile of complacency and benevolence conceals a black and most treacherous heart, and under the specious mantle of religion covers a most depraved mind, &c." It is really astonishing the distracted frenzy that disappointed rage will drive men to. One man they stigmatize as a violator of every divine precept, &c. because he does not make a specious profession of religion—another they brand with detestable hypocrisy because he makes a profession of religion, and practices the duties thereof too, with much more uprightness, at least to human appearance (and we can judge no further) than any of his calumniators can pretend to; but the more good qualities he possesses the more obnoxious he is to their envenomed malevolence; they hate him because he is a man of honesty and integrity, and dare think for himself, and avow his principles; would he prostitute his understanding to act the deceitful Parisite; the cringing tool, or fawning minion to our pretended quality. He would with the greatest alacrity be admitted "into the councils of the great," but his magnanimous soul disdains such servile disimulation. They talk of a well dressed man wrestling with a chimney sweep; this is the comparison they draw between themselves and the people. Candid public: these are the men who endeavour by fraud and force, to cram down your throats a constitution which would immediately create them your rulers; they here present you with a small specimen of what treatment you may expect when their favourite constitution becomes "the supreme law of the land." The most contemptuous and degrading epithets, is given to all such as are not of their faction; no better names than "rabble, mob, chimney sweeps, ragamuffins, vile, contemptible, senseless, ignorant, suited only by nature to a state of insignificance and contempt, is conferred on such citizens as oppose the ambitious views of this imperious junto—Rouse then my fellow citizens before it be too late; act with a spirit becoming freemen; convince the world and your adversaries to, who wish to become your tyrants—That you are not insensible of the invaluable blessings of liberty—That you esteem life and property, but secondary objects; when your liberty comes to be attacked.

Teach these domineering despots who wish to rejoice, because they have a prospect of rioting on your spoils; that you perceive their designs, that you can both read and understand their constitution, & spurn it with contempt. They make a flourish about deserting Rinn, and pray who deserted him. It is a certain fact that he was released from his chains at the request and intercession of our new federalists; that one of their champanions brought his pardon from Philadelphia,—That they hired him for five shillings to assist them, his good friends and benefactors, in carrying on their rejoicing; that they deserted him without paying him his wages, and that he, unmindful of recent favours, gratified his revenge by burning their hackney sled, and the cannon carriage. May it not then be retorted on them with the strictest propriety, "for shame! for shame! Do not act so ungratefully by your worthy friend, for whom you had so lately discovered such a kindness by procuring for him his dear bought liberty, his valiant and faithfull services in your cause, (for which you never paid him), deserve a better return; pray then do not disown your guide and Captain of Artillery. I understand the passage in their first piece "that some who opposed the rejoicing, had but lately stripped of the garb of British soldiers," is pointed to a certain gentleman who belonged to a Volunteer Company in Ireland. (Men who bravely espoused the cause of liberty in their own country; nor will they desert it here). The gentleman alluded to, challenges the Poother Anatomy who circulated the insidious falshood of a British soldier, to step forth and prove the assertion, otherwise he will be looked on with contempt, and treated accordingly. If his Pootership declines this reasonable demand, he may expect the public will consider him what he really is, a blazing meteor, or mere sky-rocket; but as the public are already in full possession of his faculty, and as he has formerly given a specimen of his vindictive, slanderous disposition, I shall dismiss him at present with wishing nothing worse to befal him, than he procured lately to a man of principles much superior to himself; this would be adding the crime of ingratitude to that of lying, defaming and cheating the hireling of his wages."

It is denied by them that the rejoicers had muskets, bayonets and bludgeons at the time of their rout, I know not what they had at the time of their rout, perhaps they threw them away that they might not incumber them in their flight; but that they had them immediately before their rout is a fact given in testimony, where no party riden lawyers were admitted as inquisitors, nor was the truth partly heard, and partly stifled, but the truth, the whole truth, and nothing but the truth was required and stated with the utmost precision; neither was self-accusation extorted from the simple and ignorant, by terror and menace, so that any person who may be solicitous to ascertain a true state of facts, may have information from other depositions besides those in the "upright magistrates" inquisition; upright indeed! rather the dupe and creature of a domineering faction. They affirm "the drum of the mob had not beat until the federalists left the ground," the drum of the mob was their own drum, but if they mean the people's drum it is a palpable falsehood; it can be proven by more than fifty witnesses, that the people's drum beat around two squares before they (the federalists) left the ground.— They seem to be mightily chagrined at calling the intended rejoicers a mob, but why so much offended, they were only acting in unison with their new federal brethren in the city, whose conduct they cordially approved chearfully recognized the authority of the mob in Philadelphia, who broke open private houses, and dragged two of the members through the streets to the State-House, and then guarded the Assembly while they were passing the resolutions for calling the state convention. The midnight mob headed by Jemey the Caledonian,[1] who attacked the lodgings of the western members of Assembly and Council, on the night of the elections for convention men, was an upright, orderly association, and highly servicable to the federal junto. The mob who insulted the western members, when advocating the rights of the people in convention, was of great utility, as they served to keep the members who were advocates for the proposed constitution, &c. in countenance when reason and argument had deserted them—In a word were it not for the mob the new constitution would not yet have been adopted in Pennsylvania; and our Carlisle rejoicers would have wanted this cause "to be pleased," and to assemble in a mobocratical manner, to express that pleasure. They further say "one of the captains had not slept off his night's drunkenness;" what more dirt yet, will the fluxion never cease. It is notoriously known that the person here alluded to, maintains a character the very reverse of what they represent; and that his opposition to the rejoicing, proceeded from that love of freedom which stimulated him, to expose himself to perils and dangers, during the late struggle for American independence; when their old man, and other ringleaders of these pretended federalists, basely sculked behind the curtain. They say, "the other was unfit to appear as he had provoked a federalist, to bung his eyes on Wednesday evening;" I expected shame would have deterred them from mentioning falsehood, as the federalist carryed the bung one of his eyes to the sham rejoicing day; and although the order appeared publickly, no such thing was to be but every thing combines to prove "the dirt came out."

The passage in one of the people, which says, "that the rejoicers had weapons and numbers more than sufficient," seems to give the dagger a violent thrust, and consequently draws forth a great eruption of dirt; they endeavour to represent it as an inconsistency with the passage, which says, "the rejoicing was contrary to the minds of three fourths of the inhabitants;" but I would wish to know where the inconsistency lies; might not three fourths of the inhabitants be against the rejoicing, and yet not one eighth of them be on the spot to oppose it; very few of the inhabitants knew any thing of the rejoicing, (the spunging club at the glimmering attorney's excepted), until it was ripe for execution; so that only a few who catched the report by chance, were on the ground to oppose it. They say, "that some of the new comers are respectable characters, and reprobate the conduct of their apostate countrymen." Yes! such of them as are under petticoat government which is certainly a very respectable situation; I think those who submit to it, may be pretty easy what constitution is the "supreme law of the land." They say "the threat in the concluding paragraph is the most despicable; they knew or might have known the authors by applying to the printers." What! is it granted that the old man was not the author, then it seems, one of the people was right in his conjecture, that the piece was a bastard, and the old man only the adopting father, or rather grandfather.—Gentlemen, apply your own proverb, "lyers should have good memories," applying to the printers for the authors names we detest. We know it is the practice of our despotic opponents; but we contend for a free press, and abhor every thing that has the least tendency to shackle it. Neither do we employ pimps and spies to catch what intelligence they can, by obtruding themselves upon companies, where their presence is as disagreeable and surfeiting as the fluxion of dirt which is emitted by the authors of another of the people.

Thus I have so far dissected this putrid carcase, were I to take notice of all the dirt which it contains, I must transcribe the whole; but this is a task by far too laborious, disagreeable and nauseous.—Other persons pointed at will therefore excuse me, if I omit saying any thing in their behalf; it greatly accelerates our business in this affair, that we have the good-will, faith, and credit of the country on our side. We are struggling for their rights and liberties, as well as our own. (Petrikin finishes with a song, "The Federal Joy.")

William Petrikin, a Philadelphia mechanic with little education, wrote from prison about the role of the Antifederalists in the Carlisle riot (see William Petrikin entry in *Biographies*). Claiming the supposed rioters had only defended themselves, he accused the Federalists of espousing class warfare. He also maintained that an aristocratic element had taken over state government. Though written after the convention had ended, Petrikin's work serves as a reminder of the unhappiness of the Antifederalists over the results.

REFERENCE

Jensen and Kaminski, *Documentary History*, vol. 2.

NOTE

1. James Wilson.

Samuel Bryan ("Centinel"), XII, "The Federalists' Conspiracy," *January 23, 1788*

TO THE PEOPLE OF PENNSYLVANIA.

Fellow-Citizens, Conscious guilt has taken the alarm, thrown out the signal of distress, and even appealed to the generosity of patriotism. The authors and abettors of the new constitution shudder at the term *conspirators* being applied to them, as it designates their true character, and seems prophetic of the catastrophe: they read their fate in the epithet.

In dispair they are weakly endeavouring to screen their criminality by interposing the shield of the virtues of a Washington, in representing his concurrence in the proposed system of government, as evidence of the purity of their intentions; but this impotent attempt to degrade the brightest ornament of his country to a base level with themselves, will be considered as an aggravation of their treason, and an insult on the good sense of the people, who have too much discernment not to make a just discrimination between the honest mistaken zeal of the patriot, and the flagitious machinations of an ambitious junto, and will resent the imposition that Machiavelian arts and consummate cunning have practised upon our *illustrious chief.*

The term *conspirators* was not, as has been alledged, rashly or inconsiderately adopted; it is the language of dispassionate and deliberate reason, influenced by the purest patriotism: the consideration of the nature and construction of the new constitution naturally suggests the epithet; its justness is strikingly illustrated by the conduct of the patrons of this plan of government, but if any doubt had remained whether this epithet is merited, it is now removed by the very uneasiness it occasions; this is a confirmation of its propriety. Innocence would have nothing to dread from such a stigma, but would triumph over the shafts of malice.

The conduct of men is the best clue to their principles. The system of deception that has been practised; the constant solicitude shewn to prevent information diffusing its salutary light, are evidence of a conspiracy beyond the arts of sophistry to palliate, or the ingenuity of falsehood to invalidate: the means practised to establish the new constitution are demonstrative of the principles and designs of its authors and abettors.

At the time, says Mr. Martin[1] (deputy from the state of Maryland in the general convention) when the public prints were announcing our perfect unanimity, discord prevailed to such a degree, that the minority were upon the point of appealing to the public against the machinations of ambition. By such a base imposition, repeated in every newspaper and reverberated from one end of the union to the other, was the people lulled into a false confidence, into an implicit reliance upon the wisdom and patriotism of the convention; and when ambition, by her deceptive wiles, had succeeded to usher forth the new system of government with apparent unanimity of sentiment, the public delusion was compleat. The most extravagant fictions were palmed upon the people, the seal of divinity was even ascribed to the new constitution; a felicity more than human was to ensue from its establishment;—overlooking the real cause of our difficulties and burthens, which have their proper remedy, the people were taught that the new constitution would prove a mine of wealth and prosperity equal to every want, or the most sanguine desire; that it would effect what can only be produced by the exertion of industry and the practice of œconomy.

The conspirators, aware of the danger of delay, that allowing time for a rational investigation would prove fatal to their designs, precipitated the establishment of the new constitution with all possible celerity; in Massachusetts the deputies of that convention, who are to give the final fiat in behalf of that great state to a measure upon which their dearest concerns depend, were elected by express in the first moments of blind enthusiasm; similar conduct has prevailed in the other states as far as circumstances permitted.

If the foregoing circumstances did not prove a conspiracy, there are others that must strike conviction in the most unsuspicious. Attempts to prevent discussion by shackling the press ought ever to be a signal of alarm to freemen, and considered as an annunciation of meditated tyranny; this is a truth that the uniform experience of mankind has established beyond the possibility of doubt. Bring the conduct of the authors and abettors of the new constitution to this test, let this be the criterion of their criminality, and every patriotic mind must unite in branding them with the stigma of conspirators against the public liberties.—No stage of this business but what has been marked with every exertion of influence and device of ambition to suppress information and intimidate public discussion; the virtue and firmness of some of the printers, rose superior to the menaces of violence, and the lucre of private interest; when every means failed to shackle the press, the free and independent papers were attempted to be demolished by withdrawing all the subscriptions to them within the sphere of the influence of the conspirators; fortunately for the cause of liberty and truth, these daring high handed attempts have failed except in one instance, where from a peculiarity of circumstances, ambition has triumphed. Under the flimsey pretence of vindicating the character of a contemptible drudge of party rendered ridiculous by his superlative folly in the late convention, of which the statement given in the Pennsylvania Herald, was confessedly a faithful representation, this newspaper has been silenced by some hundreds of its subscribers (who it seems are generally among the devoted tools of party, or those who are obliged from their thraldom to yield implicit assent to the mandates of the junto) withdrawing their support from it; by this stroke the conspirators have suppressed the publication of the most valuable debates of the late convention, which would have been given in course by the Editor of that paper, whose stipend now ceasing, he cannot afford without compensation the time and attention necessary to this business.[2]

Every patriotic person who had an opportunity of hearing that illustrious advocate of liberty and his country, Mr. Findley, must sensibly regret that his powerful arguments are not to extend beyond the confined walls of the State-House, where they could have so limitted an effect; that the United States could not have been his auditory through the medium of the press. I anticipate the answer of the conspirators; they will tell you that this could not be their motive for silencing this paper, as the whole of the debates were taken down in short hand by another person and published, but the public are not to be so easily duped, they will not receive a spurious as an equivalent for a genuine production; equal solicitude was expressed for the publication of the former as for the suppression of the latter—the public will judge of the motives.

That investigation into the nature and construction of the new constitution, which the conspirators have so long and zealously struggled against, has, notwithstanding their partial success, so far taken place as to ascertain the enormity of their criminality. That system which was pompously displayed as the perfection of government, proves upon examination to be the most odious system of tyranny that was ever projected, a many headed hydra of despotism, whose complicated and various evils would be infinitely more oppressive and afflictive than the scourge of any single tyrant: the objects of dominion would be tortured to gratify the calls of ambition and cravings of power, of rival despots contending for the sceptre of superiority; the devoted people would experience a distraction of misery.

No wonder then that such a discovery should excite uneasy apprehensions in the minds of the conspirators, for such an attempt against the public liberties is unprecedented in history, it is a crime of the blackest dye, as it strikes at the happiness of millions and the dignity of human nature, as it was intended to deprive the inhabitants of so large a portion of the globe of the choicest blessing of life and the oppressed of all nations of an asylum.

The explicit language of the Centinel during the empire of delusion was not congenial to the feelings of the people, but truth when it has free scope is all powerful, it enforces conviction in the most prejudiced mind; he foresaw the consequence of an exertion of the good sense and understanding of the people, and predicted the defeat of the measure he ventured to attack, when it was deemed sacred by most men and the certain ruin of any who should dare to lisp a word against it: he has persevered through every discouraging appearance, and has now the satisfaction to find his countrymen are aware of their danger and are taking measures for their security.

Since writing the foregoing, I am informed that the Printer of the Pennsylvania Herald is not quite decided whether he will drop his paper; he wishes, and perhaps will be enabled, to persevere; however, the conspirators have effected their purpose; the editor is dismissed and the debates of the convention thereby suppressed.

In this last "Centinel," Samuel Bryan claimed a Federalist conspiracy to undermine popular rights, as they sought to deny freedom of the press to the Antifederalists (see Samuel Bryan entry in *Biographies*). His effort circulated widely through the states, and many opponents of the Constitution used Bryan's argument for defense of free speech.

REFERENCES

Independent Gazetteer, January 23, 1788; Storing, *Complete*, vol. 3.

NOTES

1. Luther Martin, Maryland Antifederalist.
2. Eleazor Oswald, beleagured Antifederalist editor.

"Petition of the Harrisburg Convention,"
September 3, 1788

That your petitioners possess sentiments completely federal; being convinced that a confederacy of republican States, and no other, can secure political liberty, happiness, and safety throughout a territory so extended as the United States of America. They are well apprised of the necessity of devolving extensive powers to Congress, and of vesting the supreme legislature with every power and resource of a general nature; and consequently they acquiesce in the general system of government framed by the late federal convention; in full confidence, however, that the same will be revised without delay: for however worthy of approbation the general principles and outlines of the said system may be, your petitioners conceive that amendments in some parts of the plan are essential, not only to the preservation of such rights and privileges as ought to be reserved in the respective States, and in the citizens thereof, but to the fair and unembarrassed operation of the government in its various departments. And as provision is made in the constitution itself for the making of such amendments as may be deemed necessary, and your petitioners are desirous of obtaining the amendments which occur to them as more immediately desirable and necessary, in the mode admitted by such provision, they pray that your honorable House, as the Representatives of the people in this Commonwealth, will, in the course of your present session, take such measures as you in your wisdom shall deem most effectual and proper, to obtain a revision and amendment of the constitution of the United States, in such parts and in such manner as have been or shall be pointed out by the conventions or assemblies of the respective States; and that such revision be by a general convention of representatives from the several States in the union.

Your petitioners consider the amendments pointed out in the propositions hereto subjoined as essentially necessary, and as such they suggest them to your notice, submitting to your wisdom the order in which they shall be presented to the consideration of the United States.

The amendments proposed are as follows, viz:

I. That Congress shall not exercise any powers whatsoever, but such as are expressly given to that body by the constitution of the United States; nor shall any authority, power or jurisdiction, be assumed or exercised by the executive or judiciary departments of the union under color or pretense of construction or fiction. But all the rights of sovereignty, which are not by the said constitution expressly and plainly vested in the Congress, shall be deemed to remain with, and shall be exercised, by the several states in union according to their respective constitutions. And that every reserve of the rights of individuals, made by the several constitutions of the states in union to the citizens and inhabitants of each State respectively, shall remain inviolate, except so far as they are expressly and manifestly yielded or narrowed by the national constitution.

Article I, Section 2, Paragraph 3.

II. That the number of representatives be for the present one for every twenty thousand inhabitants, according to the present estimated number in the several states, and continue in that proportion till the whole number of representatives shall amount to two hundred; and then to be so proportioned and modified as not to exceed that number till the proportion of one representative for every thirty thousand inhabitants shall amount to the said number of two hundred.

Section 3.

III. That Senators, though chosen for six years, shall be liable to be recalled or superseded by other appointments, by the respective legislatures of the States, at any time.

Section 4.

IV. That Congress shall not have power to make or alter regulations concerning the time, place, and manner of electing Senators and Representatives, except in case of neglect or refusal by the State to make regulations for the purpose, and then only for such time as such neglect or refusal shall continue.

Section 8.

V. That when Congress shall require supplies, which are to be raised by direct taxes, they shall demand from the several States their respective quotas thereof, giving a reasonable time to each State to procure and pay the same; and if any State shall refuse, neglect, or omit to raise and pay the same within such limited time, then Congress shall have power to assess, levy, and collect the quota of such State, together with interest for the same from the time of such delinquency, upon the inhabitants and estates therein, in such manner as they shall by law direct, provided that no poll-tax be imposed.

Section 8.

VI. That no standing army of regular troops shall be raised or kept up in time of peace, without the consent of two-thirds of both Houses in Congress.

Section 8.

VII. That the clause respecting the exclusive legislation over a district not exceeding ten miles square, be qualified by a proviso that such right of legislation extend only to such regulations as respect the police and good order thereof.

Article I, Section 8.

VIII. That each State respectively shall have power to provide for organizing, arming, and disciplining the militia thereof, whensoever Congress shall omit or neglect to provide for the same. That the militia shall not be subject to martial law, but when in actual service in time of war, invasion or rebellion; and when not in the actual service of the United States, shall be subject to such fines, penalties, and punishments only, as shall be directed or inflicted by the laws of its own State: nor shall the militia of any State be continued in actual service longer than two months under any call of Congress, without the consent of the legislature of such State, or, in their recess, the executive authority thereof.

Section 9.

IX. That the clause respecting vessels bound to or from any one of the States, be explained.

Article 3. Section I.

X. That Congress establish no court other than the Supreme Court, except such as shall be necessary for determining causes of admiralty jurisdiction.

Section 2. Paragraph 2.

XI. That a proviso be added at the end of the second clause of the second section of the third article, to the following effect, viz.: Provided, That such appellate jurisdiction, in all cases of common law cognizance, be by writ of error, and confined to matters of law only; and that no such writ of error shall be admitted except in revenue cases, unless the matter in controversy exceed the value of three thousand dollars.

Article 6. Paragraph 2.

XII. That to article six, clause two, be added the following proviso, viz.: Provided always, That no treaty which shall hereafter be made, shall be deemed or construed to alter or affect any law of the United States, or of any particular State, until such treaty shall have been laid before and assented to by the House of Representatives in Congress.

Wanting to keep their opposition to the Constitution alive, the Antifederalists met in convention at Harrisburg in the autumn of 1788. In the "Petition," they called for another Constitutional Convention and offered amendments for the people to peruse. This petition was important because it influenced other states' Antifederalist leaders in their drafting of a bill of rights.

REFERENCES

Independent Gazetteer, September 15, 1788; Jensen and Kaminski, *Documentary History*, vol. 2.

2
Delaware

December 3–December 7, 1787

Ratification #1, December 7, 1787

In favor 30–0

James Tilton ("Timoleum"), *The Tyrant of Delaware,* (1788) (excerpts)

An indolent habit in the inhabitants of the remoter parts of New Castle County in neglecting to attend at the general election, except when a new sheriff is to be introduced, contributed very much to the success of this enterprise of DIONYSIUS.[1] This was not one of those years which brought in the remote electors. The DIONYSIANS, abounding at and about the court or place of election, and excited by extraordinary efforts of their leaders, flocked in from all quarters sufficiently numerous to carry their whole ticket, consisting of men of specious and decent appearance, but of perfectly *adjective* characters unaccustomed to stand alone, and so destitute of talents as to be admirably fitted to act by authority.

It was a great triumph to have carried the election *entirely* at New Castle. But the faction had not succeeded so well in Kent and Sussex. The cry against *Presbyterians,* though kept up with the usual officious impertinence, had by this time so far abated of its force with the sharp-sighted people of Kent that, in this county, the DIONYSIANS carried but about half their ticket.

In Sussex, the Whigs had unanimously and resolutely resolved that this election should not be carried by Refugees and other enemies to the country, who were so far from showing any repentance for their former offenses that they now acted professedly with a vindictive spirit towards the Whigs. The Whigs made public declaration of the principle from which they acted and gave full evidence of their stern purpose. Considering themselves as betrayed by the legislature, in permitting characters of a description so wicked and base to interfere in their elections, they determined the revolutionists should not be thus trampled upon by their enemies, that our constitution and laws should not be thus perverted into an engine of corruption, whereby the most bitter enemies to our liberty were enabled to avenge themselves upon those who had vanquished them in the struggle for independence; and they called upon the common sense and common feelings of mankind to justify them in the use of force, if necessary, in so good a cause. Though inferior in number, they relied on the continued favor of Heaven in finally vanquishing their mean and degenerate opponents. They made a show of arms in their previous meetings, but on the day of election appeared only with sticks in their hands (a few individuals excepted) in a connected form and with a countenance and manner resolute and determined. The sheriff, by the advice of the magistrates, adjourned the election early in the morning and kept it open from the 1st to the 15th of the month. In the meantime, the President visited the county and interposed his influence to prevent further disorder. He advised an Union Ticket consisting of equal numbers from both parties. This compromise was apparently agreed to, and it was expected the election would be held peaceably on the 15th day. The Whigs met at the usual place in Lewes, and the Tories assembled a mile or two out of town. It was soon discovered the parties had no confidence in each other. Ambassadors were mutually exchanged, and as the only means by which confidence could be ensured, it was agreed that only fifty on each side should vote, and the election be then closed. Such was the common consent to this measure that no man was prohibited from voting, who insisted upon his right. Thus was the election conducted, and the return made accordingly.

It must be noted, however, that after the election was closed, the Whigs were guilty of an indiscretion. Some angry spirits, who had bridled their passions during the election, considering the treaty as subsisting no longer, gave a loose to their resentment and called upon their companions to drive the Tories out of town. The Tories fled at the first onset, and some of the more obnoxious were caught and beaten. The Tories in return waylaid the Whigs on their return home and avenged themselves on individuals whom they caught straggling from the main body. . . .

At the first meeting of the legislature, the DIONYSIAN partisans considered their majority as secure enough. The Tory members from Sussex, willing to acquiesce in the election, expressed their desire that it should be established; and it was expected for many days that the election would be confirmed. But DIONYSIUS, upon his arrival, penetrated the members, with an eagle's eye, and found them not to his purpose. Besides the great abhorrence he had to a certain Whig of notable abilities returned from Sussex, he must have been sensible that the Kent members (with an exception or two), however returned, were too independent for him to rely upon. By an influence secret and unaccountable, a tide of opposition to the establishment of the election suddenly arose; and two of the Tory members from Sussex were sent down to hunt up petitioners against the election.

In the meantime, a law passed for lessening the quorum of the House of Assembly. This was esteemed a great piece of policy, necessary to guard against all possible obstruction to the measures intended by a secession of the minority.

The lackey members returned from Sussex with petitions signed by 121 inhabitants complaining of the manner of conducting the late election and praying relief in the premises. The House then proceeded to a formal inquiry and determined the election of members returned for Sussex to be illegal and void. Here it is to be observed that although it was given in evidence in support of the freedom of the election, that no elector was restrained or prevented from voting who insisted upon his privilege; yet the Kent members, unwilling to give any countenance to tumults or riots, with great candor acknowledged that the election was informal, and by an unanimous vote it was set aside and a new one ordered.

In Council, after examining the sheriff and his deputy and one of the inspectors, though none of them upon oath, DIONYSIUS observed that the disorders of Sussex were deeply seated in causes of long standing which ought to be thoroughly investigated. A member[2] replied that he liked the hint and proposed on this occasion a thorough inquiry, on both sides of the question, into those latent causes which produced so much mischief; that by fairly exposing their vices and prejudices, whence the evils complained of resulted, the most probable remedy might be obtained. But DIONYSIUS did not approve a cure of this sort; he changed his ground suddenly; called for a vote upon the election. It was adjudged that it was not freely, legally, and indifferently made, and that the member returned was not duly elected.

It was alleged on this occasion that, however illegal the election might be, there was no sufficient evidence before the Council to determine them in their resolution; and the member who was of this opinion offered his reasons of dissent and protest against the proceeding as partial and unprecedented. But DIONYSIUS made a motion for prohibiting all reasons of dissent and protest from being entered on the Minutes on the present or *any other occasion*. The dissenting member ridiculed the idea of restraining future Councils, who would be judges of their own privileges and would have precedents enough for the practice. But nevertheless, on this extraordinary question, whether such reasons of dissent and protest, on this *or any other occasion*, should be entered on the Minutes, *it passed in the negative.*

Having set aside the preceding election, it was consulted between the Sussex *Tories* and New Castle *Patriots* how they might secure that which was ordered. It was alleged that if the place of election could be changed from Lewes, where the Whigs abounded, to some of those swamps, where the Tories had been used to maintain their camps, they might succeed better. A few petitioners were procured for this purpose; and a bill was brought in and passed "for altering the place of election, for the county of Sussex, for the present year 1787." The place appointed by this law was the house of a noted *Refugee* and in one of the most dreary haunts of the Black Campers.

Resolutions were then entered into by both houses recommending to the inhabitants of the state to elect delegates to a state convention, who should be authorized to assent to and ratify the new Federal Constitution; and that the elections should be held on the 26th November 1787. . . .

In the recess of the legislature, the Tories went immediately to canvassing for the election of Convention men. As if by concert, they spread rumors throughout the state that the Whigs would be averse from the new Federal Constitution; and they everywhere set themselves up as the patrons of it. They asserted in the most false and scandalous manner without the least foundation, that certain respectable characters, in each county, were opposed to the Constitution. As nobody in the state opposed its establishment, their lying and slandering and affected eagerness in defense of the new Constitution could only be accounted for from a desire of gaining popularity and seizing upon the powers of the new government. The Whigs rejoiced at the prospect of any government that would probably relieve them from the wanton tyranny of DIONYSIUS. Those more adequate to the task soon determined that the new Constitution was formed on republican principles; that its powers were no more than adequate to good government; that the people were free enough, and had full powers to maintain their liberty, so long as they were virtuous. There was this odds indeed between the Whigs and Tories, that the latter approved by authority, the former from reflection and judgment. We were led to this discovery by observing that a number of the more intimate acquaintance of DIONYSIUS lamented that the government had not been more *monarchical*. This led into an inquiry into the TYRANT's own sentiments. We soon found that his wish was to bask in the sunshine of *monarchy*; that the scheme of government which he had advocated in the Convention was a *monarch chosen for life, Senators also chosen for life, and an entire abolition of state governments*. Nevertheless, his followers make a mere hobby-horse of the Federal Constitution; and, let the government be what it may, they hope to ride in chief authority.

In Sussex, they were to elect representatives as well as delegates to the state Convention. The Tory candidates had gone home from the last meeting of the legislature minutely instructed as to a plan by which they might defend the freedom of election for their Refugees and Black Campers. The constitution of the state requires that no military force shall be within a mile of the place of election. They were therefore instructed to raise what force they pleased, only to keep it a mile off to serve in case of exigency. Secure in the favor and protection of the legislature, the Tories made large provision of arms and ammunition; marked out a camp, at a proper distance, beforehand; and on the day of election, marched in companies, with drums and fifes, to the appointed field of encampment. From this place of arms, where a guard of several hundred men stood constantly paraded, they marched in companies to the place of election and carried their whole ticket of representatives and Convention men without opposition, for certain leading characters among the Whigs employed all their assiduity and address to prevent the Whigs from going to the election. They foresaw that bloodshed would be the inevitable consequence of a meeting of the parties in arms; and they could not imagine any possible event of the election to be equivalent to such a misfortune. With much difficulty the Whigs were restrained and encouraged to hope for a constitutional redress of their grievances.

At a meeting of the legislature, in January, petitions were received from 504 inhabitants of Sussex, praying to be heard by counsel, as to a variety of facts stated in their petitions showing the late election for representatives to be illegal. DIONYSIUS being absent, at the first meeting of the House of Assembly, the petitioners were permitted to be heard by counsel. This brought on the open inquiry the Whigs wished for. Many witnesses were summoned on both sides.

It was proved and admitted on all hands that, with the cognizance and concurrence of the members elected, companies of armed men, with drums and fifes, moved on from all quarters of the county and joined in full force at an old field, about a mile from the place of election; that they there formed in military array, under superior and inferior officers; that their commander in chief was a member of *Congress* and their second in command a *Refugee*; that their ostensible purpose was to protect the privileges of election; and their chief conversation consisted of cursing *Presbyterians* and *Irishmen*; that sundry of the Whigs were taken prisoners by this armed body, and could no otherwise be released but by order of the *Commander in Chief*; that the body of the Whigs of the county did not attend the election on account of this armed force; that from the field they marched in companies and voted, while a guard of several hundred remained constantly under arms. It was further proved by a respectable witness, who had himself served against the Black Campers and other insurgents, that there were not less than *sixty* of these miscreants under arms on this occasion. It was also proved, that from two hundreds only, between 40 and 50 persons voted, whose names were not in the recorded list of those who had taken the test. Many witnesses declared that a number of persons were armed at the place of election, as well as in the field; and one witness deposed that he believed half the people at the house of election were armed with clubs and other weapons. It was also given in evidence that sundry persons were insulted and violently assaulted, professedly because they were *Whigs, Presbyterians,* or *Irishmen*; that one fellow in particular, after assaulting a Whig with several blows, swore his teeth had grown an inch on that day, that he might *eat* Presbyterians and Irishmen; that some huzzaed for the *King*, and others expressed a hope that they might again come under the old government. It was agreed by all, and acknowledged by the sheriff, that, before the election was closed, he had called in 40 or 50 armed men from the field as a guard round the house where the election was held.

The counsel for the petitioners respectfully set forth the dangers of infringing the freedom of election; that from the testimony adduced, the Whigs and best citizens of the county of Sussex were manifestly restrained from attending, and the freedom of the election infringed; lastly, that calling in the aid of an armed force to protect an election in a military manner must vitiate such election. Besides the constitution and laws of the state, many learned authorities were quoted to show the great abhorrence the freedom of election had to every kind of military force. He therefore hoped and expected the Honorable House of Assembly would wisely determine the late election of Sussex to be illegal and void.

A member of the House, well acquainted with the rights of a free people, modestly observed that, waiving all personal considerations and those indiscretions which proceed from party or prejudice, he begged leave to call the attention of the House to the single circumstance of carrying the election under the *influence* of a military force. He said, however it might serve one party this year, it might serve another party next year; and he shuddered at the idea of a precedent being set for establishing such a rule of conduct throughout the state.

The returned members employed no counsel. They relied upon a speaker on the floor and were secure in a majority. It was contended on their behalf that the previous riots and disturbances were a just and reasonable apology for the measures taken at the late Sussex election, that the people had a right to assemble as they did in defense of their rights and privileges; nor did the election laws forbid whole armies from assembling, in military array, if they only kept a mile off from the place of election; that the indiscreet expression of individuals, a few clubs, pistols and swords, and even boxing and fighting about indifferent matters, were no impediments to the freedom of voting; that all present might have voted if they pleased, and all who stayed away might have come if they would. Finally with an air of triumph it was declared that the electors, on this occasion, had behaved like *genuine sons of Delaware.*

The question being put, it was *resolved*, that the several persons mentioned in the sheriff's return were duly elected. It deserves to be noted that a member from each of the counties of Kent and New Castle were absent; that another member from New Castle declined to vote because he had not been present at the examination of the witnesses; that the Speaker's vote was not required; and that, therefore, this important question was determined by the voices of ten men only, 4 against 6 for establishing the election.

The counsel for the petitioners did not think it necessary to give himself any trouble in advocating their cause before the Legislative Council. It was agreed that the depositions taken before the House of Assembly should serve as evidence before the Council. These were read and the petitions dismissed.

The reader may here indulge his own reflections in comparing the judgment on the present election with that on the last, or any former occasion, when the Tories were petitioners. We shall proceed in our narrative. No sooner was the election established than the most cordial and inviolable connection took place between the DIONYSIANS of New Castle and the Tories of Sussex. The cordiality indeed was established before: the treaty was now only to be definitively ratified. On all important questions, especially those which were intended to influence the policy of the state, they uniformly voted together. The Patriots of Kent were left to wrap themselves in their virtue; and in return for their multipliesd mortifications, to derive consolation from the approbation they might receive from distant states, or the honors paid to their recorded names, at remote periods of time. The DIONYSIAN power was now paramount in both branches of the legislature; and the leader of the faction seemed determined to exercise it in a very exemplary manner.

James Tilton, a physician and member of the Continental Congress, wrote against the power structure in Delaware and insisted the Federalist George Read and his elite cronies tried to force the Constitution on the people (see James Tilton entry in *Biographies*). Though Tilton neither served in the state ratification convention nor spoke openly against the Constitution, "Timoleum" serves as the major Delaware Antifederalist attack on the Constitution.

REFERENCES

Jensen and Kaminski, *Documentary History*, vol. 3; John A. Munroe (ed.), *Timoleon's Biographical History of Dionysius, Tyrant of Delaware* (Newark: University of Delaware Press, 1958); New-York Journal, November 1, 1787.

NOTES

1. George Read, Delaware Federalist leader.
2. Tilton.

3
New Jersey

December 11–December 18, 1787

Ratification #3, December 18, 1787

In favor 38–0

Abraham Clark, Letter to Thomas Sinnickson, *July 23, 1788*

With all these imperfections about it, I nevertheless wished it to go to the States from Congress just as it did, without any Censure or Commendation, hoping that in case of a general Adoption, the Wisdom of the States would soon amend it in the exceptionable parts; strong fears, however, remained upon my mind until I found the Custom of Recommending amendments with the Adoptions began to prevail. This set my mind at ease. . . . We have been some time in suspense about the event of the New Constitution in this State. . . . I anxiously wish every State may come into the Adoption. . . .[1]

A self-made surveyor and political leader, Abraham Clark served as a delegate to the Constitutional Convention but did not sign the document (see Abraham Clark entry in *Biographies*). A member of the Continental Congress and later of the United States House, it is unclear whether Clark supported the Constitution. (Ruth Bogin, his biographer, believes he ultimately came to support the Constitution.) In this letter to fellow New Jersey political leader Thomas Sinnickson, Clark wrote of his reservations on ratification and hoped for amendments to the Constitution before New Jersey ratified. He hesitated to make further objections, knowing that his state supported ratification overwhelmingly.

REFERENCES

Ann Clark Hart (ed.), *Abraham Clark: Signer of the Declaration of Independence* (San Francisco: The Pioneer Press, 1923); Jensen and Kaminski, *Documentary History*, vol. 3.

NOTE

1. Sinnickson, a fiscal conservative, opposed Clark and accused him of opposition to ratification.

4
Georgia

December 25–31, 1787

Ratification #4, December 29, 1787

In favor 26–0

Lachlan McIntosh, Letter to John Weriot,
December 17, 1787

I am sometimes inclined to be funny, but am now very serious with you. I hear you are Chosen one of the Convention, which I am glad of, & flatter myself you will not think it either Impertinent or Officious in a fellow Citizen to give his opinion in a business of so high Importance to ourselves & our posterity as the new Federal Constitution now Offered to your Consideration, and more especially as our Legislature have thought proper to enter upon it rather precipitately before the opinions of the other States are known.

Some of the Men who framed this Constitution are the Wisest & best that this, or perhaps any other Nation ever produced, yet with all their good intentions and Abillitys if we thought them infallible their would be no Occasion to Appeal to the States & people at large, who in Republican Governments ought at all times to think themselves the Ultimate & best Judges of their own Grievances & or Conveniencys.

The popularity of the Framers is so great, that the public Voice seems to be for adopting the Constitution in the Lump on its first appearance as a perfect System without enquiry or Limitation of time or Matter, Such hasty resolutions have Occasioned all the Misfortunes that ever happened in Governments & it is realy astonishing to see people so reluctant lately to trust Congress with only 5 per Cent duties upon Imports for a short time to pay the National Debt expressly, & so Jealous of the Sovereignty of their respective States so eager now to yield these & every thing else into their hands forever & to become *the State*, instead of United States of America. it is indeed generally agreed as we might have expected that this Constitution discovers great Judgement & Abillitys, & that the pressing exigencies of our National Affairs requires Some Speedy & effectual remedy.

If therefore we reject the whole or any part of it I fear we will remain for a Considerable time at Least, without remedy in the same unconnected State we now are in as it appears to be so constructed that the whole or none of it must stand or fall together, & should it be found Necessary to call another Convention of the United States to Amend it, we cannot expect the last illustrious Members will Serve again, & the determination of any others less dignified will not have the Same general influence and may miscarry also.

Upon the other hand, the objections made to this Constution by Mr. Gerry of Massachusetts, the Centinel of Pennsyvania, & others who dare express their Minds upon it so early, tho perhaps over Cautious appear Nevertheless to be very weighty, & if the remedy should prove Worse than the Disease, what reason will their Constituents & posterity have to blame the Convention of Georgia in whom they Confided and whose option it was, to adopt or reject it for them. in either of these determinations there appears to me the greatest wish to be in this Convento. I drew up the inclosed Compromise as a Memorandum for myself, which I had some hopes might meet with the Wishes of all parties, either with or without the Annexed Conditions & be adopted not only by our own but some other States, especially the Southern States, who are more particularly Interested, as they are, and ever will Continue from their extent & other Circumstances the Minority in Congress therefore it may be thought prudent at least for them at this time for Avoiding the rocks on both sides of the question instead of binding ourselves & posterity for ever to adopt the Constitution only for a certain period of time during which they will have a fair tryal of its Effects, & at the expiration of that time be at Liberty & have it in their own power to adopt it again if they please for another period either without or with any Amendments they may find Necessary, which probably will hereafter be done by Conventions, as the precedent is now Set which is a New & far better Method of Settling public differences than the old way of Cutting one anothers Throats; if we bind ourselves & our posterity now, by adopting this Constitution without any Conditions or Limitation of time, any efforts made there after for redress of Grievances must be termed rebellion, as it will be impossible to obtain Amendments in the Mode proposed when the majority, which is observed will ever be against the Southern States, find it their Interest to Continue them, & Men of influence are once fixed in their Saddles.

It is known to have been long the intention of the Eastern & Northern States to abolish Slavery altogether when in their power, which however Just may not be convenient for us so soon as for them especially in a New Country & hot Climate such as Georgia, Let us therefore keep the proper time for it in our own power while we have it; this Constitution prolongs the time for 20 years more, which is one reason for fixing upon that period in the Inclosed hints, as well as to pay off our National incumbrances which it is conceived may be done in that time when we have given up all our purse Strings, for that purpose, without regard to our own particular engagements.

Lachlan McIntosh was a planter and Revolutionary War officer who, because of an unfortunate duel, became for a time a pariah in Georgia (see Lachlan McIntosh entry in *Biographies*). Recouping his reputation, McIntosh rose to serve his adopted state in the Continental Congress. While not a member of the Georgia ratification convention, McIntosh in this letter reveals his worries about the Constitution. He wanted a guarantee of amendments, and he wondered whether so many different states with conflicting objectives could coexist.

REFERENCES

Lilla M. Hawes (ed.), *Lachlan McIntosh and the Politics of Revolutionary Georgia* (Athens: University of Georgia Press, 1979); original in McIntosh papers, Georgia Historical Society.

5
Connecticut

January 3–9, 1788

Ratification #5, January 9, 1788

In favor 128–40

Benjamin Gale, "Speech at the Killingworth Town Meeting," *November 12, 1787*

AT A TOWN MEETING APPOINTED BY ACT OF ASSEMBLY 12 NOVEMBER 1787.

Gentlemen, We are summoned by act of Assembly to convene upon this day, and I should be glad to know what is the business of this meeting. Perhaps our representatives can explain to us what the business of this meeting may be.

I know it has been given out that we are called together to consider the new form of government, and that it is referred back to the *people* to say whether they will adopt it or reject it, but when I come to examine the act of Assembly, you have no voice in the case. All our business, gentlemen, is to make choice of delegates to say whether you shall be made to submit to it or not—not whether you approve of it or not. That is not our business nor is it submitted to you.

The last Article of our federal Union says "The Articles of this Confederation shall be Inviolably Observed by every state and the Union shall be Perpetual, nor shall any Alteration at any time hereafter be made in Any of them, unless such Alteration be agreed to In Congress of the United States, and be Afterwards Confirmed by the Legislature of Every State." These Articles the people of these states have adopted and have sworn to support and maintain them, and by these Articles it was agreed that if any alteration was found necessary, *Congress* were first to agree to the alteration, and then afterwards that alteration was to have the sanction of the legislatures of every state. But now nine states shall bind all the rest to submission. But, gentlemen, this Convention has *fobbed* off our *assemblies*, just in the same manner as we are. It seems the Convention would not trust *our assemblies* to approve or reject their doings. They made us believe the assemblies had a right to judge of the matter, but, when all comes to all, our Assembly had no right to judge anything about it, but were permitted to order the towns to meet—but not to judge or determine anything about the Constitution, but only to choose delegates for another convention in order to judge for you, not caring to trust either you or your representatives in our assemblies to judge in this matter have left room for men of *intrigue* to get in such delegates elected for another convention as will answer their purposes, and the *job will be done.* This is the reason why, contrary to the Articles of Confederation, our assemblies might not be trusted to accept or reject this new Constitution, formed by our Convention, which without hesitation I openly declare and pronounce to be as *dark, intricate, artful, crafty, and unintelligible composition that I ever read* or *see composed by man*; and, all the time, given to the *people* to consider of it—to open their eyes or to be led into a right understanding of it by others. Is not a fortnight from the rising of our Assembly to the time of choosing our delegates either to accept or reject it. This is another *artful maneuver* of our own *domestic politicians* thus to hurry on matters before the people have time to understand it so as to be able to make a judicious choice of delegates to act conformable to their own minds.

The State of Pennsylvania, where this scheme was first planned, immediately after the declaration of peace, have outdone us by far, and they even boast of it, and say "from the time the resolution of Congress was passed till its adoption by the State of Pennsylvania was only *twenty* hours. Such is the zeal of Pennsylvania to show her attachment to a vigorous, free, and wise frame of national government." But, I must likewise tell you gentlemen, there were so many of that House that see through the whole scheme, and their unreasonable driving and pressing the matter before the people could have time to examine the new Constitution, that so many of the members withdrew from the House to prevent their hasty proceeding that there was not a quorum left so as to proceed upon business—whereupon they procured some *ruffians* to go out and pick up so many of the members as to make a quorum, dragged them into the Assembly forcibly, and there forcibly held them until the rest passed upon the new Constitution by appointing the choice of delegates. This, gentlemen, might teach us, I should think, not to think very honorably either of this new Constitution or the rectitude of the Assembly of Pennsylvania. Our Assembly, it is true, did not proceed so *violently*, but those artful politicians so managed the matter that they have not left you a fortnight to weigh and consider of the most important affair that ever came before you. Doth it appear at all likely or probable, was there not some undue measures to be pursued, that such violent measures would be pursued by legislative bodies? You may perhaps, gentlemen, wonder what such men are driving at that. I will tell you gentlemen in plain English, and would the time admit, I can prove it. But this you all know. Congress have made a grant to the officers and army of a sum of money the annual interest of which sum is £99,000. The soldiers have been told the public securities given them were good for nothing, and they have sold them from 2 to 3–4 and 5/ on the £, and the present holders of those public securities thus purchased from the soldiers well know they never can prevail with our assemblies to pay them public securities to the present possessors up to the nominal value. And the officers of the Army also well know that vote of Congress for their commutation was obtained by art and intrigue, by a pretended mutiny of the army just at the conclusion of the war, and then obtained in Congress but by a single vote, viz. of Colonel Dyer, which he immediately wrote up to our Assembly was extorted from him through fear. And they will know unless they alter our present form of government and convert it into a *military government*, they must and will finally lose their prize. Again, there are others who are promised to mount up higher in the saddle by promotion. All these combining have raised a mighty outcry of the weakness of the federal government, and they have continued it so long and so loud that many honest people are made to believe it. But gentlemen, have not we the same power we ever have had; cannot every man recover his honest just dues. If any opposition is made to government, has not our sheriffs power to call to their assistance the militia to support him in the execution of his office, and is it not so in every state in the Union. Gentlemen, this outcry of the weakness of the federal government is only a specious pretense to cover the artful schemes of *designing men* who would recover their commutation securities and the notes purchased of the soldiers. And I now will make my objections to this new form of government planned out by this Convention.

My *first* objection is to the expense of it which at the same time doth not lessen our own, which must in fact crush the common people into the dust and reduce them to a state of vassalage and slavery. By the increase of the multiplicity of new offices and officers with such salaries as Congress gives them—our ambassadors a salary of 11111 9/10 dollars per annum, exclusive of the expenses of their embassy, a large salary to their secretaries, 13000 dollars allowed to the President of Congress for to furnish his table, large salaries to the Secretary of War, Secretary for Foreign Affairs, 1900 dollars each to 13 commissioners such as Mr. Imlay at Hartford whose whole business may be executed in a month, etc., etc. And if this new form of government is adopted, a vast retinue of revenue officers must be appointed who must have ample salaries for the Southern States, who have 3, 4, 5, and six hundred slaves of their own, have high notions of things, and can bet more on a horse race than the value of one of our little farms. And 7 of the Southern States have 41 votes in Congress, while 6 of the Northern States have but 27, and the disproportion will increase so that they can forever outvote us and have just what officers they please and load us with just what taxes they please.

And here gentlemen, I must acquaint you with what I presume you do not know—that both our delegates in Congress voted against the Convention. I had it from Dr. Johnson's own mouth. He did not tell it to me in confidence, and therefore speak of it openly, and he told me at the same time it would lay a foundation for a division in the Confederation.[1]

My second objection is to the duplicity of the Articles themselves which are so artfully expressed and delegates greater power to Congress than by a common reader will readily be perceived, and seems to be artfully covered of design not to be understood. And I *now* will proceed to point out the passages severally.

Article 1. I shall consider section 1 and 8 together. My objections to them are our Congress is to consist but of 65 members which will be of the higher class of people who know but little of the poverty, straits, and difficulties of the middling and lower class of men. I have ever thought we in this state had too many representatives, but I am now confirmed in my opinion that we have not. Every town and county, their true state and ability, ought to be known, especially in matters of taxation; and it is of great service likewise to guard against the intrigues of artful, crafty, and designing men, and even then they are not always discovered in their schemes, otherwise I am persuaded our Honorable Assembly would have given the people a little more time to have understood and considered of this new plan of government before we had been called together to choose our delegates.

Section 2, 3 paragraph. My second objection. There is but *three* ways to proportion the taxes of the states justly and equitably. The *first* is according to the 8th Article of our federal Union, but that method cannot be done to satisfaction of the states. The *second* is by the number of souls in each state—the riches and strength of a state is determined by the number of the inhabitants it is capable of supporting. And the *third* way is by the number of square miles within its territorial jurisdiction. This is not so just and equitable as the other two. Consequently, I shall say nothing but with regard to the *second*, the first not being *practicable*. Here I will not only remark upon the injustice of this paragraph, but the art used to conceal the true meaning from common readers. Three-fifths of all other *persons*. Why could they not have spoke out in plain terms—*Negroes?* Were they afraid of affronting the *Negroes*, or were they ashamed to exempt 3/5 of them from taxation by outvoting. And here the language is uncertain and doubtful also I cannot say by the rules of grammar whether they are to be included or excluded from taxation. But why must our apprentices in the Northern States be all taxed and included in the capitation and 3/5ths of the Negroes in the Southern States be exempted, where it doth not cost their masters so much to keep 10 of them, as it doth here in one of our Northern States to keep one genteel horse.

I object also to the last paragraph of this section, to the small number of Representatives—a mighty empire to have but 65 Representatives—to tax by duties, impost, excise, and direct taxation, and but 27 of them in the six Northern States, and to make laws for them likewise. I would ask you, gentlemen, whether you know of any 5 men in this state who should tell you they have a right to *tax you as much as they please, to appropriate it as they please, and of the exorbitancy of their demands you have no constitutional liberty to judge*. Not only to tax you by duties, impost, and excise but to levy direct taxes upon you, and these same five men also to make all laws respecting government of the state. And if you would think it impolitic to do it for this state separately, can you think it safe to trust it in the hands of five men when linked and fettered with 41 Southern members who have no idea but that our day laborers may be treated just as they treat their African slaves.

The last clause of this paragraph limits the number of Representatives 1 to 30 thousand. At present we are allowed 5, and there be 150 thousand inhabitants in this state to entitle us to five Representatives. So that when the number of our inhabitants are taken, after all our emigrations to New York and Vermont, I suspect we shall not have more than 4 Representatives, if so many—and can you think such a representation in Congress will be sufficient thus connected with and fettered with the Southern States, where they have such high notions; not only to tax us by duties, excises, and impost, but to make laws for us, when you see by their numbers they can force us to submit to 3 fifths of their slaves exempted. It seems to me, gentlemen, this alone might convince you of the impolicy of adopting this Constitution. While I am upon the subject of *Negroes* and the artful language they use to cover their meaning, I would object to the 9th section. Why all this sly cunning and artful mode of expression unless to cover from your observation and notice that *Negroes* was intended by the word *persons*, again used on this occasion, lest it should frighten people who may have some tender feelings and a just sense of the rights of human nature. What man, that has the feelings of a man, can once think it right to send our ships across the Atlantic to tear parents from their children, children from their parents, husbands from their wives, and wives from their husbands, stifle one-half of them in their crowded ships, and the remainder sell as we do our cattle to drag out the remainder of their lives in slavery, to be whipped and lashed like horses, without being struck with horror and shudder at the deed? It might have been sufficient, one would have thought, not to have said anything about it in those articles of this blessed Constitution planned out for us by the Convention and hurried on to be established with as much precipitation as though the salvation of our souls depended upon our adopting it *immediately*. But it fills my mind with the highest resentment to read that they lay a restraint upon Congress that they shall not restrain or prohibit that antichristian and most abominable and wicked practice of trading in *bodies and souls of men* for the space of 21 years yet to come. They need not have extended it to one-half of that period, for my mind for in less than one-half of that time, if we adopt this system of government, 3/4 of us will be slaves to all intents and purposes whatsoever without any trouble or expense of sending to Africa for slaves, for it is as perfect a system of slavery as I ever saw planned out by any nation, kingdom, or state whatever. For what have we been contending and shedding our blood and wasting our substance, but to support the natural rights of men. I am told our reverend clergy in general are much engaged to support this new plan of government, but if this is really the case, they may in future preach and pray to the Africans that may be imported by virtue of this new Constitution. For my own part, any who vote for it, if I know them, will not offend my ears, neither with their prayers or preaching to the latest period of my life.

My next objection is to section 4–3. The plea has been, they wanted Congress to regulate trade, but it seems here again they make use of great art to disguise and conceal their meaning. They pretend to give us the right of election both of Senators and Representatives, and give our [state] representatives the right of elections of our Senators, but in section 4, which I have just now read to you, they tell us Congress may at any time alter both the time and manner, i.e., they may say none shall vote for Senators unless his annual income shall be worth £100 a year, and that when they may hold their seats during life.

Again under Article II, section 1 paragraph 3 they have another touch on elections for they have been extremely careful to mix everything well that the reader might not have a full view of any one topic under one head, but they have so mixed and blended everything that it requires the greatest attention imaginable to comprehend all their meaning in its full extent and latitude.

Article II, section 1. Thus it is pretended as though we chose the *President* and *Vice* President or rather the *King* and his successor. But how do we choose them? Do our representatives in General Assembly choose them? No, by no means. That would not do. Article II, section 1. But our legislature must choose 7 Electors, i.e., as many Electors as we have Representatives and Senators, which for the present we are permitted to have 5 Representatives and 2

Senators—so that after sifting the House we may perhaps get 7 men that may be trusted with the choice of a *President* or rather *King*, for the next 4 years, but if the election made by our representatives doth not happen to suit our Honorable Council, and they think he will not make a *good Elector* to choose a *President* for us or rather a *King*, they may negative the choice of our representatives, and if they cannot get those that will serve the turn, we must send a less number. To be short, all our pretended elections are so fettered and muzzled that I would as soon turn a copper for the choice as to pretend to elect, so that when we have once chose any officer, whether *President* or *Senator*, he is almost as much assured of being *reelected*, as though it was made hereditary. Indeed, I had rather have a *hereditary King* or *President* than an *Elective King*, as it will eternally embroil the states by schemers for the *outs* and *ins*, and lay the foundation of clamors, broils, and contentions that will end in *blood*.

My objection is to section 6, 7 paragraph and Article II. Congress never have informed the states what their civil list has been and I presume they never will—and I have been told by a member of Congress, that is to say by one who has been a member of Congress, that I might never expect they will ever let us know. Indeed, Congress have as good as told us so in express terms. They have told us they have an absolute discretion to determine the quantum of revenue, of appropriating it when raised, and of the exorbitancy of their demands we have no constitutional liberty to judge. The fact is, gentlemen, they never have told us in full at any time what the annual expenses of the federal government is—they never have told us what sums of money they have given away to individuals either as pensions or as presents, to show our grandeur and importance in our national character. Nor have they once told us what our quota of the public debt is, that we might fund it and make provision to pay the interest annually till the debt can be paid. They have told us that, by all we have paid, we never have lessened our foreign debt nor paid the interest of it, and they have further told us that what we do pay doth not pay the annual expenses of the federal government.

They tell us, it is true (section 9, last paragraph but one), no money shall be drawn from the public treasury but in consequence of appropriations made by law, and that the expenditures shall be published from time to time. So they told us they would transmit to each state every half year all [the?] money they borrowed or emitted. Did they ever do it? I answer, no, they never did it once, nor is it probable they ever will, and if you murmur or complain when you have taken the militia out of the hands of the governors, placed them under the President of Congress, and converted them into a standing army, and they can call them forth at any time either to *subdue Wabash Indians* or quell *insurgents* as they please, you may murmur, complain, or call for the public accounts as you will, you may as well content yourselves without complaining. Power once given up out of your hands never was given back again nor never was recovered back without *shedding of blood*. But, gentlemen, if you think you can pay such taxes to support this new federal government when it will not lessen the expenses of our own government a single copper, I am content. I promise you as a Christian, when it is once established I will not resist the *powers that be,* nor will I shed a drop of blood to recover *what I foolishly give away.* Let me recommend it to you therefore, by a friend and as a Christian, to be very careful what powers you give up and very obedient when you have done it. This shall be the line of my own conduct.

My next or 5 objection is to the regulation of the militia and taking them from under the command of the several governors and converting into a standing army which is contained in these paragraphs. Upon this head I would only observe to you—mankind, vile as they be, see the necessity of civil government and will submit to all reasonable laws and all reasonable demands of taxes to support that government, and whenever there are any stubborn refractory mortals that will not submit to civil government there are always men enough, when properly called upon, to support the civil magistrate in the execution of laws. But if the laws are oppressive and arbitrary, the public demands above the ability of the people to pay, they will eternally kick. You may depend upon it in a country where people have anything they call their own, and they must be governed by a standing army who carry with them the instruments of death if they are governed at all. But to take the militia of the state out of the command and from under the direction of our governors, place them under the President of Congress, which reduces our governors to the quality of *drill sergeants* only to discipline our militia, and fit them for the President of Congress to subdue either *Wabash Indians or quell insurgents in the County of Hampshire*—true, it may save the states the expense and trouble of declaring war against the *Wabash Indians* in future in these Northern States, when our militia, trained and well disciplined, will be ready to execute their commands. A mild government, gentlemen, wants no military force to support it, and an arbitrary and oppressive government doth not deserve it.

My 6th objection is to the 9 paragraph in the 8 section under the 1 Article and unto 1 section in the 3 Article, for I must skip about to look them up where they have scattered them in order to render them more mysterious and unintelligible, which should have been connected together if they intended they should be understood. Here they tell us of a Supreme Court to be erected somewhere, but they don't tell us where—and that they shall have a compensation for their services, but they don't tell us how much—and that they shall hold their seats during good behavior, by that I understand as long as they live or, at most, until some fitter tool to serve their purposes shall appear to oust them—and that their salaries shall not be diminished—and that Congress shall have power to erect *inferior tribunals* under the Supreme Court of their appointment. Now, gentlemen, the designs of these paragraphs is that these courts appointed by this newfangled Congress shall eat up our courts, of which our representatives have now the right of appointing the judges annually—and if it would eat up all the lawyers likewise, if they would expunge that paragraph of the Negroes. I should be tempted to vote for all the remainder. If we cannot by this Constitution eat up the lawyers, they will soon eat *us* up.

I will now, gentlemen, finish my objections by my 7th and last objection, although I could spin them out with great propriety to 20 or 30 more, which is to the 2 paragraph of the 3 section under the 4 Article. —7. I have reserved this for the last, as it is the *butt cut* for *art* and *intrigue*. Now, gentlemen, is there one in 40 of you that would judge this paragraph was a complete deed and absolute grant of all our western territory. They have taken care that we do enable them, if we adopt this new Constitution, that we resign into the hands of Congress the *impost, excise, duties,* and a power to tax us for as much more as they want, and to make all necessary laws to regulate them matters, to appoint their supreme and inferior courts, to eat up ours, and we take our militia out of the hands of our governors, reducing our governors into the quality of drill sergeants, convert our militia into a standing army.

Benjamin Gale, a physician, had served in the state legislature (see Benjamin Gale entry in *Biographies*). In this speech, he states his objections to the proposed Constitution, especially over the federal Congress regulating trade to the detriment of the state's commercial interests. He also spoke forcefully against continuing the importation of slaves. Gale spoke at the meeting also to urge the people of Killingsworth to elect Antifederalists to the state convention.

REFERENCES

Jensen and Kaminski, *Documentary History*, vol. 3; "Objections to the New Plan of Government. . . ," in Beinicke Rare Books and Manuscript Library, Yale University.

NOTE

1. William Samuel Johnson, a powerful Connecticut Federalist.

James Wadsworth, Speech in the Connecticut State Ratification Convention, *January 7, 1788*

The paragraph which respects taxes, imposts, and excises was largely debated by several gentlemen.

General James Wadsworth objected against it, because it gave the power of the purse to the general legislature; another paragraph gave the power of the sword; and that authority which has the power of the sword and purse is despotic. He objected against imposts and excises because their operation would be partial and in favor of the Southern states.

James Wadsworth, a lawyer and former member of the Continental Congress, belonged to a prominent political and commercial family (see James Wadsworth entry in *Biographies*). He opposed ratification because of the financial powers given to the federal Congress and his fear that the proposed government favored southern interests. He also feared for small farmers, believing the federal government would tax property excessively.

REFERENCES

Charles J. Hoadley and Leonard W. Labaree, *Public Records of the State of Connecticut;* Jensen and Kaminski, *Documentary History*, vol. 3.

Hugh Ledlie, Letter to John Lamb,
January 15, 1788

The length of time, since our acquaintance first commenced in N York about the years 1765 & 1766 makes me almost diffident whether you continue the same Patriot & friend to your Country; I then found you together with Sears, Robinson, Wiley, Mott, Light Scott Hazard &c &c and many others whose Names I have forgot a Committee for opposeing the diabolical and oppressive Stamp Act, when Pintard Williams &c were brought to the Stool or rather Stage or repentance for Acts of high crimes and misdemeanors committed against the then sons of liberty throughout the Continent—But to return, I say, I sho'd not have dared to Venture a line to you on the subject I am about to say a few words upon, if I had not accidentally seen your Name with others (good men) in some of our publick newspapers handled in a very rough, ungentlemanlike manner—but even then I remain'd Ignorant who those scurrilous, defamatory, backbiting writers meant, untill a few days since being in company with Genl. James Wadsworth who first told me it was you, & aded an Anecdote—the other day or some time since a gentleman one Mr. Hamilton meeting you in the street Asked you how you could be so much against the New Constitution, for it was pretty certain your old good friend Genl. Washington would in all probability be the first President under it; to which you reply'd that in that case all might be well, but perhaps after him Genl Slushington might be the next or second President. This Sir, was the very first hint I had of your opposing it and was confirmed in the same by the Approbrous indecent & I believe false speeches made use of at our late C——n[1] in this place by some sly mischevious insinuations viz that out of the impost £8000 was paid by this State Annually to the State of N York out of which you recd. upwards of £900 which enabled you & others to write the foederal farmer & other false Libels and send them into this & the Neighbouring States to poison the minds of the good people against the good C——n. They say a Lamb, a Willet, a Smith, a Clinton, & a Yates's Salleries are paid by this State through your State impost, the late C——n which Met in this town the 3d. Inst.—and Voted the New C—stn the 9th. in the evening & finished the 10th. was carried on by what I can learn with a high hand against those that disapproved thereof, for if I am not misinform'd when the Latter were speaking which by the by were far from being the best Orators (a few expected) they were brow beaten by many of those Cicero'es as they think themselves & others of Superiour rank as they call themselves, as also by the unthinking deluded Multitude who were previously convened as it is thought by many for that purpose, which together with Shuffleing & Stamping of feet, caughing talking spitting & Whispering, as well by some of the Members as Spectators with other interruptions &c &c: too many to be here inumerated which I am told is true for I was not there myself being at that time confined by a Slight touch of the Gout, all these Menaces & Stratagems were used by a Junto who tries to carry all before them in this State, as well by writing as every other diabolical & evil pretence And as the Press's in this State are open to them, but evidently shut against all those that would dare & presume to write on the other side against the N Cs———n they have greatly the Advantage & by these means Stigmatise every one they think Acts or thinks to the contrary of what they say or do. Witness our late landholder & some others of the same class against Richard Henry Lee Esqr. Mr. Mason, Mr. Geary &c &c yet notwithstanding all their long laboured scurilous, Vindictive, bitter, Malicious, & false insinuations there was found in our C n n forty one righteous men, that did not bow the knee to Baal but in the midts of all the storms of reproaches &c &c stood their ground firm tho' 127. of those (called by some of the first rank by their soft smooth speaches just at the close Voted for the New Con———n a C—n n that in the end will work the ruin of the freedom & liberty of these thirteen disunited States—I am not alone in this opinion for there are many of the first abilities in this & the Neighbouring States with whom I correspond as well by letters as otherways besides the above 41., that think this n C———n a guilded Pill, but some of them notwithstanding the guilding is so artfully laid on can discern the Arsanac & Poison through the outside colouring—and our good Printers (after the Nag was stolen I think after they had spent all their Venom which came from the Quills of the Junto in favour of the N C———n & just before the sitting of our C———n) then & not till then they published a pompious libel, that then & at all times they would publish on both sides—but the D———l trust them says many that from principle are against the N. C———n and so none that I know of was ever sent them, well knowing it must run the gauntlet through all these infernal grubstreet, hireling scurrilous scriblers, that watch & guard the posts of the Printers doors in this town, & who are daily attending for the selfsame purpose of disjointing, Mangleing & torturing every piece that don't please their pallet—This Sir, is some of the reasons why so few or none are sent—another reason is they have got almost all the best Writers (as well as speakers) on their side tho' we vie with & I believe over ballance them in point of honesty and integrity—the piece aluded to as above teems with trying to sow discord & contention between the United States, by insinuating that Richard H. Lee Esqr. has and is a great enemy to Genl. Washington & that he endeavored to get his cousin Genl. Lee to be commander of our late Army &c &c in short they leave as the old saying is no stone unturn'd but they compass Sea and land, they rake H—l and scim the D—l to make one proselite, and when they have found him, they make him two fold more the child of h. l. than he was before, this proverb is of late verified by their turning from light to darkness Copper, Wimble & some others whom at present I'll forbear to name—We that are against the N— C———n are stigmatis'd by those mighty men of Moab by the approbious Name of Wrongheads, if they are nam'd right I believe there is a Majority in this State against the N C———n for it is thought by the best judges that if the Freemen &c of this State could be convened together in one body the greatest Number would Vote against the new propos'd C——n notwithstanding all that is held out to the people at large in the publick Newspapers in this State—We wish here we had some of your good Writers and a free Press we would souse some of our upstart sons of Apollo that pretend to great things—

> One worthless man that gains what he pretends
> disgusts a thousand unpretending friends
> trials light as Air—are to the jealous confirmation strong
> as proofs of holy Writ—the Wise too Jealous are
> fools too secure—Beware beware beware
>   for I apprehend a dreadful snare
> is laid for Virtuous innocence
> under a friends false pretence—

Now Sir on the whole let me tell you, that those gentlemen at least, those that I can unite with, have no greater hope (besides that of an over ruling providence) than in the Virtue & wisdom of your State together with that of Virginia & Massachusetts not adopting the N. C——n and I have heard some of the first Characters that composed our late C——n say that if nine States did adopt the C——n and N York rejected it, they would remove into your State where they could injoy freedom & liberty, for which they had fought & Bled heretofore, and if your State is not by that means one of the most populous flourishing states on the Continent I am much Mistaken not by emigrants only that are or will be disatisfied with the N. C——n from the different states, but also from Europe, I myself if I am able to buy a small farm in your State somewhere about the South Bay Fairhaven Crownpoint, up the Mohawk river German flatts, fort Stanwix, Wood Creek, the Onoida Lake, Trouviers on the Annodanga River, Shoharyskill, Bradstreets island in Lake Ontario in the Mouth of the River St Lawrence Oswego only excepted Niagara & above all some where on the South banks of Lake Erie—most or all of those places I am acquainted with, & if the proposed C——n takes place & Providence permitts I will with others remove into your State, provided you do not adopt it for many of the Convention that attended it (for as I said before I did not attend myself in person) told me that the Conv—n was one of the most overbearing Assemblys that ever sat in this State and as the N. Cs——n gives all the power both of the Sword & purse into the hands of the C—n—ss our people reckon it leads to and opens a door for despotism Tyranny, Anarchy & confusition and every evil Work. I am afraid Sir for want of knowing whom to put confidence in you (if you sent any) sent your books into the wrong hands as they never appeared or could be seen except a few sent to Genl. J. W.[2] tho I never could see one untill a few days before our C—v—n set the rest besides those sent as above were all secreted, burnt and distributed amongst those for the N. C t. n in order to torture ridicule & make shrewd remarks & may game of, both of the pamphlet and them that wrote and sent them, all which they did not spare to do in our public Newspapers by Extracts and detach'd sentences just such as served their Vile Malignant purpose long before I or any against the C—t. n ever saw (I mean) the foederal farmer—on the whole sho'd be glad to know who those Gentlemen are whom our heads of Wit takes in hand to Villifie in our public papers besides yourself, pray Sr. who is Mr. Willet, Mr. Smith Mr. Clinton & Mr Yates—is Mr. Willet he that defended so nobly at fort Stanwix in the late War—also who is Mr Smith, and is Mr. Clinton your Worthy Govr.—and pray who is Mr Yates—two of those Names viz Judge Yates & Melankton Smith Esqr. lodged at my house upwards of 20 days in Decemr. 1787. together with Mr. Duane, your Mayor Chancellor Livingston Judge Herring, Mr. Benson your Attorney Genl. & Mr. De-Witt your Surveyor Genl. shod be glad to know which or whether all or any of the above gentlemen, are against or for the New proposed Constitution—our 41 Members of Convention that opposed the Constitution went home very heavy hearted and discouraged to think that by one stroke they had lost all their liberty & priviledges both Civil & Sacred as well as all their property money &c &c by a set of men who's aim is entirely popularity as they think will please the bulk of the people & procure them places, Sallery, & Pensions under the New Constitution, as I am inform'd that many who are now in office & who it is said were dicidedly against it untill they came to this town to Conven—n then they were told plainly, that if they did not turn & Vote for it they must not expect any places either of trust or profitt under the New Constitution, thus this capital stroke was reserved for the finishing blow, as those concerned well knew the pulse's of these sort of men—for as one of your City said att the beginning of the late War he then being on Long Island & settling some affairs from this State that he could buy any Counseller in this state for a half Joe. or a Pd. of Irish linnen—there is nothing that works so effectually as interest so it is well verified as to some of our great men in the present case some of whom I believe I could call by name but at present I'll forbear only that I will add one sentiment more & have done untill I hear from N York viz That I verily believe we have some of the most selfish, Avericious, narrow contracted set of Mortals that now exist in these thirteen disunited States you'll please to excuse some low scurrilous Vulgar language the want of diction & grammer as I am not a man of a liberal Education and only follow the plough having no other employ to get my bread but by the sweat of my brow for I injoy neither place nor pension, as they that are for the N Constitution in this state & I am sure I shall never have any except I turn to their side, which at present I have no thoughts of—Sr. you'll please to forgive this lengthy unconnected scrawl as it hastily flew from one of the pens of the family of the wrongheads so called by the tory roundheads—We this way fear this N Constitution will work much mischief before it is adopted, & the destruction & ruin of the thirteen States if it takes place. Please to give my Compliments to all the before named gentlemen and Hugh Hughes Esqr. being one of the old committee more especially to those that are decidedly against the N Constitution

Hugh Ledlie, a shopkeeper and state legislator, served in the state ratification convention (see Hugh Ledlie entry in *Biographies*). In this letter to New Yorker John Lamb, Ledlie tried to explain why Connecticut ratified the Constitution and to urge New York to stand fast in opposition to ratification.

REFERENCES

Jensen and Kaminski, *Documentary History*, vol. 3; John Lamb Papers, New York Historical Society; Isaac Q. Leake (ed.), *Memorial of the Life and Times of John Lamb* (Glendale, N.Y.: Benchmark Publication, 1970).

NOTES

1. Refers with C——n to the state convention, N. C——n refers to the Philadelphia Constitutional Convention.
2. Ally James Wadsworth.

6
Massachusetts

January 9–February 7, 1788

Ratification #6, February 6, 1788

In favor 187–168

Elbridge Gerry, Letter to the Massachusetts General Court, *November 3, 1787*

NEW-YORK, 18TH OCTOBER, 1787.

GENTLEMEN, I have the honour to inclose, pursuant to my commission, the constitution proposed by the federal Convention.

To this system I gave my dissent, and shall submit my objections to the honourable Legislature.

It was painful for me, on a subject of such national importance, to differ from the respectable members who signed the constitution: But conceiving as I did, that the liberties of America were not secured by the system, it was my duty to oppose it.—

My principal objections to the plan, are, that there is no adequate provision for a representation of the people—that they have no security for the right of election—that some of the powers of the Legislature are ambiguous, and others indefinite and dangerous—that the Executive is blended with and will have an undue influence over the Legislature—that the judicial department will be oppressive—that treaties of the highest importance may be formed by the President with the advice of two thirds of a *quorum* of the Senate—and that the system is without the security of a bill of rights. These are objections which are not local, but apply equally to all the States.

As the Convention was called for "the *sole* and *express* purpose of revising the Articles of Confederation, and reporting to Congress and the several Legislatures such alterations and provisions as shall render the Federal Constitution adequate to the exigencies of government and the preservation of the union," I did not conceive that these powers extended to the formation of the plan proposed, but the Convention being of a different *opinion*, I acquiesced in *it*, being fully convinced that to preserve the union, an efficient government was indispensibly necessary; and that it would be difficult to make proper amendments to the articles of Confederation.

The Constitution proposed has few, if any *federal* features, but is rather a system of *national* government: Nevertheless, in many respects I think it has great merit, and by proper amendments, may be adapted to the "exigencies of government," and preservation of liberty.

The question on this plan involves others of the highest importance—1st. Whether there shall be a dissolution of the *federal* government? 2dly. Whether the several State Governments shall be so altered, as in effect to be dissolved?

and 3dly. Whether in lieu of the *federal* and *State* Governments, the *national* Constitution now proposed shall be substituted without amendment? Never perhaps were a people called on to decide a question of greater magnitude— Should the citizens of America adopt the plan as it now stands, their liberties may be lost: Or should they reject it altogether Anarchy may ensue. It is evident therefore, that they should not be precipitate in their decisions; that the subject should be well understood, lest they should refuse to *support* the government, after having *hastily* accepted it.

If those who are in favour of the Constitution, as well as those who are against it, should preserve moderation, their discussions may afford much information and finally direct to an happy issue.

It may be urged by some, that an *implicit* confidence should be placed in the Convention: But, however respectable the members may be who signed the Constitution, it must be admitted, that a free people are the proper guardians of their rights and liberties—that the greatest men may err—and that their errours are sometimes, of the greatest magnitude.

Others may suppose, that the Constitution may be safely adopted, because therein provision is made to *amend* it: But cannot *this object* be better attained before a ratification, than after it? And should a *free* people adopt a form of Government, under conviction that it wants amendment?

And some may conceive, that if the plan is not accepted by the people, they will not unite in another: But surely whilst they have the power to amend, they are not under the necessity of rejecting it.

I have been detained here longer than I expected, but shall leave this place in a day or two for Massachusetts, and on my arrival shall submit the reasons (if required by the Legislature) on which my objections are grounded.

I shall only add, that as the welfare of the union requires a better Constitution than the Confederation, I shall think it my duty as a citizen of Massachusetts, to support that which shall be finally adopted, sincerely hoping it will secure the liberty and happiness of America.

A Boston merchant, major leader in the Continental Congress, member of the Philadelphia Constitutional Convention who refused to sign the Constitution, and later vice president of the United States, Elbridge Gerry was perhaps the state's most influential Antifederalist, though he did not serve in the state ratification convention (see Elbridge Gerry entry in *Biographies*). In this letter, Gerry sought to explain to the people of the state why he had refused to sign the Constitution. The letter became an influential document in behalf of the Antifederalist cause against too-powerful federal government.

REFERENCES

James T. Austin, *The Life of Elbridge Gerry* (Boston: Wells and Lilly, 1829), vol. 2; Jonathan Elliot, *The Debates in the Several State Conventions on the Adoption of the Federal Constitution* (Philadelphia: J. B. Lippincott Company, 1836), vol. 1.

William Symmes, Jr., Letter to Peter Osgood, Jr., *November 15, 1787*

According to my promise I sit down to sketch out my reasons for objecting against ye. Federal Constitution. The essay will doubtless be imperfect; but I design it for your perusal only, & I can safely rely upon your goodness for all necessary allowances.—

I will consider ye. objectionable passages in course as they occur in ye. System, as well for your convenience as my own.

1.—The apportionment of taxes.

It appears to me that this will operate unequally against ye. northern States. Let us suppose that two fifths of ye. slaves in ye. five southern states amount at least to 150,000 persons. What reason can be given why, if taxes must be proportioned by population only, this should be rejected?—That ye. profits of their labour are nothing? I deny ye. fact; for I believe that every negro that cultivates ye. valuable staples, Tobacco, Wheat, Rice, Indigo, &c raises a greater profit to his master than any white can raise from his labour here.—What then?—That ye. southern Nabobs squander it all in Luxuries, & so ye. States there are made if anything, poorer?—Very good—The Convention then have patronized Luxury, & taxed Industry & Oeconomy. [T]hree fifths include all ye. working slaves. Neither will this answer; for ye. northern States are taxed as much for an infant or a decrepid old man, as for a vigorous youth.

How then shall we be taxed? I say not in proportion to actual wealth at present, but in proportion to a State's advantages for acquiring wealth. The soil & climate of Virginia are better than those of this State—The staples of Virginia are in high demand—Its Rivers ye. finest in ye. world. How rich might Virginia be!—But Virginia is not rich—What then?—Shall a man need no better excuse from taxes than Idleness? He will hardly pay his *private* debts so easily.—

Taxes must certainly grow out of ye. ground. What then is more evident than that ye. best land & ye. best produce (supposing ye. advantages of Commerce to be equal) should pay or (if you please, produce) ye. most?—And are not our long winters in which we consume ye. labours of ye. summer, to be considered? No—But yes, I beg pardon—they *are* considered—We pay ye. more.—

But 2.—The Senate.—

To what great purpose is it that we have an equal representation in ye. House, if we are represented by States in ye. Senate. This is a great grievance in ye. present Congress. That little Delaware should weigh as much in all po-

litical debates as this State, is, in a government merely popular, quite ridiculous.—Whose voice are we supposed to hear in all public transactions?—We
accurate Republicans say, the voice of ye. people. Who are ye. people? We answer, ye. majority.—But a majority of *States* may chuse a President &c This is
a close adherence to principles.—"Two Senators from each State, & each Senator to have a vote." The present Congress *mended & made worse*, for now
seven States ~~with ye Vice-president's turning vote~~ are competent when before
it required ye. sanction of nine. But we shall have a proper House—All will be
right there. True!—& that may be a good reason why we should not have a
proper Senate—But I cannot see ye. force of it. Why any State should have
more weight in one body than in ye. other, let ye. Convention say. And yet
poor R. Island was not there to speak for herself.—

I may speak of ye. duration of offices in another place.—

3.—Congress may *make & alter* ye. times *places* & MANNER of holding elections, except ye. *place* of chusing senators.—

This is a very complaisant exception indeed—The Legislatures may sit
where they please—It means this if it means anything—And we are doubtless
much obliged to ye. Convention for this decent privelege.—But I presume ye.
time of chusing senators must be in ye. winter, for it will be too hot for a session at ye. southward in ye. summer. and ye. *place* of choosing Representatives may possibly be ye. county-town, or some place yet more remote. This
would be very convenient.—But ye. word MANNER! Oh it is an excellent
word. It would not have been half so well to have tied ye. hands of this future Congress by saying all elections shall be made *by ballot*, or as ye. several
States shall please. No—The States are to be made sensible how much this
Congress is above them in all wisdom—even to ye. knowledge of a particular
acre of ground. Nay, ye. Convention itself seems dazzled at ye. prospect of
this wisdom—for they dared not prescribe it any rules. Now that ye. future
Congress may be as wise as this Convention I have no great reason to doubt
from anything that is past—But they will certainly have a great deal more
power; & we shall shortly hear no more of *recommendations*. That they shd.
make use of their power to enlarge ye. priveleges of ye. people let anybody
expect that.—Well then! If they do not enlarge them why make provision for
altering them. That they may take them away? Oh no Never suspect such a
thing.—What then shall we think of it? That ye. Convention were fools?
Hardly—I see no other way but to recur to ye. great Wisdom of this future
Congress—It will be a wise Congress—a *very* wise Congress—Here now is a
way to get rid of every doubt.—But why need ye. Convention to care how
ye. members are chosen, if they are but sent?—Oh, Sir—it will be a very wise
Congress.—And about ye. place, if they are but chosen?—Oh Sir a very wise
Congress!—Just as good an answer as that of ye. Clown in *All's well that ends
well*, which was to everything Oh Lord, Sir!

4. The Houses to keep a journal & publish ye. same, excepting such parts
as may *in their judgment* require secrecy.

Good again. A very wise Congress! The idea used to be, except private articles in foreign treaties, secret expeditions, &c—But this Constitution excels
in ye. Laconic mode of speech. Or rather, perhaps ye. Convention were lazy
& could not conveniently go about to particularize either ye. rights of ye.

people, or ye. just prerogatives of Congress. Who can complain after this that he knows nothing of public affairs, except ye. expenditure of public monies? If Congress conceal, ye. Convention say it is best ye. people should not know— & indeed, if Congress are invested with all power, general knowledge might be inconvenient, as it could only produce discontents, & these might issue in rebellions.—

When ye. dark pages of these journals shall be inspected by some young politician of future ages, who perchance may succeed his father in ye. national council—What lessons may he not learn!—There may he observe by what steps ye. form of a Govt. is imperceptibly changed—There by what process ye. genius of a free people is altered—But I say no more.—

5. Congress shall have power, &c 1st. clause.—

To *lay*—pretty well, when you read *what & for what*—but—and to *collect*— *what?*—taxes, duties, imposts, & excises—very well! for *what ends?*—to pay ye. debts, & provide for ye. common defence & *general welfare* of ye. United States.—

A more general dedition or surrender of all ye. property in ye. United States to Congress could not perhaps have been framed. Gentlemen it is all—all yours to spend as you please, provided we may but know how you spend it—& even then you may sink as many thousands as you please under ye. heads of incidental charges, secret services, &c. Take it all.

I will paraphrase the whole of this passage in a short address from ye. States to Congress.—

Gentlemen, Having chosen you to govern us, and believing that thro' all ages you will be a disinterested body, & will always spend money, if you can get it, with rigid œconomy, we give you full power to tax us—And lest we should some of us prove refractory in ye. matter of payment from some mistaken notions that you demand it too fast, we also give you full power to collect ye. taxes you lay in ye. way most agreable to yourselves, & we will pay all your collectors, deputies, & so forth, as you shall direct. And as you have power to contract debts for us to pay, you shall have all ye. money you want to pay them—And you shall have all you want to build forts, magazines, & arsenals; buy arms & ammunition; make war & peace, & so forth—And in short, whatever you shall think will be in any degree for our good you shall have money to do, & we will never trouble you with any enquiries into ye. motives of your conduct, always relying on your wisdom with ye. most implicit confidence, & submitting our estates entirely to your disposal.

A very handsome donation! And when compared with ye. clause that throws all imposts & excises into ye. Continental treasury, produces a Query—How each state shall support its own Government?—By a dry tax, & one perhaps which cannot be collected, because ye. Federal Collectors must have ye. preference. So that we must expect to be sick of State Government as an expensive useless thing—& then Congress will help us to a Federal Intendant, perhaps, to save us the trouble of governing ourselves.—But this may be more than my text will justify.—

6. —To raise & support armies, &c,—

That ye. Federal Head should have power to raise an army for some purposes is perhaps quite necessary—Whether it is so or not, ye. present Congress have such power. But here appears to be a fault by no means singular in this constitution, viz, ye. want of limitation. All is left to ye. discretion of Congress, & there is no bar against a standing army in time of peace. For tho' no appropriation of money to this use may be for a longer term than two years, yet this is long enough, when ye. same appropriation may be continued for two years to ye. end of time. And we are to expect that this Congress will soon have such a system of policy as will bind their successors, either by ye. force of its obvious expediency, or by ye. danger of innovation, to persist in ye. same plan.—

7. To exercise exclusive legislation, &c—

I do not see so much of ye. terrible in this as some do, especially if ye. rest is granted. Congress will be secure from *little* mobs, & so it ought to be. It will be delivered from ye. persecution of ye. state in which it resides, & so it ought to be. It may build accommodations for a court which will be, as they ought to be, ye. property of ye. United States. And that a body so *powerful*, ought to be handsomely lodged, I believe every foreigner will imagine.—But how this clause came into ye. constitution I know not—for I believe any state might grant what is here demanded of ye. whole, to Congress, or any body corporate with ye. consent of Congress.—

8. No state shall emit bills of credit, or make tender-laws.—

Here I suppose ye. principal weight of opposition will hang. The point itself is of consequence, but it will receive more from ye. *prejudices* of men, & our *present embarrassed situation*. You know my sentiments are directly opposed to paper money, as they would be in almost every case in which we could *want* it.—But ye. query is whether every state shall be in a worse situation than any individual, who, if he has not ye. cash in hand, may give his promissory note. I think it ought not to be, unless ye. United States will promise to lend us money whenever we want it. But I should agree to this, that no bills of credit shall ever be a tender. This regulation would be not only just, but conformable to my notions of sound policy.—

As to other tender-laws, they are, in fact, but poor expedients—but they *are* expedients, & such as a State may possibly need. It is really better to have some kind of tender-law than to be thrown into confusion. And a State is so much a better judge of its own circumstances, that I had rather see this regulation in ye. State, than in ye. Federal Constitution. Yet, unless it were in all, some states might impose upon others, & so justice would not be equally, & universally done. I wish that ye. abolition of these abuses might be deferred till we are in a more prosperous situation—& had rather that Congress should even have power to say hereafter when they shall cease, than that they should cease immediately upon ye. adoption of any new System.—

I omit ye. next sentence, because I don't at present understand what effect it will have on ye. private debt of each particular State.—

9. No State shall without ye. consent of Congress enter into any agreement or compact with any other State.—

If I understand this, it is a curious passage. What! may we not even *agree* together—If there be a suit in ye. Federal Court between two States, may they not, like private parties, *agree*. Or in an hundred other cases of no Federal concern, may they not treat, & settle their disputes! I must have mistaken these

wise men. It cannot be so. To accuse ye. Convention of folly would be gross—
I dare say that most of them had rather be accused of design.—

10. The president may with ye. advice of two thirds of ye. senators present,
make treaties—& with ye. consent of Senate Ambassadors, &c—

The Senate—Who are ye. Senate? Look back, & you will see that a majority is a Quorum. This is fourteen, & two thirds of fourteen are ~~eight~~ ten. The
President & ten Senators may make treaties. And ye. President & senate, i.e.
by ye. same rule, eight senators may appoint Ambassadors, Ministers, Consuls,
Judges, & almost everybody else.—

Where, in God's name, did they get this?—From reason, or from history? I
fear not from ye. former, & as to ye. latter, it has not come within my reading in any Constitution where a Republican form is *guarantied*. Are we then
a Commonwealth, & shall we have no voice in treaties, but by our President
or elective King? In four years' time (with good hope of another election) cannot he pack a sufficient Senate to enable him to gratify his favourites, or sell
his country?—If this be not a servile adherence to ye. pattern of ye. King &
Privy Council of Great Britain, I confess I know not what it is. Congress may
declare war indeed, but ye. President may make peace upon what terms he shall
think proper. Is a peace of less consequence to ye. nation than a war, or is it
of more, that this power is given to one man? What is ye. privelege of declaring war, compared with ye. power of making *all kinds* of treaties? If he make
a bad treaty, what then? Why he may be impeached, if anybody dares impeach
him, before ye. very Senate that advised ye. measure. And if convicted, what?
He shall be removed from his office, & perhaps disqualified to hold any other.
And after this he may chance to lose his head by a trial at Law, if ye. Judges,
whom he has appointed, will bid ye. Jury to convict him. And so, with a great
deal of difficulty, for some (perhaps) irreparable detriment, we get ye. of-
fender's head.—Is there no better way than this?—But I must not dwell
longer.—

11. The President shall take care that ye. laws be faithfully executed.—

That there must be an executive power independent of ye. Legislative
branch, appears to have been generally agreed by ye. fabricators of modern
Constitutions. But I believe it has not till now been supposed essential that this
power should be vested in a single person. The execution of ye. Laws requires
as much prudence as any other department, & ye. pardoning or refusing to
pardon offences is a very delicate matter. Yet he has no Council, no assistance,
no restraint.—

But was ever a commission so *brief*, so *general*, as this of our President? Can
we exactly say how far a faithful execution of ye. Laws may extend—or what
may be called, or comprehended in, a faithful execution? If ye. President be
guilty of a Misdemeanor, will he not *take care* to have this excuse; & should
it turn against him, may he not plead a mistake? Or is he bound to understand
ye. Laws & their operation?—Should a Federal act happen to be as generally
expressed as ye. President's authority, must he not interpret ye. act? For in many
cases he must execute laws independently of any judicial decision.—And should
ye. Legislature direct ye. mode of executing ye. laws, or any particular law, is
he obliged to comply, if he does not think it will amount to a *faithful* execution? For to suppose that ye. Legislature can make laws to affect ye. office of

ye. President, is to destroy his independence, & in this case to supersede ye. very constitution.—Is there no instance in which he may reject ye. sense of ye. Legislature & establish his own? And so far would he not be to all intents & purposes absolute!

Doubtless it is a very good thing to have wholesome laws faithfully executed.—But where this power is given to a single person, it does not seem to me that either sufficient instructions, or a sufficient restraint, can be couched in two words.—

12. The Judicial power, &c—

"Shall extend to all cases between citizens of different States." This seems an hardship on account of ye. appeal, which will carry many men 600 miles, & cause them more expence than ye. matter in dispute may be worth. There is no reason why citizens of different states should not have as good a remedy against each other as citizens of ye. same State, nor why a Debtor in ye. one case should pay more cost than a Debtor in ye. other. And supposing that to avoid cost ye. appeal in this case should be taken away (tho by this Constitution it cannot) yet this would be very unequal.—I think this part of ye. judicial power not only very grievous, but quite unnecessary; for disputes between inhabitants of different states have hitherto been very well determined in one of ye. states.—And now all remedy for small dues is taken away in effect—for tho' judgment be obtained in ye. Infr. Court, ye. Debtor by appealing may discourage ye. Creditor from any further pursuit.—

13. The Sup. Court shall have appellate jurisdiction *both as to law & fact*, except &c—

Except what?—Here they are at it again!—"With such exceptions, & under such regulations, as *Congress* shall make." A very wise Congress!—This Convention have really saved themselves a great deal of labour by this presumption.

I confess upon ye. principle that there cannot be a fair trial before Judges chosen by ye. State in which one of ye. parties resides, juries must also be excluded. But I deny the principle, as too great a refinement.—A Federal jury in ye. Sup. Court, but especially one from ye. vicinity would be a chimera, if ye. Court be stationary. But that ye. same men shou'd be Judges of Law & fact is against reason & not congenial to a free government. Congress may make as many *exceptions* as they please—But to talk of *regulating* men's judgment of facts would be to talk nonsense.—

14. The United States shall guaranty to every State a Republican form of Govt.—

Republics are either Aristocratical or Democratical; & the United States guaranty one of these forms to every State. But I disapprove of any guaranty in ye. matter. For though it is improbable that any State will choose to alter ye. form of its govt. yet it ought to be ye. privelege of every State to do as it will in this affair. If this regulation be admitted it will be found difficult to effect any important change in State-government. For then ye. other States will have nearly as much to do with our government as we ourselves. And what Congress may see in our present constitutions, or any future amendments, not strictly republican *in their opinions*, who can tell?—Besides, it is of no importance to any State how ye. govt. in any other is administered, whether by a single House, or by two & a King.—I therefore presume that as this clause meddles too much with ye. independence of ye. several States, so also it answers no valuable end to any, or to ye. whole—

With regard to ye. Constitution taken into one view—

It is a complete system of Federal Government, every part of which is full of energy; & if established, I think it can never fail of being obeyed by ye. people, and no combination can ever be sufficiently extensive or secret to subvert it. There is some ambiguity in several important parts of it, which arises principally from ye. too general terms in which it is expressed. Too much perhaps is left for ye. future Congress to supply, which when supplied will be no part of ye. Constitution. The States are strictly confined to their own business, & even these are not a little circumscribed. And the powers of all ye. Federal departments are very ample & adequate to their ends.—In short, ye. system would make us formidable abroad, & keep us very *peaceable* at home; with some amendments might do very well for us, if we could be contented to become citizens of America, confuse ye. thirteen stripes, & change ye. stars into one glorious Sun.—

let us pause—

It is not in a few light strictures—It is not, perhaps, in ye. most acute & methodical essay—that ye. merits of this unexpected—this wonderful system can be strictly defined. Reading cannot be applied, & experience is out of ye. question. Thus much we may easily perceive—it is a great, almost a total, & probably a final change. With regard to every state, "To be or not to be—that is ye. question." So great a revolution was never before proposed to a people for their consent. In a time of profound peace, that a matter of such infinite concern should be submitted to general debate throughout such an empire as this, is a phenomenon entirely new.—Let us make a due return to that providence by which we enjoy ye. privelege, by using it like a wise, prudent, & free people. Let us equally shun a hasty acceptance or a precipitate rejection of this all-important scheme. And if our final decision be ye. effect of true wisdom, let us never doubt but that ye. end will be happy!—

Before the Massachusetts state convention, where he played a key role, William Symmes, a lawyer and Boston political leader, wrote to his friend Peter Osgood, an Andover merchant, to set out in detail his reservations about the Constitution (see William Symmes, Jr., entry in *Biographies*). His principal argument was that the Constitution was so loosely written that it ignored the need for the protection of a specific set of rights. Symmes came around to support the Constitution after the Federalists promised a bill of rights.

REFERENCES

Nathan Hazen, *Memorial of the Discourse on William Symmes* (Boston: Historical Collection of the Essex Institute, 1862); Storing, *Complete*, vol. 4.

Samuel Adams, Letter to Richard Henry Lee, *December 3, 1787*

"I have always been apprehensive that, through the weakness of the human mind, often discovered in the wisest and best of men, or the perverseness of the interested and designing, in as well as out of government, misconstructions would be given to the Federal Constitution, which would disappoint the views and expectations of the honest among those who acceded to it, and hazard the liberty, independence, and happiness of the people. I was particularly afraid that, unless great care should be taken to prevent it, the Constitution, in the administration of it, would gradually, but swiftly and imperceptibly, run into a consolidated government, pervading and legislating through all the States; not for Federal purposes *only*, as it professes, but in all cases whatsoever. Such a government would soon totally annihilate the sovereignty of the several States, so necessary to the support of the confederated commonwealth, and sink both in despotism. I know these have been called vulgar opinions and prejudices. Be it so. I think it is Lord Shaftesbury who tells us that it is folly to despise the opinions of the vulgar. This aphorism, if indeed it is his, I eagerly caught from a *nobleman* many years ago whose writings, in some accounts, I never much admired. Should a strong *Federalist*, as some call themselves, see what has now dropped from my pen, he would say that I am an Anti-Fed, an amendment-monger, &c. Those are truly vulgar terms, invented and used by some whose feelings would be sorely wounded to be ranked among such kind of men, and invented and used for the mean purpose of deceiving and entrapping others whom *they* call the vulgar. But in this *enlightened* age, one would think there was no such *vulgar* to be thus amused and ensnared.

"I mean, my friend, to let you know how deeply I am impressed with the sense of the importance of amendments; that the good people may clearly see the distinction—for there is a distinction—between the *Federal powers* vested in Congress and the *sovereign authority* belonging to the several States, which is the palladium of the private and personal rights of the citizens. I freely protest to you, that I earnestly wish some amendments may be judiciously and deliberately made, without partial or local considerations, that there may be no uncomfortable jarrings among the several powers; that the whole people may in every State contemplate their own safety on solid grounds, and the union of the States be perpetual."

The grand old man of Massachusetts radicalism, Samuel Adams served in the Continental Congress and later as governor of the state (see Samuel Adams entry in *Biographies*). In this letter to the Virginian Richard Henry Lee, Adams explained his early opposition to the Constitution in terms of the defense of state rights. Adams later voted for the Constitution because of the Federalist promise of a bill of rights. His enormous contribution to the Antifederalist cause nevertheless necessitates his inclusion in this volume.

REFERENCE

Henry A. Cushing (ed.), *Writings of Samuel Adams* (New York: Octagon Press, 1968), vol. 6.

James Winthrop ("Agrippa"), IV, VI, December 4, 14, 1787

DECEMBER 4, 1787

Having considered some of the principal advantages of the happy form of government under which it is our peculiar good fortune to live, we find by experience, that it is the best calculated of any form hitherto invented, to secure to us the rights of our persons and of our property, and that the general circumstances of the people shew an advanced state of improvement never before known. We have found the shock given by the war in a great measure obliterated, and the publick debt contracted at that time to be considerably reduced in the nominal sum. The Congress lands are fully adequate to the redemption of the principal of their debt, and are selling and populating very fast. The lands of this state, at the west, are, at the moderate price of eighteen pence an acre, worth near half a million pounds in our money. They ought, therefore, to be sold as quick as possible. An application was made lately for a large tract at that price, and continual applications are made for other lands in the eastern part of the state. Our resources are daily augmenting.

We find, then, that after the experience of near two centuries our separate governments are in full vigour. They discover, for all the purposes of internal regulation, every symptom of strength, and none of decay. The new system is, therefore, for such purposes, useless and burdensome.

Let us now consider how far it is practicable consistent with the happiness of the people and their freedom. It is the opinion of the ablest writers on the subject, that no extensive empire can be governed upon republican principles, and that such a government will degenerate to a despotism, unless it be made up of a confederacy of smaller states, each having the full powers of internal regulation. This is precisely the principle which has hitherto preserved our freedom. No instance can be found of any free government of considerable extent which has been supported upon any other plan. Large and consolidated empires may indeed dazzle the eyes of a distant spectator with their splendour, but if examined more nearly are always found to be full of misery. The reason is obvious. In large states the same principles of legislation will not apply to all the parts. The inhabitants of warmer climates are more dissolute in their manners, and less industrious, than in colder countries. A degree of severity is, therefore, necessary with one which would cramp the spirit of the other. We accordingly find that the very great empires have always been despotick. They have indeed tried to remedy the inconveniences to which the people were exposed by local regulations; but these contrivances have never answered the end. The laws not being made by the people, who felt the inconveniences, did not suit their circumstances. It is under such tyranny that the Spanish provinces languish, and such would be our misfortune and degradation, if we should submit to have the concerns of the whole empire managed by one legislature. To promote the happiness of the people it is necessary that there should be local laws; and it is necessary that those laws should be made by the representatives of those who are immediately subject to the want of them. By endeavouring to suit both extremes, both are injured.

It is impossible for one code of laws to suit Georgia and Massachusetts. They must, therefore, legislate for themselves. Yet there is, I believe, not one point of legislation that is not surrendered in the proposed plan. Questions of every kind respecting property are determinable in a continental court, and so are all kinds of criminal causes. The continental legislature has, therefore, a right to make rules *in all cases* by which their judicial courts shall proceed and decide causes. No rights are reserved to the citizens. The laws of Congress are in all cases to be the supreme law of the land, and paramount to the constitutions of the individual states. The Congress may institute what modes of trial they please, and no plea drawn from the constitution of any state can avail. This new system is, therefore, a consolidation of all the states into one large mass, however diverse the parts may be of which it is to be composed. The idea of an uncompounded republick, on an average, one thousand miles in length, and eight hundred in breadth, and containing six millions of white inhabitants all reduced to the same standard of morals, or habits, and of laws, is in itself an absurdity, and contrary to the whole experience of mankind. The attempt made by Great-Britain to introduce such a system, struck us with horrour, and when it was proposed by some theorists that we should be represented in parliament, we uniformly declared that one legislature could not represent so many different interests for the purposes of legislation and taxation. This was the leading principle of the revolution, and makes an essential article in our creed. All that part, therefore, of the new system, which relates to the internal government of the states, ought at once to be rejected.

DECEMBER 14, 1787

To prevent any mistakes, or misapprehensions of the argument, stated in my last paper, to prove that the proposed constitution is an actual consolidation of the separate states into one extensive commonwealth, the reader is desired to observe, that in the course of the argument, the new plan is considered as an intire system. It is not dependent on any other book for an explanation, and contains no references to any other book. All the defences of it, therefore, so far as they are drawn from the state constitutions, or from maxims of the common law, are foreign to the purpose. It is only by comparing the different parts of it together, that the meaning of the whole is to be understood. For instance—

We find in it, that there is to be a legislative assembly, with authority to constitute courts for the trial of all kinds of civil causes, between citizens of different states. The right to appoint such courts necessarily involves in it the right of defining their powers, and determining the rules by which their judgment shall be regulated; and the grant of the former of those rights is nugatory without the latter. It is vain to tell us, that a maxim of common law requires contracts to be determined by the law existing where the contract was made: for it is also a maxim, that the legislature has a right to alter the common law. Such a power forms an essential part of legislation. Here, then, a declaration of rights is of inestimable value. It contains those principles which the government never can invade without an open violation of the compact between them and the citizens. Such a declaration ought to have come to the new constitution in favour of the legislative rights of the several states, by which their sovereignty over their own citizens within the state should be secured. Without such an express declaration the states are annihilated in reality upon receiving this constitution—the forms will be preserved only during the pleasure of Congress.

The idea of consolidation is further kept up in the right given to regulate trade. Though this power under certain limitations would be a proper one for the department of Congress; it is in this system carried much too far, and much farther than is necessary. This is, without exception, the most commercial state upon the continent. Our extensive coasts, cold climate, small estates, and equality of rights, with a variety of subordinate and concurring circumstances, place us in this respect at the head of the union. We must, therefore, be indulged if a point which so nearly relates to our welfare be rigidly examined. The new constitution not only prohibits vessels, bound from one state to another, from paying any duties, but even from entering and clearing. The only use of such a regulation is, to keep each state in complete ignorance of its own resources. It certainly is no hardship to enter and clear at the custom-house, and the expense is too small to be an object.

The unlimitted right to regulate trade, includes the right of granting exclusive charters. This, in all old countries, is considered as one principle branch of prerogative. We find hardly a country in Europe which has not felt the ill effects of such a power. Holland has carried the exercise of it farther than any other state; and the reason why that country has felt less evil from it is, that the territory is very small, and they have drawn large revenues from their colonies in the East and West Indies. In this respect, the whole country is to be considered as a trading company, having exclusive privileges. The colonies are large in proportion to the parent state; so that, upon the whole, the latter may gain by such a system. We are also to take into consideration the industry which the genius of a free government inspires. But in the British islands all these circumstances together have not prevented them from being injured by the monopolies created there. Individuals have been enriched, but the country at large has been hurt. Some valuable branches of trade being granted to companies, who transact their business in London, that city is, perhaps, the place of the greatest trade in the world. But Ireland, under such influence, suffers exceedingly, and is impoverished; and Scotland is a mere bye-word. Bristol, the second city in England, ranks not much above this town in population. These things must be accounted for by the incorporation of trading companies; and if they are felt so severely in countries of small extent, they will operate with ten-fold severity upon us, who inhabit an immense tract; and living towards one extreme of an extensive empire, shall feel the evil, without retaining that influence in government, which may enable us to procure redress. There ought, then, to have been inserted a restraining clause, which might prevent the Congress from making any such grant, because they consequentially defeat the trade of the out-ports, and are also injurious to the general commerce, by enhancing prices, and destroying that rivalship which is the great stimulous to industry.

James Winthrop, librarian at Harvard and a brilliant mathematician, was also a bit of a gadfly (see James Winthrop entry in *Biographies*). In this essay, he expressed fear that the Massachusetts economy would suffer under the proposed Constitution.

REFERENCES

Massachusetts Gazette, December 4, 14, 1787; a complete "Agrippa" is in Storing, *Complete*, vol. 4.

Benjamin Austin, Jr.
(and Samuel Adams), ("Candidus"), II,
December 20, 1787

II
20 December 1787

In my last, I endeavoured to guard my countrymen, against the artful suggestions of many who say that the proposed Constitution is the *only one* that can be adopted: that we *must* receive it without any *amendments*; and that *anarchy and civil war*, will be the consequences of rejecting it.—The two former pleas, I contended was derogatory to freemen, and the latter affronting to our understanding.

I need not urge my countrymen, to a serious consideration of the important business before them; presuming that the wisdom and prudence which have ever been the characteristic of Americans, will lead the members of the convention to consider maturely, before they decide on so momentous a question.

Many arguments have been offered to the public, both for, and against the new Constitution; on one side we have the rapturous strains of a *Wilson*, on the other the nervous reasoning of *Brutus*.[1] But the advocates for the Constitution, have always assumed an advantage by saying, that their opposers have never offered any plan as a substitute: the following outlines are therefore submitted, not as *originating* from an individual, but as *copied* from former resolutions of Congress, and united with *some parts* of the Constitution proposed by the respectable Convention. This being the case. I presume it will not be invalidated by the cant term of antifederalism, viz.

1st. That the Legislature of *each State*, empower Congress to frame a *navigation act*, to operate uniformly throughout the States; reserving to Congress all necessary powers to *regulate our commerce with foreign nations, and among the several States, and with the Indian tribes.* The revenue arising from the *impost* to be subject to their appropriations, "to enable them to *fulfil their public engagements with foreign creditors.*"

2d. That the Legislature of each State, instruct their delegates in Congress to frame a treaty of AMITY, for the purposes of discharging each State's proportion of the public debt, and support of the foederal government. To assist each other in cases of *insurrections* and *invasion:* and in case any State within the confederacy should be *delinquent* in discharging their proportion of the public debt, either *foreign or domestic*, to enforce (if necessary) their immediate payment. Each State *obligating themselves in the treaty of amity*, to furnish (whenever required by Congress) a proportionate number of the Militia, who are ever to be well organized and disciplined, for the purposes of repelling any invasion; suppressing any insurrection; or reducing any delinquent State within the confederacy, to a compliance with the foederal treaty of commerce and amity.—Such assistance to be furnished by the *Supreme Executive* of each State, on the application of Congress.—The troops in cases of *invasion* to be under the command of the Supreme Executive of the State immediately in danger; but in cases of *insurrection*, and *when employ'd against any delinquent State in the confederacy*, the troops to be under the command of Congress.

3d. That such States as did not join the confederacy of *commerce and amity*, should be considered as *aliens*; and any goods brought from such State into any of the confederated States, together with their vessels, should be subject to heavy extra duties.

4th. The treaty of amity, agreed to by the several States, should expressly declare, that no State (without the consent of Congress) should enter into any treaty, alliances or confederacy, grant letters of marque and reprisal; make any thing but gold and silver coin a tender in payment of debts; pass any bill of attainder; expost facto law, impairing the obligations of contracts; engage in war, or declare peace.

5th. A Supreme Judicial Court to be constituted for the following *foederal purposes*, viz. To extend to all treaties made previous to, or which shall be made under the authority of the confederacy. All cases affecting Ambassadors, and other public Ministers and Consuls; controversies between two or more States; and between citizens of the same State, claiming lands under grants of different States.—To define and punish piracies, and felonies committed on the high seas, and offences against the law of nations.

6th. That it be recommended to Congress, that the said *navigation act*, and *treaty of amity*, be sent to the Legislatures (or people) of the several States, for their assenting to, and ratifying the same.—The ratification of nine States, to be sufficient for the establishment of such a navigation act, and treaty of amity, between the States, so ratifying the same.

7th. A regular statement and account of the receipt and expenditures, of all public monies, should be published from time to time.

The above plan it is humbly conceived secures the *internal government* of the several States, promotes the *commerce* of the whole union; preserves a due degree of *energy*, lays restraints on *aliens*; secures the several States against *invasions* and *insurrections*, by a MILITIA, rather than a STANDING ARMY; checks all *expost facto* laws; cements the States by certain *foederal restrictions*; confines the judiciary powers to *national matters*; provides for the public information of *receipts* and *expenditures*: in a word, places us in a compleat *foederal state*.

Every man must be sensible, that a foederal system, is of the utmost importance to our national prosperity.—The deranged situation of our public affairs, now calls on us to adopt such measures as will relieve the distresses of the PEOPLE, and establish upon a permanent basis the COMMERCE of these States.

The encouragement of a beneficial commerce must be acknowledged, to be of the greatest public utility; as the value of our produce and our lands, must either rise or fall in proportion to the prosperous, or adverse state of trade. This essential concern, has ever claimed the particular attention of Congress; their earnest solicitations to vest them with sufficient powers for this purpose, fully evince of what importance they considered this object. Provided their requisitions had been complied with, our trade would probably have been upon a respectable footing,—and foreigners would largely have contributed to the payment of our national debt.

The question now is, what public measures must be adopted to restore our decayed commerce, and give energy to government? These I presume, are the great objects to be considered: And, provided this business is earnestly undertaken, every embarrassment we now experience would subside; our public credit would revive; our government would receive every support; a circulation of currency would ensue; our taxes would be quickly collected; the husbandman, merchant and tradesman, would experience the salutary effects; and *public confidence*, which has long been wanting among us, would be again restored.

Notwithstanding the many advocates for the adoption of the new Constitution. I cannot but doubt, whether this establishment will remedy our complaints. It is true the government of these States has been for many years in a decline; *for want of a federal system*, all our measures to promote the public interest have proved abortive. But in order to remedy these evils, shall we now pass to the other extreme; and, from denying Congress every power whatever, wantonly surrender into their hands our *Excises*, and submit to their *direct taxation?* with powers to raise armies. &c. &c.

The readiness of the people to adopt the new Constitution, arises in a great degree from the apprehension that *no other mode* can be adopted: But this is a mistaken idea, as Congress a few years since, pointed out a mode similar to a part of the plan now offered.—which they recommended to the several States for their adoption.

The resolves of Congress, 18th April, 1783, "recommends to the several States, to invest them with powers to levy for the use of the United States, certain duties upon goods, imported from any foreign port, island or plantation;" which measure is declared by them, "To be a system more free, from well founded exceptions, and is better calculated to receive the approbation of the several States, *than any other, that the wisdom of Congress could devise; and if adopted, would enable them to fulfil their public engagements with their foreign creditors.*"

The address of the General Court of this Commonwealth, to the people, 30th October, 1786, fully evinces, that measure much short of the proposed Constitution, would restore these States to the highest degree of harmony and respectability.

They say "Of the *national debt*, that part which is due to foreigners, must be paid in gold and silver;—if the *Continental Impost*, should take place, which there is much reason to expect, *it would immediately discharge us from the principal of this debt*; with respect to the *Continental domestic debt*, Congress have resolved that the lands ceded to them, by the individual States, shall be disposed of, *for the payment of that debt; the particular debt of this Commonwealth,* is almost wholly due to its citizens; considerable sums are expected from the sale of lands in the easterly part of this State."

From the above quotations, it does appear, that the *Continental Impost*, is fully adequate to enable Congress to fulfil their engagements with their *foreign Creditors*. The *lands ceded to Congress*, are to be disposed of, for the payment of the *Continental domestic debt*. And the *particular debt of this State*, will probably, (exclusive of the Western territory) be discharged in a great measure, from the sale of the *Eastern lands*. If then, these three great national objects, can be accomplished, without a total surrender of the Sovereignty of these States, why should each State with such *alacrity*, reduce themselves to mere corporations,— and submit their *Excises*, with every other tax, to the unlimited controul of Congress? This conduct in the American annals, may appear as inglorious, as King *John's* resignation of the Crown, to the *Pope's Legate*. The magnitude of the surrender is expressed most forcibly by Mr. *Wilson*, when he says, "Thirteen Sovereign States, some of which, in territorial jurisdiction, *population*, and *resource*, equal the most respectable nations of Europe; but likewise myriads of citizens, who in future ages, shall inhabit the vast uncultivated regions of the Continent." Certainly then, the importance of the business before us, ought to "fill our minds with awe and apprehension."[2]

The creditors of the particular States, would become great sufferrers, if the *Excises* are wholly subject to the use of Congress. The interest of the State debt must remain for many years unpaid; as the necessary arrangements of Congress; the pay of their officers; the great expences naturally attending so extensive a system of government; the parade and pagentry necessary to keep up the etiquette of *Dignities*; together with the enormous expenditures, within the confines of the Federal town, will call for the greatest part of the money that can be for many years collected.

Provided the Constitution should be adopted in *all its parts*, the Congressional Body, would have so many important matters to consider, that the most essential object of *Commerce* might not claim that particular attention, which our present situation requires. The merchant and tradesman, might be waiting with earnest expectations for some commercial regulations, while Congress were busily engaged in framing other systems of legislation.

When we consider the great revenue requisite to support the proposed Constitution, we ought to reflect whether the *abilities* of the people are proportionate. How can the tradesman, farmer and merchant in the present feeble state of their several occupations, and employments, be able to support the immediate expences of the new Constitution? The demands on them, would be *hastily* made; and they must be answered, even before any beneficial operations could arise from the establishment; and after those great advances of taxes, it is quite uncertain, whether we should not be disappointed in our expectations, of the revival of our commerce.

But should we adopt the plan proposed by Congress, in their resolves of the 18th April, 1783, (already mentioned) no extraordinary expences would arise, and Congress having but *one object* to attend, every commercial regulation would be uniformly adopted; the duties of impost and excise, would operate equally throughout the States; our ship-building and carrying trade, would claim their immediate attention. And in consequence thereof, our agriculture, trade and manufactures would revive and flourish. No acts of legislation, independent of this great business, would disaffect one State against the other; but the whole, uniting in one Federal System of commerce, would serve to remove all local attachments, and establish our navigation upon a most extensive basis. The powers of Europe, would be alarmed at our Union, and would fear lest we should retaliate on them by laying restrictions on their trade.

These being the probable consequences of a commercial system, the questions are, Whether it is necessary, to adopt the Constitution proposed; or whether each State, complying with the request of Congress, together with the other parts of the plan proposed, would not answer every purpose we would wish to effect? If the latter is competent to these purposes, why should we be so urgent to adopt a plan of government, among other defects, destitute of that basis of freedom, A BILL OF RIGHTS; and which exposes every man, within these States, to be drag'd hundreds of miles, to a Federal Judicial Court?

The Constitution proposed, may aggrandize a few individuals: *The offices of honor and profit, may please the AMBITION of some, and relieve the EMBARRASSMENTS of others.* It may serve to multiply Judicial controversies, and embarrass the citizens of the several States, by appeals to a Federal Court. It may give an undue influence to Congress, by the appointment of a numerous Body of officers. It may discourage *Industry,* by promoting an infinite train of dependants and seekers.—But the great object of commerce,—our national respectability,—together with industry and frugality, would probably be the happy consequences of a Commercial Confederation.

These States, by the blessing of Heaven, are now in a very tranquil state.—This government in particular, has produced an instance of ENERGY, in suppressing late Rebellion, &c. which no absolute Monarchy can boast: And, notwithstanding the insinuations of a *"small party,"* who are ever branding the PEOPLE, with the most approbious Epithets; representing them as aiming to level all distinctions; emit paper money; encourage the Rebellion. Yet the present General Court, the voice of that Body, whom they have endeavoured to stigmatize, have steadily pursued measures foreign from the suggestions of such revilers. And the public credit has been constantly appreciating since the present Administration.

Let us then be cautious how we disturb this general harmony. Every exertion is now making, by the people, to discharge their taxes. Industry and frugality prevail. Our commerce is every day encreasing by the enterprize of our Merchants.—And above all, the PEOPLE of *the several States are convinced of the necessity of adopting some Federal Commercial Plan.*

Benjamin Austin, Jr., a Boston merchant and member of the state senate, was a close colleague of Samuel Adams (see Benjamin Austin entry in *Biographies*). In this article published on December 20, 1787, Austin proposed a plan for amending the proposed economic, taxing, and import restrictions of the federal Constitution. Austin believed amendments necessary because an unrevised Constitution encouraged the desire for gain and would turn the young republic into a country driven by the desire for wealth.

REFERENCES

Independent Chronicle, December 20, 1787; Storing, *Complete*, vol. 4 shows Austin's relationship with Adams.

NOTES

1. Robert Yates of New York.
2. Federalist James Wilson of Pennsylvania.

James Warren ("Helvidius Priscus"), December 27, 1787

INDEPENDENT CHRONICLE
27 December 1787

Mr. Wilson observes, in his late celebrated speech, "that after a lapse of six thousand years, America has now presented the first instance of a people asembled to weigh deliberately, and calmly, and to decide leisurely, and peaceably, on a form of government, by which they shall bind themselves and their posterity."[1] Has he not here suggested the strongest reason that can be urged, for postponing the adoption of the new system? If the assertion is true, is it prudent for this extensive Continent implicitly to accept, and rapidly and irrevocably adopt, the propositions of thirty or forty men, some of whom were infants, when the principles of the late revolution animated the patriots of this country to a noble resistance, and led them to bear the bold arm to shake the sceptre of foreign dominion: And as Mr. WILSON himself observers, "Government is a science as yet in infancy; and with all its various modifications, has been the result of force, fraud or accident." May not these gentlemen be considered as yet in their pupilage, with regard to the origin, the end, and the most perfect mode of civil government? It is also well known, that some of the late Convention were the professed advocates of the British system; that others stood suspended in equilibrio, uncertain on which side to declare, until the scale of fortune balanced in favour of America; that the political manoeuvres of some of them have always sunk in the vortex of private interest, and that the immense wealth of others has set them above all principle. These several classes selected, a correspondent would inquire; how many of the disinterested worthies who ventured every thing for the support of the rights of their country, and the liberties of mankind, will be left to adorn that assembly, who have ambitiously and daringly presumed (without any commission for that purpose) to annihilate the sovereignties of the thirteen United States; to establish a DRACONIAN CODE; and to bind posterity by their *secret councils*? It may perhaps be replied that one third part of the body were of this generous description. Let us candidly grant it and examine their conduct; several of them left the assembly in disgust before the decision of the question. Others expressly reprobated the proceedings of a *conclave*, where it has been ridiculously asserted all the wisdom of America was con-centered; and a RANDOLPH, MASON, and GERRY, had the firmness to avow their dissent; to support their opinions in the Legislatives of their several States; and submit them to the observation of the world. It is true indeed that the *ancient Doctor*, who has been always republican in principle and conduct, doubted, trembled, hesitated, wept, and signed: While the illustrious President, not called upon to decide or necessitated to give his opinion, kept the chair, but undoubtedly painfully agitated for the fate of a country he had heroically lent his arm to defend. All the powers of eloquence are exerted to catch the ear; and the utmost pathos of expression employed to warm the imagination, in Mr. WILSON's insidious speech; but as it will doubtless be the subject of critical discussion by those who have leisure to examine both its principles, and its tendency, I will but cursorily observe that he discovers no less *dexterity* and *address*, in his oratorical explanation of the system, then he acknowledges was necessary to *reconcile the jarring interests that opposed it*—and finally to prevail with several whose objections were insurmountable, to lend their signature to an instrument for which he is obliged to ransack the annals of ancient and modern story to find a name. But he acknowledges that neither *Rome*, nor *Britain*, nor *Switzerland*, or *Holland*, bear much resemblance to the newly fabricated *federal republic*.—And that he cannot find a precedent any where for the *Heterogeneous Monster*, unless it may be admitted in the *Lycian league* of the *Amphictionic Council*. It is here natural for every one acquainted with ancient history to turn their thoughts to the miserable fate of the *Lycians*. They were a sober, and virtuous people, who maintained their independence, and their freedom, for several centuries; and supported their own simple institutions, under twenty-three distinct sovereignties; until the reign of *Leomitian*, when they fell under the Roman yoke, with other cities of Greece, while the *tyrant* alledged the same excuse for his encroachment, that we hear hacknied in the streets of our capitals, for subjugating the Americans to the arms of power *because they were no longer capable of enjoying their liberties.* Nor is *Mr. Wilson* more fortunate in calling our attention to the ruin of the Amphictionic union. Every one will recollect that the *Locrians*, (a people bearing a strong resemblance to a party in America) had crept in among them, and that an ambitious *Phillip* had his emisaries in that body, who by political intrigue, and well-timed *plausible speeches*, enabled him by the aid of a *standing army*, to set himself at the head of the Grecian States; to annihilate their constitutions, and to degrade them to the most abject submission to the will of a despotic tyrant. The application and the semblance is left for the consideration of every lover of his country.

America has fought for her liberties; she has purchased them by the most costly sacrifices; she embarked in the enterprize with a spirit that gained her the applauses of mankind; and procured her emancipation from tyranny by the blood of her heroes, and her friends. And shall her honour, her character, her freedom, be sported away by the duplicity, and the intrigues of those, who never participated in her sufferings? Or by the machinations of such as have no pole star for their guide, but the mad ambition of a mind ready to sacrifice the finest feelings of humanity for its gratification? FORBID IT HEAVEN! and may the people awake from a kind of apathy which seems to pervade them, before they are aroused by the thunder of arms, or the insolence of dragooning parties, to arrest from the peasant, and the mechanic, the last farthing of their hard earnings, to support the splendid fabrick of *Mr. Wilson's* FEDERAL REPUBLIC. What an insiduous term! But this people are too wise to be long deceived by the extortion, or misapplication of words. Let the youth of America, who are yet ignorant of the characters, and the causes that occasioned the dismemberment of the United States from the crown of Britain, read for themselves the many excellent publications, on the origin of government, and the rights of human nature, that appeared between the year 1763 and 1775. And instead of indulging a raptuous admiration for the modern superficial speechifyers in favour of an American monarchy: let them examine the principles of the late glorious revolution, and see how far they comport with the opinions in vogue. And before they embrace the chains of survitude, let them scrutinize their own hearts, and inquire, if their pride and their independency of spirit, will suffer them to lick the hand of a despotic master. And may the delegates for the ensuing convention consider well the importance of their decision. They will be applauded by the admiring world for making a stand at this critical conjuncture; or they will be execrated by all posterity for co-operating with the ambitious and intriguing spirits, who wish for the sake of their own advancement, to manacle a free and independent people, who have made the most astonishing and successful exertions to support their own rights, and to establish their rank among the nations. And when they shall have time to look around and be convinced, even *Mr. Wilson* acknowledges, *"they will then spurn at every attempt to shackle them with despotic power."*

Let them call for the name of the audacious man, who dared to say to his associates, in the late convention, *"that unless they hurried the constitution through before the people had time for consideration, there was no probability that it would ever be adopted."* And let him be stigmatized with the odium that is due to the base betrayer of the rights of his country, and not absurdly trusted, though he may artfully have obtained an election, to decide a second time on a question in which he is so manifestly interested.

It is obvious that there is not the smallest propriety that any of the members of that body, who have held out a system for the people to judge of, should themselves set in any of the State conventions, and have a voice to enforce their own alarming proceedings.

Let the old Patriots come forward, and instead of secretly wraping up their opinions within their own breasts, let them lift up the voice like a trumpet, and shew this people their folly, and the trembling *Columbia*, her impending danger.

In this letter, James Warren, a Boston merchant and intellectual, wrote to the public to warn of a loss of personal liberty in the federal Constitution (see James Warren entry in *Biographies*). In this way, he contributed to the language the conventions' delegates used to write a bill of rights to add to the Constitution. Warren also feared that the gains made for republican government in separation from England could be lost if the Constitution was ratified.

REFERENCES

Independent Chronicle, December 27, 1787; Storing, *Complete*, vol. 4.

NOTE

1. James Wilson, Pennsylvania Federalist.

Thomas B. Wait, Letter to George Thatcher,[1]
January 8, 1788

My dear friend—

My opposition to the proposed plan of Continental Govt. does not, as you suppose, arise from *"violence of passion."*—

On reception of the Report of the Convention, I perused, and admired it:— Or rather, like many who still *think* they admire it, I loved Geo. Washington— I venerated Benj. Franklin—and therefore concluded that I must love and venerate all the works of their hands:—This, if you please my friend, was *"violence of passion"*—and to this very *violence of passion* will the proposed Constitution owe its adoption—i.e.—should the people ever adopt it. The honest and uninformed *freemen* of America entertain the same opinion of those two gentlemen as do European *slaves* of their Princes,—*"that they can do no wrong"*—

On the unprecedented Conduct of the Pennsylvania Legislature, I found myself disposed to lend an ear to the arguments of the opposition—not with an expectation of being convinced that the new Constitution was defective; but because I thought the minority had been ill used; and I felt a little curious to hear the particulars.

The address of the Seceders was like the Thunder of Sinai—it's lightnings were irresistible; and I was obliged to acknowledge, not only that the conduct of the majority was highly reprehensible, but that the Constitution itself might possibly be defective.—My mind has since been open to conviction—I have read & heard every argument, on either side, with a degree of candour, of which I never, on any other occasion, felt myself possessed—And, after this cool and impartial examination I am constrained—I repeat it, my dear friend— I am constrained to say, that I am dissatisfied with the proposed Constitution.—

Your arguments against the necessity of a Bill of Rights are ingenious; but, pardon me my friend, they are not convincing.—You have traced the origin of a Bill of Rights accurately.—The People of England, as you say, undoubtedly made use of a Bill of Rights to obtain their liberties of their soverigns; but is this an argument to prove that they ought not now to make use of Bills in defence of those liberties?—shall a man throw away his sword, and refuse to defend a piece of property, for no other reason than that his property was obtained by that very sword?—Bills of Rights have been the happy instruments of wresting the privileges and rights of the people from the hand of Despotism; and I trust God that Bills of Rights will still be made use of by the people of America to defend them against future encroachments of despotism—Bills of Rights, in my opinion, are the grand bulwarks of freedom.

But, say some, however necessary in state Constitutions, there can be no necessity for a Bill of Rights in the Continental plan of Govt.—because every Right is reserved that is not *expressly* given up—Or, in other words, Congress have no powers but those *expressly* given by that Constitution.—This is the *doctrine* of the *celebrated* Mr. Wilson; and as you, my friend, have declared it *orthodox*, be so good as to explain the meaning of the following Extracts from the Constitution—Art. I Sect. 9.—"The privilege of the writ of Habeas Corpus shall *not* be suspended &c."—"*No* bill of attainder or ex post facto law shall be passed."—"*No* money shall be drawn from the treasury" &c.—"*No* title of nobility shall be granted by the United states."—Now, how absurd—how grosly absurd is all this, if Congress, in reality, have no powers but those particularly specified in the Constitution!—

It will not do, my friend—for God's sake let us not deny self-evident propositions—let us not sacrifice the truth, that we may establish a favourite hypothesis;—in the present case, the liberties and happiness of a world may also be sacrificed.—

There is a certain darkness, duplicity and studied ambiguity of expression running thro' the whole Constitution which renders a Bill of Rights peculiarly necessary.—As it now stands but very few individuals do, or ever will understand it.—Consequently, Congress will be its own *interpreter*—The article respecting taxation and representation is neither more or less than a *puzling Cap*; and you, my friend, had the pleasure of *wearing* it, at my office, an hour or two—and then pulled it off, *just as wise* as when you put it on.—But you will now perhaps tell me that you can explain it entirely to my satisfaction—possibly you can; but that may not happen completely to satisfy Congress—if it should not, why they will put a different one,—one that may not satisfy *either you or me*—But Some persons have *guessed* the meaning to be this—that *taxation and representation should be in proportion to all the freemen and slaves in each state—counting five of the latter to three of the former*—If these were the ideas of the Convention, what a strange collection of words do we find in the Constitution to express them!—Who, in the name of God, but the *majority* of that honl. body, would ever have tho't of expressing like ideas in like words!—But bad as may be the *mode* of *expression*, the *ideas*, in my opinion, are worse—

By this *interpretation* the article in question is an egregious imposition on the northern states—Tell me, if you can, why a southern *negro*, in his present debased condition, is any more intitled to representation, than a northern *Bullock?*—Both are mere pieces of property—and nothing more!—The latter is equally a *free agent* with the former.— . . .

And now let me beseech you, not obstinately to defend your present notions of the new Constitution tho' they may be all the *ton* in the *great* world, till you have examined every argument that has been used against it—pay particular attention to the Debates of the Pennsylvania Convention; and I am certain that you must acknowledge if the Constitution is good, that it by no means appears so from any arguments made use of by the majority of that body—they are lighter than straws.—

How can you, after *perusing* the arguments of Crazy Jonathan, approve of the abolition of juries in civil causes—If the Genl. Court of this state are insurgents for depriving the subject of that right in 110 actions out of 120—what shall we say to the Constitution that evidently deprives the subject of that right altogether?—O, my good friend, that cursed Small pox has made a crazy Jonathan of you in good earnest.—But your life is spared—and I am happy— . . .

We continued as perfectly happy as was possible in the absence of our *friend*, our *Uncle* and our *father*, until sunday noon;—at which time Jeremiah Hill, Esq. made his appearance—from that time till after tea, (which we drank at his house) we eat and drank and talked politicks. The Squire, you must know, is a professed Constitutionalist—Silas and myself were *Anti's*—so we had nothing to do but fall at it *hammer & tongs*,—Had you been within hearing, you would have wished the new Constitution, or its advocate, or both, at the Devil—We *roasted* him—we *basted* him, till he became quite a *crisp*; and, had we tarried the evening, we should certainly have *devoured* him—We took pity upon, and left him directly after tea—returned to your house, and were again happy. . . .

You say nothing of a Post to Pownalboro'—The people at the Eastward are amazingly impatient—It is an important period; and they are almost totally ignorant of every public transaction—Five Delegates in six, from these three Counties are opposed to the new plan of Cont. Government—Genl. Thompson and your *Brother* Widgery are warm in the opposition, and both are Conventioners—[2]

Just before the state convention began, Thomas B. Wait, a radical Maine newspaper editor, explained to the Federalist George Thatcher why his opposition to the Constitution was considered and judgmental (see Thomas Baker Wait entry in *Biographies*). Wait had previously given unconditional support for the Constitution. But, after consideration of its lack of protection for civil rights, he explained to Thatcher, he had turned to the Antifederalists.

REFERENCES

Bailyn, *Debate*, vol. 1; George Thatcher Papers, Boston Public Library.

NOTES

1. Thatcher was a prominent Massachusetts Federalist.
2. Samuel Thompson and William Widgery, Maine Antifederalists.

Nathaniel Barrell, Letter to George Thatcher, *January 15, 1788*

I can assure my friend Thatcher, his letter of 22d. ultimo was peculiarly flat-
tering, and should have been answered before, but for a variety of reasons any
of which I persuade myself you will be satisfied with, when you come to be informed of them, but which I have not time now to mention—I am pleasd with
the open freedom with which you touch political matters, and however we may
differ on that point I hope we shall always view each other as friends to good
Government—at present I confess to you we are not altogether agreed in sentiment respecting the federal frame which brings me to this town—the pamphlet you were pleased to enclose on that subject I think is wrote in that easy
familiar stile which is ever pleasing to me, but tho it has a tendency to eluci-
date if not remove some objections to the federal constitution, yet I dare not
say 'tis a full answer to the many objections against it, however I think with
you a great part of those objections are founded on remote possibilities—do
realy what you so humourously define, spring from that doctrine I have heard
you reprobate, as originating in the heart which we are told by him who made
it, is as you say—but tho I give more credit to this declaration than you do,
yet I would by no means treat congress, or such men as my friend Thatcher,
as *"tho they were rogues"*—nay I have such an opinion of you Sir, that I would
cheerfully consent to your being a leading man in the first congress, after we
adopt the federal Government—I hope you will not think me to familiar if I
should say the manner in which you treat this subject is rather laughfable than
serious—and that it is much easier to tell the objectors to turn their representatives out, than to do it—I cant but think you know how difficult it is to turn
out a representative who behaves ill, even tho chosen but for one year—think
you not 'twould be more dificult to remove one chosen for two years?—I could
wish to lay my objections before you in the same familiar manner you have
been pleasd to set me the example, but for want of your talents, I will do it in
my own way, which are such as if not removd will prevent my acceeding to
it—because after all the Willsonian orotary—after all the learned arguments I
have seen written—after all the labord speeches I have heard in its defence—
and after the best investigation I have been able to give it—I see it pregnant
with the fate of our libertys and if I should not live to feel its baneful effects,
I see it intails wretchedness on my posterity—slavery on my children—for as it
now stands congress will be vested with much more extensive powers than ever
great Britain exercised over us—too great to intrust with any set of men, let
their talents & vertues be ever so conspicuous—even tho composed of such

exalted amiable characters as the great Washington—for while we consider
them as men of like passion the same spontaneous inherent thirst for power
with ourselves—great & good as they may be when they enter upon this important charge, what dependance can we have on their continuing so?—but
were we sure they would continue the faithful guardians of our libertys, & prevent any infringments on the priviledges of the people—what assurance can we
have that such men will always hold the reins of Government?—that their successors will be such—history tells us Rome was happy under Augustus, tho
wretched under Nero, who could have no greater power than Augustus—and
that the same Nero when young in power could weep at signing a death warrant, tho afterwards became so callous to the tender feelings of humanity as to
behold with pleasure Rome in flames.—but Sir I am convincd such that six
years is too long a term for any set of men to be at the helm of Government
for in that time they will get so firmly rooted their influence will be so great
as to continue them for life—because Sir I am persuaded we are not able to
support the additional charge of such a Government and that when our State
Government is annihilated this will not suit our local concerns so well as what
we now have—because I think 'twill not be so much for our advantage to have
our taxes imposd & levied at the pleasure of Congress as the method now pursued—and because Sir I think a Continental collector at the head of a standing army will not be so likely to do us justice in collecting the taxes, as the
mode of colecting now practicd—and to crown all sir, because I think such a
Government impracticable among men with such high notions of liberty as we
americans. these are the general objections as they occur to my mind, the per-
ticulars I cant bring within the bounds of a letter, all which convince me the
federal constitution as it now stands, needs much amendment before 'twill be
safe for us to adopt it—therefore as wise men—as the faithful guardians of the
peoples libertys—and as we wish well to posterity it becomes to reject it unless such amendments take place as will secure to us & ours that liberty without which life is a burthen.—

Nathaniel Barrell, a Boston merchant and political leader, strongly opposed the
Constitution (see Nathaniel Barrell entry in *Biographies*). In this letter, he sum-
marized his comments in the state convention in which he called the federal
Congress aristocratic. Lack of turnover in office, control of when elections
would be held, and the costs of elections all influenced his judgement.

REFERENCES

Bradford K. Peirce (ed.), *Debates and Proceedings in the Convention of the Commonwealth of Massachusetts* (Boston: William White, 1856); George Thatcher papers, Boston
Public Library.

James Warren ("A Republican Federalist"), *January 19, 1788*

TO THE MEMBERS OF THE CONVENTION
OF MASSACHUSETTS

Honourable Friends, and Fellow Citizens.

The proceedings of the federal Convention, having, as has been shewn, originated in usurpation, and being founded in tyranny, cannot be ratified by the State Convention, *without breaking down the barriers of liberty; trampling on the authority of federal and State Constitutions, and annihilating in America, governments founded in compact.* In this predicament, there appears but two measures which can with safety be adopted by the Convention of this State. One has been hinted at, *an adjournment,* until the sense of Virginia can be known. The great danger in this business is, from *precipitation, not* from *delay:* The *latter* cannot injure whilst the *former* may *irretrievably* ruin us; an adjournment would not only ripen the judgment of our own citizens, but give them an opportunity of benefiting by the opinions of those States, which are attentive to, but not *extravagantly* zealous in this matter. The other measure is, to return the proceedings of the federal Convention to the legislature of this State, to be by them transmitted to Congress, and *amended* agreeably to the articles of Confederation: For the system being *improperly* before the State Convention, and they being *incompetent* to a ratification of it, cannot thereby bind the citizens of Massachusetts. Had the system been in itself unobjectionable, it is evident from what has been said, that the sentiments of the qualified voters *on the necessity* of revision, *must* have been taken, and two thirds of them *must* have been in favour of it, before a State Convention could be called for amending the Constitution much more for dissolving the government.

Let us once more particularly attend to the system itself. It begins. "We the People of the United States, in order to form a more perfect union," &c. "do ordain and establish this Constitution for the United States of America"—In other words, *We the people, do hereby publickly declare the violation of the faith which we have solemnly pledged to each other—do give the most unequivocal evidence, that we cannot ourselves, neither can any others, place the least confidence in our most solemn covenants, do effectually put an end in America, to governments founded in compact—do relinquish that security for life, liberty and property, which we had in the Constitutions of these States, and of the Union—do give up governments which we well understood, for a new system which we have no idea of—and we do, by this act of ratification and political suicide, destroy the new sys-*

tem itself, and prepare the way for a despotism, if agreeable to our rulers. All this we do, for the *honour of having a system of consolidation formed by us the people.* This is not *magnifying*, for such are the facts, and such will be the consequences. Indeed we find *despotism* not only in contemplation of the Pennsylvanians, but openly avowed in their State Convention, in the words following—"Despotism, if wisely administered, is the best system invented by the ingenuity of man." This was declared by chief justice M'Kean; and in such an high office, we must suppose him a man of too much precaution to have made the declaration, had he not known, that a majority of the Convention, and of the citizens, who so highly applauded his speeches, were of his opinion. M. Montesquieu, in his "Spirit of Laws," 1st vol. book 3, chap. 9, says, "As *virtue* is necessary in a *republick*, and *honour* in a *monarchy, so fear* is necessary in a *despotick* government: With regard to *virtue*, there is no occasion for it, and *honour* would be extremely dangerous." Thus has a declaration been made in Pennsylvania, in favour of a government which substitutes *fear* for *virtue*, and reduces men *from rational beings* to the *level of brutes:* and if the citizens of Massachusetts are disposed to follow the example, and *submit their necks to the yoke*, they must expect to be governed by the *whip* and *goad*. But it is remarkable, that the resolution of the federal Convention, for transmitting the system to the people, provided, "that the Constitution should *be laid before the United States in Congress assembled*, and afterwards submitted to a Convention of Delegates, chosen in each State by the people thereof, *under the recommendation of its legislature;* thus making Congress and the legislatures, *vehicles of conveyance*, but precluding them from passing their judgments on the system. Had it been submitted to their consideration, their members were men of such discernment, that the *defects* as well as *excellencies* of the plan, would have been clearly explained to the people; but immediately on the publication of it, we find measures were taken to prejudice the people against all persons in the legislative, executive and judicial departments of the States and Confederacy (if opposed to the plan) as being actuated by motives of private interest. Mr. Wilson, a member of the federal and Pennsylvanian Convention, in his town meeting speech, adopted this practice, which, to say the least of it, was very *illiberal*. Indeed, it is but justice to observe, that many artful advocates of this plan, to cover their designs of creating a government which will afford *abundance of legislative offices for placemen and pensioners, proclaimed suspicions* of others, and diverted the attention of the people from themselves, on whom the odium should fall.

Let us now proceed to the provision in the system for a representation of the people, which is the *corner stone* of a free government. The Constitution provides, art 1st. sect. 2, "that representatives and direct taxes shall be apportioned among the several States, which may be included within this union, according to their respective numbers, which shall be determined by adding to the whole number of free persons, including those bound to service for a term of years, and excluding Indians not taxed, three fifths of all other persons." Representatives then are to be "apportioned among the several States, according to their respective numbers," and *five* slaves, in computing those numbers, are to be classed with *three* freemen—By which rule, fifty thousand slaves, having neither *liberty or property*, will have a representative in that branch of the legislature—to which more especially will be committed, the *protection of the liberties*, and *disposal of all the property* of the freemen of the Union—for thus stands the new Constitution. Should it be said, that not *the slaves* but their *masters* are to send a representative, the answer is plain—If the *slaves* have a *right* to be represented, they are *on a footing* with *freemen, three of whom* can then have no more than an equal right of representation with *three slaves*, and these when qualified by property, may elect or be elected representatives, *which is not the case:* But if they have not a right to be represented, their masters can have no right derived from their *slaves*, for *these* cannot transfer to others what they have not themselves. Mr. Locke, in treating of political or civil societies, chap. 7. sect. 85, says, that men "being in the state of slavery, not capable of any property, cannot, in that state, be considered as any part of civil society, the chief end whereof, is the preservation of property."[1] If slaves, then, are no part of civil society, there can be no more reason in admitting them, than there would be in admitting the *beasts* of the field, or *trees* of the forest, to be classed with *free electors*. What covenant are the freemen of Massachusetts about to ratify? A covenant that will degrade them to the *level of slaves*, and give to the States who have as many blacks as whites, *eight* representatives, *for the same number of freemen* as will enable this State to elect *five*—Is this an *equal*, a *safe*, or a *righteous* plan of government? Indeed it is not. But if to encrease these objections, it should be urged, "that representation being regulated by the same rule as taxation, and taxation being regulated by a rule intended to as-certain the relative property of the States, representation will then be regulated by the principle of property." This *answer* would be the only one that could be made, for representation, according to the new Constitution is to be regu-lated, either by *numbers or property*.

Let us now inquire of those who take this ground, what right they have to put a construction on the constitution, which is repugnant to the express terms of the Constitution itself? This provides, "that representatives shall be appor-tioned among the several States, *according to their respective numbers*." Not a word of *property* is mentioned, but the word "numbers" is repeatedly ex-pressed—Admitting however that property was intended by the Constitution as the rule of representation, does this *mend the matter?* it will be but a short time, after the adoption of the new Constitution, before the State *legislatures*, and *establishments in general* will be so *burthensome* and *useless* as to make the people desirous of being rid of them, for they will not be able to support them. The *State appointment* of Representatives will then cease, but *the principle of representation according to property*, will undoubtedly be retained, and before *it is established* it is necessary to consider whether it is a just *one*, for if *once* it is *adopted* it will *not be easily altered*. According to this principle, a man worth £50,000, is to have as many votes for representatives in the new Congress, as *one thousand men*, worth £50 each: And *sixty such nabobs* may send *two* repre-sentatives, while *sixty thousand* freemen having £50 *each* can only send the same number. Does not this establish in the representative branch of the new Con-gress, a principle of aristocracy, with a vengeance? The Constitution of the sev-eral States, admit of no such principle, neither can any freeman with safety thus surrender, not only the intire disposition of their property, but also, the con-troul of their liberties and lives to a few opulent citizens. Should it be said that the rule of federal taxation, being advantageous to the State, it should be content with the same rule for representation. The answer is plain, the rule gives no advantage, but is supposed to be advantageous to Massachusetts, and to be an accommodation very beneficial to the southern States: But admiting this State will be benefited by the rule, is it disposed to sell its birthright, the right of an equal representation in the federal councils *for so small a consideration?* Would this State give up that right to any State that would pay our whole proportion of *direct* and *indirect taxes?* Shall we relinquish some of the most essential rights of government, which are our only security for every thing dear to us, to avoid our proportion of the publick expense? shall we give up all we have, for a small part of it? This if agreed to, would be no great evidence of our wisdom or foresight. But it is not probable, in the opinion of some of the ablest advocates for the new system, that *direct taxes* will ever be levied on the States, and if not, the provision for levying such taxes will be *nugatory:* We shall receive no kind of benefit from it, and shall have committed ourselves to the mercy of the states having slaves, *without any consideration whatever.* Indeed, should direct taxes be necessary, shall we not by increasing the representation of those States, put it in their power to prevent the levying such taxes, and thus defeat our own purposes? Certainly we shall, and having given up a substantial and *essential* right, shall in lieu of it, have a mere *visionary advantage.* Upon the whole then, it must be evident, that we might as well have committed ourselves to the parliament of Great-Britain, under the idea of a *virtual representation* as in this manner resign ourselves to the federal government.

James Warren wrote to the Massachusetts convention delegates of his worries that the Constitution condoned slavery and, moreover, that the Southern slave states would control the new government (see James Warren entry in *Biographies*). With the use of the slave population in the federal census, the Southerners added to their numbers of members in Congress. Thus, the Southern agricultural exporting interests would dominate the policies of the new government to the detriment of the economies of the rest of the nation.

REFERENCES

Independent Gazette, January 19, 1788; Storing, *Complete*, vol. 4.

NOTE

1. Refers to the English political philosopher John Locke.

Martin Kinsley, Speech in the Massachusetts State Ratification Convention, *January 21, 1788*

Mr. President, after so much has been said on the powers to be given to Congress, I shall say but a few words on the subject. By the articles of confederation the people have three checks on their delegates in Congress; the annual election of them, their rotation, and the power to recall any, or all of them, when they see fit: in view of our federal rulers, they are the servants of the people: in the new constitution, we are deprived of annual elections, have no rotation, and cannot recall our members; therefore our federal rulers will be masters and not servants. I will examine what powers we have given to our masters. They have power to lay and collect all taxes, duties, imposts and excises; raise armies, fit out navies, to establish themselves in a federal town of ten miles square, equal to four middling townships, erect forts, magazines, arsenals, &c.—Therefore, should the Congress be chosen of designing and interested men, they can perpetuate their existence, secure the resources of war; and the people will have nothing left to defend themselves with. Let us look into ancient history.—The Romans, after a war, thought themselves safe in a government of ten men, called the Decemviri: these ten men were invested with all powers, and were chosen for three years. By their arts and designs they secured their second election; but finding, from the manner in which they had exercised their power, they were not able to secure their third election, they declared themselves masters of Rome, impoverished the city, and deprived the people of their rights. It has been said that there was no such danger here; I will suppose they were to attempt the experiment, after we have given them all our money, established them in a federal town, given them, the power of coining money, and raising a standing army; and to establish their arbitrary government; what resources have the people left? I cannot see any.—The parliament of England was first chosen annually, they afterwards lengthened their duration to three years; and from triennial they became septennial. The government of England has been represented as a good and happy government, but some parts of it, their greatest political writers much condemn: especially that of the duration of their Parliaments: Attempts are yearly made to shorten their duration, from septennial to triennial; but the influence of the ministry is so great, that it has not yet been accomplished. From this duration, bribery and corruption are introduced. Notwithstanding they receive no pay, they make great interest for a seat in Parliament, one or two years before its dissolution, and give from five to twenty guineas, for a vote; and the candidates sometimes expend from 10,000l to 30,000l. Will a person throw away such a fortune—and waste so much time, without the probability of replacing such a sum with interest? Or can there be security in such men? Bribery may be introduced here as well as in Great-Britain—and Congress may equally oppress the people—because we cannot call them to an account; considering that there is no annual election—no rotation—no power to recall them, provided for.

Martin Kinsley, a physician who later served in the federal House of Representatives, spoke of excessive powers given to the federal Congress (see Martin Kinsley entry in *Biographies*). What would happen to the state legislatures that more nearly reflected the will of the people? he wondered. Kinsley also feared that the Constitution enabled leaders to hold power too long, thus creating a government conducive to tyranny.

REFERENCE

Benjamin Russell, *Debates, Resolutions, and Other Proceedings, of the Convention of the Commonwealth of Massachusetts* (Boston: Adams and Nourse, 1788).

Amos Singletary, Speech in the Massachusetts State Ratification Convention,
January 25, 1788

Mr. President, I should not have troubled the Convention again, if some gentlemen had not called upon them that were on the stage in the beginning of our troubles, in the year 1775. I was one of them—I have had the honour to be a member of the court all the time, Mr. President, and I say, that if any body had proposed such a Constitution as this, in that day, it would have been thrown away at once—it would not have been looked at. We contended with Great-Britain—some said for a three-penny duty on tea, but it was not that—it was because they claimed a right to tax us and bind us in all cases whatever. And does not this Constitution do the same? does it not take away all we have—all our property? does it not lay *all* taxes, duties, imposts and excises? and what more have we to give? They tell us Congress won't lay dry taxes upon us, but collect all the money they want by impost. I say there has always been a difficulty about impost. Whenever the General Court was a going to lay an impost they would tell us it was more than trade could bear, that it hurt the fair trader, and encouraged smuggling; and there will always be the same objection; they won't be able to raise money enough by impost and then they will lay it on the land, and take all we have got. These lawyers, and men of learning, and monied men, that talk so finely and gloss over matters so smoothly, to make us poor illiterate people swallow down the pill, expect to get into Congress themselves; they expect to be the managers of this Constitution and get all the power and all the money into their own hands, and then they will swallow up all us little folks, like the great *Leviathan,* Mr. President, yes, just as the whale swallowed up *Jonah.*

A farmer and member of the state senate, Amos Singletary claimed that the Constitution allowed nontrading states to impose import taxes to raise revenue, which therefore damaged the trading states (see Amos Singletary entry in *Biographies*). He also feared the states with western interests would then dominate the seaboard states.

REFERENCES

Elliot, *Debates,* vol. 2; Russell, *Debates, Resolutions, and Other Proceedings.*

Samuel Nasson, Speech in the Massachusetts State Ratification Convention, *February 1, 1788*

Mr. President—I feel myself happy, that your Excellency has been placed by the free suffrages of your fellow-citizens, at the head of this government: I also feel myself happy, that your Excellency has been placed in the chair of this Hon. Convention: And I feel a confidence, that the proposition submitted to our consideration yesterday by your Excellency, has for its object the good of your country: But, sir, as I have not had an opportunity leisurely to consider it, I shall pass it over, and take a short view of the Constitution at large, which is under consideration, though my abilities, sir, will not permit me to do justice to my feelings—or to my constituents. Great-Britain, sir, first attempted to enslave us, by declaring her laws supreme, and that she had a right to bind us in all cases whatever. What, sir, roused the Americans to shake off the yoke preparing for them?—It was this measure, the power to do which we are now about giving to Congress—And here, sir, I beg the indulgence of this hon. body, to permit me to make a short apostrophe to Liberty.—Oh! Liberty—thou greatest good—thou fairest property! with thee I wish to live—with thee I wish to die! Pardon me if I drop a tear on the peril to which she is exposed: I cannot, sir, see this brightest of jewels tarnished! a jewel worth ten thousand worlds! And shall we part with it so soon?—Oh, No. Gentlemen ask, can it be supposed, that a Constitution so pregnant with danger, could come from the hands of those who framed it? Indeed, sir, I am suspicious of my own judgment, when I contemplate this idea—when I see the list of illustrious names annexed to it:—But, sir, my duty to my constituents, obliges me to oppose the measure they recommend, as obnoxious to their liberty and safety.

When, sir, we dissolved the political bands which connected us with Great-Britain, we were in a state of nature—we then formed and adopted the Confederation, which must be considered as a sacred instrument; this confederated us under one head, as sovereign and independent States. Now, sir, if we give Congress power to dissolve that Confederation, to what can we trust? If a nation consent thus to treat their most solemn compacts, who will ever trust them? Let us, sir, begin with this Constitution, and see what it is—and first, "We the People of the United States, do," &c. If this, sir, does not go to an annihilation of the state governments, and to a perfect consolidation of the whole union, I do not know what does. What! shall we consent to this? Can 10, 20, or 100 persons in this State, who have taken the oath of allegiance to it, dispense with this oath. Gentlemen may talk as they please of dispensing in certain cases with oaths; but, sir, with me they are sacred things: We are under oath; we have sworn that Massachusetts is a sovereign and independent State—How then, can we vote for this Constitution, that destroys that sovereignty? . . .

Let us consider the Constitution without a Bill of Rights. When I give up any of my natural rights, it is for the security of the rest: But here is not one right secured, although many are neglected.

With respect to biennial elections, the paragraph is rather loosely expressed; I am a little in favour of our ancient custom. Gentlemen say they are convinced that the alteration is necessary: It may be so: When I see better, I will join with them.

To go on. Representation and taxation to be apportioned according to numbers. This, sir, I am opposed to; it is unequal. I will shew an instance in point—We know for certainty, that in the town of Brooklyn, persons are better able to pay their taxes, than in the parts I represent: Suppose the tax is laid on polls: Why the people of the former place will pay their tax ten times as easy, as the latter—thus helping that part of the community, which stands in the least need of help: On this footing the poor pay as much as the rich: And in this a way is laid, that five slaves shall be rated no more than three children. Let gentlemen consider this—a farmer takes three small orphans, on charity, to bring up—they are bound to him—when they arrive at 21 years of age, he gives each of them a couple suits of clothes, a cow, and two or three young cattle—we are rated as much for these, as a farmer in Virginia is for five slaves, whom he holds for life—they and their posterity—the male and the she ones too. The senate, Mr. President, are to be chosen two from each State. This, sir, puts the smaller States on the footing with the larger—when the States have to pay according to their numbers—New-Hampshire does not pay a fourth part as much as Massachusetts. We must, therefore, to support the *dignity* of the union, pay four times as much as New-Hampshire, and almost fourteen times as much as Georgia—who, we see, are equally represented with us.

The term, sir, for which the senate is chosen, is a grievance—it is too long to trust any body of men with power: It is impossible but that such men will be tenacious of their places; they are to be raised to a lofty eminence, and they will be loth to come down; and in the course of six years, may by management, have it in their power to create officers, and obtain influence enough, to get in again, and so for life.—When we felt the hand of British oppression upon us, we were so jealous of rulers, as to declare them eligible but for three years in six. In this Constitution we forget this principle. I, sir, think that rulers ought at short periods, to return to private life, that they may know how to feel for, and regard their fellow creatures. In six years, sir, and at a great distance, they will quite forget them.

"For time and absence cure the purest love"

We are apt to forget our friends, except when we are conversing with them.

We now come, sir, to the 4th section. Let us see—the times, places and manners of holding elections, shall be prescribed in each State by the legislature thereof. No objections to this: but, sir, after *the flash of lightening comes the peal of thunder;* "but Congress may at any time, alter them, &c." Here it is, Mr. President: this is the article which is to make Congress omnipotent. Gentlemen say, this is the greatest beauty of the Constitution—this is the great security for the people—this is the all in all. Such language have I heard in this house: but, sir, I say, by this power Congress may, if they please, order the election of federal representatives for Massachusetts, to be at Great-Barrington, or Machias: And at such a time too, as shall put it in the power of a few artful, and designing men, to get themselves elected at their pleasure.

The 8th sect. Mr. President, provides that Congress shall have power to lay and collect taxes, duties, imposts, excises, &c. We may, sir, be poor; we may not be able to pay these taxes, &c.—we must have a little meal, and a little meat, whereon to live; and save a little for a rainy day: But what follows? Let us see. To raise and support armies. Here, sir, comes the key to unlock this cabinet: Here is the mean by which you will be made to pay your taxes? But will ye, my countrymen, submit to this. Suffer me, sir, to say a few words on the fatal effects, of standing armies, that bane of republican governments! A standing army! Was it not with this that Cæsar passed the *Rubicon*, and laid prostrate the liberties of his country? By this has seven eighths of the once free nations of the globe, been brought into bondage! Time would fail me, were I to attempt to recapitulate the havock made in the world, by standing armies. Britain attempted to inforce her arbitrary measures, by a standing army. But, sir, we had patriots then who alarmed us of our danger—who shewed us the serpent, and bid us beware of it. Shall I name them? I fear I shall offend your Excellency? But I cannot avoid it? I must. We had an HANCOCK, an ADAMS, and a WARREN—our sister States too, produced a RANDOLPH, a WASHINGTON, a GREENE, and a MONTGOMERY, who lead us in our way—Some of these have given up their lives in defence of the liberties of their country; and my prayer to God is, that when this race of illustrious patriots, shall have bid adieu to the world; that from their dust, as from the sacred ashes of the Phoenix, another race may arise, who shall take our posterity by the hand, and lead them to trample on the necks of those who shall dare to infringe on their liberties— Sir, had I a voice like Jove, I would proclaim it throughout the world—and had I an arm like Jove, I would hurl from the globe those villains that would dare attempt to establish in our country a standing army. I wish, sir, that the gentlemen of Boston, would bring to their minds the fatal evening of the 5th of March 1770—when by standing troops they lost five of their fellow townsmen—I will ask them what price can atone for their lives? What money can make satisfaction for the loss? The same causes produces the same effects. An army may be raised on pretence of helping a friend, or many pretences might be used; that night, sir, ought to be a sufficient warning against standing armies, except in cases of great emergency—they are too frequently used for no other purpose than dragooning the people into slavery, but I beseech you, my countrymen, for the sake of your posterity, to act like those worthy men, who have stood forth in defence of the rights of mankind; and shew to the world, that you will not submit to tyranny. What occasion have we for standing armies? We fear no foe—If one should come upon us, we have a militia, which is our bulwark. Let Lexington witness that we have the means of defence among ourselves. If during the last winter there was not much alacrity shewn by the militia, in turning out, we must consider that they were going to fight their countrymen. Do you, sir, suppose, that had a British army invaded us at that time, that such supineness would have been discovered. No, sir, to our enemies dismay, and discomfort, they would have felt the contrary: But against deluded, infatuated men they did not wish to exert their valour or their strength. Therefore, sir, I am utterly opposed to a standing army, in time of peace.

The paragraph that gives Congress power to suspend the writ of habeas corpus, claims a little attention—This is a great bulwark—a great privilege indeed—we ought not, therefore, to give it up, on any slight pretence. Let us see—how long it is to be suspended? As long as rebellion or invasion shall continue. This is exceeding loose. Why is not the time limitted, as in our Constitution? But, sir, its design would then be defeated—It was the intent, and by it we shall give up one of our greatest privileges.

A powerful Maine political leader, Samuel Nasson entitled his widely printed speech "Pathetick Apostrophe" (see Samuel Nasson entry in *Biographies*). He argued against the powers given to the federal Congress at the expense of state government, which Nasson envisioned would create a strong federal government similar to that of the hated British government. He also called for a bill of rights to protect individual rights against the oppressive central government.

REFERENCES

Elliot, *Debates*, vol. 2; Russell, *Debates, Resolutions, and Other Proceedings*.

James Winthrop ("Agrippa"), XVI,
February 5, 1788

TO THE MASSACHUSETTS CONVENTION

GENTLEMEN,

In my last address I ascertained, from historical records, the following principles, that, in the original state of government, the whole power resides in the whole body of the nation; that when a people appoint certain persons to govern them, they delegate their whole power; that a constitution is not itself a bill of rights; and that, whatever is the form of government, a bill of rights is essential to the security of the persons and property of the people. It is an idea favourable to the interest of mankind at large, that government is founded in compact. Several instances may be produced of it; but none is more remarkable than our own. In general I have chosen to apply to such facts as are in the reach of my readers. For this purpose I have chiefly confined myself to examples drawn from the history of our own country, and to the old testament. It is in the power of every reader to verify examples thus substantiated. Even in the remarkable argument on the fourth section, relative to the power over election, I was far from stating the worst of it, as it respects the adverse party. A gentleman, respectable in many points, but more especially for his systematick and perspicuous reasoning in his profession, has repeatedly stated to the Convention among his reasons in favour of that section, that *the Rhode-Island assembly have for a considerable time past had a bill lying on their table for altering the manner of elections for representatives in that state.* He had stated it with all the zeal of a person, who believed his argument to be a good one. But surely a *bill lying on a table* can never be considered as any more than an *intention* to pass it, and nobody pretends that it ever actually did pass. It is in strictness only the intention of a part of the assembly, for nobody can aver that it ever will pass. I write not with an intention to deceive, but that the whole argument may be stated fairly. Much eloquence and ingenuity have been employed in shewing that side of the argument in favour of the proposed constitution; but it ought to be considered, that if we accept it upon mere verbal explanations, we shall find ourselves deceived. I appeal to the knowledge of every one, if it does not frequently happen, that a law is interpreted in practice very differently from the intention of the legislature. Hence arises the necessity of acts to amend and explain former acts. This is not an inconvenience in the common and ordinary business of legislation; but is a great one in a constitution. A constitution is a legislative act of the whole people. It is an excellence that it should be permanent, otherwise we are exposed to perpetual insecurity from the fluctuation of government. We should be in the same situation as under absolute government, sometimes exposed to the pressure of greater, and sometimes unprotected by the weaker power in the sovereign.

It is now generally understood, that it is for the security of the people, that the powers of the government should be lodged in different branches. By this means publick business will go on, when they all agree, and stop when they disagree. The advantage of checks in government is thus manifested, where the concurrence of different branches is necessary to the same act; but the advantage of a division of business is advantageous in other respects. As in every extensive empire, local laws are necessary to suit the different interests, no single legislature is adequate to the business. All human capacities are limitted to a narrow space; and as no individual is capable of practising a great variety of trades no single legislature is capable of managing all the variety of national and state concerns. Even if a legislature was capable of it, the business of the judicial department must, from the same cause, be slovenly done. Hence arises the necessity of a division of the business into national and local. Each department ought to have all the powers necessary for executing its own business, under such limitations as tend to secure us from any inequality in the operations of government. I know it is often asked against whom in a government by representation is a bill of rights to secure us? I answer, that such a government is indeed a government by ourselves; but as a just government protects all alike, it is necessary that the sober and industrious part of the community should be defended from the rapacity and violence of the vicious and idle. A bill of rights therefore ought to set forth the purposes for which the compact is made, and serves to secure the minority against the usurpation and tyranny of the majority. It is a just observation of his excellency doctor Adams in his learned defence of the American constitutions, that unbridled passions produce the same effect whether in a king, nobility, or a mob. The experience of all mankind has proved the prevalence of a disposition to use power wantonly. It is therefore as necessary to defend an individual against the majority in a republick, as against the king in a monarchy. Our state constitution has wisely guarded this point. The present confederation has also done it.

I confess that I have yet seen no sufficient reason for not amending the confederation, though I have weighed the argument with candour. I think it would be much easier to amend it than the new constitution. But this is a point on which men of very respectable character differ. There is another point in which nearly all agree, and that is, that the new constitution would be better in many respects if it had been differently framed. Here the question is not so much what the amendments ought to be, as in what manner they shall be made; whether they shall be made as conditions of our accepting the constitution, or whether we shall first accept it, and then try to amend it. I can hardly conceive that it should seriously be made a question. If the first question, whether we will receive it as it stands, be negatived, as it undoubtedly ought to be, while the conviction remains that amendments are necessary; the next question will be, what amendments shall be made? Here permit an individual, who glories in being a citizen of Massachusetts, and who is anxious that the character may remain undiminished, to propose such articles as appear to him necessary for preserving the rights of the state. He means not to retract any thing with regard to the expediency of amending the old confederation, and rejecting the new one totally; but only to make a proposition which he thinks comprehends the general idea of all parties. If the new constitution means no more than the friends of it acknowledge, they certainly can have no objection to affixing a declaration in favour of the rights of states and of citizens, especially as a majority of the states have not yet voted upon it.

"Resolved, that the constitution lately proposed for the United States be received only upon the following conditions:

"1. Congress shall have no power to alter the time, place or manner of elections, nor any authority over elections, otherwise than by fining such state as shall neglect to send its representatives or senators, a sum not exceeding the expense of supporting its representatives or senators one year.

"2. Congress shall not have the power of regulating the intercourse between the states, nor to levy any direct tax on polls or estates, nor any excise.

"3. Congress shall not have power to try causes between a state and citizens of another state, nor between citizens of different states; nor to make any laws relative to the transfer of property between those parties, nor any other matter which shall originate in the body of any state.

"4. It shall be left to every state to make and execute its own laws, except laws impairing contracts, which shall not be made at all.

"5. Congress shall not incorporate any trading companies, nor alienate the territory of any state. And no treaty, ordinance or law of the United States shall be valid for these purposes.

"6. Each state shall have the command of its own militia.

"7. No continental army shall come within the limits of any state, other than garrison to guard the publick stores, without the consent of such states in time of peace.

"8. The president shall be chosen annually and shall serve but one year, and shall be chosen successively from the different states, changing every year.

"9. The judicial department shall be confined to cases in which ambassadours are concerned, to cases depending upon treaties, to offences committed upon the high seas, to the capture of prizes, and to cases in which a foreigner residing in some foreign country shall be a party, and an American state or citizen shall be the other party; provided no suit shall be brought upon a state note.

"10. Every state may emit bills of credit without making them a tender, and may coin money, of silver, gold or copper, according to the continental standard.

"11. No powers shall be exercised by Congress or the president but such as are expressly given by this constitution and not excepted against by this declaration. And any offices of the United States offending against an individual state shall be held accountable to such state as any other citizen would be.

"12. No officer of Congress shall be free from arrest for debt by authority of the state in which the debt shall be due.

"13. Nothing in this constitution shall deprive a citizen of any state of the benefit of the bill of rights established by the constitution of the state in which he shall reside, and such bills of rights shall be considered as valid in any court of the United States where they shall be pleaded.

"14. In all those causes which are triable before the continental courts, the trial by jury shall be held sacred."

These at present appear to me the most important points to be guarded. I have mentioned a reservation of excise to the separate states, because it is necessary, that they should have some way to discharge their own debts, and because it is placing them in an humiliating & disgraceful situation to depute them to transact the business of internal government without the means to carry it on. It is necessary also, as a check on the national government, for it has hardly been known that any government having the powers of war, peace, and revenue, has failed to engage in needless and wanton expense. A reservation of this kind is therefore necessary to preserve the importance of the state governments; without this the extremes of the empire will in a very short time sink into the same degradation and contempt with respect to the middle state as Ireland, Scotland, & Wales, are in with regard to England. All the men of genius and wealth will resort to the seat of government, that will be center of revenue, and of business, which the extremes will be drained to supply.

This is not mere vision, it is justified by the whole course of things. We shall therefore, if we neglect the present opportunity to secure ourselves, only encrease the number of proofs, already too many, that mankind are incapable of enjoying their liberty. I have been the more particular in stating the amendments to be made, because many gentlemen think it would be preferrable to receive the new system with corrections. I have by this means brought the corrections into one view, and shewn several of the principal points in which it is unguarded. As it is agreed, at least professedly, on all sides, that those rights should be guarded, it is among the inferiour questions in what manner it is done, provided it is absolutely and effectually done. For my own part, I am fully of opinion, that it would be best to reject this plan, and pass an explicit resolve, defining the powers of Congress to regulate the intercourse between us and foreign nations, under such restrictions as shall render their regulations equal in all parts of the empire. The impost, if well collected, would be fully equal to the interest of the foreign debt, and the current charges of the national government. It is evidently for our interest that the charges should be as small as possible. It is also for our interest that the western lands should, as fast as possible, be applied to the purpose of paying the home debt. Internal taxation and that fund have already paid two thirds of the whole debt, notwithstanding the embarrassments usual at the end of a war.

We are now rising fast above our difficulties, every thing at home has the appearance of improvement, government is well established, manufactures increasing rapidly, and trade expanding. Till since the peace we never sent a ship to India, and the present year, it is said, sends above a dozen vessels from this state only, to the countries round the Indian ocean. Vast quantities of our produce are exported to those countries. It has been so much the practice of European nations to farm out this branch of trade, that we ought to be exceedingly jealous of our right. The manufactures of the state probably exceed in value one million pounds, for the last year. Most of the useful and some ornamental fabricks are established. There is great danger of these improvements being injured unless we practice extreme caution at setting out. It will always be for the interest of the southern states to raise a revenue from the more commercial ones. It is said that the consumer pays it; But does not a commercial state consume more foreign goods than a landed one? The people are more crouded, and of consequence the lands is less able to support them. We know it is to be a favourite system to raise the money where it is. But the money is to be expended at another place, and is therefore so much withdrawn annually from our stock. This is a single instance of the difference of interest; it would be very easy to produce others. Innumerable as the differences of manners, and these produce differences in the laws. Uniformity in legislation is of no more importance than in religion; Yet the framers of this new constitution did not even think it necessary that the president should believe, that there is a God, although they require an oath of him. It would be easy to shew the propriety of a general declaration upon that subject. But this paper is already extended too far.

Another reason which I had in stating the amendments to be made, was to shew how nearly those who are for admitting the system with the necessary alterations, agree with those who are for rejecting this system and amending the confederation. In point of convenience, the confederation amended would be infinitely preferable to the proposed constitution. In amending the former, we know the powers granted, and are subject to no perplexity; but in reforming the latter, the business is excessively intricate, and great part of the checks on Congress are lost. It is to be remembered too, that if you are so far charmed with eloquence, and misled by fair representations and charitable constructions, as to adopt an undefined system, there will be no saying afterwards that you were mistaken, and wish to correct it. *It will then be the constitution of our country, and entitled to defence.* If Congress should chuse to avail themselves of a popular commotion to continue in being, as the fourth section justifies, and as the British parliament has repeatedly done, the only answer will be, that it is the constitution of our country, and the people chose it. It is therefore necessary to be exceedingly critical.

James Winthrop proposed amending the Constitution to include a bill of rights (see James Winthrop entry in *Biographies*). Following on his earlier fear of loss of liberties gained from the Revolutionary War, Winthrop wanted to make certain that the laws protected personal freedoms of religion and public opinion.

REFERENCES

Massachusetts Gazette, February 5, 1788; for the complete "Agrippa" see Paul L. Ford, *Essays on the Constitution* (Brooklyn, N.Y.: Historical Printing Club, 1892).

William Symmes, Jr., Speech in the Massachusetts State Ratification Convention, *February 6, 1788*

Mr. President: I hope, sir, the Convention will indulge me with a few words, and I promise I will not detain them long. It may be known to your excellency, that I have heretofore had the honor to address the Convention in opposition to a certain paragraph in the Constitution. That fact is the sole occasion of my craving a turn to be heard again.

Sir, it never was my opinion that we ought, entirely, to abandon this Constitution. I thought it had great defects: and I still think it by no means free from blemishes; but I ever expected the worst consequences to follow a total rejection of it. I always intended to urge amendments, and was in hopes that the wisdom of this assembly would devise a method to secure their adoption. Therefore, when your excellency came forward, as well became your high office, in the character of a mediator, a ray of hope shone in upon the gloom that overspread my heart—of hope that we should still be united in the grand decision.

Sir, a mortal hatred, a deadly opposition, can be deserved by no government but the tyranny of hell, and perhaps a few similar forms on earth. A government of that complexion, in the present enlightened age, could never enter the heart of man; and if it could, and impudence enough were found to propose it,—nay, if it should be accepted,—I affirm, sir, that in America it would never operate a moment. I should glory in debating on my grounds for this assertion; but who will dare to question the truth of it?

Mr. President, so ample have been the arguments drawn from our national distress, the weakness of the present Confederation, the danger of instant disunion, and perhaps some other topics not included in these, that a man must be obstinate indeed, to say, at this period, that a new government is needless. One is proposed. Shall we reject it totally, or shall we amend it? Let any man recollect or peruse the debates in this assembly, and I venture to say, he shall not be a moment, if he loves his country, in making his election. He would contemplate the idea of rejection with horror and detestation. But, sir, it has been alleged that the necessary amendments cannot be obtained in the way your excellency has proposed. This matter has been largely debated. I beg a moment to consider it. Our committee, sir, were pretty well agreed to the amendments necessary to be made, and, in their report, it appears that these amendments are equally beneficial to all the citizens of America. There is nothing local in them. Shall we, then, totally reject the Constitution, because we are only morally certain that they will be adopted? Shall we choose certain misery in one way, when we have the best human prospect of enjoying our most sanguine wishes in another? God forbid!

But, sir, a great deal has been said about the amendments. Here again I refer to the debates. Such has been said to have been the past prevalence of the Northern States in Congress, the sameness of interest in a majority of the states, and their necessary adhesion to each other, that I think there can be no reasonable doubt of the success of any amendments proposed by Massachusetts. Sir, we have, we do, and we *shall,* in a great measure, give birth to all events, and hold the balance among the United States.

The honorable gentlemen, my respected friend from Scituate, has so fully entered into the expediency of ratifying the Constitution upon the basis of the report, and so ably stated the unanswerable reasons he finds for giving his sanction to it, notwithstanding his former different opinion, that I may decently waive a task I could not half so well perform.

Upon the whole, Mr. President, approving the amendments, and firmly believing that they will be adopted, I recall my former opposition, such as it was, to this Constitution, and shall—especially as the amendments are a standing instruction to our delegates until they are obtained—give it my unreserved assent.

In so doing, I stand acquitted to my own conscience; I hope and trust I shall to my constituents, and I know I shall before God.

Here William Symmes explained why, after speaking forcefully against the Constitution, he had decided to vote for ratification (see William Symmes, Jr., entry in *Biographies*). He really believed the delegates had promised to amend the Constitution. For his perfidy, Symmes's constituents retired him from public life.

REFERENCE

Russell, *Debates, Resolutions, and Other Proceedings.*

Mercy Otis Warren ("A Columbian Patriot"), *Observations on the Constitution*, published in *February 1788*

Mankind may amuse themselves with theoretick systems of liberty, and trace its social and moral effects on sciences, virtue, industry, and every improvement of which the human mind is capable; but we can only discern its true value by the practical and wretched effects of slavery; and thus dreadfully will they be realized, when the inhabitants of the Eastern States are dragging out a miserable existence, *only* on the gleanings of their fields; and the Southern, blessed with a softer and more fertile climate, are languishing in hopeless poverty; and when asked, what is become of the flower of their crop, and the rich produce of their farms—they may answer in the hapless stile of the Man of *La Mancha*,—"The steward of my Lord has seized and sent it to *Madrid*."—Or, in the more literal language of truth, The *exigencies* of government require that the collectors of the revenue should transmit it to the *Federal City*.

Animated with the firmest zeal for the interest of this country, the peace and union of the American States, and the freedom and happiness of a people who have made the most costly sacrifices in the cause of liberty,—who have braved the power of Britain, weathered the convulsions of war, and waded thro' the blood of friends and foes to establish their independence and to support the freedom of the human mind; I cannot silently witness this degradation without calling on them, before they are compelled to blush at their own servitude, and to turn back their languid eyes on their lost liberties—to consider, that the character of nations generally changes at the moment of revolution.—And when patriotism is discountenanced and publick virtue becomes the ridicule of the sycophant—when every man of liberality, firmness, and penetration, who cannot lick the hand stretched out to oppress, is deemed an enemy to the State—then is the gulph of despotism set open, and the grades to slavery, though rapid, are scarce perceptible—then genius drags heavily its iron chain—science is neglected, and real merit flies to the shades for security from reproach—the mind becomes enervated, and the national character sinks to a kind of apathy with only energy sufficient to curse the breast that gave it milk, and as an elegant writer observes, "To bewail every new birth as an encrease of misery, under a government where the mind is necessarily debased, and talents are seduced to become the panegyrists of usurpation and tyranny." He adds, "that even sedition is not the most indubitable enemy to the publick welfare; but that its most dreadful foe is despotism, which always changes the character of nations for the worse, and is productive of nothing but vice, that the tyrant no longer excites to the pursuits of glory or virtue; it is not talents, it is baseness and servility that he cherishes, and the weight of arbitrary power destroys the spring of emulation."[1] If such is the influence of government on the character and manners, and undoubtedly the observation is just, must we not subscribe to the opinion of the celebrated *Abbé Mablé?* "That there are disagreeable seasons in the unhappy situation of human affairs, when policy requires both the intention and the power of doing mischief to be punished; and that when the senate prescribed the memory of *Cæsar* they ought to have put *Anthony* to death, and extinguished the hopes of *Octavius.*" Self defence is a primary law of nature, which no subsequent law of society can abolish; this primæval principle, the immediate gift of the Creator, obliges every one to remonstrate against the strides of ambition, and a wanton lust of domination, and to resist the first approaches of tyranny, which at this day threaten to sweep away the rights for which the brave sons of America have fought with an heroism scarcely paralleled even an ancient republicks. It may be repeated, they have purchased it with their blood, and have gloried in their independence with a dignity of spirit, which has made them the admiration of philosophy, the pride of America, and the wonder of Europe. It has been observed, with great propriety, that "the virtues and vices of a people when a revolution happens in their government, are the measure of the liberty or slavery they ought to expect—An heroic love for the publick good, a profound reverence for the laws, a contempt of riches, and a noble haughtiness of soul, are the only foundations of a free government." Do not their dignified principles still exist among us? Or are they extinguished in the breasts of Americans, whose fields have been so recently crimsoned to repel the potent arm of a foreign Monarch, who had planted his engines of slavery in every city, with design to erase the vestiges of freedom in this his last asylum. It is yet to be hoped, for the honour of human nature, that no combinations either foreign or domestick have thus darkened this Western hemisphere.—On these shores freedom has planted her standard, diped in the purple tide that flowed from the veins of her martyred heroes; and here every uncorrupted American yet hopes to see it supported by the vigour, the justice, the wisdom and unanimity of the people, in spite of the deep-laid plots, the secret intrigues, or the bold effrontery of those interested and avaricious adventurers for place, who intoxicated with the ideas of distinction and preferment, have prostrated every worthy principle beneath the shrine of ambition. Yet these are the men who tell us republicanism is dwindled into theory—that we are incapable of enjoying our liberties—and that we must have a master.—Let us retrospect the days of our adversity, and recollect who were then our friends; do we find them among the sticklers for aristocratick authority? No, they were generally the same men who now wish to save us from the distractions of anarchy on the one hand, and the jaws of tyranny on the other; where then were the class who now come forth importunately urging that our political salvation depends on the adoption of a system at which freedom spurns?—Were not some of them hidden in the corners of obscurity, and others wrapping themselves in the bosom of our enemies for safety? Some of them were in the arms of infancy; and others speculating for fortune, by sporting with public money; while a few, a very few of them were magnanimously defending their country, and raising a character, which I pray heaven may never be sullied by aiding measures derogatory to their former exertions. But the revolutions in principle which time produces among mankind, frequently exhibits the most mortifying instances of human weakness; and this alone can account for the extraordinary appearance of a few names, once distinguished in the honourable walks of patriotism, but now found on the list of the Massachusetts assent to the ratification of a Constitution, which, by the undefined meaning of some parts, and the ambiguities of expression in others, is dangerously adapted to the purposes of an immediate *aristocratic tyranny;* that from the difficulty, if not impracticability of its operation, must soon terminate in the most *uncontrouled despotism.*

All writers on government agree, and the feelings of the human mind witness the truth of these political axioms, that man is born free and possessed of certain unalienable rights—that government is instituted for the protection, safety, and happiness of the people, and not for the profit, honour, or private interest of any man, family, or class of men—That the origin of all power is in the people, and that they have an incontestible right to check the creatures of their own creation, vested with certain powers to guard the life, liberty and property of the community: And if certain selected bodies of men, deputed on these principles, determine contrary to the wishes and expectations of their constituents, the people have an undoubted right to reject decisions, to call for a revision of their conduct, to depute others in their room, or if they think proper, to demand further time for deliberation on matters of the greatest moment: it therefore is an unwarrantable stretch of authority or influence, if any methods are taken to preclude this reasonable, and peaceful mode of enquiry and decision. And it is with inexpressible anxiety, that many of the best friends to the Union of the States—to the peaceable and equal participation of the rights of nature, and to the glory and dignity of this country, behold the insidious arts, and the strenuous efforts of the partisans of arbitrary power, by their vague definitions of the best established truths, endeavoring to envelope the mind in darkness the concomitant of slavery, and to lock the strong chains of domestic despotism on a country, which by the most glorious and successful struggles is but newly emancipated from the sceptre of foreign dominion.— But there are certain seasons in the course of human affairs, when Genius, Virtue, and Patriotism, seems to nod over the vices of the times, and perhaps never more remarkably, than at the present period; or we should not see such a passive disposition prevail in some, who we must candidly suppose, have liberal and enlarged sentiments; while a supple multitude are paying a blind and idolatrous homage to the opinions of those who by the most precipitate steps are treading down their dear bought privileges; and who are endeavouring by all the arts of insinuation, and influence, to betray the people of the United States, into an acceptance of a most complicated system of government; marked on the one side with the *dark, secret* and *profound intrigues,* of the statesman, long practised in the purlieus of despotism; and on the other, with the ideal projects of *young ambition,* with its wings just expanded to soar to a summit, which imagination has painted in such gawdy colours as to intoxicate the *inexperienced votary,* and send *him* rambling from State to State, to collect materials to construct the ladder of preferment.

1. But as a variety of objections to the *heterogeneous phantom,* have been repeatedly laid before the public, by men of the best abilities and intentions; I will not expatiate long on a Republican *form* of government, founded on the

principles of monarchy—a democratick branch with the *features* of aristocracy—and the extravagance of nobility pervading the minds of many of the candidates for office, with the poverty of peasantry hanging heavily on them, and
insurmountable, from their taste for expence, unless a generous provision
should be made in the arrangement of the civil list, which may enable them
with the champions of their cause to *"sail down the new pactolean channel."*
Some gentlemen with laboured zeal, have spent much time in urging the necessity of government, from the embarrassments of trade—the want of respectability abroad and confidence in the public engagements at home:—These
are obvious truths which no one denies; and there are few who do not unite
in the general wish for the restoration of public faith, the revival of commerce,
arts, agriculture, and industry, under a lenient, peaceable and energetick government: But the most sagacious advocates for the party have not by fair discussion, and rational argumentation, evinced the necessity of adopting this
many-headed monster; of such motley mixture, that its enemies cannot trace a
feature of Democratick or Republican extract; nor have its friends the courage
to denominate it a Monarchy, an Aristocracy, or an Oligarchy, and the favoured
bantling must have passed through the short period of its existence without a
name, had not Mr. *Wilson,* in the fertility of his genius, suggested the happy
epithet of a *Federal Republic.*—But I leave the field of general censure on the
secrecy of its birth, the rapidity of its growth, and the fatal consequences of
suffering it to live to the age of maturity, and will particularize some of the
most weighty objections to its passing through this continent in a gigantic
size.—It will be allowed by every one that the fundamental principle of a free
government, is the equal representation of a free people—And I will *first* observe with a justly celebrated writer, "That the principal aim of society is to
protect individuals in the absolute rights which were vested in them by the immediate laws of nature, but which could not be preserved in peace, without
the mutual intercourse which is gained by the institution of friendly and social
communities." And when society has thus deputed a certain number of their
equals to take care of their personal rights, and the interest of the whole community, it must be considered that responsibility is the great security of integrity and honour; and that annual election is the basis of responsibility.—Man
is not immediately corrupted, but power without limitation, or amenability,
may endanger the brightest virtue—whereas a frequent return to the bar of
their Constituents is the strongest check against the corruptions to which men
are liable, either from the intrigues of others of more subtle genius, or the
propensities of their own hearts,—and the gentlemen who have so warmly advocated in the late Convention of the Massachusetts, the change from annual
to biennial elections, may have been in the same predicament, and perhaps with
the same views that Mr. *Hutchinson* once acknowledged himself, when in a letter to *Lord Hillsborough,* he observed, "that the grand difficulty of making a
change in government against the general bent of the people had caused him
to turn his thoughts to a variety of plans, in order to find one that might be
executed in spite of opposition," and the first he proposed was that, "instead
of annual, the elections should be only once in three years:" but the Minister
had not the hardiness to attempt such an innovation, even in the revision of
colonial charters: nor has any one ever defended Biennial, Triennial, or Septen-

nial, Elections, either in the British House of Commons, or in the debates of Provincial assemblies, on general and free principles: but it is unnecessary to dwell long on this article, as the best political writers have supported the principles of annual elections with a precision, that cannot be confuted, though they may be darkened, by the sophistical arguments that have been thrown out with design, to undermine all the barriers of freedom.

2. There is no security in the profered system, either for the rights of conscience, or the liberty of the Press: Despotism usually while it is gaining ground, will suffer men to think, say, or write what they please; but when once established, if it is thought necessary to subserve the purposes of arbitrary power, the most unjust restrictions may take place in the first instance, and an *imprimator* on the Press in the next, may silence the complaints, and forbid the most decent remonstrances of an injured and oppressed people.

3. There are no well defined limits of the Judiciary Powers, they seem to be left as a boundless ocean, that has broken over the chart of the Supreme Lawgiver *"thus far shalt thou go and no further,"* and as they cannot be comprehended by the clearest capacity, or the most sagacious mind, it would be an Herculean labour to attempt to describe the dangers with which they are replete.

4. The Executive and the Legislative are so dangerously blended as to give just cause of alarm, and every thing relative thereto, is couched in such ambiguous terms—in such vague and indefinite expression, as is a sufficient ground without any other objection, for the reprobation of a system, that the authors dare not hazard to a clear investigation.

5. The abolition of trial by jury in civil causes.—This mode of trial the learned Judge Blackstone observes, "has been coeval with the first rudiments of civil government, that property, liberty and life, depend on maintaining in its legal focus the constitutional trial by jury." He bids his readers pauze, and with Sir Matthew Hale observes, how admirably this mode is adapted to the investigation of truth beyond any other the world can produce. Even the party who have been disposed to swallow, without examination, the proposals of the *secret conclave,* have started on a discovery that this essential right was curtailed; and shall a privilege, the origin of which may be traced to our Saxon ancestors—that has been a part of the law of nations, even in the fewdatory systems of France, Germany and Italy—and from the earliest records has been held so sacred, both in ancient and modern Britain, that it could never be shaken by the introduction of Norman customs, or any other conquests or change of government—shall this inestimable privilege be relinquished in America—either thro' the fear of inquisition for unaccounted thousands of public monies in the hands of some who have been officious in the fabrication of the *consolidated system,* or from the apprehension that some future delinquent possessed of more power than integrity, may be called to a trial by his peers in the hour of investigation?

6. Though it has been said by Mr. *Wilson* and many others, that a Standing-Army is necessary for the dignity and safety of America, yet freedom revolts at the idea, when the Divan, or the Despot, may draw out his dragoons to suppress the murmurs of a few, who may yet cherish those sublime principles which call forth the exertions, and lead to the best improvement of the human mind.

It is hoped this country may yet be governed by milder methods than are usually displayed beneath the bannerets of military law.—Standing armies have been the nursery of vice and the bane of liberty from the Roman legions, to the establishment of the artful Ximenes, and from the ruin of the Cortes of Spain, to the planting the British cohorts in the capitals of America:—By the edicts of authority vested in the sovereign power by the proposed constitution, the militia of the country, the bulwark of defence, and the security of national liberty is no longer under the controul of civil authority; but at the rescript of the Monarch, or the aristocracy, they may either be employed to extort the enormous sums that will be necessary to support the civil list—to maintain the regalia of power—and the splendour of the most useless part of the community, or they may be sent into foreign countries for the fulfilment of treaties, stipulated by the President and two thirds of the Senate.

7. Notwithstanding the delusory promise to guarantee a Republican form of government to every State in the Union—If the most discerning eye could discover any meaning at all in the engagement, there are no resources left for the support of internal government, or the liquidation of the debts of the State. Every source of revenue is in the monopoly of Congress, and if the several legislatures in their enfebled state, should against their own feelings be necessitated to attempt a dry tax for the payment of their debts, and the support of internal police, even this may be required for the purposes of the general government.

8. As the new Congress are empowered to determine their own salaries, the requisitions for this purpose may not be very moderate, and the drain for public moneys will probably rise past all calculation: and it is to be feared when America has consolidated its despotism, the world will witness the truth of the assertion—"that the pomp of an eastern monarch may impose on the vulgar who may estimate the force of a nation by the magnificence of its palaces; but the wise man, judges differently, it is by that very magnificence he estimates its weakness. He sees nothing more in the midst of this imposing pomp, where the tyrant sets enthroned, than a sumptuous and mournful decoration of the dead; the apparatus of a fastuous funeral, in the centre of which is a cold and lifeless lump of unanimated earth, a phantom of power ready to disappear before the enemy, by whom it is despised!"

9. There is no provision for a rotation, nor any thing to prevent the perpetuity of office in the same hands for life; which by a little well timed bribery, will probably be done, to the exclusion of men of the best abilities from their share in the offices of government.—By this neglect we lose the advantages of that check to the overbearing insolence of office which by rendering him ineligible at certain periods, keeps the mind of man in equilibrio, and teaches him the feelings of the governed, and better qualifies him to govern in his turn.

10. The inhabitants of the United States, are liable to be draged from the vicinity of their own county, or state, to answer to the litigious or unjust suit of an adversary, on the most distant borders of the Continent: in short the appelate jurisdiction of the Supreme Federal Court, includes an unwarrantable stretch of power over the liberty, life, and property of the subject, through the wide Continent of America.

11. One Representative to thirty thousand inhabitants is a very inadequate representation; and every man who is not lost to all sense of freedom to his country, must reprobate the idea of Congress altering by law, or on any pretence whatever, interfering with any regulations for the time, places, and manner of choosing our own Representatives.

12. If the sovereignty of America is designed to be elective, the circumscribing the votes to only ten electors in this State, and the same proportion in all the others, is nearly tantamount to the exclusion of the voice of the people in the choice of their first magistrate. It is vesting the choice solely in an aristocratic junto, who may easily combine in each State no place at the head of the Union the most convenient instrument for despotic sway.

13. A Senate chosen for six years will, in most instances, be an appointment for life, as the influence of such a body over the minds of the people will be coequal to the extensive powers with which they are vested, and they will not only forget, but be forgotten by their constituents—a branch of the Supreme Legislature thus set beyond all responsibility is totally repugnant to every principle of a free government.

14. There is no provision by a bill of rights to guard against the dangerous encroachments of power in too many instances to be named: but I cannot pass over in silence the insecurity in which we are left with regard to warrants unsupported by evidence—the daring experiment of granting *writs of assistance* in a former arbitrary administration is not yet forgotten in the Massachusetts; nor can we be so ungrateful to the memory of the patriots who counteracted their operation, as so soon after their manly exertions to save us from such a detestable instrument of arbitrary power, to subject ourselves to the insolence of any petty revenue officer to enter our houses, search, insult, and seize at pleasure. We are told by a gentleman of too much virtue and real probity to suspect he has a design to deceive—"that the whole constitution is a declaration of rights"—but mankind must think for themselves, and to many very judicious and discerning characters, the whole constitution with very few exceptions appears a perversion of the rights of particular states, and of private citizens.—But the gentleman goes on to tell us, "that the primary object is the general government, and that the rights of individuals are only incidentally mentioned, and that there was a clear impropriety in being very particular about them." But, asking pardon for dissenting from such respectable authority, who has been led into several mistakes, more from his predilection in favour of certain modes of government, than from a want of understanding or veracity. The rights of individuals ought to be the primary object of all government, and cannot be too securely guarded by the most explicit declarations in their favor. This has been the opinion of the Hampdens, the Pyms, and many other illustrious names, that have stood forth in defence of English liberties; and even the Italian master in politicks, the subtle and renouned Machiavel acknowledges, that no republic ever yet stood on a stable foundation without satisfying the common people.

15. The difficulty, if not impracticability, of exercising the equal and equitable powers of government by a single legislature over an extent of territory that reaches from the Mississippi to the Western lakes, and from them to the

Atlantic ocean, is an insuperable objection to the adoption of the new system.—
Mr. *Hutchinson*, the great champion for arbitrary power, in the multitude of his
machinations to subvert the liberties of this country, was obliged to acknowledge in one of his letters, that, "from the extent of country from north to south,
the scheme of one government was impracticable."[2] But if the authors of the
present visionary project, can by the arts of deception, precipitation and address,
obtain a majority of suffrages in the conventions of the states to try the haz-
ardous experiment, they may then make the same inglorious boast with this insidious politician, who may perhaps be their model, that "the union of the
colonies was pretty well broken, and that he hoped never to see it renewed."

16. It is an indisputed fact, that not one legislature in the United States had
the most distant idea when they first appointed members for a convention, entirely commercial, or when they afterwards authorized them to consider on
some amendments of the Federal union, that they would without any warrant
from their constituents, presume on so bold and daring a stride, as ultimately
to destroy the state governments, and offer a *consolidated system*, irreversible
but on conditions that the smallest degree of penetration must discover to be
impracticable.

17. The first appearance of the article which declares the ratification of nine
states sufficient for the establishment of the new system, wears the face of dis-
sention, is a subversion of the union of the Confederated States, and tends to
the introduction of anarchy and civil convulsions, and may be a means of involving the whole country in blood.

18. The mode in which this constitution is recommended to the people to
judge without either the advice of Congress, or the legislatures of the several
states, is very reprehensible—it is an attempt to force it upon them before it
could be thoroughly understood, and may leave us in that situation, that in the
first moments of slavery the minds of the people agitated by the remembrance
of their lost liberties, will be like the sea in a tempest, that sweeps down every
mound of security.

But it is needless to enumerate other instances, in which the proposed constitution appears contradictory to the first principles which ought to govern
mankind; and it is equally so to enquire into the motives that induced to so
bold a step as the annihilation of the independence and sovereignty of the thirteen distinct states.—They are but too obvious through the whole progress of
the business, from the first shutting up the doors of the federal convention and
resolving that no member should correspond with gentlemen in the different
states on the subject under discussion; till the trivial proposition of *recommending* a few amendments was artfully ushered into the convention of the
Massachusetts. The questions that were then before that honorable assembly
were profound and important, they were of such magnitude and extent, that
the consequences may run parallel with the existence of the country, and to
see them waved and hastily terminated by a measure too absurd to require a
serious refutation, raises the honest indignation of every true lover of his country. Nor are they less grieved that the ill policy and arbitrary disposition of some
of the sons of America has thus precipitated to the contemplation and discussion of questions that no one could rationally suppose would have been agitated among us, till time had blotted out the principles on which the late

revolution was grounded; or till the last traits of the many political tracts, which defended the separation from Britain, and the rights of men were consigned to everlasting oblivion. After the severe conflicts this country has suffered, it is presumed that they are disposed to make every reasonable sacrifice before the altar of peace.—But when we contemplate the nature of men and consider them originally on an equal footing, subject to the same feelings, stimulated by the same passions, and recollecting the struggles they have recently made, for the security of their civil rights; it cannot be expected that the inhabitants of the Massachusetts, can be easily lulled into a fatal security, by the declamatory effusions of gentlemen, who, contrary to the experience of all ages would perswade them there is no danger to be apprehended, from vesting discretionary powers in the hands of man, which he may, or may not abuse. The very suggestion, that we ought to trust to the precarious hope of amendments and redress, after we have voluntarily fixed the shackles on our own necks should have awakened to a double degree of caution.—This people have not forgotten the artful insinuations of a former Governor, when pleading the unlimited authority of parliament before the legislature of the Massachusetts; nor that his arguments were very similar to some lately urged by gentlemen who boast of opposing his measure, "*with halters about their necks.*"

We were then told by him, in all the soft language of insinuation, that no form of government of human construction can be perfect—that we had nothing to fear—that we had no reason to complain—that we had only to acquiesce in their illegal claims, and to submit to the requisitions of parliament, and doubtless the lenient hand of government would redress all grievances, and remove the oppressions of the people:—Yet we soon saw armies of mercenaries encamped on our plains—our commerce ruined—our harbours blockaded—and our cities burnt. It may be replied, that this was in consequence of an obstinate defence of our privileges; this may be true; and when the "*ultima ratio*" is called to aid, the weakest must fall. But let the best informed historian produce an instance when bodies of men were intrusted with power, and the proper checks relinquished, if they were ever found destitute of ingenuity sufficient to furnish pretences to abuse it. And the people at large are already sensible, that the liberties which America has claimed, which reason has justified, and which have been so gloriously defended by the sword of the brave; are not about to fall before the tyranny of foreign conquest: it is native usurpation that is shaking the foundations of peace, and spreading the sable curtain of despotism over the United States. The banners of freedom were erected in the wilds of America by our ancestors, while the wolf prowled for his prey on the one hand, and more savage man on the other; they have been since rescued from the invading hand of foreign power, by the valor and blood of their posterity; and there was reason to hope they would continue for ages to illumine a quarter of the globe, by nature kindly separated from the proud monarchies of Europe, and the infernal darkness of Asiatic slavery.—And it is to be feared we shall soon see this country rushing into the extremes of confusion and violence, in consequence of the proceedings of a set of gentlemen, who disregarding the purposes of their appointment, have assumed powers unauthorised by any commission, have unnecessarily rejected the confederation of the United States, and annihilated the sovereignty and independence of the individual governments.

The causes which have inspired a few men assembled for very different purposes with such a degree of temerity as to break with a single stroke the union
of America, and disseminate the seeds of discord through the land may be easily investigated, when we survey the partizans of monarchy in the state conventions, urging the adoption of a mode of government that militates with the
former professions and exertions of this country, and with all ideas of republicanism, and the equal rights of men.

Passion, prejudice, and error, are characteristics of human nature; and as it
cannot be accounted for on any principles of philosophy, religion, or good policy; to these shades in the human character must be attributed the mad zeal of
some, to precipitate to a blind adoption of the measures of the late federal convention, without giving opportunity for better information to those who are
misled by influence or ignorance into erroneous opinions.—Litterary talents
may be prostituted, and the powers of genius debased to subserve the purposes
of ambition, or avarice; but the feelings of the heart will dictate the language
of truth, and the simplicity of her accents will proclaim the infamy of those,
who betray the rights of the people, under the specious, and popular pretence
of *justice, consolidation,* and *dignity.*

It is presumed the great body of the people unite in sentiment with the
writer of these observations, who most devoutly prays that public credit may
rear her declining head, and remunerative justice pervade the land; nor is
there a doubt if a free government is continued, that time and industry will
enable both the public and private debtor to liquidate their arrearages in the
most equitable manner. They wish to see the Confederated States bound together by the most dissoluble union, but without renouncing their separate
sovereignties and independence, and becoming tributaries to a consolidated
fabrick of aristocratick tyranny.—They wish to see government established,
and peaceably holding the reins with honour, energy, and dignity; but they
wish for no *federal city* whose *"cloud cap't towers"* may screen the state culprit from the hand of justice; while its exclusive jurisdiction may protect the
riot of armies encamped within its limits.—They deprecate discord and civil
convulsions, but they are not yet generally prepared with the ungrateful Is-
raelites to ask a King, nor are their spirits sufficiently broken to yield the best
of their olive grounds to his servants, and to see their sons appointed to run
before his chariots—It has been observed by a zealous advocate for the new
system, that most governments are the result of fraud or violence, and this
with design to recommend its acceptance—but has not almost every step towards its fabrication been fraudulent in the extreme? Did not the prohibition
strictly enjoined by the general Convention, that no member should make
any communication to his Constituents, or to gentlemen of consideration and
abilities in the other States, bear evident marks of fraudulent designs?—This
circumstance is regretted in strong terms by Mr. Martin, a member from
Maryland, who acknowledges "He had no idea that all the wisdom, integrity,
and virtue of the States was contained in that Convention, and that he wished
to have corresponded with gentlemen of eminent political characters abroad,
and to give their sentiments due weight"—he adds, "so extremely solicitous
were they, that their proceedings should not transpire, that the members were

prohibited from taking copies of their resolutions, or extracts from the Journals, without express permission, by vote."[3]—And the hurry with which it has been urged to the acceptance of the people, without giving time, by adjournments, for better information, and more unanimity *has a deceptive appearance;* and if finally driven to resistance, as the only alternative between that and servitude, till in the confusion of discord, the reins should be seized by the violence of some enterprizing genius, that may sweep down the last barrier of liberty, it must be added to the score of criminality with which the fraudulent usurpation at Philadelphia, may be chargeable.—Heaven avert such a tremendous scene! and let us still hope a more happy termination of the present ferment:—may the people be calm, and wait a legal redress; may the mad transport of some of our infatuated capitals subside; and every influential character through the States, make the most prudent exertions for a new general Convention, who may vest adequate powers in Congress, for all national purposes, without annihilating the individual governments, and drawing blood from every pore by taxes, impositions and illegal restrictions.—This step might again re-establish the Union, restore tranquility to the ruffled mind of the inhabitants, and save America from distresses, dreadful even in contemplation.—"The great art of governing is to lay aside all prejudices and attachments to particular opinions, classes or individual characters; to consult the spirit of the people; to give way to it; and in so doing, to give it a turn capable of inspiring those sentiments, which may induce them to relish a change, which an alteration of circumstances may hereafter make necessary."—The education of the advocates for monarchy should have taught them, and their memory should have suggested that "monarchy is a species of government fit only for a people too much corrupted by luxury, avarice, and a passion for pleasure, to have any love for their country, and whose vices the fear of punishment alone is able to restrain; but by no means calculated for a nation that is poor, and at the same time tenacious of their liberty—animated with a disgust to tyranny—and inspired with the generous feelings of patriotism and liberty, and at the same time, like the ancient Spartans have been hardened by temperance and manly exertions, and equally despising the fatigues of the field, and the fear of enemies,"—and while they change their ground they should recollect, that Aristocracy is still a more formidable foe to public virtue, and the prosperity of a nation—that under such a government her patriots become mercenaries—her soldiers, cowards, and the people slaves.—Though several State Conventions have assented to, and ratified, yet the voice of the people appears at present strong against the adoption of the Constitution.—By the chicanery, intrigue, and false colouring of those who plume themselves, more on their education and abilities, than their political, patriotic, or private virtues—by the imbecility of some, and the duplicity of others, a majority of the Convention of Massachusetts have been flattered with the ideas of amendments, when it will be too late to complain—While several very worthy characters, too timid for their situation, magnified the hopeless alternative, between the dissolution of the bands of all government, and receiving the proffered system *in toto,* after long endeavouring to reconcile it to their consciences, swallowed the indigestible penacea, and in a kind of sudden desperation lent their signature to the dereliction of the honorable station they held in the Union, and have broken over the solemn compact, by which they were bound to support their own excellent constitution till the period of revision.—Yet Virginia, equally large and respectable, and who have done honour to themselves, by their vigorous exertions from the first dawn of independence, have not yet acted upon the question; they have wisely taken time to consider before they introduce innovations of a most dangerous nature:—her inhabitants are brave, her burgesses are free, and they have a Governor who dares to think for himself, and to speak his opinion (without first pouring libations on the altar of popularity) though it should militate with some of the most accomplished and illustrious characters.

Maryland, who has no local interest to lead her to adopt, will doubtless reject the system—I hope the same characters still live, and that the same spirit which dictated to them a wise and cautious care, against sudden revolutions in government, and made them the last State that acceded to the independence of America, will lead them to support what they so deliberately claimed.—Georgia apprehensive of a war with the Savages, has acceded in order to insure protection.—Pennsylvania has struggled through much in the same manner, as Massachusetts, against the manly feelings, and the masterly reasonings of a very respectable part of the Convention: They have adopted the system, and seen some of its authors burnt in effigy—their towns thrown into riot and confusion, and the minds of the people agitated by apprehension and discord.

New-Jersey and Delaware have united in the measure, from the locality of their situation, and the selfish motives which too generally govern mankind; the Federal City, and the seat of government, will naturally attract the intercourse of strangers—the youth of enterprize, and the wealth of the nation to the central States.

Connecticut has pushed it through with the precipitation of her neighbour, with few dissentient voices;—but more from irritation and resentment to a sister State, perhaps partiality to herself in her commercial regulations, than from a comprehensive view of the system, as a regard to the welfare of all.—But New-York has motives, that will undoubtedly lead her to a rejection, without being afraid to appeal to the understanding of mankind, to justify the grounds of their refusal to adopt a Constitution, that even the framers dare not risque to the hazard of revision, amendment, or reconsideration, least the whole superstructure should be demolished by more skilful and discreet architects.—I know not what part the Carolinas will take; but I hope their determinations will comport with the dignity and freedom of this country—their decisions will have great weight in the scale.—But equally important are the small States of New-Hampshire and Rhode-Island:—New-York, the Carolinas, Virginia, Maryland, and these two lesser States may yet support the liberties of the Continent; if they refuse a ratification, or postpone their proceedings till the spirit of the community have time to cool, there is little doubt but the wise measure of another federal convention will be adopted, when the members would have the advantage of viewing, at large, through the medium of truth, the objections that have been made from various quarters; such a measure might be attended with the most salutary effects, and prevent the dread consequences of civil feuds.—But even if some of those large states should hastily accede, yet we have frequently seen in the story of revolution, relief spring from a quarter least expected.

Though the virtues of a Cato could not save Rome, nor the abilities of a Padilla defend the citizens of Castile from falling under the yoke of Charles; yet a *Tell* once suddenly rose from a little obscure city, and boldly rescued the liberties of his country.—Every age has its Bruti and its Decii, as well as its Cæsars and Sejani:—The happiness of mankind depends much on the modes of government, and the virtues of the governors; and America may yet produce characters who have genius and capacity sufficient to form the manners and correct the morals of the people, and virtue enough to lead their country to freedom. Since her dismemberment from the British empire, America has, in many instances, resembled the conduct of a restless, vigorous, luxurious youth, prematurely emancipated from the authority of a parent, but without the experience necessary to direct him to act with dignity or discretion. Thus we have seen her break the shackles of foreign dominion, and all the blessings of peace restored on the most honourable terms: She acquired the liberty of framing her own laws, choosing her own magistrates, and adopting manners and modes of government the most favourable to the freedom and happiness of society. But how little have we availed ourselves of these superior advantages: The glorious fabric of liberty successfully reared with so much labour and assiduity totters to the foundation, and may be blown away as the bubble of fancy by the rude breath of military combinations, and politicians of yesterday.

It is true this country lately armed in opposition to regal despotism—impoverished by the expences of a long war, and unable immediately to fulfil their public or private engagements, have appeared in some instances, with a boldness of spirit that seemed to set at defiance all authority, government, or order, on the one hand; while on the other, there has been, not only a secret wish, but an open avowal of the necessity of drawing the reins of government much too taught, not only for republicanism, but for a wise and limited monarchy.— But the character of this people is not averse to a degree of subordination: the truth of this appears from the easy restoration of tranquility, after a dangerous insurrection in one of the states; this also evinces the little necessity of a complete revolution of government throughout the union. But it is a republican principle that the majority should rule; and if a spirit of moderation could be cultivated on both sides, till the voice of the people at large could be fairly heard it should be held sacred.—And if, on such a scrutiny, the proposed constitution should appear repugnant to their character and wishes; if they, in the language of a late elegant pen, should acknowledge that "no confusion in my mind, is more terrible to them than the stern disciplined regularity and vaunted police of arbitrary governments, where every heart is depraved by fear, where mankind dare not assume their natural characters, where the free spirit must crouch to the slave in office, where genius must repress her effusions, or like the Egyptian worshippers, offer them in sacrifice to the calves in power, and where the human mind, always in shackles, shrinks from every generous effort." Who would then have the effrontery to say, it ought not to be thrown out with indignation, however some respectable names have appeared to support it.—But if after all, on a dispassionate and fair discussion, the people generally give their voice for a voluntary dereliction of their privileges, let every individual who chooses the active scenes of life, strive to support the peace and unanimity of his country, though every other blessing may expire—And while the statesman is plodding for power, and the courtier practising the arts of dissimulation without check—while the rapacious are growing rich by oppression, and fortune throwing her gifts into the lap of fools, let the sublimer characters, the philosophic lovers of freedom who have wept over her exit, retire to the calm shades of contemplation, there they may look down with pity on the inconsistency of human nature, the revolutions of states, the rise of kingdoms, and the fall of empires.

Published after the Massachusetts convention, in late February, this influential pamphlet was seen and used by a number of other Antifederalists. A playwright and later famous historian, Mercy Otis Warren argued against the excessive powers given to the federal government, in violation of the American Revolution's protection of the rights of the people in their states (see Mercy Otis Warren entry in *Biographies*). She believed that the Constitution did not promote civic responsibility. Instead it contributed to the potential corruption in leaders, especially since they could hold office for long periods of time.

REFERENCE

Mercy Otis Warren, *Observations on the New Constitution* (Boston: Adams and Rhoades, 1788).

NOTES

1. Quotes her husband, James Warren.
2. Quotes Thomas Hutchinson, governor of Massachusetts just before the Revolution, hated by the Warrens and their revolutionary allies.
3. Luther Martin, fellow Antifederalist from Maryland.

Nathan Dane, Letter to Melancton Smith, *July 3, 1788*

In my last letter I briefly gave my opinion on the questions you stated to me; now being more at leisure sensible that the peculiar situation of our Government at this time is a matter of common concern and highly interesting to us all; and that we have the same object in view, the peaceable establishment of a general Government on genuine federal and republican principles, I shall in this be more particular, and submit to your consideration several observations with that candor and frankness with which we have always communicated our sentiments to each other relative to the important subject in question—

The Constitution of the United States is now established by the people of ten States, and a day of course must soon be fixed, when all proceedings under the Confederation shall cease—The line of conduct which shall now be pursued by the three States which have not as yet ratified is become particularly and deeply interesting to them, and to the whole Confederacy—As things are now circumstanced will it not be clearly for their interest and happiness, as well as for the interest and happiness of all the union to adopt the Constitution proposing such amendments as they may think essential—the situation of the States is now critical—as the Constitution is already established there can be no previous amendments; and a State which has not ratified, and wishes to be in the union, appears to have but this alternative before her;—either to accede with recommending certain alterations, or to make them a condition of her accession, and the probable consequence of either Step must be considered—I take it for granted that New York and the other two States wish to form a part of an American Confederacy—the readiness with which they Joined in the revolution, and acceded to the articles of Confederation; their open and general professions, and their past exertions to the support of the union Justify the opinion—In all our late political discussions, a separation of the States, or Separate Confederacies, have Scarcely, to my knowledge, been Seriously mentioned—Admitting that Rhode Island, New York, and North Carolina all withhold their assent to the Constitution, and propose similar amendments, their situation is such, far removed from each other, and surrounded by ratifying States, that they never can think of confederating among themselves— Each one of them must be considered as Standing alone—but we have no reason to suppose that any one of those States has a wish to Stand alone, in Case she can Confederate on principles agreeable to her—If I understand the politics of these three States, they are Strongly attached to governments founded in freedom and compact, and possess a Just aversion to those which are the result of force and violence—they will, therefore, be the last States which will adopt measures tending to foment parties, and give passion an ascendancy over reason, or to hazard Steps that may, in the end, lead to a civil war, and consequently to the Government of the prevailing party established by the longest Sword—It is not to be pretended that the ratifying States will have any Just cause to make war upon any non ratifying State, merely because she does not accede to a national compact, where she has a right to act according to her discretion—nor ought we to presume that hostilities will be commenced by any party without some plausible or Just provocation—But the ratifying and non ratifying States will immediately have opposite Interests, which, in the nature of things, they will pursue—the longer they shall remain Separate the more their assertions and friendship for each other will decrease—and counteracting laws and a disposition for coercive measures will take place—the affairs of the Country will have a propensity to extremities and a thousand accidents may give rise to hostilities—The question in the ratifying States being settled, it is probable the parties in them will gradually unite—In the States where the question shall remain unsettled, and the contest continue between the parties in them, as it undoubtedly will, in what manner they shall Join the union, they will grow under which the people may, with Safety, relax in any considerable degree in their attention to public measures?—can they be secure under any Constitution unless attentive themselves, and unless some of their able leaders are their real friends and their faithful guardians

Tho I think our people have examined the system in question with candor and freedom and discovered a strong attachment to liberty—Yet I would by no means so far rely upon their exertions and vigilance as to lose sight of those Constitutional securities which may be obtained by time and experience—while we view the conduct of rulers with candor, we ought to watch their movements with an Eagle's eye, and guard and secure the temple of freedom with unceasing attention—

To conclude ought we not now to give additional weight to the plea in favor of the Constitution drawn from the peculiarity of our situation, and which when less urgent and pressing appears again and again to have saved the system? and tho the system may be abused by bad men, ought we not to recollect that the road to lasting fame in this Country has generally been Justice, and Integrity, prudence and moderation, political information and industry & that there is more than an equal chance that this will continue to be the case? Attempts to palm upon our people vice for virtue, the mere shew of talents for real abilities, and the arts and puffs of party for a well earned reputation have generally failed—and what is wanting but to excite the attention of this intelligent people to render such attempts always unsuccessful? all these and many other considerations ought to have their Just weight in deciding the great question before us—

Nathan Dane, a former member of the Continental Congress from Massachusetts and skeptic about the Constitution, lived in New York during that state's debates over ratification (see Nathan Dane entry of *Biographies*). To his friend Melancton Smith, the powerful New York Antifederalist, Dane wrote that he had reconciled himself to the Constitution. Dane's letter no doubt showed the changes in Massachusetts after the state convention and certainly influenced Smith's own shift in position. Both men came to believe that the Constitution, though a dangerous document for state's rights, would be ratified, and they wanted to place their energies into advocating future amendments.

REFERENCES

Bailyn, *Debate*, vol. 2; Thornton Papers, New England Historic Genealogical Society.

7
New Hampshire

February 13–adjourned February 22, 1788,

June 18–21, 1788

Ratification #9, June 29, 1788

In favor 57–47

Joshua Atherton, Speech in the New Hampshire State Ratification Convention,
February 1788

Mr. President,—I cannot be of the opinion of the honorable gentleman who last spoke, that this paragraph is either so just or so inoffensive as they seem to imagine, or that the objections to it are so totally void of foundation. The idea that strikes those who are opposed to this clause so disagreeably and so forcibly is, hereby it is conceived (if we ratify the Constitution) that we become consenters to and partakers in the sin and guilt of this abominable traffic, at least for a certain period, without any positive stipulation that it shall even then be brought to an end. We do not behold in it that valuable acquisition so much boasted of by the honorable member from Portsmouth, "that an end is then to be put to slavery." Congress may be as much or more puzzled to put a stop to it then, than we are now. The clause has not secured its abolition.

We do not think ourselves under any obligation to perform works of supererogation in the reformation of mankind; we do not esteem ourselves under any necessity to go to Spain or Italy to suppress the Inquisition of those countries, or of making a journey to the Carolinas to abolish the detestable custom of enslaving the Africans; but, Sir, we will not lend the aid of our ratification to this cruel and inhuman merchandise, not even for a day. There is a great distinction in not taking a part in the most barbarous violation of the sacred laws of God and humanity, and our becoming guarantees for its exercise for a term of years. Yes, Sir, it is our full purpose to wash our hands clear of it; and however unconcerned spectators we may remain of such predatory infractions of the laws of our nature, however unfeelingly we may subscribe to the ratification of man-stealing, with all its baneful consequences, yet I cannot but believe, in justice to human nature, that if we reverse the consideration, and bring this claimed power somewhat nearer to our own doors, we shall form a more equitable opinion of its claim to our ratification.

Let us figure to ourselves a company of these man-stealers, well equipped for the enterprise, arriving on our coast. They seize or carry off the whole or part of the town of Exeter. Parents are taken and children left; or possibly they may be so fortunate as to have a whole family taken and carried off together by these relentless robbers. What must be their feelings in the hands of their new and arbitrary masters? Dragged at once from every thing they held dear to them, stripped of every comfort of life, like beasts of prey, they are hurried on a loathsome and distressing voyage to the coast of Africa, or some other quarter of the globe where the greatest price may waft them. And here, if any thing can be added to their miseries, comes on the heart-breaking scene! A parent is sold to one, a son to another, a daughter to a third. Brother is cleft from brother, sister from sister, and parents from their darling offspring. Broken with every distress that human nature can feel, and bedewed with tears of anguish, they are dragged into the last stage of depression and slavery, never, never to behold the faces of one another again. The scene is too affecting,—I have not fortitude to pursue the subject.

Joshua Atherton, a lawyer and later state attorney general, spoke against the state ratifying the Constitution because it condoned the expansion of slavery (see Joshua Atherton entry in *Biographies*). His work is eloquent and compassionate, but there remains some question whether he ever delivered it as printed.

REFERENCE

Joseph B. Walker, *A History of the New Hampshire Convention for the Investigation, Discussion, and Decision of the Federal Constitution* (Boston: Supples and Hurd, 1888).

Joshua Atherton, Letter to John Lamb (and other New York delegates), *June 11, 1788*

I have the honor to recognize the reception of your very great favor, which came to hand yesterday. Long anxiously desirous of the communication proposed, I shall leave nothing unattempted in my power, to effect a unanimity of sentiment with respect to amendments. I cannot persuade myself however, that the method adopted by the Convention of Massachusetts, is by any means eligible: to ratify, and then propose amendments, is to surrender our all, and then to ask our new masters, if they will be so gracious as to return to us some, or any part of our most important rights and privileges. Can this be the part of wisdom or good policy? I have the honor, Gentlemen, perfectly to coincide with you in sentiment, that the amendments should be procured, previous to the adoption of the new system, and all local advantages, rejected as unworthy the attention of those, who are contending for the general liberty.

There has hitherto been a fair majority in the Convention of New Hampshire, as far as their sentiments could be collected (for the decisive question has not been put) against ratifying the proposed Constitution in its present form; this the candid consolidarians confess; but I need not inform you, how many arts are made use of to increase their party. The presses are in a great measure, secured to their side; inevitable ruin is held up, on non-compliance; while the new system is fraught with every species of happiness. The opponents are enemies to their country, and they often make them say what they never thought.

In the Exeter Advertiser, (New Hampshire), they had the disingenuity to say, that "Mr. Atherton, seemed to give up the idea of all cases between citizens of different states, originating in the federal courts, &c., &c." Nothing can be the more reverse of truth than this assertion. Their views are obvious; but I will not trouble you with particulars. I flatter myself some future publications will brush off the mask of falsehood. Permit me to hope you will lead the way, and delineate the method of a correspondence between the states, who have not yet resigned their lives, liberties, and properties, into the hands of this new and unlimited sovereignty. Your central situation, and your great importance as a state, gives us a right to expect it of you: While nothing shall be wanting here, to second such a desirable event; nor indeed shall any part of your public spirited, and benevolent proposals, want the attention they so highly merit.

No amendments being yet fixed on here, or even attempted, that subject must be left for future consideration. Could our convention receive your resolution not to adopt without the necessary amendments, before they have proceeded too far, together with your amendments; I have not the least doubt but a great majority would immediately close with your views and wishes. The Convention of this state, sits next Wednesday at Concord, by adjournment: on the conclusion of which session, I will cause to be transmitted to the Anti-Federal Committee of the county of Albany, the result of our deliberations, who will be good enough to forward them to you. The subject of amendments shall not be forgot.

June 14th.—I yesterday received the supplement to the Albany Journal, of the tenth instant, by which it appears you will have a majority of two to one, at least, against adoption. I congratulate you on so fortunate an event, and have the highest confidence that the power and opportunity, thus put into your hands to save our devoted country from impending ruin, will be exercised with firmness, integrity, and wisdom.

I am, Gentlemen, with great esteem and respect,

Your most humble & most ob't serv't,

Joshua Atherton.

In this letter, Atherton questioned Massachusetts' decision to adopt the Constitution with only the promise of amendment (see Joshua Atherton entry in *Biographies*). He believed Massachusetts harmed the New Hampshire Antifederalists, and he wanted New York to stand fast in opposition.

REFERENCE

Charles A. Atherton, *Memoir of Joshua Atherton* (Boston: Crosby, Nichols, 1852).

Announcement to Congress from the Second
New Hampshire Convention,
June 21, 1788

In Convention of the Delegates of the People of the State of New Hampshire, June 21st, 1788:—

The Convention having impartially discussed and fully considered the Constitution for the United States of America, reported to Congress by the Convention of Delegates from the United States of America, and submitted to us by a Resolution of the General Court of said State passed the fourteenth day of December last past, and acknowledging with grateful hearts the Goodness of the Supreme Ruler of the Universe in affording the People of the United States, in the course of his Providence, an opportunity, deliberately and peaceably, without fraud or surprise, of entering into an explicit and solemn compact with each other, by assenting to and ratifying a new Constitution, in order to form a more perfect union, establish justice, insure domestic tranquillity, provide for the common defence, promote the general welfare and secure the blessings of Liberty to themselves and their posterity, Do in the name and in behalf of the people of the State of New Hampshire, assent to and ratify the said Constitution for the United States of America; and as it is the opinion of this Convention, that certain amendments and alterations in the said Constitution would remove the fears and quiet the apprehensions of many of the good people of this State, and more effectually guard against an undue administration of the federal Government, the Convention do therefore recommend that the following alterations and provisions be introduced into the said Constitution:

First, That it be explicitly declared that all powers not expressly and particularly delegated by the aforesaid Constitution, are reserved to the several States to be by them exercised.

Secondly, That there shall be one Representative to every thirty Thousand persons according to the Census mentioned in the Constitution, until the whole number of Representatives amounts to two hundred.

Thirdly, That Congress do not exercise the power vested in them by the fourth Section of the first Article, but in cases when a State shall neglect or refuse to make the regulations therein mentioned, or shall make regulations subversive of the rights of the people to a free and equal representation in Congress, nor shall Congress in any case make regulations contrary to a free and equal representation.

Fourthly, That Congress do not lay direct Taxes but when the money arising from the impost excise and their other resources are insufficient for the
public exigencies; nor then, until Congress shall have first made a requisition
upon the States to assess, Levy and pay their respective proportions of such
requisition agreeably to the census fixed in the said Constitution, in such way
and manner as the Legislature of the State shall think best; and in such case,
if any State shall neglect, then Congress may assess and Levy such State's proportion, together with the interest thereon at the rate of six pr. cent pr. Annum
from the time of payment prescribed in such requisition.

Fifthly, That Congress erect no company of Merchants with exclusive advantages of commerce.

Sixthly, That no person shall be tried for any crime by which he may incur
an infamous punishment or loss of life until he be first indicted by a grand
jury—except in such cases as may arise in the government and regulation of
the land and naval forces.

Seventhly, All common law cases between citizens of different States shall
be commenced in the Common Law Courts of the respective States, and no
appeal shall be allowed to the federal Courts in such cases, unless the sum or
value of the thing in controversy amount to three hundred dollars.

Eighthly, In civil actions between citizens of different States, every issue of
fact arising in actions at common law, shall be tried by a jury if the parties or
either of them request it.

Ninthly, Congress shall at no time consent that any person holding an office of trust or profit under the United States, shall accept a title of nobility or
any other title or office, from any king, prince or foreign State.

Tenthly, That no standing army shall be kept up in time of peace, unless
with the consent of three fourths of the members of each branch of Congress;
nor shall soldiers in a time of peace, be quartered upon private houses without the consent of the owners.

Eleventhly, Congress shall make no Laws touching religion or to infringe
the rights of conscience.

Twelfthly, Congress shall never disarm any citizen, unless such as are or have
been in actual rebellion.

And the Convention do, in the name and in behalf of the people of this
State enjoin it upon their Representatives in Congress, at all times, until the
alterations and provisions aforesaid have been considered, agreeably to the fifth
article of the said Constitution, to exert all their Influence and use all reasonable and legal methods to obtain a Ratification of the said alterations and provisions in such manner as is provided in the said article.

And that the United States in Congress Assembled may have due notice of
the assent and ratification of the said Constitution by this Convention:—

It is Resolved, That the assent and ratification aforesaid, be engrossed on
parchment, together with the recommendation and Injunction aforesaid, and
with this Resolution; and that John Sullivan Esq[r]. President of Convention,
and John Langdon, Esq[r]. President of the State, transmit the same counter-
signed by the Secretary of Convention and the Secretary of the State under
their hands and seals, to the United States in Congress assembled.

This announcement reveals the continuing reservations the New Hampshire delegation had over the Constitution. Many members of the delegation still feared for the rights of state government. But they bowed to the obvious, once their powerful neighbor, Massachusetts, had voted to ratify.

REFERENCE

Journal of the Proceedings of the Convention of the State of New Hampshire, Which Adopted the Federal Constitution (Concord: State Historical Society, 1876).

8
Rhode Island

March 4, 1788 popular referendum rejects
the Constitution,
May 29, 1790
Ratification #13, May 29, 1790
In favor 34–32

Rhode Island State Legislature Refusal to Call a State Ratifying Convention, *February 29, 1788*

A Motion was made by Mr. *Sayles* and seconded by Mr. *Childs* that the House do now proceed to the Consideration of the Dispatches from Congress, on the Subject of the proposed Federal Constitution.—Upon which Mr. Joslyn made a Motion to the following Purport:—"That the Constitution for the United States, proposed by the late Federal Convention, be submitted to the Freemen of the several Towns in this State, in Town-Meetings assembled, for their Decision; and that the Yeas and Nays be registered in the several Towns, in the same Manner as it is now done for the Choice of General Officers."—This Motion was seconded by Mr. *Hazard*.

After a pretty lengthy Discussion of the Propriety of submitting it in this Way, the Vote was finally put—Whether it should be submitted to a Convention, chosen as in the other States—or to the People at large, and was carried against a Convention, by a Majority of 28—15 voting for a Convention, and 43 for submitting it to the People at large.

In Course of discussing this Question, it was observed—That by the proposed Constitution the People were called upon to surrender a Part of their Liberties; that they were the best Judges what Part they ought to give up:—That the Legislature had no legal Right to appoint a Convention to alter the Constitution:—That they were not deputed for that Purpose:—That the Citizens of some other States, had by the Means of appointing Conventions, been decoyed into an Adoption of the Constitution, when, it was asserted, at least Two-Thirds of the Inhabitants of some of the States that had agreed to it, were against the Constitution:—That submitting it to every Individual Freeholder of the State was the only Mode by which the *true* Sentiments of the People could be collected.—It was replied—That this Mode was without Precedent on the Face of the Earth:—That all the United States, except this, had appointed Conventions; and that we ought to pay some Deference to the Opinions, at least of those in the different States who oppose the new Constitution, if not of those who wish it adopted—in not one of which such a Motion as this had been made:—That by Meeting in Convention the Sentiments of the best Men in the State would be collected;—the different *Interests* would there be represented—the *Mechanics* might there shew how far it would be advantageous or disadvantageous for *their* particular Interest to have it adopted or rejected: The *Farmers*—the *Merchants*—might in the same Manner be satisfied:

All this would be lost by Meeting in the different Towns, in each of which but *one Interest* or at most but *two*, could be considered.

The two state legislators, Thomas Joslyn, who was later a delegate to the state convention, and Jonathan Hazard, a lawyer and member of the Continental Congress, succeeded in getting a popular referendum on the Constitution (see Thomas Joslyn and Jonathan J. Hazard entries in *Biographies*). In this they followed, Hazard claimed, in a longstanding tradition of allowing the voice of the people to prevail over any elected delegation.

REFERENCE

Jensen and Kaminski, *Documentary History*, vol. 3.

David Howell ("Solon, Junior")
Letter in Providence *Gazette*,
August 9, 1788

Under all governments where the people have any considerable influence, but especially under democracies, there is a pervading influential principle superior to all constitutions and laws on paper—I mean, *the spirit of the times.*

The constitution of England has been nearly the same for ages, yet how different the condition of the people under it in different reigns? Even some of their laws lie dormant at times, maugre all their armies. There is a majesty in the people, and a sovereignty in their voice, that prostrate all other authority. Hardy indeed is that Magistrate, who dare execute a law against the decided opinion of all his neighbours.

I shall not undertake to assert, that this *popular impetus* is always right—I well know, that bad Kings and bad Ministers in England have executed the most villainous measures amidst the acclamations of the people. But these delusions are short-lived, as being commonly founded in misinformation—or at least a false notion of their interest; and as soon as the veil is removed from the minds of the people, their resentment falls on the authors of the cheat.

The grievances, frauds and irregularities, of the present day, are the natural result of the depravity of manners and idleness let in upon us by the late war.—It is no less folly to charge the whole of them on the deficiency of our present governments or constitutions, than it is to expect a radical cure from any constitution whatever.—They are evils that grow out of the manners and habits of the mass of the people—they flow from causes too operative, it is to be feared, to be suddenly checked by *any* form of government.

Will not the administration of the new government receive its tincture from this spirit of the times? Will not the people appoint men to administer it in conformity to their views? I am not yet convinced that any government can save us without reformation of manners.

A careful education of youth, and strict family government, will operate like leaven—and lay a foundation to hope for better fruit from the rising generation, than ought to have been expected from the generality of those at present on the stage, had we considered the dissipation of the times when their manners were forming. Children that are taught obedience to their parents, and subordination to their superiors, and in early life initiated in habits of virtue and industry, will not fail to make good citizens.—Civil government may lop off the excrescences of vice; but good education establishes principles in the mind, and prevents the vicious shoots. Let every man, therefore, who glories in being a federalist, consider that true federalism, like charity, ought to begin *at home*.

An abundance of proof lies within our own observation, of the prevalance of the spirit of the times over the dead letter of laws and constitutions.—During the war, and while that was the rage of the day, was not an act passed for putting every freeman in the State under martial law, to be inflicted by a General over whom even the Legislature had no controul?—yet the people bore it—and those who complained of its being *unconstitutional* were answered, that *the safety of the people is the highest law*.

A more recent instance is also in point.—When the rage of the times turned on forcing paper money into circulation—the principles of the *penal laws* became *constitutional*—a trial by jury must be laid aside.—Hardy indeed was that Court, and obstinate to a great degree, which opposed the tide of power—and gave up themselves a sacrifice to a cause by which they could gain nothing! Such were and such are the times—while to fill up the measure of absurdity, the same men who framed that *penal law*, and demolished that Court for not executing it, cry down the New Federal Constitution, because it does not secure *a trial by jury in all cases!*

Had that privilege been ever so safe on paper, and had a phrenzy seized the administration familiar to that under which this State at a certain time laboured, could not a penal law have passed Congress, and been enforced by a Federal Court—or a Federal Army—unless, indeed, they should have found the unconquerable spirit of an ADAMS in that Court, to humble the pride of trumped power?

Whatever the New Federal Constitution is in itself, *its administration* is all that can ever affect the people.—That may be made *safe and easy*—or *cruel and oppressive,* by the administrators for the time being—and much will depend on the *spirit of the times*.

As this Constitution provides the means of altering itself—supposing it right now, the principles and manners of the times would be our chief security for its remaining so—and admitting it to be defective now, is there not reason to hope, that it will soon be made such as the good sense and virtue of the people choose to have it?

> "For *forms of government* let fools contest:
> That form that's *best administer'd* is best."

While others sharpen the point of the satyric pen, and by stirring up the angry passions of men add fuel to the flame of party—to sooth and sweeten the tempers of fellow-citizens—to warm their bosoms with brotherly love, and to unite them in pursuing the real good of their distracted country, shall be the pleasing task of

SOLON, *junior.*

David Howell, a teacher and lawyer, served in the Continental Congress and later as a state judge (see David Howell entry in *Biographies*). In this letter, Howell rejected the Constitution out of fear that it rolled back the great gains of the American Revolution that made a free people. He also opposed joining a nation that condoned and supported the growth of slavery.

REFERENCES

Bailyn, *Debate*, vol. 2; Providence *Gazette*, August 9, 1788.

Jonathan Hazard, Debate at the Rhode Island Ratification Convention, Proposed Amendments to the Constitution, *May 1790*

Jon. Hazzard Wishes to propose Amendts in which we may be contended. The South States must answer for themselves. They must conduct their own Legislation as they please. They can regulate their Trade as they please. We are not interested one Hand nor answerable in our Consciences on the other. They must answer for own Crimes. The southern states will seperate from us before they will agree to this Alternate proposed. They will say That They do not interfere with our Legislatures—Why should we with theirs. The Constitution does not prevent any of the States from suppressing the Trade—to move for this Amendt will be to abridge the Sovereignty of the States. . . .

I am Sory to rise again. It is not for the Interest of this State to ask for Amendt concerning. The Gentlemen who have spoken have acted on right Principle. I must Rely on it that the Motion is contesting the Advantag we now have. It will be Stabbing to the Vitals the S. States. Do of the Word/Common Law of England/reported it be altered & read as follows: and hath been exercised by us and our Ancestors from the Time whereof the memory of Man is not to the Contrary. . . .

AMENDMENTS TO BE PROPOSED TO THE FEDERAL CONSTITUTION

Article First. The United States shall guarantee to each state, its sovereignty, freedom and independence, and every power, jurisdiction and right, which is not by this Constitution expressly delegated to the United States.

Second. There shall be one representative for every thirty thousand free inhabitants, including those bound to service for a term of years, and excluding all slaves and Indians, until the whole number of representatives amount to two hundred, after which, that number shall be continued or increased as Congress shall direct, but shall not be diminished.

Second. That Congress shall not alter, modify, or interfere in the times, places, or manner of holding elections for senators and representatives, or either of them, except when the legislature of any state, shall neglect, refuse, or be disabled by invasion or rebellion, to prescribe the same; or in case when the provision made by the states is so imperfect, as that no consequent election is had, and then, only in that the legislature of such state shall make provision in the premises.

Third. It is declared by the Convention, that the judicial power of the United States, in cases in which a state may be a party, does not extend to criminal prosecutions, or to authorize any suit by any person against a state, but to remove all doubts or controversies respecting the same, that it be expressly expressed as a part of the Constitution of the United States, that Congress shall not directly or indirectly, either by themselves or through the judiciary, interfere with any one of the states in the redemption of paper money already emitted and now in circulation; or in liquidating and discharging the public securities of any one state, and that each and every state shall have the exclusive right of making such laws and regulations, for the before mentioned purpose, as they shall think proper.

Fourth. That no amendments of the Constitution of the United States shall take effect or become a part of the Constitution of the United States, after the year one thousand and seven hundred and ninety-three without the consent of eleven of the states heretofore united under one Confederation.

Fifth. That the judicial powers of the United States shall extend to no possible case, where the cause of action shall have originated before the ratification of this Constitution, except in dispute between states about their territory, disputes between persons claiming lands under grants of different states and debts due to the United States.

Sixth. That no person shall be compelled to do military duty, otherwise than by voluntary enlistment, except in cases of general invasion, anything in the second paragraph of the sixth article of the Constitution, or any law made under the Constitution of the United States, to the contrary notwithstanding.

Seventh. That no capitation or poll tax shall ever be laid by Congress.

Eighth. In cases of direct taxes, the Congress shall first make requisitions on the several states, to assess, levy and pay their respective proportions to such requisitions, in such way and manner as the legislatures of the several states shall judge best; and in case any state shall refuse or neglect to pay its proportion, pursuant to such requisition, then Congress may assess and levy such state's proportion, together with interest at the rate of six per cent, per annum, from the time prescribed in such requisition.

Ninth. That Congress shall lay no direct taxes, without the assent of the legislatures of the three-fourths of the states in the Union.

Tenth. That the journals of the proceedings of the Senate and House of Representatives, shall be published as soon as conveniently may be, at least once in every year, except such parts thereof relating to treaties, alliances or military operations as, in their judgment, may require secrecy.

Eleventh. That regular accounts of the receipts and expenditures of all public moneys, shall be published, at least, once in every year.

Twelfth. As standing armies, in time of peace, are dangerous to liberty, and ought not to be kept up, except in cases of necessity, and as, at all times, the military should be under strict subordination to the civil powers, that, therefore, no standing army or regular troops shall be raised or kept up in time of peace.

Thirteenth. That no moneys be borrowed on the credit of the United States, without the assent of two-thirds of the senators and representatives present, in each House.

Fourteenth. That the Congress shall not declare war, without the concurrence of two-thirds of the senators and representatives present, in each House.

Fifteenth. That the words "without the consent of Congress," in the seventh clause in the ninth section of the first article of the Constitution, be expunged.

Sixteenth. That no judge of the Supreme Court of the United States, shall hold any other office under the United States or any of them; nor shall any officers appointed by Congress, be permitted to hold any office under the appointment of any of the States.

Seventeenth. As a traffic tending to establish or continue slavery of any part of the human species, is disgraceful to the cause of liberty and humanity, that Congress shall, as soon as may be, promote and establish such laws and regulations as may effectually prevent the importation of slaves, of every description, into the United States.

Eighteenth. And that the amendments proposed by Congress, in March, 1789, be adopted by this Convention, except the second article therein contained.

The courtly party leader Jonathan Hazard listed the amendments he proposed to the federal Constitution (see Jonathan J. Hazard entry in *Biographies*). He continued his argument from 1788, as he wrote against a strong government's ability to tax the people, especially the small farmers.

REFERENCE

Theodore Foster (ed.), *The Minutes of the Rhode Island Convention of 1790* (Providence: Rhode Island Historical Society, 1929).

9
Maryland

April 21–26, 1788

Ratification #7, April 26, 1788

In favor 63–11

Luther Martin ("The Genuine Information"), I, *December 28, 1787*, and II, *January 1, 1788*

1

Mr. Speaker, Since I was notified of the resolve of this Honourable House, that we should attend this day, to give information with regard to the proceedings of the late convention, my time has necessarily been taken up with business, and I have also been obliged to make a journey to the Eastern-Shore: These circumstances have prevented me from being as well prepared as I could wish, to give the information required—However, the few leisure moments I could spare, I have devoted to refreshing my memory, by looking over the papers and notes in my possession; and shall with pleasure, to the best of my abilities, render an account of my conduct.

It was not in my power to attend the convention immediately on my appointment—I took my seat, I believe, about the eighth or ninth of June. I found that Governor Randolph, of Virginia, had laid before the convention certain propositions for their consideration, which have been read to this House by my Honourable colleague, and I believe, he has very faithfully detailed the substance of the speech with which the business of the convention was opened, for though I was not there at the time, I saw notes which had been taken of it.—The members of the convention from the States, came there under different powers.

The greatest number, I believe under powers, nearly the same as those of the delegates of this State—Some came to the convention under the former appointment, authorising the meeting of delegates merely to regulate trade.— Those of Delaware were *expressly instructed to agree to no system which should take away from the States, that equality of suffrage secured by the original articles of confederation.* Before I arrived, a number of rules had been adopted to regulate the proceedings of the convention, by one of which, seven States might proceed to business, and consequently four States, the majority of that number, might eventually have agreed upon a system which was to effect the whole Union. By another, *the doors were to be shut,* and the *whole proceedings were to be kept secret;* and so far did this rule extend, that we were thereby prevented from corresponding with gentlemen in the different States upon the subjects under our discussion—a circumstance, Sir, which I confess, I greatly regretted—I had no idea that all the wisdom, integrity, and virtue of this State, or of the others, were centered in the convention—I wished to have corresponded freely, and confidentially, with eminent political characters in my own, and other States, not implicitly to be dictated to by them, but to give their sentiments due weight and consideration. So *extremely solicitous* were they, that their proceedings should not transpire, that *the members were prohibited even from taking copies of resolutions, on which the convention were deliberating, or extracts of any kind from the journals without formally moving for, and obtaining permission, by a vote of the convention for that purpose.*

You have heard, Sir, the resolutions which were brought forward by the honourable member from Virginia—let me call the attention of this House, to the conduct of Virginia, when our confederation was entered into—That State then proposed, and obstinately contended, *contrary to the sense of, and unsupported by the other States, for an inequality of suffrage* founded on *numbers, or some such scale,* which should give *her,* and certain other States, *influence in the Union over the rest*—pursuant to that spirit which then characterized her, and uniform in her conduct, the very second resolve, is calculated expressly for that purpose *to give her a representation proportioned to her numbers,* as if the *want of that* was the *principle defect* in our original system, and this alteration the great means of remedying the evils we had experienced under our present government.

The object of *Virginia* and *other large States, to increase their power and influence over the others,* did not escape observation—The subject, however, was discussed with great coolness in the committee of the whole House (for the convention had resolved itself into a committee of the whole to deliberate upon the propositions delivered in by the honourable member from Virginia). Hopes were formed, that the farther we proceeded in the examination of the resolutions, the better the House might be satisfied of the impropriety of adopting them, and that they would finally be rejected by a majority of the committee—If on the contrary, a majority should report in their favour, it was considered that it would not preclude the members from bringing forward and submitting any other system to the consideration of the convention; and accordingly, while those resolves were the subject of discussion in the committee of the whole House, a number of the members who disapproved them, were preparing *another system,* such as *they thought more conducive to the happiness and welfare of the States*—The propositions originally submitted to the convention having been debated, and undergone a variety of alterations in the course of our proceedings, the committee of the whole House by a *small majority* agreed to a *report,* which I am happy, Sir, to have in my power to lay before you—It was as follow:

1. *Resolved,* That it is the opinion of this committee, that a *national* government ought to be established, consisting of a supreme, legislative, judiciary and executive.

2. That the legislative ought to consist of *two branches.*

3. That the members of the first branch of the national legislature ought to be elected by the people of the several States, for the term of three years, to receive fixed stipends, by which they may be compensated for the devotion of their time to public service, to be paid out of the national treasury, to be ineligible to any office established by a particular State, or under the authority of the United States, except those particularly belonging to the functions of

the first branch, during the term of service, and under the national government, for the space of one year after its expiration.

4. That the members of the second branch of the legislature ought to be chosen by the individual legislatures, to be of the age of thirty years at least, to hold their offices for a term sufficient to ensure their independency, namely, seven years, one third to go out biennially, to receive fixed stipends, by which they may be compensated for the devotion of their time to public service, to be paid out of the national treasury, to be ineligible to any office by a particular State, or under the authority of the United States, except those peculiarly belonging to the functions of the second branch, during the term of service, and under the national government, for the space of one year after its expiration.

5. That each branch ought to possess the right of originating acts.

6. That the national legislature ought to be empowered to enjoy the legislative rights vested in Congress by the confederation, and *moreover, to legislate in all cases to which the separate States are incompetent,* or in which the *harmony of the United States may be interrupted, by the exercise of individual legislation*; to *negative* all laws passed by the *several States,* contravening, in the *opinion* of the *legislature* of the *United States,* the articles of union, or any treaties subsisting under the authority of the Union.

7. That the *right of suffrage* in the *first* branch of the national legislature, *ought not to be according to the rule established in the articles of confederation,* but according to some equitable rate of representation, namely, *in proportion to the whole number of white, and other free citizens and inhabitants of every age, sex and condition, including those bound to servitude for a term of years, and three fifths of all other persons,* not comprehended in the foregoing description, except Indians not paying taxes in each State.

8. That the *right of suffrage* in the *second branch* of the national legislature, *ought to be according to the rule established in the first.*

9. That a national executive be instituted to consist of a single person, *to be chosen by the national legislature* for the term of seven years, with power to carry into execution the national laws, *to appoint to offices* in cases not otherwise provided for, to be ineligible a second time, and to be removable on impeachment and conviction of malpractice or neglect of duty, to receive a fixed stipend, by which he may be compensated for the devotion of his time to public service—to be paid out of the national treasury.

10. That the national executive shall have a right to *negative any legislative act which shall not afterwards be passed, unless by two third parts of each branch of the national legislature.*

11. That a national judiciary be established, to consist of one supreme tribunal, the judges of which, to be appointed *by the second branch* of the national legislature, to hold their offices during good behaviour, and to receive punctually, at stated times, a fixed compensation for their services, in which no increase or diminution shall be made, so as to affect the persons actually in office at the time of such increase or diminution.

12. That the *national legislature* be empowered to *appoint inferior tribunals.*

13. That the jurisdiction of the *national* judiciary shall extend to cases which

respect the collection of the national revenue; cases arising under the laws of the United States—impeachments of any national officer, *and questions which involve the national peace and harmony.*

14. *Resolved,* That provision ought to be made for the admission of States lawfully arising within the limits of the United States whether from a voluntary junction of government, territory, or otherwise, with the consent of a number of voices in the national legislature less than the whole.

15. *Resolved,* That provision ought to be made for the continuance of Congress, and their authority and privileges, until a given day after the reform of the articles of union shall be adopted, and for the completion of all their engagements.

16. That a republican constitution and its existing laws ought to be guaranteed to each State by the United States.

17. That provision ought to be made for the amendment of the articles of union, whensoever it shall seem necessary.

18. That the legislative, executive and judiciary powers, within the several States, ought to be bound by oath to support the articles of the union.

19. That the amendments which shall be offered to the confederation by this convention, ought, at a proper time or times, after the approbation of Congress, to be submitted to an assembly or assemblies, recommended by the legislatures, to be expressly chosen by the people to consider and decide thereon.

These propositions, Sir, were *acceded to* by a *majority of the members of the committee*—a system by which the *large States were to have not only an inequality of suffrage in the first branch,* but also *the same inequality* in the *second branch,* or senate; however, it was not designed the second branch should consist of the same *number* as the first. It was proposed that the senate should consist of *twenty-eight members,* formed on the following scale—Virginia to send *five,* Pennsylvania and Massachusetts each *four,* South-Carolina, North-Carolina, Maryland, New-York, and Connecticut *two* each, and the States of New-Hampshire, Rhode-Island, Jersey, Delaware, and Georgia each of them *one;* upon this plan, the three large States, Virginia, Pennsylvania, and Massachusetts, would have *thirteen* senators out of *twenty-eight,* almost *one half of the whole number*—Fifteen senators were to be a quorum to proceed to business; those *three States* would, therefore, have *thirteen* out of that quorum. Having this inequality *in each branch* of the legislature, it must be evident, Sir, that *they would make what laws they pleased, however disagreeable or injurious to the other States,* and that *they would always prevent the other States from making any laws, however necessary and proper, if not agreeable to the views of those three States*—They were not only, Sir, by this system, to have such an undue superiority in making laws and regulations for the Union, but to have the same superiority in the *appointment* of the *president,* the *judges,* and all *other officers* of government. Hence, those three States would in reality have the appointment of the president, judges, and all the other officers. This president, and these judges, so appointed, we may be morally certain would be citizens of one of those three States; and the president, as appointed by them, and a citizen of one of them, would espouse their interests and their views, when they came in competition with the views and interests of the other States. This president, so appointed by the three large States, and so unduly under their influence, was to have a negative upon every law that should be passed, which, if negatived by him, was not to take effect, unless assented to by two thirds of each branch of the legislatures, a provision which deprived ten States of even the faintest shadow of liberty; for if they, by a miraculous unanimity, having all their members present, should outvote the other three, and pass a law contrary to their wishes, those three large States need only procure the president to negative it, and thereby prevent a possibility of its ever taking effect, because the representatives of those three States would amount to much more than one third (almost one half) of the representatives in each branch. And, Sir, this government, so organized with all this undue superiority in those three large States, was as you see to have a power of negativing the laws passed by every State legislature in the Union. Whether, therefore, laws passed by the legislature of Maryland, New-York, Connecticut, Georgia, or of any other of the ten States, for the regulation of their internal police, should take effect, and be carried into execution, was to depend on the good pleasure of the representatives of Virginia, Pennsylvania and Massachusetts.

This system of slavery, which bound hand and foot ten States in the Union, and placed them at the mercy of the other three, and under the most abject and servile subjection to them, was approved by a majority of the members of the convention, and reported by the committee.

On this occasion, the House will recollect, that the convention was resolved into a committee of the whole—of this committee Mr. Gorham was chairman—The honorable Mr. Washington was then on the floor, in the same situation with any other member of the convention at large, to oppose any system he thought injurious, or to propose any alterations or amendments he thought beneficial, to these propositions so reported by the committee, no opposition was given by that illustrious personage, or by the president of the State of Pennsylvania. They both appeared cordially to approve them, and to give them their hearty concurrence; yet this system, I am confident, Mr. Speaker, there is not a member in this house would advocate, or who would hesitate one moment in saying it ought to be rejected. I mention this circumstance in compliance with the duty I owe this honorable body, not with a view to lessen those exalted characters, but to shew how far the greatest and best of men may be led to adopt very improper measures, through error in judgment, State influence, or by other causes, and to shew that it is our duty not to suffer our eyes to be so far dazzled by the splendor of names, as to run blindfolded into what may be our destruction.

Mr. Speaker, I revere those illustrious personages as much as any man here. No man has a higher sense of the important services they have rendered this country. No member of the convention went there more disposed to pay a deference to their opinions; but I should little have deserved the trust this State reposed in me, if I could have sacrificed its dearest interests to my complaisance for their sentiments.

(*To be continued.*)

II

Mr. MARTIN's *Information to the House of Assembly, continued.*

When contrary to our hopes it was found, that a majority of the members of the convention had in the committee agreed to the system, I have laid before you, we then thought it necessary to bring forward the propositions, which such of us who disapproved the plan before had prepared—The members who had prepared these resolutions were principally of the Connecticut, New York, Jersey, Delaware and Maryland delegations.—The honorable Mr. Patterson, of the Jerseys, laid them before the convention—of these propositions I am in possession of a copy, which I shall beg leave to read to you.

These propositions were referred to a committee of the whole house.— Unfortunately the New-Hampshire delegation had not yet arrived, and the sickness of a relation of the honorable Mr. M'Henry, obliged him still to be absent, a circumstance, Sir, which I considered much to be regretted, as Maryland thereby was represented by only two delegates, and they unhappily differed very widely in their sentiments.

The result of the refference of these last propositions to a committee, was a speedy and hasty determination to reject them—I doubt not, Sir, to those who consider them with attention, so sudden a rejection will appear surprising; but it may be proper to inform you, that on our meeting in convention, it was soon found there were among us three parties of very different sentiments and views.

One party, whose object and wish it was to abolish and annihilate all State governments, and to bring forward one general government over this extensive continent of a monarchical nature, under certain restrictions and limitations:—Those who openly avowed this sentiment were, it is true, but few, yet it is equally true, Sir, that there was a considerable number who did not openly avow it, who were by myself, and many others of the convention, considered as being in reality favourers of that sentiment, and acting upon those principles, covertly endeavouring to carry into effect what they well knew openly and avowedly could not be accomplished.

The second party was not for the abolition of the State governments, nor for the introduction of a monarchical government under any form; but they wished to establish such a system as would give their own States undue power and influence in the government over the other States.—A third party was what I considered truly federal and republican—This party was nearly equal in number with the other two, and were composed of the delegations from Connecticut, New-York, New-Jersey, Delaware, and in part from Maryland; also of some individuals from other representations.—This party, Sir, were for proceeding upon terms of *federal equality,* they were for taking our present *federal system* as the basis of their proceedings, and as far as experience had shewn us that there were defects, to remedy those defects, as far as experience had shewn that other powers were necessary to the federal government, to give those powers—They considered this, the object for which they were sent by their State, and what their States expected from them—They urged, that if after doing this, experience should shew that there still were defects in the system (as no doubt there would be) the same good sense that induced this convention to be called, would cause the States when they found it necessary to call another; and if that convention should act with the same moderation, the members of it would proceed to correct such errors and defects as experience should have brought to light—That by proceeding in this train, we should have a prospect at length of obtaining as perfect a system of federal government, as the nature of things would admit. On the other hand, if we, contrary to the purpose for which we were intrusted, considering ourselves as master-builders, too proud to amend our original government, should demolish it entirely, and erect a new system of our own, a short time might shew the new system as defective as the old, perhaps more so—Should a convention be found necessary again, if the members thereof acting upon the same principles, instead of amending and correcting its defects, should demolish that entirely, and bring forward a third system, that also might soon be found no better than either of the former, and thus we might always remain young in government, and always suffering the inconveniences of an incorrect, imperfect system.

But, Sir, the favourers of monarchy, and those who wished the total abolition of State governments, well knowing that a government founded on *truly federal principles,* the basis of which were the *Thirteen State governments, preserved in full force and energy,* would be destructive of their views; and knowing they were too weak in numbers, openly to bring forward their system, conscious also that the people of America would reject it if proposed to them, joined their interest with that party, who wished a system, giving *particular States* the *power* and *influence over the others,* procuring in return mutual sacrifices from them, in giving the government *great* and *undefined powers* as to its *legislative* and *executive,* well knowing that by *departing from a federal system,* they paved the way for their favourite object, the *destruction of the State governments,* and the *introduction of monarchy*—And hence, Mr. Speaker, I apprehend, in a great measure, arose the objections of those honorable members Mr. Mason and Mr. Gerry. In every thing that tended to give the *large States power* over the *smaller,* the *first* of those gentlemen could not forget he belonged to the *ancient dominion,* nor could the *latter* forget that he represented Old Massachusetts; that part of the system which tended to give those States power over the others, met with their *perfect approbation;* but when they viewed it charged with *such powers* as would *destroy all State governments,* their *own* as well as the *rest*—when they saw a president so constituted as to differ from a monarch, scarcely but in name, and having it in his power to become such in reality when he pleased; they being *republicans* and *federalists* as far as an attachment to their own States would permit them, they warmly and zealously opposed those parts of the system. From these different sentiments, and from this combination of interest, *I apprehend,* Sir, proceeded the fate of what was called the Jersey resolutions, and the report made by the committee of the whole house.

The Jersey propositions being thus rejected, the convention took up those reported by the committee, and proceeded to debate them by paragraphs—It was now that they who disapproved the report found it necessary to make a *warm* and *decided opposition,* which took place upon the discussion of the seventh resolution, which related to the *inequality* of representation in the *first* branch.—Those who advocated this inequality, urged, that when the articles of confederation were formed, it was *only* from *necessity* and *expediency* that the States were admitted *each* to have an *equal vote*; but that our situation was *now altered*, and therefore those States who considered it contrary to their interest, would *no longer abide* by it. They said no State ought to wish to have influence in government, except in proportion to what it contributes to it; that if it contributes but little, it ought to have but a small vote; that taxation and representation ought always to go together; that if one State had *sixteen times as many inhabitants* as another, or was *sixteen times as wealthy*, it ought to have *sixteen times as many votes*; that an inhabitant of Pennsylvania ought to have as much weight and consequence as an inhabitant of Jersey or Delaware; that it was contrary to the feelings of the human mind—what the *large States* would *never* submit to; that the *large States* would have *great objects* in view, in which they would never permit the *smaller States* to thwart them; that *equality of suffrage* was the rotten part of the constitution, and that this was a happy time to get clear of it. In fine, that it was the poison which contaminated our whole system, and the source of all the evils we experienced.

This, Sir, is the substance of the arguments, if arguments they can be called, which were used in favour of *inequality of suffrage.*—Those, who advocated the *equality of suffrage*, took the matter up on the original principles of government—They urged that all men considered in a state of nature, before any government formed, are equally free and independent, no one having any right or authority to exercise power over another, and this *without any regard to difference in personal strength, understanding, or wealth*—That when such individuals enter into government, they have *each* a right to an *equal voice* in its first formation, and afterwards have *each* a right to an *equal vote* in every matter which relates to their government—That if it could be done conveniently, they have a right to exercise it in person—Where it cannot be done in person but for convenience, representatives are appointed to act for them, *every person* has a *right* to an *equal vote* in choosing that representative who is entrusted to do for the whole, that which the whole, if they could assemble, might do in person, and in the transacting of which each would have an equal voice— That if we were to admit, because a man was *more wise, more strong*, or *more wealthy*, he should be entitled to *more votes* than another, it would be *inconsistent with the freedom and liberty* of *that other*, and would reduce him to *slavery*—Suppose, for instance, ten individuals in a state of nature, about to enter into government, *nine* of whom are *equally wise, equally strong*, and *equally wealthy*, the *tenth is ten times as wise*, ten times as *strong* or ten times as *rich*; if for this reason he is to have *ten votes* for *each vote of either of the others*, the *nine* might as well have *no vote at all*, since though the *whole nine* might assent to a measure, yet the *vote of the tenth* would *countervail*, and *set aside all their votes*—If this *tenth* approved of what *they* wished to adopt, it would be well, but if he disapproved, he could prevent it, and in the same manner he could carry into execution *any measure he wished contrary to the opinion of all the others, he* having *ten votes*, and the *other* all together *but nine*—It is evident, that on these principles, *the nine* would have *no will nor discretion of their own*, but must be *totally dependent* on the *will* and *discretion* of the *tenth*, to *him they* would be as *absolutely slaves* as any *negro* is to his *master*.— If *he* did not attempt to carry into execution any measures injurious to the *other nine*, it could only be said that *they* had a *good master*, they would not be the *less slaves*, because *they* would be *totally dependent* on the *will* of *another*, and not on *their own will*—They might not *feel their chains*, but they would notwithstanding *wear them*, and whenever their *master* pleased he might draw them so tight as to gall them to the bone. Hence it was urged the *inequality of representation*, or giving to one man more votes than another on account of his wealth, &c. was *altogether inconsistent with the principles of liberty*, and in the *same proportion as it should be adopted*, in favour of *one* or *more*, in *that proportion are the others inslaved*—It was urged that though every individual should have an equal voice in the government, yet, even then superiour wealth, strength or understanding, would give great and undue advantages to those who possessed them. That wealth attracts respect and attention; superior strength would cause the weaker and more feeble to be cautious how they of-fended, and to put up with small injuries rather than to engage in an unequal contest—In like manner superior understanding would give its possessor many opportunities of profiting at the expence of the more ignorant.—Having thus established these principles with respect to the *rights* of *individuals* in a *state of nature*, and what is due to *each* on entering into government, principles es-tablished by every writer on liberty, they proceeded to shew that *States*, when *once formed*, are considered *with respect* to *each other as individuals* in a state of nature—That, like individuals, each *State* is considered *equally free* and *equally independent*, the *one* having no right to exercise authority over the *other*, though more *strong, more wealthy*, or *abounding with more inhabitants*—That when a number of *States* unite themselves under a *federal government*, the *same principles apply* to *them* as when a *number* of *individual men* unite themselves under a *State government*—That every argument which shews *one man* ought not to have *more votes* than *another*, because he is *wiser, stronger* or *wealthier*, proves that *one State* ought not to have *more votes* than *another*, because it is *stronger, richer, or more populous*—And that by *giving one State*, or *one or two States more votes* than the *others*, the *others* thereby are *enslaved to such State or States*, having the *greater number of votes*, in the *same manner* as in the case before put of *individuals* where *one* has *more votes than the others*—That the reason why each individual man in forming a State government should have an equal vote is, because each individual before he enters into government is *equally free* and *independent*—So *each State*, when *States enter* into a *federal government*, are entitled to an *equal vote*, because before they entered into such federal government, *each State* was *equally free* and *equally independent*—That *adequate* representation of *men formed into a State government*, consists in *each man* having an *equal voice* either personally, or if by representatives, that he should have an equal voice in choosing the representative—So adequate rep-resentation of *States* in a *federal government*, consists in *each State* having an *equal voice* either in person or by its representative in every thing which relates to the federal government—That this *adequacy of representation* is *more im-portant* in a *federal*, than in a *State* government, because the members of a State government, the *district* of which is *not very large*, have generally such a *common interest*, that laws can scarcely be made by *one* part *oppressive* to the *others*, without *their suffering in common*; but the *different States* composing an *extensive federal empire*, widely distant, *one* from the *other*, may have *interests so totally distinct*, that the *one* part might be greatly *benefited* by what would be *destructive* to the *other*.

They were not satisfied by resting it on principles; they also appealed to history—They shewed that in the amphyctionic confederation of the Grecian cities, *each city* however *different* in *wealth, strength*, and other *circumstances*, sent the same *number* of deputies, and had *each* an *equal voice* in every thing that related to the common concerns of Greece. It was shewn that in the seven provinces of the United Netherlands, and the confederated Cantons of Switzerland, *each Canton* and *each province* have an *equal vote*, although there are as great distinctions of wealth, strength, population, and extent of territory among those provinces and *those Cantons*, as among *these States*. It was said, that the maxim that taxation and representation ought to go together, was true so far, that no person ought to be *taxed* who is not *represented*, but not in the extent insisted upon, to wit, that the *quantum* of *taxation* and *representation* ought to be the *same*; on the contrary, the *quantum* of *representation* depends upon the quantum of *freedom*, and therefore *all*, whether *individual States*, or individual *men*, who are *equally free*, have a right to *equal representation*—That to those who insist that he who pays the greatest share of taxes, ought to have the greatest number of votes; it is a sufficient answer to say, that *this rule* would be *destructive* of the *liberty* of the *others*, and would render *them slaves* to the *more rich* and *wealthy*—That if one man pays *more taxes* than another, it is because he has *more wealth* to be protected by government, and he receives greater benefits from the government—So if one State pays more to the federal government, it is because as a State, she enjoys greater blessings from it; she has more wealth protected by it, or a greater number of inhabitants, whose rights are secured, and who share its advantages.

Luther Martin, a brilliant lawyer and member of the Continental Congress, later served as a state judge (see Luther Martin entry in *Biographies*). In "Genuine Information," twelve articles published in the Maryland *Gazette*, between December 28, 1787, and February 8, 1788, and widely reprinted and circulated as a pamphlet throughout the states, Martin developed a lawyer's argument against ratification of the Constitution. I print #1 and #2, in which he defended individual rights, and worried about how such a small state as Maryland could function in a large republic.

REFERENCES

Ford, *Essays on the Constitution*; Storing, *Complete*, vol. 5; Elliot, *Debates*, vol. 1.

John Francis Mercer, *Essays by a Farmer*, I, *February 15, 1788* (partial)

When men, to whom the guardianship of public liberty has been committed, discover a neglect if not contempt for a bill of rights—when they answer reasons by alledging a fact,—which fact too, is no fact at all—it becomes a duty to bear testimony against such conduct, for silence and acquiescence in political language are synonimous terms.

If men were as anxious about reality as appearance, we should have fewer professions of disinterested patriotism—true patriotism like true piety, is incompatible with an ostentatious personal display.

In a world more cautious than correct, the intrusion of private names in a public cause, is generally considered as a sacrifice of prudence to vanity, and not unfrequently censured as impertinent—in either view it is unreasonable to require it—It is more, it is inadmissible—it would be betraying one of those inestimable rights of an individual, over which society should have no controul—the freedom of the press—and the only recompence for the treason, would be a boundless increase of private malice.

That men who profess an attachment to the liberty of the press, should also require names, is one of those instances of human weakness and inconsistency, that deserves rather pity than resentment. Political as well as religious freedom has ever been and forever will be destroyed by that invariable tendency of enthusiasts and bigots to mark out as objects of public resentment and persecution, those who presume to dispute their opinions or question their infallibility—and whilst there are men, enthusiasm and bigotry will prevail—it is the natural predominance of the passions over reason—The citizens of America are not yet so agitated by the phrenzy of innovation as to forget—that the object of public inquiry is, or ought to be, *truth*—that to convert *truth* into *falsehood*, *right* into *wrong*, is equally beyond the reach of the *good*, the *bad*, the *great* and the *humble*—A great name may indeed *impose falsehood* for *truth*—*wrong* for *right*—and whenever such voluntarily offer themselves, there may be ground for suspicion—But the people may listen with safety to those, who assert no other claim to their attention, than the *reason* and *merit* of their remarks.

To assert that bills of rights have always originated from, or been considered as grants of the King or Prince, and that the liberties which they secure are the gracious concessions of the sovereign, betrays an equal ignorance of history and of law, or what in effect amounts to the same thing a violent and precipitate zeal.

I believe no writer in the most venal age, has ever openly asserted this doctrine, but the prostituted, rotten Sir Robert Filmer, and Aristides—And the man who at this day would contend in England that their bill of rights is the grant of the King, would find the general contempt his only security—in saying this, I sincerely regret that the name of Aristides should be joined with that of Sir Robert Filmer, and I freely acknowledge that no contemptible degree of talents, and integrity render him who uses it, much more worthy of the very respectable association he has selected for himself—But the errors of such men alone are dangerous—the man who has too much activity of mind, or restlessness to be quiet, qualities to engage public and private esteem, talents to form and support an opinion, fortitude to avow it, and too much pride to be convinced, will at all times have weight in a free country, (especially where indolence is the general characteristic) though that weight he will always find impaired in proportion as he indulges levity, caprice and passion.

I will confine my inquiry to the English constitution—Example *there*, is in a great measure law *here*—and the authority of an American judge on a point of English law, should be digested with coolness and promulgated with caution, because it is frequently conclusory.

The celebrated and only bill of rights of Great-Britain, which is considered as the supreme law of the land, and not to be questioned or impeached in their courts, was the work of that convention of lords and commons in 1688, which declared that *King James 2d, had abdicated the crown, and that the throne had thereby become vacant*, and who after they had compleated and asserted this glorious declaration of the unalienable rights of their fellow citizens, pursuing the peculiar duty of a convention, conferred the crown of the three kingdoms on an alien and foreigner, William the 3d.

Can any man imagine that this convention could at that time, have considered these rights as the grant of a King, whom they previously declared to have abdicated the throne, or the gracious concessions of a Prince whom they were about to deprive forever of the crown? Or could they have considered this bill of rights as the concession of Prince William, at that time a foreigner and alien, not entitled to hold a foot of land, or any of the common rights of citizenship, and who could afterwards only derive his title to the crown from the same source, which gave authority and sanction to this fundamental and most inestimable law? or, could the British nation at that time, or ever since, have viewed this declaration, as the grant and concession of a King or Prince, when no King or Prince was at that time in existence?—But should there remain any minds yet unsatisfied, I refer such to the debates of that convention, which are preserved in Grey's debates in parliament, and there will be found in them, the principles of equal liberty, the inherent and unalienable rights of men, as amply and ably discussed, and as fully recognized by the authors of that blessing, the artists of that British palladium, as ever they have since been by the animated patriots of America, or the present age.—I also refer them to an inestimable little treatise composed on this occasion by that accomplished lawyer and patriot, afterwards the Lord Somers—High Chancellor of Great-Britain—then a member of the convention, and chiefly instrumental in their great work—a pamphlet that should find a place in the library of every American judge at least—Whoever peruses these, will discover undeniable evidence, that the

British convention, considered this their declaration, as the concession of no Prince, but the Prince of Heaven—whom alone they acknowledged as the author of their liberties—they will there find that a bill of rights, is an enumeration of those conditions on which the individuals of the empire agreed to confirm the social compact; and consequently that no power, which they thus conditionally delegated to the majority (in whatever form organized) should be so exercised as to infringe and impair these their natural rights—not vested in SOCIETY, but reserved to each member thereof.

This was not the doctrine of that period alone—It was the common law and constitution of England, so asserted and maintained by the ablest lawyers of every age of the empire.—The petition of right, which came forward in the reign of Charles 1st, said to have been originally penned by the celebrated Lord Coke—although in its title a contradiction in terms, is yet in substance equally strong and clear—asserting the rights of the people to be coeval with the government—We find this principle strenuously and ably maintained through all the works of this great man, and to this doctrine he finally, with the devotion of a freeman, and the fortitude of an Englishman, sacrificed his vanity, his ambition and his avarice—This last act of an aged and venerable judge, has obliterated the errors of a youthful courtier—it has made his peace with posterity, who with gratitude and indulgence has forgiven the conduct of a court lawyer, which she might have punished with detestation, although she could not correct.

Here I cannot but observe what strenuous bill of rights men, all the great luminaries of the English law have been: to Lord Coke and Lord Somers. Sir Matthew Hale, in whom were united true Christian piety, Roman fortitude, and an understanding more than human.

This perfect man although firmly opposed to the violences of the mad fanatics of the age, stood up almost alone in that parliament which restored the regal government, in favor of a bill of rights—but the tide of popular rage, hastening to place the worthless Charles on the throne of his more worthless ancestors, was too strong, and the voice of that man could not be heard, who was the delight of his own and the admiration of succeeding ages.

It is true, that something like the doctrine of Aristides was frequently the language of courtiers and sycophants in the feeble reigns of the arbitrary Stuarts—times of impotent and impudent usurpation—and they grounded their assertions on the form of the statute of magna charta, a statute much estemed for the many valuable rights it ascertains—the enacting words of which imply it to be an act of the King—But Aristides must know that this was the frequent form of the ancient statutes, sometimes it is the King alone enacts, sometime the King with advice and consent of the great men and Barons, and sometimes the three estates—Even at this day, the King uses these words in passing laws that bear the same implication; and we see even in America acts of authority issue under the name and signature of the Governor alone, who has not a voice unless the council are divided—But as to the legal and acknowledged authority of the King at the time of enacting magna charta, there can remain but little doubt. Henry Bracton a contemporary lawyer and judge, who has left us a compleat and able treatise on the laws of England, is thus clear and express— *Omnes quidem sub rege, ipse autem sub lege*, all are subject to the King, but the

King is subject to the law—It will hardly then be imagined, that the supreme law and constitution were the grants and concessions of a Prince, who was thus in theory and practice, subject himself to ordinary acts of legislation—But all these things are so amply discussed and the authorities so accurately collected in the publication of my Lord Somers, that a reference must be much more satisfactory than a repetition.

If I understand Aristides, he says that it would have been considered as an arrogant usurpation of sovereign rights in the members of convention, to have affixed a bill of rights—Can be reconcile this position with another opinion in his remarks, where he maintains that in offering this constitution, they could only act as private individuals, any of whom have a right to propose a constitution to the Americans to adopt at their discretion—In this view they could only have proposed—it is certain they could not have enacted a bill of rights—Nor would there have been any usurpation in WE *the people, of the States of New Hampshire, Massachusetts, &c. securing to ourselves and our posterity the following unalienable rights, &c.* which is the stile of the new constitution—The convention have actually engrafted some of these natural rights, yet no one calls it an usurpation—nor can I believe that any of my fellow-citizens of the United States, would have discovered the least indignation, had they engrafted them all—The universal complaint has been that they have enumerated so few—But says Aristides, it would have been a work of great difficulty, if not impossible to have ascertained them—Are the fundamental rights of mankind at this day unknown? Are they so soon forgot? If they are not imprinted on our hearts, they are in several of the constitutions—Although various in form, they are certainly not contradictory in substance—It did not require the wisdom of a national convention to have reduced them into order, and such as would not have gained the suffrage of a majority, would never have been regretted by America—or, I will venture to assert, what I shall never believe, that the majority were very unworthy of the trust reposed in them—Nor yet can I believe, that the late convention were incompetent to a task that has never been undertaken in the separate States without success.

This constitution is to be the act of the individual members of the American empire—the highest source of terrestrial power with us—As it is a subsequent act, it not only repeals all prior acts of the same authority where it interferes with them—But being a government of the people of all the States, I do not know what right the citizens of Maryland for instance, have to expect that the citizens of Connecticut or New-Jersey, will be governed by the laws or constitution of Maryland—or what benefit a citizen of Maryland could derive from his bill of rights in a court of the United States, which can only be governed by the constitution and laws of the United States—Nor will it help the question to say, what will certainly be denied, that the future Congress may provide by law for this,—that an ordinary law of the United States can make, is an admission that it can unmake, and to submit the bills of rights of the separate States to the power of every annual national parliament, is a very uncertain tenure indeed.

If a citizen of Maryland can have no benefit of his own bill of rights in the confederal courts, and there is no bill of rights of the United States—how could he take advantage of a natural right founded in reason, could he plead it and produce Locke, Sydney, or Montesquieu as authority?[1] How could he take advantage of any of the common law rights, which have heretofore been considered as the birthright of Englishmen and their descendants, could he plead them and produce the authority of the English judges in his support? Unquestionably not, for the authority of the common law arises from the express adoption by the several States in their respective constitutions, and that in various degrees and under different modifications—If admitted at all, I do not see to what extent, and if admitted, it must be admitted as unalterable by ordinary acts of legislation, which would be impossible—and it could never be of use to an individual, but in combating some national law infringing natural right.— To render this more intelligible—suppose for instance, that an officer of the United States should force the house, the asylum of a citizen, by virtue of a general warrant, I would ask, are general warrants illegal by the constitution of the United States? Would a court, or even a jury, but juries are no longer to exist, punish a man who acted by express authority, upon the bare recollection of what once was law and right? I fear not, especially in those cases which may strongly interest the passions of government, and in such only have general warrants been used—Suppose a case that must and will frequently happen, for such happen almost daily in England—That an officer of the customs should break open the dwelling, and violate the sanctuary of a freeman, in search for smuggled goods—impost and revenue laws are and from necessity must be in their nature oppressive—in their execution they may and will become intolerable to a free people, no remedy has been yet found equal to the task of detering and curbing the insolence of office, but a jury—It has become an invariable maxim of English juries, to give ruinous damages whenever an officer has deviated from the rigid letter of the law, or been guilty of any unnecessary act of insolence or oppression—It is true these damages to the individual, are frequently paid by government, upon a certificate of the judge that there was probable cause of suspicion—But the same reasons that would induce an English judge to give this certificate, would probably lead an American judge, who will be judge and jury too, to spare the public purse, if not favour a brother officer.

I could proceed with an enumeration of familiar instances that must and will happen, that would be as alarming as prolix; but it is not my intention to ring an alarm bell—If I know myself I would rather conciliate than divide—But says Aristides the government may establish for such cases, though not commanded; what they will do I will not presume to say; but I can readily and will hereafter prove if they do, they will violate the constitution; and even admitting their power, it would be but a slender thread.[2]

A lawyer and planter who had recently moved to Maryland from Virginia, John Francis Mercer served in the Continental Congress and later as a reform governor of Maryland (see John Francis Mercer entry in *Biographies*). His first essay demanded a bill of rights to protect individual liberties. Mercer feared arbitrary federal government as a threat to the natural rights of the people. Like other Maryland Antifederalists, he also worried about whether the Constitution would violate the historic rights of the people to trial by jury.

REFERENCES

Maryland *Gazette*, February 15, 1788; Storing, *Complete*, vol. 5.

NOTES

1. The brilliant Mercer refers often to English and Continental political and legal thinkers.

2. Much of the remainder of the essay is illegible. The gist of the argument here calls for a bill of rights.

Samuel Chase, "Notes of Speeches Delivered to the Maryland Ratifying Convention," *April 1788*

I
The Constitutional Convention

Authority of Delegates to Convention.

Act of appointment.

No authority from legislature to annihilate Confederation and form a Constitution for the United States. Legislature could not grant such power. Deputies acted as mere individuals and not in official or delegated capacity. Express object of delegates to *revise* Confederacy.

Act done—a general or *national* government is formed—the separate sovereignty and independence of each state, and their union by a confederate league is destroyed and they are melted down and consolidated into one *National* Government. In Confederation—*We the States*—in Proposed Constitution—*We the People*—the first is a true *federal government of states* and has no power over the *individual citizens* of any of the states—the latter a national one by express compact of all the people; it establishes a supreme power over the *individuals* of the states.

It annuls the confederacy. See Art. 13.

It swallows up the state governments and state legislatures—it alters our Constitution and annuls our Bill of Rights in many of its most essential parts—How justify this Convention on the principles of Aristides—People no right to interfere, etc.

Aristides p. 9. Amendent in parliamentary language means striking out the *whole*. Convention has only advised—and so might an individual.

Wilson—Convention did not act upon the powers given them by the States but they proceeded upon *original principles*—Independent Gazetteer, 29 Nov.[1]

McKean—State Convention no right to inquire into power of late convention, or to alter or amend their work. Sole question whether to ratify or reject the whole system. Could convention lessen the *rights* of the people? their right to lessen never surrendered to Convention. People must have a *right* to judge of the Government proposed. No man can controvert the right of proposing amendments. Whether proper and necessary the only question. Aristides 30.

1st. Question. Whether a federal or national government proper for America. S.C. for the former. Because an extensive country (like United States) on democratical principles only by a Confederation of small republics exercising all the powers of *internal* government, but united by league as to their *external* foreign concerns.—A national or general government however constructed over so extensive a country as America must end in despotism.—If instituted on principles of freedom, not competent to the local wants and concerns of the remote parts of the empire. Montesquieu Vol. I. ch. 16. Brutus No. 1. Cato No. 3.

2nd Question—If *national* whether the one proposed ought to be ratified without any previous amendments. 1. The question is the most important that ever came before an assembly for decision. It involves the happiness or misery of millions yet unborn. The decision requires all the consideration that the utmost exertion of the powers of the mind can bestow.

The present and future generations will bless or execrate us. We have a solemn crisis—and the magnitude of the subject requires that it should be deliberately considered and fully considered with temper and moderation.—

II A
THE PRESENT GOVERNMENT OF THE U.S.: EXCELLENCE OF STATE GOVERNMENTS

I am a friend to our present state government because it is wisely calculated to secure all the civil and *religious* rights of the people and fully adequate for *all internal state* purposes, and our *state* Constitution and laws afford security to property and ample protection to the poor from abuse by the officers of our state government and from any oppression of the poor by the rich and powerful. *There is no injury for which our present laws do not provide a remedy.*— There are some few, and not very capital, defects in our form of Government and they may at any time be amended with prudence and sense without any division or commotion—in a word; We might be happy under our present state government, if we knew our own good, and would be contented. I am opposed—averse from the proposed national government, because it *immediately* takes away the power from our *state* legislature to protect the *personal* liberty of the citizen, and I am convinced in my judgment that it will in a few years entirely absorb and swallow up the state legislature.

Our Bill of Rights which is part of our Constitution provides—

Sect. 2. That the people of this state ought to have the sole and exclusive right of regulating the internal government and police thereof.

Sect. 3. That the inhabitants are entitled to the Trial by Jury according to the course of common law, not only in criminal cases but in all cases between Government and its officers—cause etc.

Sect. 17. Every freeman for any injury to person or property ought to have remedy by the law of the land.

Sect. 18. Trial of facts where they arise is one of the greatest securities of the lives, liberties and estate of the people.

Sect. 23. All warrants without oath to search, etc.

Sect. 13.—Laying taxes by the poll is grievous and oppressive and ought to be abolished.

Sect. 25. Militia proper and natural defence of a free government.

Sect. 26. Standing armies.—27.—28. No soldier to be quartered in any house *in time of peace* without the consent of the owner, and in time of war in such manner only as the legislature shall direct.

Sect. 38. The liberty of the press ought to be inviolably preserved.

Sect. 33. Securing religious rights of conscience.

By our present form of government, the legislature is not supreme but bound by the Constitution.

II B

The Present Government of the U.S.: Reform of the Articles of Confederation

The greatest happiness of a people is to govern themselves. Their greatest misery to be governed by others;—Our *state* government is fully competent to all *internal state purposes.*

For the safety and happiness of the people of this and the other states, *external* objects, or such for which the state governments are not competent are to be provided for.

1. To provide a form to regulate commerce among the states and to preserve peace between the states—resort against domestic enemies, with Indian tribes, and to coin money and to regulate the value thereof, and of foreign coin and to fix the standard of weights and measures—to establish post offices and post roads—may be called a *general internal or continental object.*

2. To preserve all the states from injury or violence from the foreign powers of Europe and to shield them against foreign hostility may be called a *general external or foreign object.*

3. To regulate the trade of the States with foreigners, by Acts of Navigation and by treaties of Commerce with the powers of Europe may be also called a general external or foreign object.

I am for the establishment of power in Congress for all the above or similar purposes.

The 1st—to preserve peace between the states, etc. may be provided for without much difficulty (and about which there never has been nor can be much difference in opinion) by establishing a supreme power to decide all controversies between the states, to coin money, etc., etc. and by a Bill of Rights declaring what the states shall *not* do—as, e.g. not to enter into any treaty, keep troops, coin money, or do any of the above or other acts which the supreme power of all the states are authorized to do.

The 2nd—to preserve all the states etc.—This necessarily includes the power of war;—and the means to carry it on—i.e. to raise money, to maintain troops and to provide a navy.—and it includes the jurisdiction of piracies and felonies on the high seas and of all offences against the law of nations. This also includes the payment of the debt contracted by the United States.

This power is necessary, not immediately pressing—consider the situation of Confederation—but attended with some difficulty. It requires a legislative, an executive and a judicial authority.

Every legislative power should be vested in two, if not three Branches, and they ought to be the *real*, and not the *fictitious* representative of the people. Their numbers ought to be sufficient to know the wants and the wishes of those they represent—too numerous to be corrupted and not so great as to be a mob.

The *Executive* of the States ought to be in a Supreme Magistrate or president—ineligible after a limited time with a Council of short duration and responsible for their advice.

The *Judicial* should be confined to the decision of cases arising on treaties. The great question is in what manner the legislative of the states shall raise taxes on the people of the several states.

I would not give this power only on default of a state to raise its quota as required. If neglected, I would authorise the legislative to lay and collect imposts and duties on tonnage without limitation, provided they be uniform in all the states; also taxes not exceeding limited sums on enumerated Articles of Exports, and stamp and post office duties. If they not sufficient, an excise. Provided they be the same in all the states and that Congress officers be held to account for abuse of authority in the states. And if all not sufficient, a tax on land not exceeding ½ d. per acre.

I would give the above power of taxation without requisition being first made to the states. It is difficult to say what taxes the legislative may lay, but some limitation is necessary.

The Third—to regulate trade—

I am against giving this power—but if it is given let it be to ⅔ of the Senate.

III
THE TENDENCY OF THE CONSTITUTION TO
ANNIHILATE STATE GOVERNMENTS

The National Government will in its operation and effects annihilate the State Governments.

1. National Government has unlimited power, legislative, executive and judicial, as to every object to which it extends by the Constitution.

2. The powers of the National legislature extend to every case of the least consequence—it may make laws to affect the lives, liberty and property of every citizen in America, nor can the Constitution of any State prevent the Execution of any power given to the National legislature.

3. The National legislature may impose every species of taxes external and internal (except only on Exports) *excise, land tax*, poll tax, stamps etc. to *any extent*, and may raise and collect them as they please, without any previous requisition to the State legislatures who have nothing to say to the laws for imposing or collecting taxes—

4. The power to impose and collect taxes is the most important of all powers a people can grant—it absorbs all other powers—Maxim—Money finds Men and Troops will find money—The power of taxation is the highest object of legislation—it is the necessary means of protection and safety to the people in a *good* government and it ever has been and will be the instrument of oppression and tyranny in a *bad* government.

5. No state can emit paper money—nor without consent of Congress lay any duties on Imports or *Exports* or Tonnage except for executing its inspection laws, and in such cases the net produce is for the use of the United States—Therefore no state can pay its debts—or support its government but only by *direct* taxes on Property—Congress can lay all indirect taxes, and also *direct* taxes when they exercise this power in all its extent. The state legislatures will

find it impossible to raise money by *direct* taxes to pay their debts and support their governments—the consequence is certain—without money they will be as Congress is now,—without power, or respect and despised—they will sink to nothing, and be absorbed in the general government.—The people will not bear the expense of two governments. The state government may come in for some time to carry into execution the National Government—even this may be taken away. Art. 1. Sect. 4. See Aristides 37. Impost 38. Farmer's Letters 9 p. 37. Will impost pay interest of *national foreign and domestic debt* and expenses of new government?

6. The power of the national legislature to raise troops in *peace* (as well as war) without any limitation as to number, or with consent of more than a Majority in Congress or a Majority of the state legislature and to levy money for their support for two years—to control the Militia will also to swallow up the state governments—

7. The supreme and inferior federal courts will have the same effect by absorbing the state courts—One must be in each state.

8. The power to make laws—e.g. The state lays a direct tax to pay its debts or to support its government—Congress thinks proper to lay tax on *same property* and as both cannot be paid cannot Congress repeal the State law, or will not their judges declare it void. Will not this conduct deprive the state of all support?

9. The little power reserved to the states will be an object of jealousy to Congress. The whole Constitution breathes a jealousy of the states— its judges and juries. Truth confirmed by experience of ages that every *individual*, and all bodies of men invested with power, always attempt to increase it, and never part with any it but by force. It is the very nature of man. The National government will possess this desire and having the means it will in time carry it into execution. I think the people themselves will assent and may be persuaded to call for the abolition of the state governments. It is at this moment the wish of many men in America and some in this state.

IV A
OBJECTIONS TO THE NEW GOVERNMENT: GENERAL

I am opposed to the new Government:—

1. Because it gives Congress a power without any limitation to lay any kind of taxes that the invention of Man can suggest—indirect and direct. I particularly object to the power to lay taxes on our lands without any limitation and according to our numbers including ⅗ of our slaves. Also to an Excise and the power to excise officers to enter and search and no remedy by such in state courts—and *Verdict by a Jury;* as under the British government. Also to a poll tax which Congress is *expressly* authorized—Art. 1. Sect. 9.—to lay on all our whites and ⅗ of our slaves—the most fatal and oppressive of all taxes. N.B. A favorite tax with Congress and R.M.[2]

2. Because Congress will have a *right* to keep any army in time of peace without number.

3. Because Congress will have a right to quarter soldiers in our *private* houses, not only in time of war, but also in time of *peace*. Bill of Rights 28.

4. Because Congress will have authority over our Militia, and may if they please, march any of them without regard to scruples of conscience against bearing arms, to any part of the United States.

5. Because the inferior federal courts will have the exclusive jurisdiction—Art. 3. Sect. 2 of every controversy between the citizens of the different States—and so trial by Jury. Blackstone 3. c. 33.

6. Because these courts will have the same jurisdiction in controversies between our citizens and subjects of Great Britain or any other foreign state—Tobacco shipped. N.B. An appeal in both cases.

7. Because the Senators or Representatives may be appointed to civil offices under the United States not created or the emoluments increased during the time for which he was elected.

8. Because Congress are to ascertain their own salaries. Art. 1. Sect. 6.

9. Because the Senate are too few in number—only two from each state. 26 at present—a Majority, a Quorum—14—ergo 8 may make a law—liable to corruption—France, Great Britain.

10. Because the Senate are a perpetual body and never die a civil death, although ⅓ is to be chosen every second year—because after first six years there will always be ⅔ of the body in existence—⅓ of which ⅔ will always have served two years and other four years and after first rotation every Senator may serve 6 years.

11. Because ⅔ of the Senate *present* and the president may make treaties of commerce, and the treaties are to be the supreme laws of the land.

12. Because the Representatives are too few in number—1 for 30,000—whites and ⅗ slaves—65 at present—a majority, a quorum 33.—ergo 17 may make a law—liable to corruption.

13. The House of Representatives will not be chosen by the people. Art. 1. Sect. 2.

Maryland is to choose 6 representatives—Every person qualified to elect members to our House of Delegates to be entitled to vote—our legislature is to prescribe the *time, place* and *manner* of electing representatives. Art. 1. Sect. 4—Either the people at large of the whole state must choose the six representatives—or the state must be divided into six districts—say 2 on Eastern and 4 on Western shore.

14. Because Congress may alter the *time, place* and *manner* of choosing representatives. Art. 1. Sect. 4 proceedings Boston 47—51.

15. Because Congress may alter the time and manner of choosing Senators—the place where is not to be altered.

Massachusetts propose to restrict this power to cases expressed.

16. Because the *president* will *not* be chosen by the people *immediately*—that is by electors chosen by the people—as pretended. Art. 2. Sect. 2. The legislature are to direct *who are to be* electors, but the number is fixed to be equal to the whole number of Senators and Representatives—e.g. in this state 8—in all 91. Congress are to determine the *time* of choosing electors and the *day* on which they shall elect the president which shall be the same day in all the states.

The electors are to choose by ballot *two* persons. The person having a *majority* of all the electors to be president and if no person has a majority—which is most improbable, except in first instance then from the *five* highest on the list the House of Representatives to choose the President—each State to have a vote.

17. Because the powers of the President are dangerous. Power of nominating to office. Of pardoning *before* conviction.

18. Because he is eligible for life and he ought to be ineligible after a given number of years.

19. Because the *Judicial* Power extends to controversies between citizens of different states and between citizens of the states and subjects of foreign states and in such cases the trial by Jury is taken away.

20. It is said by the advocates for the new government that we are without a government. Ans. They mean a general or national government—not a state government. The former is wanted to make the *states* do their duty, and pay their Quota to discharge the debt contracted during the war—and to protect the states against the Powers of Europe and to regulate trade—If admitted—yet no necessity much less wisdom to do more than is necessary to answer these objects—powers for these purposes can be given without surrendering up our liberties.

21. The new government will take the burthen from the farmer and planter, and the poor people and place it on trade—because duties on imports and tax on *Excise* will be adopted. Ans. Why cannot state governments do the same?—In truth it is only changing *in part* the mode of taxation—Explain it. *Why poll tax* is not for the benefit of the poor.

22. Regulations of trade and treaties of commerce will bring in money—employ our Merchants—shipbuilders. Ans. if true, give those powers but not those granted.

23. The people can't be worse. Ans. Why are they distressed?—many from their *private debts*—some from taxes—all from the scarcity of money. Will new government pay private debts? Will it lessen taxes? It will make our Continental debt specie—it is now at 8 for 1. £200,000 would pay the proportion of this state—it was proposed by *an emission*—Consider the Expenses of National government.

24. The government is calculated for a few rich and ambitious men—and speculators in certificates—

25. Merchants are for it. Ans. consider them. Birds of passage.

26. General Washington et al. for it.

27. May amend afterwards. Ans. The amendments proposed prove that these are capital defects. Should amend before adoption—1. because it is easy to grant and very difficult to recall power which from its nature is ever encroaching. 2. No wise people ever gave power over their liberties with a view of getting back the power. 3. It is now in the power of five states to obtain amendments—afterwards there must be nine.—4. a bad government becomes more feared every day by its officers. 5. why not *another convention?* Who is violent for it—Ans. Rich Men and speculators and office hunters.

Call on friends to give reasons for new government.

IV B
OBJECTIONS TO THE NEW GOVERNMENT: EXPENSE

Expense of National Government.

Civil List—President—Vice-President—Senators—Representatives—Ambassadors—Judicial Department—Judges, Justices, Chanellor, Clerks, Sheriffs. Excise officers, Naval officers—Locusts—Policy to institute a number of lucrative new offices to increase their influence in the States—Army will provide for many expectants.

IV C
OBJECTIONS TO THE NEW GOVERNMENT: LIBERY OF THE PRESS

Bill or Declaration of Rights.

Liberty of Press.

1. The Constitution gives no power to Congress *express* or *implied* to abridge or take away the liberty of the press.

2. Art. 1. Sect. 8. Congress have power to promote Science and it is impossible to promote Science and at same time destroy the liberty of the press—under this clause may write what they please about Government. There is no Bill or Declaration of Rights to restrain Congress—They will have the power and it remains in their discretion when they will exercise it.

V
REPRESENTATION

Representation.

1. A fact—the continent will be governed by 65. Six northern states—35-seven southern states—30.

2. I do not object that the states have not an equal representation in the second branch or House of Representatives.

3. I object because the representatives will not be the representatives of the people at large but really of a few rich men in each state. A representative should be the image of those he represents. He should know their sentiments and their wants and desires—he should posses their feelings—he should be governed by their interests with which his own should be inseparably connected. The representatives of so extensive a country—consequently such numbers should be numerous.—A few men cannot possibly represent the *opinions*, wishes, and *interests* of great numbers. It is impossible for a few men to be acquainted with the sentiments and interests of the United States, which contains many different classes or orders of people—Merchants, farmers, planters, mechanics and gentry or wealthy men. To form a proper and true representation each order ought to have an opportunity of choosing from each a person as their representative; this is impossible from the smallness of the number—65. Can six men be found in Maryland who understand the interests of the several orders of men in this state and are acquainted with their situation, wants and would act with a proper sense and zeal to promote their prosperity—If such could be found will they be chosen by the people? No—but few of the Merchants and those only of the

opulent and ambitious will stand any chance. The great body of farmers and planters cannot expect any of their order—the station is too elevated for them to aspire to—the distance between the people and their representatives will be so very great that there is no probability of a farmer or planter being chosen.—Mechanics of every branch will be excluded by a general voice from a seat—only the *gentry*, the *rich* and well born will be elected. Wealth creates power—the wealthy always have a number of dependents—they always favor each other—it is their interest to combine and they will consequently always unite their efforts to procure those of their own order or rank to be elected and they will generally succeed. The station is too high and elevated to be filled but by the *first men* in the state in point of fortune and influence. In fact no order or class of the people will be represented in the House of Representatives—called the Democratic branch—but the rich and wealthy. They will be ignorant of the sentiments of the middling class of citizens, strangers to their ability, unacquainted with their wants, difficulties and distress and need of sympathy and fellow feeling.

4. The numbers are too few. It is to consist at first of 65—and cannot exceed 1 for 30,000 inhabitants—whites and ⅗ slaves—a majority, a quorum 33—ergo 17 may make a law—liable to bribery and corruption. G.B. and F.[3] will endeavor to obtain an influence to procure treaties of commerce, and alliances offensive and defensive—they will practice the means—Holland is a proof.

This objection applies to the Senate—at first 26—14 a majority—8 may make a law—liable to same bribery and corruption. Madness to vest 25 men with absolute power—no free people ever reposed power in so small a number. The Executive will corrupt them—they are not excluded from office.

The last House of Commons above 500 members. Number of inhabitants about 8 millions—1 for little above 14,000—The numbers in the Democratic branches in 13 states amount to 2,000. The numbers should be too great to be corrupted and not so great as to be a mob.

5. The House of Representatives will *not* be chosen by the people. Art. 1. Sect. 2.

Maryland is to choose 6 representatives—every person qualified to elect members of our House of Delegates is to be entitled to vote. Our legislature is to prescribe the time, place and manner of electing representatives. Art. 1. Sect. 4. Aristides 9. Either the people at large of the whole state must choose the six representatives, or the state must be divided into six Districts for each to elect one man.—Say 2 on Eastern and 4 on Western shore.

If the whole people choose they will meet in their counties on the same day; this is proposed by some—consider such an election.

If in districts the inconvenience—and the last who vote will elect—and choice like as if all chose. Suppose our delegates chosen in this manner. On the whole I am convinced, 1st That the representation will be merely nominal from the persons and the numbers elected; 2nd That the right of electing is nugatory and cannot be effectually exercised—it is only a *fallacious participation* by the people at large in the national legislature.

6. There is no security even for this nugatory right.

7. I have said the *Senate* are too few in number.

8. The *Senate* are a perpetual *body* and never die a civil death (as in this State) although ⅓ is to be chosen every second year, because after the *first six* years there will always be ⅔ of the body in existence—⅓ of which ⅔ will always have served 2 years; and the other ⅓ will have served 4 years and after the first rotation every Senator may serve six years.—The body is permanent—will act by system—⅓ at end of every second year may be different men if legislature pleases.

9. In classing, the Senator who pleases will not be put in the class to go out before six years. Vide Boston Debates.

Samuel Chase was a lawyer, a member of the Continental Congress, and later a justice of the United States Supreme Court (see Samuel Chase entry in *Biographies*). A controversial leader, in these notes Chase discussed the need for better representation of the people in the proposed federal government. His speeches in the state convention built upon these valuable notes.

REFERENCES

Draft of notes in Bancroft Papers, New York Public Library; Storing, *Complete*, vol. 5.

NOTES

1. Chase often cites "Aristides," Maryland's Federalist Alexander C. Hanson, as well as Pennsylvania's James Wilson as those with whom he disagrees.

2. Robert Morris, Pennsylvania Federalist.

3. Refers to Great Britain and France.

William Paca, et al., "Address of the Minority of the Maryland Ratifying Convention," *Maryland Gazette,* May 6, 1788

TO THE PEOPLE OF MARYLAND.

The following facts, disclosing the conduct of the late convention of Maryland, is submitted to the serious consideration of the citizens of the state.

On Monday, the 21st of April, the convention met in Annapolis, and elected the Hon. George Plater, Esq. president. On Tuesday they established rules for the conduct of the business; and on the same day the following question was propounded to the convention:—

"When a motion is made and seconded, the matter of the motion shall receive a determination by the question, or be postponed by general consent, or the previous question, before any other motion shall be received."

And the following question, viz.

"Every question shall be entered on the journal, and the yeas and nays may be called for by any member on any question, and the name of the member requiring them shall be entered on the journal."

Which two questions the convention determined in the negative.

On Wednesday, the proposed plan of government was read the first time, and thereupon it was resolved, "That this convention will not enter into any resolution upon any *particular part* of the proposed plan of federal government, for the United States, but that the *whole* thereof shall be read through a second time, after which the subject may be fully debated and considered, and then the president shall put the question. That this convention do assent to and ratify the same constitution? On which question the yeas and nays shall be taken."

On Thursday, the members who were opposed to the ratification of the constitution, without such *previous* amendments could be obtained as they thought essentially necessary to secure the liberty and happiness of the people (being confined by the last resolution to consider in one view the whole of the plan of government) stated some of their objections to the constitution.—The convention met in the evening, when Mr. Paca, member from Harford, having just taken his seat, rose and informed the president, that he had great objection to the constitution proposed, in its present form, and meant to propose a variety of amendments, not to prevent, but to accompany, the ratification, but, having just arrived, he was not ready to lay them before the house, and requested indulgence until the morning for that purpose.—The proposal being seconded, and the house asked if they would give the indulgence, it was granted without a division, and they adjourned *for that purpose.*—On Friday, at the meeting of the house, Mr. Paca rose and informed the president, that, in consequence of the permission of the house given him the preceding evening, he had prepared certain amendments, which he would read in his place and then lay on the table, when he was interrupted, and one member from each of the following counties, viz Frederick, Talbot, Charles, Kent, Somerset, Prince-George's, Worcester, Queen-Anne's, Corchester, Calvert and Caroline, and one member from the city of Annapolis, and one from Baltimore-Town, arose in their places, and declared for themselves and their colleagues, *"that they were elected and* INSTRUCTED *by the people they represented, to ratify the proposed constitution, and that as speedily as possible, and to do no other act; that after the ratification their power ceased, and they did not consider themselves as authorised by their constituents to consider any amendments."*—After this Mr. Paca was not permitted even to *read* his amendments.—The opponents continued to make their objections to the constitution until Saturday noon. The advocates of the government, although repeatedly called on, and earnestly requested, to answer the objections, if not just, remained inflexibly silent, and called for the question, that "the convention assent to and ratify the proposed plan of federal government for the United States?" Which was carried in the affirmative by 63 to 11.

The vote of ratification having thus passed, Mr. Paca again arose and laid before the convention his propositions for amending the constitution thus adopted; which he had prepared by leave of the house, declaring that he had only given his assent to the government under the firm persuasion, and in full confidence, that such amendments would be peaceably obtained, as to enable the people to live happy under the government;—that the people of the county he represented, and that he himself, would support the government with such amendments, but without them, not a man in the State, and no people, would be more firmly opposed to it than himself and those he represented. Sentiments highly favourable to amendments were expressed, and a general murmur of approbation seemed to arise from all parts of the house, expressive of a desire to consider amendments, either in their characters as members of convention, or in their individual capacities as citizens; and the question was put on the following motion:

"*Resolved,* That a committee be appointed to take into consideration and report to this house on Monday morning next, a draught of such amendments and alterations as may be thought necessary, in the proposed constitution for the United States, if approved of by this convention; and Mr. Paca, Mr. Johnson, Mr. S. Chase, Mr. Potts, Mr. Mercer, Mr. Goldsborough, Mr. J. Tilghman, Mr. Hanson, Mr. J. T. Chase, Mr. Lee, Mr. W. Tilghman, Mr. McHenry and Mr. G. Gale, were appointed a committee for that purpose."

A division was called for on this resolution, when there appeared 66 members for, and not more than 7 against, it.

And then it was resolved. "That the amendments proposed to the constitution by the delegate from Harford-county, should be referred to the above committee."

The committee thus appointed, and the convention adjourned to give them time to prepare their propositions; they proceeded with every appearance of unanimity to execute the trust reposed in them.

The following amendments for the proposed constitution were separately agreed to by the committee, most of them by an *unanimous* vote, and all of them by a *great majority:*

1. That Congress shall exercise no power but what is expressly delegated by this constitution.

By this amendment, the general powers given to Congress, by the first and last paragraphs of the 8th sect. of art. 1, and the second paragraph of the 6th article, would be in a great measure restrained: those dangerous expressions by which the bills of rights and constitutions of the several states may be repealed by the laws of Congress, in some degree moderated, and the exercise of *constructive* powers wholly prevented.

2. That there shall be a trial by jury in all criminal cases, according to the course of proceeding in the state where the offence is committed; and that there be no appeal from matter of fact, or second trial after acquittal; but this provision shall not extend to such cases as may arise in the government of the land or naval forces.

3. That in all actions on debts or contracts, and in all other controversies respecting property, of which the inferior federal courts have jurisdiction, the trial of facts shall be by jury, if required by either party; and that it be expressly declared, that the State courts, in such cases, have a concurrent jurisdiction with the federal courts, with an appeal from either, only as to matter of law, to the supreme federal court, if the matter in dispute be of the value of   dollars.

4. That the inferior federal courts shall not have jurisdiction of less than   dollars; and there may be an appeal in all cases of revenue, as well to matter of fact as law, and Congress may give the State courts jurisdiction of revenue cases, for such sums, and in such manner, as they may think proper.

5. That in all cases of trespasses done within the body of a county, and within the inferior federal jurisdiction, the party injured shall be entitled to trial by jury in the State where the injury shall be committed; and that it be expressly declared, that the State courts, in such cases, shall have concurrent jurisdiction with the federal courts; and there shall be no appeal from either, except on matter of law; and that no person be exempt from such jurisdiction and trial but ambassadors and ministers privileged by the law of nations.

6. That the federal courts shall not be entitled to jurisdiction by fictions or collusion.

7. That the federal judges do not hold any other office of profit, or receive the profits of any other office under Congress, during the time they hold their commission.

The great objects of these amendments were, 1st. To secure the trial by jury in all cases, the boasted birth-right of Englishmen, and their descendants, and the palladium of civil liberty; and to prevent the *appeal from fact*, which not only destroys that trial in civil cases, but by *construction*, may also exclude it in criminal cases; a mode of proceeding both expensive and burthensome; and also by blending law with fact, will destroy all check on the judiciary authority, render it almost impossible to convict judges of corruption, and may lay the foundation of that gradual and silent attack on individuals, by which the approaches of tyranny become irresistable. 2d. To give a concurrent jurisdiction to the State courts, in order that Congress may not be compelled, as they will be under the present form, to establish inferior federal courts, which if not numerous will be inconvenient, and if numerous very expensive; the circumstances of the people being unequal to the increased expence of double courts, and double officers; an arrangement that will render the law so complicated and confused, that few men can know how to conduct themselves with safety to their persons or property, the great and only security of freemen. 3dly, To give such jurisdiction to the State courts, that transient foreigners, and persons from other States, committing injuries in this State, may be amenable to the State, whose laws they violate, and whose citizens they injure. 4thly, To prevent an extension of the federal jurisdiction, which may, and in all probability will, swallow up the State jurisdictions, and consequently sap those rules of descent and regulations of personal property, by which men now hold their estates; and lastly, To secure the independence of the federal judges, to whom the happiness of the people of this great continent will be so greatly committed by the extensive powers assigned them.

8. That all warrants without oath, or affirmation of a person conscientiously scrupulous of taking an oath, to search suspected places, or to seize any person or his property, are grievous and oppressive; and all general warrants to search suspected places; or to apprehend any person suspected, without naming or describing the place or person in special, are dangerous, and ought not to be granted.

This amendment was considered indispensible by many of the committee, for Congress having the power of laying excises, the horror of a free people, by which our dwelling-houses, those castles considered so sacred by the English law, will be laid open to the insolence and oppression of office, there could be no constitutional check provided, that would prove so effectual a safeguard to our citizens. General warrants too, the great engine by which power may destroy those individuals who resist usurpation, are also hereby forbid to those magistrates who are to administer the general government.

9. That no soldier be enlisted for a longer time than four years except in time of war, and then only during the war.

10. That soldiers be not quartered in time of peace upon *private* houses, without the consent of the owners.

11. That no mutiny bill continue in force longer than two years.

These were the only checks that could be obtained against the unlimited power of raising and regulating standing armies, *the natural enemies to freedom*, and even with these restrictions, the new Congress will not be under such constitutional restraints as the parliament of Great-Britain; restraints which our ancestors have bled to establish, and which have hitherto preserved the liberty of their posterity.

12. That the freedom of the press be inviolably preserved.

In prosecutions in the federal courts for libels, the constitutional preservation of this great and fundamental right, may prove invaluable.

13. That the militia shall not be subject to martial law, except in time of war, invasion or rebellion.

This provision to restrain the powers of Congress over the militia, although by no means so ample as that provided by magna charta, and the other fundamental constitutional laws of Great-Britain, (it being contrary to magna charta to punish a freeman by martial law in time of peace, and murder to execute him,) yet it may prove an inestimable check; for all other provisions in favour of the rights of men, would be vain and nugatory, if the power of subjecting all men able to bear arms to martial law at any moment, should remain vested in Congress.

Thus far the amendments were agreed to.

The following amendments were laid before the committee, and negatived by a majority.

1. That the militia, unless selected by lot, or voluntarily enlisted, shall not be marched beyond the limits of an adjoining State, without the consent of their legislature or executive.

2. That Congress shall have no power to alter or change the time, place or manner, of holding elections for senators or representatives, unless a State shall neglect to make regulations, or to execute its regulations, or shall be prevented by invasion or rebellion; in which cases only Congress may interfere, until the cause be removed.

3. That, in every law of Congress imposing *direct* taxes, the *collection* thereof shall be *suspended* for a reasonable certain time therein limited, and on payment of the sum by any State, by the time appointed, such taxes shall not be collected.

4. That no standing army shall be kept up *in time of peace*, unless with the consent of two thirds of the members present of each branch of Congress.

5. That the president shall not command the army in person, without the consent of Congress.

6. That no treaty shall be effectual to repeal or abrogate the *constitutions or bills of rights* of the States, or any part of them.

7. That no regulation of commerce, or navigation act, shall be made, unless with the consent of two thirds of the members of each branch of Congress.

8. That no member of Congress shall be eligible to any office of profit under Congress during the time for which he shall be appointed.

9. That Congress shall have no power to lay a *poll-tax*.

10. That no person, conscientiously scrupulous of bearing arms in any case, shall be compelled *personally* to serve as a soldier.

11. That there be a responsible council to the president.

12. That there be no national religion established by law, but that all persons be equally entitled to protection in their religious liberty.

13. That all imposts and duties laid by Congress shall be placed to the credit of the State in which the same be collected, and shall be deducted out of such State's quota of the common or general expences of government.

14. That every man hath a right to petition the legislature for the redress of grievances in a peaceable and orderly manner.

15. That it be declared, that all persons intrusted with the legislative or executive powers of government are the *trustees* and *servants* of the public, and as such accountable for their conduct. Wherefore, whenever the ends of gov-

ernment are perverted, and public liberty manifestly endangered, and all other means of redress are ineffectual, the people may, and of right ought, to reform the old, or establish a new government; the doctrine of non-resistance against arbitrary power and oppression, is absurd, slavish, and destructive of the good and happiness of mankind.

The committee having proceeded thus far, all the members who voted for the ratification declared, that they would engage themselves under every tie of honour to support the amendments they had agreed to, both in their public and private characters, until they should become a part of the general government; but a great majority of them insisted on this *express* condition, that none of the propositions rejected, or any others, should be laid before the convention for their consideration, except those the committee had so agreed to.

The gentlemen of the minority, who had made the propositions which had been rejected, reduced to the necessity of accommodating their sentiments to the majority, through fear of obtaining no security whatever for the people— notwithstanding they considered *all* the amendments as highly important to the welfare and happiness of the citizens of the States, yet to conciliate, they agreed to confine themselves to the first three of those propositions, and solemnly declared and pledged themselves, that if these were added, and supported by the other gentlemen, they would not only cease to oppose the government, but give all their assistance to carry it into execution so amended. Finally, they only required liberty to take the sense of the convention on the three first propositions, agreeing that they would hold themselves bound by the decision of a majority of that body.

The first of these objections concerning the militia they considered as essential, for to march beyond the limits of a neighbouring State, the general militia, who consist of so many poor people that can illy be spared from their families and domestic concerns, by power of Congress, who could know nothing of their circumstances, without consent of their own legislature or executive, ought to be restrained.

The second objection respecting the power of Congress to alter elections, they thought indispensible. Montesquieu says, that the rights of election should be established unalterably by fundamental laws in a free government.

The third objection concerning previous requisition, they conceived highly important; they thought if money required by *direct* taxation could be paid with certainty and in due time to Congress, that every good consequence would be secured to the union, and the people of the State thereby relieved from the great inconvenience and expence of a double collection and a double set of tax-gatherers, and they might also get rid of those odious taxes by exise and poll, without injury to the general government.

William Paca practiced law, and served as governor and later as a district judge (see William Paca entry in *Biographies*). The principal author of the "Address," he summed up why the Antifederalists opposed ratification. He wanted to protect an independent judiciary, to limit the powers of a standing army, and to protect personal rights to freedom of speech.

REFERENCES

The "Address" was also printed in the Maryland *Gazette* in May 1788; Elliot, *Debates*, vol. 2.

John Francis Mercer, Address (Letter) to the Members of the New York and Virginia Conventions, *May 1788*

Gentlemen

The galling Chains of Despotizm under the oppressive weight of which nine tenths of our Fellow Mortals groan—the Tortures which unfeeling Tyranny has invented and fearlessly practiced in every Age and every Clime, are melancholy and terrifying proofs of the Incapacity of the *many* to defend those rights, which God and Nature gave them, from the artful and unceasing usurpations of the *Few:*—and they are frightful Lessons to teach us a watchful Jealousy of great and unnecessary Grants of Power and of Changes in a State of Society which we know to be mild and free—Still there are moments of national Languor and Lethargy which the Ambitious ever enterprizing mark with Alacrity and use with Success.—The People long unaccustomed in a good and guarded Government, to bold and selfish Designs in their Rulers, look up with an unsuspicious Confidence, to any alteration, which those entrusted with Power may propose—however unconstitutional the changes, if recommended by Men used to govern them, they seem to come forward under the Sanction of legal authority—if prepared in Secrecy—the public mind taken by surprize, and every Engine previously set in Motion—the unconcerted and unconnected Defence of Individuals is branded with the opprobrious Epithet of *Opposition* and overwhelmed in the directed Tide of popular Clamour—a clamour which a Number of wealthy Men may at all Times command at a small Expence from the most indigent of the Populace.

We forbear to remark on the Manner in which the Constitution proposed for the United States came forward—as the Circumstances are known to you, your own Feelings will render any Observations unnecessary.

The Object of our present Address is to prevent your forming unjust Conclusions from the Adoption of the Constitution in the State of Maryland by so large a Majority of the Convention and the subsequent dissolution of that Body, without proposing any Amendments.

Permit us to assure You that the Torrent which burst forth at the Birth of the Constitution had but little Effect on the Minds of many of us—and altho' it might prevent our having that weight with our Countrymen, in the first Paroxisms of Phrenzy which forever accompany great and sudden Revolutions in Government—we were yet determined not to be wanting in our Duty to the Republic, at that Moment when Reason should resume her Empire over the unagitated Minds of our fellow Citizens—from many Circumstances we despaired of this in Maryland untill the adoption of the Constitution—At that Period, when our Efforts could not be subjected to Calumniating Misrepresentation,—we expected that an Appeal to the reflection of our Countrymen, would be listened to with attention and produce those Effects which unanswered and unanswerable Reasons ought to command—All opposition being thus postponed and every necessary Step to inform the minds of our Citizens on one Side neglected while unremitting Exertions by a Number of wealthy and respectable Characters were continued on the other—it cannot be surprizing that the Elections were generally favorable to the Constitution—In a very few of the Counties did any Candidates propose themselves against it—very few voted and even in those Counties where the Opposition succeeded by such a decided Majority—those Gentlemen's offering was merely accidental. They had refused every Solicitation of the People and had actually determined not to serve in Convention until within 6 Days before the Election—

That the People of the State would have made alterations and amendments a Condition of Adoption, is a Question which from the above Circumstances it is impossible to decide—but that four fifths of the people of Maryland are now in favor of considerable Alterations and Amendments, and will insist on them,—we dont hesitate to declare (as our Opinion) to You and the world.— The difference between amending *before or after* adoption (provided it is amended) is certainly not worth a Distinction.—

We are persuaded that the People of so large a Continent, so different in Interests, so distinct in Habits, cannot in all cases legislate in one Body by themselves or their Representatives—By themselves it is obviously impracticable—By their Representatives it will be found on Investigation equally so— for if these representatives are to pursue the general Interest without Constitutional checks and restraints—it must be done by a mutual Sacrifice of the Interests, wishes and prejudices of the parts they represent—and then they cannot be said to represent those Parts, but to misrepresent them.—Besides as their Constituents cannot judge of their Conduct by their own Sense of what is right and proper—and as a representative can always in this view screen his abuse of Trust under the Cloak of Compromize, we do not see what check can remain in the Hands of the Constituents—for they cannot know how far the Compromise was necessary, and the representative wrong— and to turn out and disgrace a Man when they cannot prove him wrong, and when he will have of Course the voice of the Body he is a Member of in his Favor, would in the Event be found subversive of the Principles of good Government.—

Thus then the pursuit of the general Interest produces an unchecked Misrepresentation—but if Representatives are to pursue the partial Interests of the Districts they represent (which to recommend themselves to their Constituents it is most probable they will do) then the Majority must ruin the Minority, for the Majority will be found interested to throw the Burthens of Government upon that Minority which in these States present a fair Opening by difference of *Cultivation—Importation* and *property*—In such extensive Territories governed by one Legislature, the Experience of Mankind tells us that if not by Preference the People will at least be led gradually to confide the legislative

Power to the Hands of one Man and his Family—who alone can represent the whole, without partial Interests and this is or leads to unlimited Despotizm—

We have not that permanent and fixed distinction of ranks or orders of Men among us, which unalterably seperating the interests and views, produces that division in pursuits, which is the great security of the mixed Government we seperated from, and which we now seem so anxiously to copy:— . . . the New Senate of the United States will be really opposite in their pursuits and views from the Representatives, have they not a most dangerous power, of interesting foreign Nations by Treaty to support *their* views?—for instance the relinquishment of the navigation of Mississippi—And yet these Treaties are expressly declared paramount to the Constitutions of the several States and being the *Supreme Law*, must of course control the national legislature, if not supercede the Constitution of the United States itself—[T]he check of the President over a Body, with which he must act in concert, or his influence and power be almost annihilated, can prove no great Constitutional security; And even the Representative body itself—and much more the Senate—are not sufficiently numerous to secure them from corruption—for all Governments tend to corruption, in proportion as power concentrating in the hands of the *few*, renders them objects of corruption to Foreign Nations and among themselves—

For these and many other reasons we are for preserving the Rights of the State Governments, where they must not be necessarily relinquished for the welfare of the Union—and where so relinquished the line should be definitely drawn under the proposed Constitution the States exercise any Power, it would seem to be at the mercy of the General Government—for it is remarkable that the clause securing to them those rights not expressly relinquished in the old Confoederation, is left out in the new Constitution; And we conceive that there is not Power which Congress may *think* necessary to exercise for the *general welfare*, which they may not assume under this Constitution—and this *Constitution* and the Laws made under it are declared paramount even to the unalienable rights, which have heretofore been assured to the Citizens of these States by their Constitutional compacts.—

Altho' this new Constitution can boast indeed of a Bill of Rights of seven Articles—yet of what nature is that Bill of Rights? to hold out such a security to the rights of property as might lead very wealthy and influential Men and Families into a blind compliance and adoption—whilst the Rights that are essential to the great body of Yeomanry of America are entirely disregarded.—

Moreover those very powers, which are to be expressly vested in the new Congress, are of a nature most liable to abuse—They are those which tempt the avarice and ambition of Men to a violation of the rights of their fellow Citizens, and they will be screend under the sanction of an undefined and unlimited authority—Against the *abuse* and *improper* exercise of these special powers, the People have a right to be secured by a sacred Declaration, defining the rights of the Individual and limiting by them, the extent of the exercise. The People were secured against the abuse of those Powers by fundamental Laws and a Bill of Rights, under the Government of Britain and under their own Constitutions—That Government which permits the abuse of Power, recommends it; and will deservedly experience the tyranny which it authorizes; for the history of Mankind establishes the truth of this political adage—*that in Government what may be done will be done.*

The most blind admirer of this Constitution must in his heart confess that it is as far inferior to the British Constitution, of which it is an imperfect imitation as darkness is to light—In the British Constitution, the rights of Men, the primary objects of the social Compact—are fixed on an immoveable foundation and clearly defined and ascertained by their Magna Charta, their Petition of Rights and Bill of Rights and their Effective administration by ostensible Ministers, secures Responsibility—In this new Constitution—a complicated System sets responsibility at defiance and the Rights of Men, neglected and undefined are left at the mercy of events; We vainly plume ourselves on the safeguard alone of Representation, forgetting that it will be a Representation on principles inconsistent with true and just Representation—that it is but a delusive shadow of Representation proffering in theory what can never be fairly reduced to practice;—And after all Government by Representation (unless confirmed in its views and conduct by the constant inspection, immediate superintendance, and frequent interference and control of the People themselves on one side, or an hereditary nobility on the other, both of which orders have fixed and permanent views) is really only a scene of perpetual rapine and confusion.—and even with the best checks it has failed in all the Governments of Europe, of which it was once the basis, except that of England.—

When We turn our Eyes back to the scenes of blood and desolation which we have waded through to separate from Great Britain—we behold with manly indignation that our blood and treasure have been wasted to establish a Government in which the Interest of the *few* is preferred to the Rights *of the Many*—When We see a Government so every way inferior to that we were born under, proposed as the reward of our sufferings in an eight years calamitous war—our astonishment is only equalled by our resentment—On the conduct of Virginia and New York, two important States the preservation of Liberty in a great measure depends—the chief security of a Confoederacy of Republics was boldly disregarded and the old Confoederation violated by requiring Nine instead of 13 voices to alter the Constitution.—still the resistance of either of these States, in the present temper of America (for the late conduct of the Party here must open the eyes of the People in Massachusetts with respect to the fate of their amendments) will secure all that we mean to contend for—*The natural and unalienable Rights of Men* in a constitutional manner—At the distant appearance of danger to these. We took up arms in the late Revolution—and may we never have cause to look back with regret on that period when connected with the Empire of Great Britain, We were *happy, secure,* and *free.*

Mercer here demonstrates how states that ratified continued to argue against the Constitution and to influence the state conventions that had not yet voted (see John Francis Mercer entry in *Biographies*). Mercer had many friends in New York and Virginia, and in his address he attempted to offer his views about the excessive powers given to the federal government over the states.

REFERENCES

Storing, *Complete*, vol. 5; notes in Etting Collection, Mercer Papers, Historical Society of Pennsylvania.

10
South Carolina

May 12–23, 1788

Ratification #8, May 23, 1788

In favor 149–73

Rawlins Lowndes, Debate in the
South Carolina Legislature,
January 16, 1788

Mr. Lowndes desired gentlemen to consider that his antagonists were mostly gentlemen of the law, who were capable of giving ingenious explanations to such points as they wished to have adopted. He explained his opinion relative to treaties to be, that no treaty concluded contrary to the express laws of the land could be valid. The king of England, when he concluded one, did not think himself warranted to go further than to promise that he would endeavor to induce his parliament to sanction it. The security of a republic is jealousy; for its ruin may be expected from unsuspecting security; let us not therefore receive this proferred system with implicit confidence, as carrying with it the stamp of superior perfection; rather let us compare it with what we already possess with what we are offered for it. We are now under government of a most excellent constitution—one that had stood the test of time, and carried us through difficulties generally supposed to be insurmountable—one that had raised us high in the eyes of all nations, and given to us the enviable blessings of liberty and independence—a constitution sent like a blessing from heaven, yet we were impatient to change it for another, that vested power in a few men to pull down that fabric which we had raised at the expence of our blood. Charters ought to be considered as sacred things; in England an attempt was made to alter the charter of the East India company, but they invoked heaven and earth in their cause—moved lords, nay even the king in their behalf, and thus averted the ruin with which they were threatened. It had been said, that this new government was to be considered as an experiment; he really was afraid it would prove a fatal one to our peace and happiness—an experiment! what risque the loss of political existence on experiment? No, Sir, if we are to make experiments, rather let them be such as may do good, but which cannot possibly do any injury to us or our posterity. So far from having any expectation of success from such experiments, he sincerely believed that when this new constitution should be adopted, the sun of the southern states would set never to rise again. To prove this, he observed, that six of the eastern states formed a majority in the house of representatives (in the enumeration he passed Rhode Island, and included Pennsylvania.) Now was it consonant with reason—with wisdom—with policy, to suppose that in a legislature where a majority of persons sat whose interests were greatly different from ours, that we had the smallest chance of receiving adequate advantages? certainly not. He believed the gentlemen that went from this state to represent us in the convention, pos-

sessed as much integrity, and stood as high in point of character as any gentlemen that could have been selected; and he also believed, that they had done
every thing in their power to procure for us a proportionate share in this new
government; but the very little they had gained proved what we might expect
in future; and that the interest of the Northern states would so predominate,
as to divest us of any pretensions to the title of a republic. In the first place,
what cause was there for jealousy of our importing negroes? Why confine us
to 20 years, or rather why limit us at all? For his part he thought this trade
could be justified on the principles of religion, humanity and justice; for certainly to translate a set of human beings from a bad country to a better, was
fulfilling every part of these principles. But they don't like our slaves, because
they have none themselves, and therefore want to exclude us from this great
advantage; why should the southern states allow of this without the consent of
nine states? (Judge Pendleton observed, that only three states, Georgia, South
Carolina, and North Carolina, allowed the importation of negroes, Virginia
had a clause in her constitution for this purpose, and Maryland, he believed,
even before the war, prohibited them.) Mr. Lowndes observed, that we had a
law prohibiting the importation of negroes for three years, a law he greatly approved of, but there was no reason offered why the southern states might not
find it necessary to alter their conduct, and open their ports.—Without negroes
this state would degenerate into one of the most contemptible in the union,
and cited an expression that fell from general Pinckney, on a former debate,
that whilst there remained one acre of swamp land in South Carolina, he should
raise his voice against restricting the importation of negroes. Even in granting
the importation for 20 years, care had been taken to make us pay for this indulgence, each negro being liable on importation to pay a duty not exceeding
ten dollars, and in addition to this were liable to a capitation tax. Negroes were
our wealth, our only natural resource, yet behold how our kind friends in the
North were determined soon to tie up our hands, and drain us of what we
had.—The Eastern states drew their means of subsistence in a great measure
from their shipping, and on that head they had been particularly careful not to
allow of any burthens—they were not to pay tonnage or duties, no not even
the form of clearing out—all ports were free and open to them! Why then call
this a reciprocal bargain, which took all from one party to bestow it on the
other? (Major Butler observed, that they were to pay five per cent. impost)
This Mr. Lowndes proved must fall upon the consumer. They are to be the
carriers, and we being the consumers, therefore all expences would fall upon
us. A great number of gentlemen were captivated with this new constitution,
because those who were in debt would be compelled to pay; others pleased
themselves with the reflection that no more confiscation laws could be passed;
but those were small advantages in proportion to evils that might be apprehended from the laws that might be passed by Congress, whenever there was
a majority of representatives from the Eastern states, who were governed by
prejudices and ideas extremely different from ours. He was afraid in the present instance that so much partiality prevailed for this new constitution, that
opposition from him would be fruitless; however he felt so much the importance of the subject, that he hoped the house would indulge him in a few words
to take a view comparatively of the old constitution and the new one, in point

of modesty.—Congress, labouring under many difficulties, asked to regulate commerce for 21 years, when the power reverted into the hands of those who originally gave it; but this infallible new constitution eased us of any more trouble, for it was to regulate commerce *ad infinitum*; and thus called upon us to pledge ourselves and posterity forever in support of their measures; so that when our local legislature had dwindled down to the confined powers of a corporation, we should be liable to taxes and excise; not perhaps payable in paper, but in specie. However they need not be uneasy, since every thing would be managed in future by great men, and great men every body knew were incapable of acting under influence of mistake or prejudice—they always were infallible—so that if at any future period we should smart under laws which bore hard upon us, and think proper to remonstrate, the answer would probably be—Go, you are totally incapable of managing for yourselves—go mind your private affairs—trouble not yourselves with public concerns—*mind your business*—the latter expression was already the motto of some coppers in circulation, and he thought it would soon be the style of language held out towards the southern states. The honorable member apologized for going into the merits of this new constitution, when it was ultimately to be decided on by another tribunal, but understanding that he differed in opinion with his constituents, who were opposed to electing any person as a member of the convention that did not approve of the proposed plan of government; he should not therefore have an opportunity of expressing those sentiments which occurred to him on considering the plan for a new federal government. But if it was sanctioned by the people it would have his hearty concurrence and support. He was very much originally against a declaration of independency—he also opposed the instalment law, but when they received the approbation of the people, it became his duty as a good citizen to promote their due observance.

A Charleston lawyer, planter, and state senator, Rawlins Lowndes became a leading Antifederalist spokesman in heavily Federalist Charleston (see Rawlins Lowndes entry in *Biographies*). In this speech, Lowndes explained that the flawed Constitution had not taken into consideration the many differences among the states. Lowndes understood that conflicting economic interests were irreconcilable, and he desperately wanted to protect those of his own region. He feared northern attacks on slave states and for that reason opposed ratification.

REFERENCE

R. Haswell (comp.), *Debates Which Arose in the South Carolina House of Representatives* (Charleston: City Gazette Printing Office, 1788).

James Lincoln, Debate in the South Carolina Legislature,
January 18, 1788

Hon. JAMES LINCOLN, of *Ninety-six*, declared, that if ever any person rose in a public assembly with diffidence, he then did; if ever any person felt himself deeply interested in what he thought a good cause, and at the same time lamented the want of abilities to support it, it was he. On a question on which gentlemen, whose abilities would do honor to the senate of ancient Rome, had enlarged with so much eloquence and learning, who could venture without anxiety and diffidence? He had not the vanity to oppose his opinion to such men; he had not the vanity to suppose he could place this business in any new light; but the justice he owed to his constituents—the justice he owed to his own feelings, which would perhaps upbraid him hereafter, if he indulged himself so far as to give merely a silent vote on this great question—impelled him, reluctantly impelled him, to intrude himself on the house. He had, for some years past, turned his thoughts towards the politics of this country; he long since perceived that not only the federal but the state Constitution required much the hand of correction and revision. They were both formed in times of confusion and distress, and it was a matter of wonder they were so free from defects as we found them. That they were imperfect, no one would deny; and that something must be done to remedy those imperfections, was also evident; but great care should be taken that, by endeavoring to do some good, we should not do an infinite deal of mischief. He had listened with eager attention to all the arguments in favor of the Constitution; but he solemnly declared that the more he heard, the more he was persuaded of its evil tendency. What does this proposed Constitution do? It changes, totally changes, the form of your present government. From a well-digested, well-formed democratic, you are at once rushing into an aristocratic government. What have you been contending for these ten years past? Liberty! What is liberty? The power of governing yourselves. If you adopt this Constitution, have you this power? No: you give it into the hands of a set of men who live one thousand miles distant from you. Let the people but once trust their liberties out of their own hands, and what will be the consequence? First, a haughty, imperious aristocracy; and ultimately, a tyrannical monarchy. No people on earth are, at this day, so free as the people of America. All other nations are, more or less, in a state of slavery. They owe their constitutions partly to chance, and partly to the sword; but that of America is the offspring of their choice—the darling of their bosom: and was there ever an instance in the world that a people in this situation, possessing all that Heaven could give on earth, all that human wisdom and valor could procure—was there ever a people so situated, as calmly and deliberately to convene themselves together for the express purpose of considering whether they should give away or retain those inestimable blessings? In the name of God, were we a parcel of children, who would cry and quarrel for a hobby-horse, which, when we were once in possession of, we quarrel with and throw it away? It is said this Constitution is an experiment; but all regular-bred physicians are cautious of experiments. If the constitution be crazed a little, or somewhat feeble, is it therefore necessary to kill it in order to cure it? Surely not. There are many parts of this Constitution he objected to: some few of them had not been mentioned; he would therefore request some information thereon. The President holds his employment for four years; but he may hold it for fourteen times four years: in short, he may hold it so long that it will be impossible, without another revolution, to displace him. You do not put the same check on him that you do on your own state governor—a man born and bred among you; a man over whom you have a continual and watchful eye; a man who, from the very nature of his situation, it is almost impossible can do you any injury: this man, you say, shall not be elected for more than four years; and yet this mighty, this omnipotent governor-general may be elected for years and years.

He would be glad to know why, in this Constitution, there is a total silence with regard to the liberty of the press. Was it forgotten? Impossible! Then it must have been purposely omitted; and with what design, good or bad, he left the world to judge. The liberty of the press was the tyrant's scourge—it was the true friend and firmest supporter of civil liberty; therefore why pass it by in silence? He perceived that not till almost the very end of the Constitution was there any provision made for the nature or form of government we were to live under: he contended it should have been the very first article; it should have been, as it were, the groundwork or foundation on which it should have been built. But how is it? At the very end of the Constitution, there is a clause which says,—"The Congress of the United States shall guaranty to each state a republican form of government." But pray, who are the United States?—A President and four or five senators? Pray, sir, what security have we for a republican form of government, when it depends on the mere will and pleasure of a few men, who, with an army, navy, and rich treasury at their back, may change and alter it as they please? It may be said they will be sworn. Sir, the king of Great Britain, at his coronation, swore to govern his subjects with justice and mercy. We were then his subjects, and continued so for a long time after. He would be glad to know how he observed his oath. If, then, the king of Great Britain forswore himself, what security have we that a future President and four or five senators—men like himself—will think more solemnly of so sacred an obligation than he did?

Why was not this Constitution ushered in with the bill of rights? Are the people to have no rights? Perhaps this same President and Senate would, by and by, declare them. He much feared they would. He concluded by returning his hearty thanks to the gentleman who had so nobly opposed this Constitution: it was supporting the cause of the people; and if ever any one deserved the title of man of the people, he, on this occasion, most certainly did.

James Lincoln, a farmer and legislator, spoke against the Constitution in the state legislature and later at the state ratification convention because he feared a distant government could not protect personal liberties (see James Lincoln entry in *Biographies*). He also claimed that the distant government would breed a detached aristocracy with no responsibility to the voters.

REFERENCE

Haswell (comp.), *Debates Which Arose in the South Carolina House of Representatives.*

Patrick Dollard, Speech in the South Carolina State Ratification Convention, *May 21, 1788*

I rise with the greatest diffidence to speak on this occasion, not only knowing myself unequal to the task, but believing this to be the most important question that ever the good people of this state were called together to deliberate upon. This constitution has been ably supported, and ingeniously glossed over by many able and respectable gentlemen in this house, whose reasoning, aided by the most accurate eloquence, might strike conviction even in the pre-determined breast, had they a good cause to support. Conscious that they have not, and also conscious of my inabilities to point out the consequences of its defects, which have in some measure been defined by able gentlemen in this house, I shall therefore confine myself within narrow bounds, that is, concisely to make known the sense and language of my constituents. The people of Prince Frederick's parish, whom I have the honor to represent, are a brave, honest and industrious people. In the late bloody contest they bore a conspicuous part, when they fought, bled and conquered, in defence of their civil rights and privileges, which they expected to transmit untainted to their posterity. They are nearly to a man opposed to this new constitution, because, they say, they have omitted to insert a bill of rights therein, ascertaining and fundamentally establishing the unalienable rights of men, without a full, free and secure enjoyment of which there can be no liberty, and over which it is not necessary that a good government should have the controul. They say, that they are by no means against vesting congress with ample and sufficient powers, but to make over to them or any set of men, their birthright comprized in Magna Charta, which this new constitution absolutely does, they can never agree to. Notwithstanding this they have the highest opinion of the virtue and abilities of the honorable gentlemen from this state, who represented us in the general convention; and also a few other distinguished characters, whose names will be transmitted with honor to future ages; but I believe at the same time, they are but mortal, and therefore liable to err; and as the virtue and abilities of those gentlemen will consequently recommend their being first employed in jointly conducting the reins of this government, they are led to believe it will commence in a moderate aristocracy, but that it will in its future operations produce a monarchy, or a corrupt and oppressive aristocracy they have no manner of doubt. Lust of dominion is natural in every soil, and the love of power and superiority is as prevailing in the United States at present as in any part of the earth; yet in this country, depraved as it is, there still remains a strong regard for liberty: an American bosom is apt to glow at the sound of it, and the splendid merit of preserving that best gift of God, which is mostly expelled every country in Europe, might stimulate indolence, and animate even luxury herself to consecrate at the altar of freedom. My constituents are highly alarmed at the large and rapid strides which this new government has taken towards despotism. They say it is big with political mischiefs, and pregnant with a greater variety of impending woes to the good people of the southern states, especially South-Carolina, than all the plagues supposed to issue from the poisonous box of Pandora. They say it is particularly calculated for the meridian of despotic aristocracy—that it evidently tends to promote the ambitious views of a few able and designing men, and enslave the rest; that it carries with it the appearance of an old phrase formerly made use of in despotic reigns, and especially by archbishop Laud in the reign of Charles the 1st, that is "*non resistance.*" They say they will resist against it—that they will not accept of it unless compelled by force of arms, which this new constitution plainly threatens; and then, they say, your standing army, like Turkish Janizaries enforcing despotic laws, must ram it down their throats with the points of Bayonets. They warn the gentlemen of this convention, as the guardians of their liberty, to beware how they will be accessary to the disposal of, or rather sacrificing their dear bought rights and privileges. This is the sense and language, Mr. President, of the people; and it is an old saying, and I believe, a very true one, that the general voice of the people is the voice of God. The general voice of the people to whom I am responsible is against it; I shall never betray the trust reposed in me by them, therefore shall give it my hearty dissent.

As the state convention neared its inevitable conclusion, Patrick Dollard, a planter and later state judge, claimed the Constitution created a corrupt aristocracy (see Patrick Dollard entry in *Biographies*). Speaking to the people who elected him to the convention, Dollard insisted he would never betray their trust. Since small government and the protection of their rights were important to them, he vowed to vote against the Constitution.

REFERENCE

Elliot, *Debates*, vol. 4.

Aedanus Burke, Letter to John Lamb,
June 23, 1788

Your favour of the 19th. of May I received the 18th. of June inst. That it came not to hand sooner, I cannot account for; however, it came too late; for our Convention had acceded to the new Constitution on the 24th. of May by a Majority of   The minority consisting of 73.

(It is now unnecessary perhaps to state to you the different causes, whereby the new Plan has been carried in South Carolina, notwithstanding ⅘ of the people do, from their Souls detest it.) I am convinced, from my Knowledge of the Country, that I am rather under, than over, that proportion. In the first place, we in the Opposition, had not, previous to our Meeting, either wrote, or spoke, hardly a word against it, nor took any one step in the matter. We had no principle of concert or union, while its friends and abettors left no expedient untried to push it forward. All the rich, leading men, along the seacoast, and rice settlements; with few exceptions, Lawyers, Pysicians and Divines, the merchants, mechanicks, the Populace, and mob of Charleston. I think it worthy of Observation that not a single instance in So. Carolina of a Man formerly a Tory, or British adherent, who is not loud and zealous for the new Constitution. From the British Consul (who is the most violent Man I know for it) down to the British Scavenger, all are boisterious to drive it down. Add to this, the whole weight and influence of the *Press* was in that Scale. Not a printing press, in Carolina, out of the City. The printers are, in general, British journeymen, or poor Citizens who are afraid to offend the great men, or Merchants, who could work their ruin. Thus, with us, the press is in the hands of a junto, and the Printers, with most servile insolence discouraged Opposition, and pushed forward publications in its favour; for no one wrote against it.

But the principle cause was holding the Convention in the City, where there are not fifty Inhabitants who are not friendly to it. The Merchants and leading Men kept open houses for the back and low country Members during the whole time the Convention sat. The sixth day after we sat, despatches arrived, bringing an account that Maryland had acceded to the Scheme. This was a severe blow to us; for next day, one of our best speakers in the Opposition, Doctor Fousseaux, gave notice he would quit that ground, as Maryland had acceded to it. Upon which we were every day afterwards losing ground & numbers going over to the Enemy, on an idea that further Opposition was useless. But notwithstanding these Misfortunes, the few of us who spoke, General Sumpter, Mr. John Bowman, a gentleman of fortune and fine talents, of the low-country; myself and a few of the back country men, found it necessary, in supporting the Opposition, to exert the greater spirit and resolution, as our difficulties increased. (Our Minority is a respectable one, and I can with great truth assure you, that it represents by far a greater number of Citizens than the Majority— The minority are chiefly from the back country where the Strength and numbers of our republick lie—And although the Vote of the Convention has carried it, that has not changed the opinion of the great body of people respecting its evil tendency. In the interiour Country, all is disgust, sorrow, and vindictive reproaches against the System, and those who voted for it. It is true, the ratification of it was solemnized in our City, with splended procession and shew. We hear from the back Country, however That in some places the people had a Coffin painted black, which, borne in funeral procession, was solemnly buried, as an emblem of the dissolution and interment of publick Liberty. You may rely upon it if a fair Opportunity offers itself to our back Country men they will join heart and hand to bring Ruin on the new Plan unless it be materially altered. They declare so publickly: They feel that they are the very men, who, as mere Militia, half-armed and half-clothed have fought and defeated the British regulars in sundry encounters—They think that after having disputed and gained the Laurel under the banners of Liberty, now, that they are likely to be robbed both of the honour and the fruits of it, by a Revolution purposely contrived for it. I know some able Men among us, or such as are thought so, affect to despise the general Opinion of the Multitude: For my own part I think that that Government rests on a very sandy foundation, the Subjects whereof are convinced that it is a bad one.) Time alone will convince us.

This is the first time that I ever put pen to paper on the subject, and it is not for want of inclination to do it. Nobody views this matter from the point of light and view in which I see it; or if any one did, he must be crazy, if he told his mind. The true, open, rising ground, no one has dared to take, or will dare to do it,'till the business is all over. If you live two or three years, you will find the World will ascribe to the right Author, this whole affair, and put the saddle on the right Horse, as we say. I find myself approaching too near to forbidden ground, and must desist. I am sorry it hath been my Lot not to be able to serve the Repub. on the present Business, Virginia and New York adopting it (and of which I have no doubt) they will proceed to put it into Motion, and then you, and I, and all of us, will be obliged to take it, as we take our Wives, "for better, for worse". I have only one remark to make—Should any event turn up with you, that would require to be known to our republican Friends here, only make us acquainted with it. Should either Virginia or New York State reject it, the system will fall to pieces, tho other nine States may agree to it, and in such an Event, or in any other that may give us an occasion to serve the Repub. your communication will be duly attended to by me. I forgot to mention, that Mr Lowndes, would not serve in the Convention, declining to take his Seat; out of disgust to some leading men in the parish that sent him, he abandoned a Cause, which, I believe, he thought a just one.[1]

The Irish immigrant Aedanus Burke rose as a Charleston lawyer and political leader and later served in the United States House (see Aedanus Burke entry in *Biographies*). In this letter to New York's John Lamb, later printed in a New York Antifederalist paper and widely seen, Burke explained why South Carolina ratified the Constitution and why he continued to oppose it. He lamented South Carolina Antifederalists' powerlessness but urged the New York delegation to continue to argue for a bill of rights.

REFERENCES

John Lamb Papers, New York Historical Society; New York *Journal*, July 10, 1788.

NOTE

1. Lowndes said he had been defeated for election.

11
Virginia

June 2–27, 1788

Ratification #10, June 25, 1788

In favor 89–79

Richard Henry Lee, Letter to George Mason,
October 1, 1787

I have waited until now to answer your favor of Septr. 18th from Philadelphia, that I might inform you how the Convention plan of Government was entertained by Congress. Your prediction of what would happen in Congress was exactly verified—It was with us, as with you, this or nothing; & this urged with a most extreme intemperance—The greatness of the powers given & the multitude of Places to be created, produces a coalition of Monarchy men, Military Men, Aristocrats, and Drones whose noise, impudence & zeal exceeds all belief—Whilst the Commercial plunder of the South stimulates the rapacious Trader. In this state of things, the Patriot voice is raised in vain for such changes and securities as Reason and Experience prove to be necessary against the encroachments of power upon the indispensable rights of human nature. Upon due consideration of the Constitution under which we now Act, some of us were clearly of opinion that the 13th article of the Confederation precluded us from giving an opinion concerning a plan subversive of the present system and eventually forming a New Confederacy of Nine instead of 13 States. The contrary doctrine was asserted with great violence in expectation of the strong majority with which they might send it forward under terms of much approbation. Having procured an opinion that Congress was qualified to consider, to amend, to approve or disapprove—the next game was to determine that tho a right to amend existed, it would be highly inexpediant to exercise that right, but merely to transmit it with respectful marks of approbation—In this state of things I availed myself of the Right to amend, & moved the Amendments copy of which I send herewith & called the ayes & nays to fix them on the journal—This greatly alarmed the Majority & vexed them extremely—for the plan is, to push the business on with great dispatch, & with as little opposition as possible; that it may be adopted before it has stood the test of Reflection & due examination—They found it most eligible at last to transmit it merely, without approving or disapproving; provided nothing but the transmission should appear on the Journal—This compromise was settled and they took the opportunity of inserting the word *Unanimously*, which applied only to simple transmission, hoping to have it mistaken for an Unanimous approbation of the thing—It states that Congress having Received the Constitution unanimously transmit it &c.—It is certain that no Approbation was given—This constitution has a great many excellent Regulations in it and if it could be reasonably amended would be a fine System—As it is, I think 'tis past doubt, that if it should be established, either a tyranny will result from it, or it will be prevented by a Civil war—I am clearly of opinion with you that it should be sent back with amendments Reasonable and Assent to it with held until such amendments are admitted—You are well acquainted with Mr. Stone & others of influence in Maryland—I think it will be a great point to get Maryld. & Virginia to join in the plan of Amendments & return it with them—if you are in correspondence with our Chancelor Pendleton it will be of much use to furnish him with the objections, and if he approves our plan, his opinion will have great weight with our Convention, and I am told that his relation to Judge Pendleton of South Carolina has decided weight in that State & that he is sensible & independent—How important will it be then to procure his union with our plan, which might probably be the case, if our Chancelor was to write largely & pressingly to him on the subject; that if possible it may be amended there also. It is certainly the most rash and violent proceeding in the world to cram thus suddenly into Men a business of such infinite Moment to the happiness of Millions. One of your letters will go by the Packet, and one by a Merchant Ship. . . .

Suppose when the Assembly recommended a Convention to consider this new Constitution they were to use some words like these—It is earnestly recommended to the good people of Virginia to send their most wise & honest Men to this Convention that it may undergo the most intense consideration before a plan shall be without amendments adopted that admits of abuses being practised by which the best interests of this Country may be injured and Civil Liberty greatly endanger'd.—This might perhaps give a decided Tone to the business—

Richard Henry Lee wrote from New York to George Mason, just after the Confederation Congress had sent the Constitution to the states for their votes (see Richard Henry Lee entry in *Biographies*). A wealthy planter and senior leader of the Virginians in national government, Lee went on to serve in the first United States Senate. In this letter to his colleague and friend, Lee wrote of his desire to amend the Constitution, something he had been unable to persuade the Continental Congress to do. Lee's main concern was the protection of minority rights. He believed the Constitution provided for majority rule but made no provision for the minority.

REFERENCES

James C. Ballagh (ed.), *The Letters of Richard Henry Lee* (New York: Macmillan Co., 1911); George Mason Papers, Library of Congress.

George Mason, "Objections to the Constitution," circulated early
October 1787

There is no declaration of rights; and the laws of the general government being paramount to the laws and constitutions of the several States, the declarations of rights in the separate States are no security. Nor are the people secured even in the enjoyment of the benefits of the common law, which stands here upon no other foundation than its having been adopted by the respective acts forming the constitutions of the several States.

In the House of Representatives there is not the substance, but the shadow only of representation; which can never produce proper information in the Legislature, or inspire confidence in the people; the laws will therefore be generally made by men little concerned in, and unacquainted with their effects and consequences.

The Senate have the power of altering all money-bills, and of originating appropriations of money, and the salaries of the officers of their own appointment in conjunction with the President of the United States; although they are not the representatives of the people, or amenable to them.

These with their other great powers (viz. their power in the appointment of ambassadors and other public officers, in making treaties, and in trying all impeachments) their influence upon and connection with the supreme executive from these causes, their duration of office, and their being a constant existing body almost continually sitting, joined with their being one complete branch of the Legislature, will destroy any balance in the government, and enable them to accomplish what usurpations they please upon the rights and liberties of the people.

The judiciary of the United States is so constructed and extended as to absorb and destroy the judiciaries of the several States; thereby rendering law as tedious, intricate and expensive, and justice as unattainable by a great part of the community, as in England, and enabling the rich to oppress and ruin the poor.

The President of the United States has no constitutional council (a thing unknown in any safe and regular government) he will therefore be unsupported by proper information and advice; and will be generally directed by minions and favorites—or he will become a tool to the Senate—or a Council of State will grow out of the principal officers of the great departments; the worst and most dangerous of all ingredients for such a council in a free country; for they may be induced to join in any dangerous or oppressive measures, to shelter themselves, and prevent an inquiry into their own misconduct in office; whereas had a constitutional council been formed (as was proposed) of six members, viz. two from the eastern, two from the middle, and two from the southern States, to be appointed by vote of the States in the House of Representatives, with the same duration and rotation in office as the Senate, the Executive would always have had safe and proper information and advice, the President of such a council might have acted as Vice-President of the United States, pro tempore, upon any vacancy or disability of the chief Magistrate; and long continued sessions of the Senate would in a great measure have been prevented.

From this fatal defect of a constitutional council has arisen the improper power of the Senate, in the appointment of public officers, and the alarming dependence and connection between that branch of the Legislature and the supreme Executive.

Hence also sprung that unnecessary and dangerous officer the Vice-President; who for want of other employment is made President of the Senate; thereby dangerously blending the executive and legislative powers; besides always giving to some one of the States an unnecessary and unjust preeminence over the others.

The President of the United States has the unrestrained power of granting pardons for treason; which may be sometimes exercised to screen from punishment those whom he had secretly instigated to commit the crime, and thereby prevent a discovery of his own guilt.

By declaring all treaties supreme laws of the land, the Executive and the Senate have, in many cases, an exclusive power of legislation; which might have been avoided by proper distinctions with respect to treaties, and requiring the assent of the House of Representatives, where it could be done with safety.

By requiring only a majority to make all commercial and navigation laws, the five southern States (whose produce and circumstances are totally different from that of the eight northern and eastern States) will be ruined; for such rigid and premature regulations may be made, as will enable the merchants of the northern and eastern States not only to demand an exorbitant freight, but to monopolize the purchase of the commodities at their own price, for many years: To the great injury of the landed interest, and impoverishment of the people: And the danger is the greater, as the gain on one side will be in proportion to the loss on the other. Whereas requiring two-thirds of the members present in both houses would have produced mutual moderation, promoted the general interest and removed an insuperable objection to the adoption of the government.

Under their own construction of the general clause at the end of the enumerated powers, the Congress may grant monopolies in trade and commerce, constitute new crimes, inflict unusual and severe punishments, and extend their power as far as they shall think proper; so that the State Legislatures have no security for the powers now presumed to remain to them; or the people for their rights.

There is no declaration of any kind for preserving the liberty of the press, the trial by jury in civil causes; nor against the danger of standing armies in time of peace.

The State Legislatures are restrained from laying export duties on their own produce.

The general Legislature is restrained from prohibiting the further importation of slaves for twenty odd years; though such importations render the United States weaker, and more vulnerable, and less capable of defence.[1]

Both the general Legislature and the State Legislatures are expressly prohibited making ex post facto laws; though there never was nor can be a Legislature but must and will make such laws, when necessity and the public safety require them, which will hereafter be a breach of all the constitutions in the Union, and afford precedents for other innovations.

This government will commence in a moderate aristocracy; it is at present impossible to foresee whether it will, in its operation, produce a monarchy, or a corrupt oppressive aristocracy; it will most probably vibrate some years between the two, and then terminate between the one and the other.

The shy but brilliant political thinker George Mason had served in the state legislature and had resigned from the Constitutional Convention refusing to vote in its favor (see George Mason entry in *Biographies*). In this article, later reprinted and circulated widely, Mason argued that the proposed Constitution created an aristocratic form of government rather than a republic. He claimed the lower house had too little power to counter the proposed Senate's authority to control money bills. Above all, Mason opposed the Constitution because it lacked a bill of rights such as Virginia had written in its state constitution.

REFERENCES

Elliot, *Debates*, vol. 1; printed more than thirty times, including in the *Massachusetts Sentinel*, November 21, 1787 (see Saul Cornell, *The Other Founders*); *Virginia Journal*, October 1787.

NOTE

1. Mason's own questioning of slavery's future is here apparent.

Joseph Jones, Letter to James Madison, *October 29, 1787*

DEAR SIR,—On my arrival in Richmond the other day I found your favor of the 7th from New York, with some newspapers inclosed. Mr. Thomas Pleasants who called on me the next day inquired whether I had lately heard from you, which being acknowledged brought forward a conversation on the new constitution, and finding him a strenuous advocate for it I asked if he had seen or read some pieces in favor of it under the signature of an American citizen. He said he had not. I then informed him I had received some papers from you, which contained three numbers on the subject and did not doubt he would be pleased with the perusal of them; whereupon he signified his desire to possess them. When I delivered them to him I told him it would not I thought be amiss if they were put into the printer's hands, that he might, if he thought proper, insert them in the newspaper here. He said he would think of it, and I have not seen him since. I shall speak to him on the subject as soon as I meet with him, but have no doubt he will endeavour to have them printed.

I must confess I see many objections to the constitution submitted to the conventions of the States. That which has the greatest weight with me lies against the constitution of the Senate, which being both legislative and executive, and in some respects judiciary, is I think radically bad. The President and the Senate too may in some instances legislate for the Union, without the concurrence of the popular branch, as they may make treaties and alliances which when made are to be paramount [with] the law of the land. The State spirit will also be preserved in the Senate, as they are to have equal numbers and equal votes. It is to be feared this body united with the President, as on most occasions it is to be presumed they will act in concert, will be an overmatch for the popular branch. Had the Senate been merely legislative even proportioned as they are to the States, it would have been less exceptionable; and the President with a member from each State as a privy council to have composed the Executive. There is also a strong objection against the appellate jurisdiction over law and fact, independent of a variety of other objections, which are and may be raised against the judiciary arrangements, and the undefined powers of that Department. I own I should have been pleased to see a declaration of rights accompany this constitution, as there is so much in the execution of the government to be provided for by the legislature, and that body possessing too great assertion of aristocracy. The legislature may, and will probably make proper and wise regulations in the judiciary, as in the execution of that branch of power the citizens of all the States will generally be equally affected.

But the reflection that there exists in the constitution a power that may oppress, makes the mind uneasy, and that oppression may and will result from the appellate power of unsettling facts does to me appear beyond a doubt. To rehearse the doubts and difficulties that arise in my mind when I reflect on this part of the judiciary power would I am sure to you be unnecessary.

It would be more troublesome than useful to recite the variety of objections that some raise; some of more, others of inconsiderable weight. Could I see a change in the constitution of the Senate and the right of unsettling facts removed from the Court of Appeals, I could with much less reluctance yield my assent to the system. I could wish, I own, to see some other alterations take place, but for the accomplishment of them, I would trust to time and the wisdom and moderation of the legislature, rather than impede the putting the new plan in motion, was it in my power, because I well know our desperate situation under the present form of government. It is at this time very difficult to inform you what is the prevalent opinion among the people. If we are to judge of them at large from their representatives here, they must be very much divided and I think the advocates for the new plan rather diminish than increase in number. You will have from the Executive an account of the proceedings of the Houses on the report of the Convention. I think they have taken a wise course in delivering it over to the people without conveying sentiments of approbation or disapprobation. At present nothing of consequence except the referring to the people the new constitution has been done in the Assembly. Tomorrow they are to discuss the recommendation of Congress respecting British debts. I think there will be a majority in the delegates for the repeal of the laws. How it will go down in the Senate, I am unable to calculate. You shall be occasionally informed how we go on.

Joseph Jones, a lawyer-planter and former member of the Continental Congress, served in the state ratification convention and later as a state judge (see Joseph Jones entry in *Biographies*). Jones wrote to his friend James Madison of the rising tide of Antifederalism in Virginia because of the threat to state government. Jones also wanted to have a declaration of rights appended to the Constitution.

REFERENCE

Worthington C. Ford (ed.), *Letters of Joseph Jones of Virginia, 1777–1787* (Washington: Department of State, 1889).

Arthur Lee (?) ("Cincinnatus"), I,
November 1, 1787

Sir, You have had the graciousness, Sir, to come forward as the defender and panegyrist of the plan of a new Constitution, of which you was one of the framers. If the defence you have thought proper to set up, and the explanations you have been pleased to give, should be found, upon a full and fair examination, to be fallacious or inadequate; I am not without hope, that candor, of which no gentleman talks more, will render you a convert to the opinion, that some material parts of the proposed Constitution are so constructed—that a *monstrous aristocracy springing from it, must necessarily swallow up the democratic rights of the union, and sacrifice the liberties of the people to the power and domination of a few.*

If your defence of this new plan of power, has, as you say, been matured by four months constant meditation upon it, and is yet so very weak, as I trust will appear, men will begin to think, that—the thing itself is indefensible. Upon a subject so momentous, the public has a right to the sentiments of every individual that will reason: I therefore do not think any apology necessary for appearing in print; and I hope to avoid, at least, the indiscriminate censure which you have, with so much candor and liberality, thrown on those who will not worship *your idol*—"that they are industriously endeavouring to prevent and destroy it, by insidious and clandestine attempts." Give me leave just to suggest, that perhaps these clandestine attempts might have been owing to the terror of *your mob*, which so nobly endeavoured to prevent all freedom of action and of speech. The *reptile Doctor* who was employed to blow the trumpet of persecution, would have answered the public reasoning of an opponent, by hounding on him the rage of a deluded populace.

It was to such men, and under such impressions, that you made the speech which I am now to examine; no wonder then that it was received with loud and unanimous testamonies of their approbation. They were vociferating through you the panegyric of their own intemperate opinions.

Your first attempt is to apologize for so very obvious a defect as—the omission of a declaration of rights. This apology consists in a very ingenious discovery; that in the state constitutions, whatever is not reserved is given; but in the congressional constitution, whatever is not given, is reserved. This has more the quaintness of a conundrum, than the dignity of an argument. The conventions that made the state and the general constitutions, sprang from the same source, were delegated for the same purpose—that is, for framing rules by which we should be governed, and ascertaining those powers which it was necessary to vest in our rulers. Where then is this distinction to be found, but in your assumptions? Is it in the powers given to the members of convention? no—Is it in the constitution? not a word of it:—And yet on this play of words, this dictum of yours, this distinction without a difference, you would persuade us to rest our most essential rights. I trust, however, that the good sense of this free people cannot be so easily imposed on by professional figments. The confederation, in its very outset, declares—that what is not expressly given, is reserved. This constitution makes no such reservation. The presumption therefore is, that the framers of the proposed constitution, did not mean to subject it to the same exception.

You instance, Sir, the liberty of the press; which you would persuade us, is in *no* danger, though not secured, because there is no express power granted to regulate literary publications. But you surely know, Sir, that where general powers are expressly granted, the particular ones comprehended within them, must also be granted. For instance, the proposed Congress are empowered— to define and punish offences against the law of nations—mark well, Sir, if you please—to *define* and punish. Will you, will any one say, can any one even think that does not comprehend a power to define and declare all publications from the press against the conduct of government, in making treaties, or in any other foreign transactions, an offence against the law of nations? If there should ever be an influential president, or arbitrary senate, who do not choose that their transactions with foreign powers should be discussed or examined in the public prints, they will easily find pretexts to prevail upon the other branch to concur with them, in restraining what it may please them to call—the licentiousness of the press. And this may be, even without the concurrence of the representative of the people; because the president and senate are empowered to make treaties, and these treaties are declared the supreme law of the land.

What use they will make of this power, is not now the question. Certain it is, that such power is given, and that power is not restrained by any declaration—that the liberty of the press, which even you term, the sacred palladium of national freedom, shall be forever free and inviolable. I have proved that the power of restraining the press, is necessarily involved in the unlimited power of defining offences, or of making treaties, which are to be the supreme law of the land. You acknowledge, that it is not expressly excepted, and consequently it is at the mercy of the powers to be created by this constitution.

Let us suppose then, that what has happened, may happen again: That a patriotic printer, like Peter Zenger, should incur the resentment of our new rulers, by publishing to the world, transactions which they wish to conceal. If he should be prosecuted, if his judges should be as desirous of punishing him, *at all events*, as the judges were to punish Peter Zenger, what would his innocence or his virtue avail him? This constitution is so admirably framed for tyranny, that, by clear construction, the judges might put the verdict of a jury out of the question. Among the cases in which the court is to have appellate jurisdiction, are—controversies, to which the United States are a party:—In this appellate jurisdiction, the judges are to determine, *both law and fact*. That is, the court is both judge and jury. The attorney general then would have only to move a question of law in the court below, to ground an appeal to the supreme judicature, and the printer would be delivered up to the mercy of his judges. Peter Zenger's case will teach us, what mercy he might expect. Thus, if the president, vice-president, or any officer, or favorite of state, should be censured in print, he might effectually deprive the printer, or author, of his trial by jury, and subject him to something, that will probably very much resemble the—Star Chamber of former times. The freedom of the press, the sacred palladium of public liberty, would be pulled down;—all useful knowledge on the conduct of government would be withheld from the people—the press would become subservient to the purposes of bad and arbitrary rulers, and imposition, not information, would be its object.

The printers would do well, to publish the proceedings of the judges, in Peter Zenger's case—they would do well to publish lord Mansfield's conduct in, the King against Woodfall;—that the public mind may be properly warned of the consequences of agreeing to a constitution, which provides no security for the freedom of the press, and leaves it controversial at least—whether in matter of libels against any of our intended rulers; the printer would even have the security of trial by jury. Yet it was the jury only, that saved Zenger, it was a jury only, that saved Woodfall, it can only be a jury that will save any future printer from the fangs of power.

Had you, Mr. Wilson, who are so unmerciful against what you are pleased to call, the disingenuous conduct of those who dislike the constitution; had you been ingenuous enough to have stated this fairly to our fellow citizens; had you said to them—gentlemen, it is true, that the freedom of the press is not provided for; it is true, that it may be restrained at pleasure, by our proposed rulers; it is true, that a printer sued for a libel, would not be tried by a jury; all this is true, nay, worse than this is also true; but then it is all necessary to what I think, *the best form of government that has ever been offered the world*.

To have stated these truths, would at least have been acting like an honest man; and if it did not procure you such unanimous testimonies of approbation, what you would have received, would have been *merited*.

But you choose to shew our fellow citizens, nothing but what would flatter and mislead them. You exhibited, that by a rush-light only, which, to dissipate its darkness, required the full force of the meridian sun. When the people are fully apprized of the chains you have prepared for them, if they choose to put them on, you have nothing to answer for. If they choose to be tenants at will of their liberties, by the new constitution; instead of having their freehold in them, secured by a declaration of rights; I can only lament it. There was a time, when our fellow citizens were told, in the words of Sir Edward Coke—For a man to be tenant at will of his liberty, I can never agree to it—*Etiam si* Dominus *non sit molestus, tamen miserremum est*, posse, *se vebit*—Though a despot may not act tyrannically; yet it is dreadful to think, that if he *will*, he *may*. Perhaps you may also remember, Sir, that our fellow citizens were then warned against those—"smooth words, with which the most dreadful designs may be glossed over." You have given us a lively comment on your own text. You have varnished over the iron trap that is prepared, and *bated with some illustrious names, to catch the liberties of the people*.

Arthur Lee, from a wealthy family, served in foreign service and in the Continental Congress (see Arthur Lee entry in *Biographies*). In this brilliant article, Lee attacked the Pennsylvania Federalist James Wilson, calling him a supporter of aristocratic government. Lee also claimed that Wilson did not care to protect individual liberties, and he called for the Constitution to include a declaration of rights.

REFERENCES

Richard Henry Lee, *Life of Arthur Lee*, 2 vols. (Boston: Wells and Lilly, 1829); New York *Journal*, November 1, 1787; Storing, *Complete*, vol. 6.

George Lee Turberville, Letter to James Madison, *December 11, 1787*

Will you excuse an abrupt tresspass upon your leizure—which has its rise from a desire to promote the welfare of Virginia & the Union a cause that has so long been the object of your pursuits—& that has already received so many beneficial supports from your attention—& still expects to receive so much future aid—from your Counsel—Assiduity & patriotism—?

Tis not sir to draw from you—your opinions—but merely to be informed of some parts of the Plan of Government proposed by the convention at Philadelphia—which appear obscure to a Reader that I have ventured to interrupt you, seeing that it is impossible to receive any information in the circle here—but what manifestly bears ye Stamp of faction—rancour—or intemperance—

Upon a question of Such importance—(on which perhaps it may be my lot to have a Vote) you will therefore excuse me for endeavoring to understand the subject as well as possible to the end that I may be enabled to form cooly & deliberately—such an opinion of it as my best abilities—aided by extreme attention—& all the information I can obtain—will admit—without further apology therefore I will proceed to mention such parts of the plan as appear obscure to me—always premising that it is not my wish to draw from you your own opinions, but only the reasonings thereon—& the objects thereof that weighed with the convention—

The principal objection that the opponents bring forward against this Constitution, is the total want of a Bill of Rights—this they build upon as an essential—and altho' I am satisfied that an enumeration of those priviledges which we retained—wou'd have left floating in uncertainty a number of non enumerated contingent powers and priviledges—either in the powers granted or in those retained—thereby indisputably trenching upon the powers of the states—& of the Citizens—insomuch as those not specially retained might by just implication have been consider'd as surrender'd—still it wou'd very much assist me in my determination upon this subject if the sense of the Convention and their opinion upon it cou'd be open'd to me—

Another objection (and that I profess appears very weighty with me) is the want of a Council of State to assist the President—to detail to you the various reasons that lead to this opinion is useless. You have seen them in all the publications almost that pretend to analyse this system—most particularly in Colo. Masons We have heard from *private persons* that a system of government was engrossed—which had an Executive council—and that the priviledge of importing slaves (another great evil) was not mention'd in it—but that a Coalition took place between the members of the small states—& those of the southern states—& they barter'd the Council for the Priviledge—and the present plan thus defective—owes it origin to this Junction—if this was the case it takes greatly off from the confidence that I ever conceived to be due to this Convention—such conduct wou'd appear rather like the attempt of a party to carry an interested measure in a state legislature than the production of the United Wisdom—Virtue—& Uprightness of America called together to deliberate upon a form of Government that will affect themselves & their latest Posterity.—

The operation of the Judiciary is a matter so far beyond the reach of most of our fellow Citizens that we are bounden to receive—& not to originate our opinions upon this branch of ye Federal government—Lawyers alone conceive themselves masters of this subject & they hold it forth to us *danger* & *distress* as the inevitable result of the new system—& that this will proceed from the immense power of the general Judiciary—which will pervade the states from one extremity to the other & will finally absorb—& destroy the state Courts— But to me their power seem's very fairly defined by the clauses that constitute them—& the mention of Juries, in criminal cases—seeming therefore by implication in civil cases—not to be allowed, is the only objection *I* have to this Branch—

Why shou'd the United states in Congress Assembled be enabled to fix on the places of choosing the Representatives?

Why shou'd the Laws of the Union operate agt. & supercede—the state Constitutions?

Wou'd not an uniform duty—impost—or excise of £5. pr. hhd on Tobo. exported—throughout the United states—operate upon the tobo. states alone? & have not the U.S. the power of levying this impost?

Why shou'd the states be prevented from raising a Revenue by Duties or Taxes—on their own Exports? Are the states not bound down to direct Taxation for the support of their police & government?

Why was not that truely republican mode of forcing the Rulers or sovereigns of the states to mix after stated Periods with the people again—observed—as is the case with the present members of Congress—Governors of this state &c &c—?

For what Reason—or to answer what republican View is it, that the way is left open for the importation of Negro slaves for twenty one Yrs?

May not the powers of the Congress from the clause which enables them to pass all Laws necessary to carry this system into effect—& that clause also which declares their Laws to be paramount to the Constitutions of the states— be so operated upon as to annihilate the state Governments?

If the Laws of the United states are to be superior to the Laws & Constitutions of the several states, why was not a Bill of Rights affixed to this Constitution by which the Liberties of individuals might have been secured against the abuse of Fœderal Power?

If Treaties are to be the Laws of the Land and to supercede all laws and Constitutions of the states—why is the Ratification of them left to the senate & President—and not to the house of Representatives also?

These queries if satisfactorily answer'd will defeat all the attempts of the opposition—many of them I can readily answer to satisfy myself—but I still doubt whether my fondness for the new government may not make me as improper a Judge in its favor, as the rage of the opposition renders those who are under its influence inadequate to decide even agt. it—

You will I hope my good sir excuse this scrawl which is scarcely legible it has been written by peice meals—& as I cou'd snatch an opportunity from the hurry of business—& from the noise & clamour of the disputants at ye house in which I lodge—the Mail is just going out and I have not time—to add the detail of State politics—but as I have written on the subject of the federal Constitution—I will Just detain you for a moment on ye present Situation of it in this state—

The people in the Country generally for it—the doctrine of amendments exploded by them—the Assembly I fear agt. it—Mr. Henry—Mr. Harrison—Mr. smith—All the Cabells & Colo. Mason—agt. or at least favorer's of the Amendatory system—& notwithstanding our Resolutions of the 25th. of October—I fear we shall still pass some measure that may have an influence unwarrantable & derogatory. Mr. Henry has declared his intention (and perhaps this day may see his plan effectuated) of bringing in a bill for the purpose of promoting a second Convention at Philadelphia to consider amendments—& that the speakers of the two houses shou'd form a Committee of Correspondence to communicate with our sister states on that subject—You know the force of this wonderful mans oratory upon a Virginia house of Delegates—& I am sure will with me lament that that force shou'd be ever erroneously or injudiciously directed—[1]

George Lee Turberville, a planter and state legislator, wrote to James Madison of his reservations about the Constitution and, in particular, the powers of the presidency and the dangers of the slave trade (see George Lee Turberville entry in *Biographies*). Turberville also lamented the absence of a bill of rights to protect individual freedoms.

REFERENCES

Bailyn, *Debate*, vol. 1; James Madison Papers, New York Public Library.

NOTE

1. Here Turberville has listed the state's major Antifederalists.

Spencer Roane ("A Plain Dealer"),
February 13, 1788

After a long and general expectancy of some dissertation on the subject of the proposed Fœderal Constitution, worthy the first magistrate of the respectable state of Virginia, a letter of his Excellency Governor Randolph, of Oct. 10, 1787, is at length presented to the public. Previous to the appearance of this letter, various opinions were prevailing in different parts of this country respecting that gentleman's *real* opinion on the subject of the said Constitution; and it became difficult for many to conjecture how his Excellency would devise a middle course, so as to catch the spirit of all his countrymen, and to reconcile himself to all parties. It was not known to me, at least, that his Excellency felt an "unwillingness to disturb the harmony of the legislature" on this important subject; nor could I conceive that the sentiments of even the ablest man among us could "excite a contest unfavorable" to the fairest discussion of the question. On the other hand, I thought it right that the adversaries of the Constitution, as well as its framers, should candidly avow their real sentiments as early and decidedly as possible, for the information of those who are to determine. It is true, his Excellency was prevented declaring his opinion sooner, "by motives of delicacy arising from two questions depending before the General Assembly, one respecting the Constitution, the other respecting himself;" but I am of opinion that during the pendency of a question concerning the Constitution, every information on that subject is most properly to be adduced; and I did not know that the being or not being Governor of Virginia, (an office in a great degree nominal) was sufficient to deter a real patriot from speaking the warning voice of opposition, in behalf of the liberties of his country.

The letter above-mentioned can derive no aid from panegyric, as to the brilliancy and elegance of its stile, for unlike the thread-bare discourses of other statesmen on the dry subject of government, it amuses us with a number of fine words. But how shall I express my dislike of the ultimatum of his Excellency's letter, wherein he declares "that if after our best efforts for amendments, they cannot be obtained, he will adopt the Constitution as it is." How is this declaration reconcilable to a former opinion of his Excellency's, expressed to the Honorable Richard Henry Lee, and repeated by the latter gentleman in his letter, as printed in the public papers, "that either a monarchy or an aristocracy will be generated from the proposed Constitution." Good God! how can the first Magistrate and Father of a free republican government, after a feeble parade of opposition, and before his desired plan of amendments has been determined upon, declare that he will accept a Constitution which is to beget a monarchy or an aristocracy? How can such a determination be reconcilable to the feelings of Virginia, and to the principles which have prevailed in almost every legislature of the union, who looked no farther than the amendment of our present republican confederation? I have charity to believe that the respectable characters who signed this Constitution did so, thinking that neither a monarchy nor an aristocracy would ensue, but that they should thereby preserve and ameliorate the republic of America; but never until now, that his Excellency has let the cat out of the bag, did I suppose that any member of the Convention, at least from the republican state of Virginia, would accept a Constitution, whereby the republic of his constituents is to be sacrificed in its infancy; and before it has had a fair trial. But his Excellency will adopt this Constitution, "BECAUSE HE WOULD REGULATE HIMSELF BY THE SPIRIT OF AMERICA." But is his Excellency a prophet as well as a politician—can he foretell future events? How else can he at this time discover what the spirit of America is? But admitting his infallibility for a moment, how far will his principle carry him?—why, that if the dominion of Shays, instead of that of the new Constitution, should be generally accepted, and become the spirit of America, his Excellency, too, would turn Shayite!— and yet this question of the Constitution, is "ONE ON WHICH THE FATE OF THOUSANDS YET UNBORN DEPENDS." It is his Excellency's opinion, as expressed in the aforesaid letter, that the powers which are acknowledged necessary for supporting the Union, cannot safely be entrusted to our Congress as at present constituted; and his vain objection is "that the representation of the states bears no proportion to their importance." This is literally true; but is equally true of the Senate of the proposed Constitution, which is to be an essential part of the legislature; and yet his Excellency will accept the latter, and not agree to invest the necessary powers in the former, although the above objection equally applies to both. Nay, I am inclined to believe that the injurious consequences of this unequal representation will operate more strongly under the new government—for under the present confederation the members of Congress are removable at the pleasure of their constituents;—whereas under the proposed Constitution, the only method of removing a wicked, unskilful or treacherous senator, will be by impeachment before the senate itself, of which he is a member.

These, Mr. Printer, are some of the inconsistencies which even a slight observation of the above letter will suggest. It is not my purpose to oppose now, or to investigate, the merits of the Constitution. This I leave to abler pens, and to the common sense of my countrymen. The science of government is *in itself* simple and plain; and if in the history of mankind no perfect government can be found, let it be attributed to the chicane, perfidy and ambition of those who fabricate them; and who are more or less, in common with all mankind, infected with a lust of power. It is, however, certainly not consistent with sound sense to accept a Constitution, knowing it to be imperfect; and his Excellency acknowledges the proposed one to have radical objections. A Constitution ought to be like Cæsar's wife, not only good, but unsuspected, since it is the highest compact which men are capable of forming, and involves the dearest rights of life, liberty and property. I fear his Excellency has done no service to his favorite scheme of amendments (and he too seems to be of the same opinion) by his very candid declaration at the end of his letter. Subtlety and chicane in politics, are equally odious and dishonorable; but when it is considered that the present is not the golden age—the epoch of virtue, candor and integrity—that the views of ambitious and designing men are continually working to their own aggrandizement and to the overthrow of liberty, and that the discordant interests of thirteen different commonwealths are to be reconciled and promoted by one general government; common reason will teach us that the utmost caution, secrecy, and political sagacity is requisite to secure to each the important blessings of a good government.

I shall now take my leave of his Excellency and the above-mentioned letter, declaring my highest veneration for his character and abilities; and it can be no impeachment of the talents of any man who has not served a regular apprenticeship to politics, to say, that his opinions on an intricate political question are erroneous. For if, as the celebrated Dr. Blackstone observes, "in every art, occupation, or science, commercial or mechanical, some method of instruction or apprenticeship is held necessary, how much more requisite will such apprenticeship be found to be, in the science of government, the noblest and most difficult of any!"

Spencer Roane, a young lawyer and state legislator, later became a famous state's rights judge in Virginia (see Spencer Roane entry in *Biographies*). Here he attacks Governor Edmund Randolph for joining the Federalists. He feared Virginians would be deprived of their rights in the new nation. That led to Roane's accusation that an aristocracy, perpetually reelected, would dominate the rights of individual states which had little power in the proposed government. One sees emerging here Roane's later defense of state's rights.

REFERENCE

Ford, *Essays on the Constitution.*

Richard Henry Lee, Letter to Edmund Pendleton, *May 26, 1788*

The manner in which we have together struggled for the just rights of human nature, with the friendly correspondence that we have maintained, entitles us, I hope, to the most unreserved confidence in each other upon the subject of human rights and the liberty of our country. It is probable that yourself, no more than I do, propose to be hereafter politically engaged; neither therefore expecting to gain or fearing to loose, the candid part of mankind will admit us to be *impartial* Judges, at least of the arduous business that calls you to Richmond on the 2d. of next month.

I do not recollect to have met with a sensible and candid Man who has not admitted that it would be both safer and better if amendments were made to the Constitution proposed for the government of the U. States; but the friends to the idea of amendments divide about the mode of obtaining them—Some thinking that a second Convention might do the business, whilst others fear that the attempt to remedy by another Convention would risk the whole. I have been informed that you wished Amendments, but disliked the plan of another Convention. The just weight that you have Sir in the Councils of your Country may put it in your power to save from Arbitrary Rule a great and free people. I have used the words Arbitrary Rule because great numbers fear that this *will* be the case, when they consider that it *may* be so under the new proposed System, and reflect on the unvarying progress of power in the hands of frail Man. To accomplish the ends of Society by being equal to Contingencies infinite, demands the deposit of power great and extensive indeed in the hands of Rulers. So great, as to render abuse probable, unless prevented by the most careful precautions: among which, the freedom & frequency of elections, the liberty of the Press, the Trial by Jury, and the Independency of the Judges, seem to be so capital & essential; that they ought to be secured by a Bill of Rights to regulate the discretion of Rulers in a legal way, restraining the progress of Ambition & Avarice within just bounds. Rulers must act by subordinate Agents generally, and however the former may be secure from the pursuits of Justice, the latter are forever kept in Check by the trial by jury where that exists "in all its Rights". This most excellent security against oppression, is an universal, powerful and equal protector of *all*. But the benefit to be derived from this System is most effectually to be obtained from a well informed and enlightened people. Here arises the necessity for the freedom of the Press, which is the happiest Organ of communication ever yet devised, the quickest & surest means of conveying intelligence to the human Mind.

I am grieved to be forced to think, after the most mature consideration of the subject, that the proposed Constitution leaves the three essential Securities before stated, under the mere pleasure of the new Rulers! And why should it be so Sir, since the violation of these cannot be necessary to *good* government, but will be always extremely convenient for bad. It is a question deserving intense consideration, whether the State Sovereignties ought not to be supported, perhaps in the way proposed by Massachusetts in their 1st. 3d. & 4th Amendments. Force & Opinion seem to be the two ways alone by which Men can be governed—the latter appears the most proper for a free people—but remove that and obedience, I apprehend, can only be found to result from *fear* the Offspring of *force*. If this be so, can Opinion exist among the great Mass of Mankind without competent knowledge of those who govern, and can that knowledge take place in a Country so extensive as the territory of the U. States which is stated by Capt. Hutchins at a Million of square miles, whilst the empire of Germany contains but 192,000, and the kingdom of France but 163,000 square miles. The almost infinite variety of climates, Soils, productions, manners, customs & interests renders this still more difficult for the general government of one Legislature; but very practicable to Confederated States united for mutual safety & happiness, each contributing to the federal head such a portion of its sovereignty as would render the government fully adequate to these purposes and *No more.* The people would govern themselves more easily, the laws of each State being well adapted to its own genius and circumstances; the liberties of the U. States would probably be more secure than under the proposed plan, which, carefully attended to will be found capable of annihilating the State Sovereignties by finishing the operation of their State governments under the general Legislative right of commanding Taxes without restraint. So that the productive Revenues that the States may happily fall upon for their own support can be seized by superior power supported by the Congressional Courts of Justice, and by the sacred obligation of Oath imposed on all the State Judges to regard the laws of Congress as supreme over the laws and Constitutions of the States! Thus circumstanced we shall probably find resistance vain, and the State governments as feeble and contemptible as was the Senatorial power under the Roman Emperors—The *name* existed but the *thing* was gone. I have observed Sir that the sensible and candid friends of the proposed plan agree that amendments would be proper, but fear the consequences of another Convention. I submit the following as an effectual compromise between the Majorities, and the formidable Minorities that generally prevail.

It seems probable that the determinations of four States will be materially influenced by what Virginia shall do—This places a strong obligation on our country to be unusually cautious and circumspect in our Conventional conduct. The Mode that I would propose is something like that pursued by the Convention Parliament of England in 1688. In our Ratificaton insert plainly and strongly such amendments as can be agreed upon, and say; that the people of Virginia do insist upon and mean to retain them as their undoubted rights and liberties which they intend not to part with; and if these are not obtained and secured by the Mode pointed out in the 5th article of the Convention plan in two years after the meeting of the new Congress, that Virginia shall be considered as disengaged from this Ratification. In the 5th. article it is stated that two thirds of Congress may propose amendments, which being approved by three fourths of the Legislatures become parts of the Constitution— So that the new Congress may obtain the amendments of Virginia without risking the convulsion of Conventions. Thus the beneficial parts of the new System may be retained, and a just security be given for Civil Liberty; whilst the friends of the System will be gratified in what they say is necessary, to wit, the putting the government in motion, when, as they again say, amendments may and ought to be made. The good consequences resulting from this method will probably be, that the undetermined States may be brought to harmonize, and the formidable minorities in many assenting States be quieted by so friendly and reasonable an accommodation. In this way may be happily prevented the perpetual opposition that will inevitably follow (the total adoption of the plan) from the State Legislatures; and united exertions take place. In the formation of these amendments Localities ought to be avoided as much as possible. The danger of Monopolized Trade may be avoided by calling for the consent of 3 fourths of the U. States on regulations of Commerce. The trial by Jury to be according to the course of proceeding in the State where the cause criminal or civil is tried, and confining the Supreme federal Court to the jurisdiction of Law excluding Fact. To prevent surprises, and the fixing of injurious laws, it would seem to be prudent to declare against making laws until the experience of two years at least shall have their utility. It being much more easy to get a good Law than a bad one repealed. The amendments of Massachusetts to be good so far as they go, except the 2d. and extending the 7th. to foreigners as well as the Citizens of other States in this Union. For their adoption the aid of that powerful State may be secured. The freedom of the Press is by no means sufficiently attended to by Massachusetts, nor have they remedied the want of responsibility by the impolitic combination of President & Senate. No person, I think, can be alarmed at that part of the above proposition which proposes our discharge if the requisite Amendments are not made; because, in all human probability it will be the certain means of securing their adoption for the following reasons—N.C. N.Y. R.I. & N.H. are the 4 States that are to determine after Virginia, and there being abundant reason to suppose that they will be much influenced by our determination; if they, or 3 of them join us, I presume it cannot be fairly imagined that the rest, suppose 9, will hesitate a moment to make Amendments which are of general nature, clearly for the safety of Civil Liberty against the future designs of despotism to destroy it; and which indeed is requir'd by at least half of most of those States who have adopted the new Plan; and which finally obstruct not good but bad government.

It does appear to me, that in the present temper of America, if the Massachusetts amendments, with those herein suggested being added, & were inserted in the form of our ratification as before stated, that Virginia may safely agree, and I believe that the most salutary consequences would ensue.[1] I am sure that America and the World too look with anxious expectations at us, if we change the Liberty that we have so well deserved for elective Despotism we shall suffer the evils of the change while we labor under the contempt of Mankind—I pray Sir that God may bless the Convention with wisdom, maturity of Counsel, and constant care of the public liberty; and that he may have you in his holy keeping. I find that as usual, I have written to *you* a long letter—but you are good and the subject is copious—I like to reason with a reasonable Man, but I disdain to notice those Scribblers in the Newspapers altho they have honored me with their abuse—My attention to them will never exist whilst there is a Cat or a Spaniel in the House!

In this thoughtful analysis of the various states' positions on ratification, Richard Henry Lee planned amendments to the Constitution (see Richard Henry Lee entry in *Biographies*). Here Lee also lays out his reasons why a large republic would be unable to reflect the will of the many different constituencies in the country. Soil differences, manners, and customs all made for conflicts no government could arbitrate. That is why Lee called for formal protection of the interests and values of the minority in the nation.

REFERENCE

Ballagh, *Letters of Richard Henry Lee*, vol. 2.

NOTE

1. Lee here is referring to the Massachusetts Antifederalists' proposal for a bill of rights.

James Monroe, *Some Observations on the Constitution*, *May 1788*

Gentlemen.

When you did me the honour to elect me into the Convention, to decide
for you upon the constitution submitted to the states from Philadelphia, I had
not at that time examined it with that attention its importance required, and
of course could give you no decided opinion respecting it. Other cares had unavoidably taken my attention from it. After you had reposed that trust in me
it became my duty to pay it a more serious attention. Having given it the best
investigation that my limited capacity is capable of, and perhaps formed in some
measure my opinion respecting it, subject however to alteration when I shall
be convinced that I am in an error, I should think myself unpardonable if I
withheld it from you. To you it belongs to approve or correct this opinion, for
although it would give me pain to be compelled to take a course which my
own mind did not approve, yet I have too high a respect for your rights, too
just a sense of my duty, and too strong an impression of gratitude for the confidence you have reposed in me, to act contrary to your wishes. Under this impression I have thought proper to make to you the following unreserved
communication of my sentiments upon this all important subject.

It will readily occur to you that this plan of government is not submitted
for your decision in an ordinary way; not to one branch of the government in
its legislative character and confined under the constitution to the sphere it has
assigned it; but to the people to whom it belongs and from whom all power
originates, in convention assembled. In this situation your present state constitution was, or should have been, formed, and in this situation you are of
course able to alter, or change it at pleasure. You are therefore to observe that
whatever act you now enter into, will be paramount to all others either of law
or constitution, and that in adopting this it becomes in reality the constitution
of the state, and binding on you as such. Whether it will absolutely annul and
do away that of the state is perhaps doubtful; my own apprehension is it will
not, except in those cases wherein they disagree; in these it will of course prevail, and controul all the departments of the state government, being the ul-
terior act of the people. You will therefore perceive it is a subject of great extent
and importance upon which you have to decide, and that you owe it to your
country, yourselves, and posterity, that it be well examined in all its consequences before it is determined.

When we contemplate the causes that might probably have contributed to make it necessary to submit to your decision the propriety of such a change in your political situation, we are naturally led into one of the following conclusions—either that the morals of the people have become corrupted—that the passions of mankind by nature render them unfit for the enjoyment of equal liberty, or that the form of the government itself under which we live is radically defective, and capable of such improvement, as will extend to us its blessings in a higher degree, and make them of longer duration. Believing firmly that the body of the people are virtuous, at least sufficiently so to bear a free government; that it was the design of their Creator in forming such an order of beings that they should enjoy it, and that it is only by a strange and unaccountable perversion of his benevolent intentions to mankind, that they are ever deprived of it, I will proceed to examine the latter hypothesis which supposes such defects in the present form, as to make a change adviseable. If we find that they really do exist, I will then proceed to suggest such remedies as will enable us comparitively to determine on the merits of that proposed to be substituted in its stead. I feel myself deeply impressed with the importance of this undertaking and am too well acquainted with my own inability, even to hope that I shall conduct myself with propriety through it, but from a sincere desire to establish a perfect good understanding between us, and prevent the possibility of any future and anxiety on this subject, I find myself constrained however painful it may be, and however ungracefully I may do it, not only to avow my sentiments respecting it, but the principles on which they are founded.

The present states were separate, from their first colonial establishments until the encroachments of Great Britain, compelled them into an union for their defence. But as their combined efforts soon promised to erect them into independent governments, the consideration which had united them for a time, and for the accomplishment of one object only, became perpetual, and the wisdom of their councils suggested the propriety of provisions that would secure them from like dangers for ever—under this impression they entered into the articles of confederation on the——day of——, 178 .[1] To this instrument or bond of union therefore we are to look for the strength, or imbecility, for the perfection or demerits, of the present fœderal government. As this is the system whose defects we have to remedy, it will be proper to present to your view concisely a summary of its powers.

The powers which have been given by these articles of agreement or confederation to the general government are extensive. They are to be found principally in the 9th and the 6th articles, in the former positively, and in the latter negatively by a qualification of the rights of the individual states. By the 9th, the United States are authorised to make war and peace—send and receive ambassadors—enter into treaties and alliances, provided that no treaty of commerce shall be made whereby the legislature of the respective states shall be restrained from imposing such duties on foreigners as their own people are subject to, or from prohibiting the importation or exportation of any species of goods or commodities whatsoever—establishing rules for deciding what captures shall be legal by land and water, and how appropriated; grant letters of marque and reprisal in time of peace—appoint courts for determining finally in all cases of captures; appoint courts for the decision of territorial controversies between states and individuals claiming lands under different grants from two or more states, whose jurisdictions respecting such lands have already been adjusted by the said court;—coin and regulate exclusively the value of coin throughout the United States—fix the standard of weights and measures—regulate the trade with the Indians not members of a particular state—establish and regulate post-offices—appoint all officers of land and sea forces, except regimental; make rules for their government and regulation and direct their operations—ascertain the necessary sums of money to be raised for the service of the United States appropriate, and apply the same—borrow money and emit bills of credit on the faith of the United States—build and equip a navy—agree on the number of land forces and make requisitions for the same. Provided that none of the said powers shall be exercised without the consent of nine states. By the 6th, the individual states are prohibited from sending or receiving embassies, entering into conferences, treaties or alliances with any foreign power, and the servants of the United States or individual states from holding offices of profit or trust under any foreign prince or potentate whatever—from partial confederacies without consent of Congress—from keeping up troops or vessels of war in time of peace except such as shall be approved by Congress—entering into a war with a foreign power unless invaded by an enemy—from granting letters of marque or reprisal except after declaration of war by the United States and then under particular restrictions only.

These articles give all the efficient powers to the United States—The 1st, 3d, 4th, 7th and 8th, although they establish some fundamental principles on which the government is to move, and especially the 8th the rule of apportionment, yet they give no real power; they are rather the rule by which the power already given is to be used than that they give any themselves. The 10th, 11th, 12th and 13th, fall still more under this exception or regulate other inferior objects of compact. But the 2d and 5th are of a different impression. By the former, each state retains its sovereignty, freedom and independence, and every power, jurisdiction and right, not expressly delegated to the United States and by the latter, that of appointing, continuing, or removing its own delegates at pleasure. These are the powers, and this the form, of the present government.

An attentive view of the subject will satisfy us that these powers are really great and extensive; they appear to have contemplated the greater part of those concerns wherein it might be supposed they had a national interest. Having made the United States the sovereign arbiters of war and peace, given them the right to require men and money, equip fleets and armies, to send and receive ambassadors, make treaties of alliance and commerce, with the very extensive catalogue which I have already enumerated, except the regulation of trade there seemed to be little left of external policy to the individual states. It is not my object to inquire here whether these powers should be more extensive. I may in the course of these observations; at present I shall examine more particularly the effect or operation of a government organised like this.

It is to be observed that by the 2d article the individual states retain their respective sovereignties, jurisdictions and rights in all cases not expressly ceded to the confederacy. And by the 5th they reserve the right of appointing, continuing or removing their respective delegations at pleasure. To these articles we are to look for the tone and character of this government, for upon these does its good or bad qualities depend. It is upon this point, that the present commotion hath taken place in America, and upon the merits of which we have to decide.

The deputies from each state being amenable for their conduct, and depending on it for their hopes and prospects, necessarily negotiate for its interests. This property or distinction pervades the whole body, and thus their general council or the Congress becomes a diplomatick corps, or a corps formed of ministers or representatives from sovereign states acting for the particular advantage of that to which they belong. The efforts therefore of each state, whatever may be the powers of the union over the several members that compose it, will be to shield itself from the common burdens of the government; and to effect this all the arts of intrigue and negotiation will be constantly exerted. What is the obvious course of a government organised on such principles? Are not the seeds of dissolution deeply ingrafted in it? The most powerful principles of human action the hope of reward and the fear of punishment are in the hands of each state, and whilst mankind are subject to their influences, or the passions and affections of the human heart continue as they have been, its course will always be the same. This government it is manifest can never be an efficient one. Strong necessity and emminent danger may make it so occasionally, but whenever this cause ceases to operate, its repellent principles will prevail. If this position is just, I am perhaps right in supposing it a consequence necessarily resulting from it, that the stronger the powers of the government are, the more repellent will its qualities be, and the sooner its dissolution; at least certain it is that the conflict between the general and state governments, will be proportionally more violent, and its or their ruin the sooner accomplished, for it must soon terminate either in that of the one or the other, I mean as an efficient government. The higher toned those of the states were the more rapid would the progress be. I think I may venture to affirm that a confederacy formed of principalities would not last long, for the pride of princes would not brook those familiarities and insults which a free discussion of rights and interests, especially if they interfere, sometimes unavoidably occasions; and when an absolute prince takes offence he wields the state with him. But this is not the case with democracies, for although their chief magistrates may be offended, yet it is difficult for them to communicate at the same time, the same passions and dispositions to the whole community which they themselves possess. This is a caution however which I hope it is not necessary to suggest here, for I am satisfied the state governments will never take this turn of themselves, nor whilst that of the confederacy is preserved and properly supported. But to carry this government a little further into practice.

Let us submit the concerns and interests of different states or individuals within them to this corps formed of representatives from each negociating for that to which they respectively belong, and what kind of justice may we expect from its decisions? If magazines were to be established or troops raised and stationed in some quarter of the union for public defence, might we not expect that these arrangements would take stronger byas, from the combination of the day, than any sentiment of propriety? If states or individuals within them had claims founded on the same principles with those upon which a decision had already been had in favour of others, are we to calculate with certainty upon a similar decree? In short apply it to every case that may possibly arise, either of states or individuals, in the full scope of its powers, and we shall find its decisions depend, more upon negociation, the bargain of the day, than any established maxim of justice or policy.

On the other hand how are its treaties, laws, or ordinances to be carried into effect? Are they of authority and in force immediately within the states as soon as they are passed? Or does it require the intervention of a state law to give them validity? And if the law is necessary may not the state refuse to pass it, and if she does how shall she be compelled? It is well known from the practice of all the states in the confederacy that no act of Congress, of what nature soever it may be, is of force within them, until it is recognized by their own legislatures, prior to that event it is a nullity, and to that only does it owe its authority. This view of the subject demonstrates clearly that the present government, in its ordinary administration, though a league of independent states for common good, and possessed of extensive powers, must always be void of energy, slow in its operation, sometimes oppressive, and often altogether suspended—that it can never be calculated on by foreign powers, and of course that they will form no treaties or compacts whatever with it, that stipulate any thing, at least on equal terms, that in fine very little dependence can be placed in it by the states themselves, for destitute of the power of coercion, to say nothing as to the justice or propriety of the measures themselves, these will not be forward to comply with its demands, whilst those may refuse with impunity. On the other hand the illustrious event which hath placed them in the rank of independent states demonstrates with equal certainty, that it is competent to external defence, and perfect security from abroad, for how otherwise could it have been achieved? These are the defects or the principal defects in the form of the present government, and they are inseparable from the league of independent states, for to that circumstance, and that alone they are to be attributed. We have then to weigh these evils, and compare them with the probable benefits and dangers that may accompany a change, and then see in which scale the balance preponderates.

It may be now asked are we reduced to this alternative either to subvert the state sovereignties or submit to these evils? Is the state sovereignty a vain and illusory hope, is it incompatible with its own and the general interests of the confederacy? Or is there any other alternative? The practice of nations and the field of enquiry is open before us, and we have every thing that is sacred and dear to mankind depending on the event. Two species of remedy only present themselves to my mind, and these contemplate either a complete annihilation of the state governments, or a partial one or considerable reduction of their powers. A complete annihilation and the organization of a general government over the whole, would unquestionably remove all the objections which have been stated above, and apply to it as a fœderal government; and I will be free to own that if it were in reality a practicable thing, there is no object which my mind has ever contemplated, the attainment of which would give it such high gratification. To collect the citizens of America, who have fought and bled together, by whose joint and common efforts they have been raised to the comparatively happy and exalted theatre on which they now stand; to lay aside all those jarring interests and discordant principles, which state legislatures if they do not create, certainly foment and increase, arrange them under one government and make them one people, is an idea not only elevated and sublime, but equally benevolent and humane. Whether it contains within it a territory as extensive as the Russian or German empires, or is confined in its operation to the narrow scale of their smallest principallities or provinces, yet it is the business of state legislation to pursue its destined course "the interests of those who live under it." For a legislature to contemplate other objects, and make a sacrifice of their own for the good of other people, or even decline availing itself of the legitimate exercise of its powers for that purpose, upon every opportunity which chance or fortune may present in its way, is a degree of liberality to which the human heart hath not as yet attained. A society of philosophers of the ancient stoick sect might perhaps be capable of such extended philanthropy, but this sect is now altogether at an end, and at its height, never formed but an inconsiderable part of any community, and was by all the rest of the world considered as affecting objects without the pale of human nature. How much more delightful therefore is it to the mind to contemplate one legislature organized over the whole continent, containing all the free inhabitants of the American states within it, nourishing, protecting, and promoting their interests in every line and extending its genial influence to every part; commerce flourishing, and increasing, lands rising in value, with all those other happy concomitants that attend a well formed and wisely directed government, than thirteen different legislatures, in pursuit of local objects, acting upon partial and confined considerations, without system or policy, jealous of their particular rights, dissatisfied with, and preying upon each other. If it were practicable, I should embrace this change with the utmost pleasure, and consider it the goal at which all our efforts should bend, the polar star that should direct all our movements. I should consider the abolition of the state legislatures as a most fortunate event for America, and congratulate my country on the commencement of a new area in her affairs from whence to date the dawn of better hopes and happier days. But is it practicable, can it be accomplished? Can a legislature be organized upon such principles as to comprehend the territory lying between the Mississippi, the St. Lawrence, the Lakes, and the Atlantic ocean, with such a variety of soil and climate, contain within it all the vital parts of a democracy, and those provisions which the wisdom of ages has pointed out as the best security for liberty, and be at the same time a strong, efficient, and energetic government? Would it be possible to form in every respect a complete consolidation of interest and how otherwise would its operation affect the weaker party? Or to accommodate its legislative acts so as to suit those of a local kind that were variant in the nature of things? To form a system of revenue, by direct taxation and excise, regulate the mode of collection, supervise it, without the establishment of a train of officers and tribunal under tribunal, that would not be enormously expensive, free from more than ordinary imposition, and preserve the spirit of the government? Separated at the distance of near 1200 miles, suppose the dispositions to do right the best that nature can infuse into the human heart, generally speaking in the operation of the government, will the man of Georgia possess sufficient information to legislate for the local concerns of New-Hampshire? Or of New-Hampshire for those of Georgia? Or to contract it to a smaller space of New-York for those of Vir-

ginia? Will not of course most of its measures be taken upon an imperfect view
of the subject? A wise legislator should possess a precise knowledge of the situation and interests of all the territory and of the state of society, manners, and
dispositions of the people within it committed to his care. Some men perhaps
to whom a kinder fortune had dispensed her more liberal gifts, who had devoted their earlier life to travels, general science, and those researches that were
particularly necessary for it, might succeed, but unfortunately for us the most
sanguine admirer of this plan, could not promise to America that her national
councils, should always be filled with men of this stamp. I would not wish to
discolour this plan of a complete national government, acting in all cases for
the common good, to the exclusion of subordinate legislatures, so delightful
in theory, with the reverse of this picture, nor to depaint those consequences
which might result from its maladministration, if instead of the best qualities
that are the portion of humanity, it should be its fortune to have its councils
filled, with men remarkable for their ignorance, or any great malignity of heart,
contending against difficulties, under its best form and with its best hopes,
which perhaps are insurmountable, what would be its situation and issue in
that event? As this subject is of great importance and leads to a decision upon
an important trait in the plan of government now before you, it will be proper
to give it a more particular investigation.

   Perhaps an attention for a moment in this respect to those political establishments which have been erected in different quarters of the globe, in ancient and modern times, may furnish an instructive lesson, upon the present
occasion. In but few instances, and those at distant intervals of time, hath a
democracy or government of the people ever been established. To what cause
it is to be attributed, philosophers and statesmen may differ, but it is an un-
questionable truth, that there hath been a constant effort in all societies, to ex-
terpate it from off the face of the earth. The contest hath been often violent,
and the manly exertions which the friends of equal liberty have made against
this disease of human nature, is the great, the instructive subject of history.
They have had to contend against difficulties thrown in their way by all ranks
of society: If the poor and those in moderate circumstances only, where an
union might have been expected had united, a tyranny had never been erected.
But the ignorance, the folly, and often times the vices of the lower classes have
perhaps favoured this tendency as strongly as the lust for dominion and power
in the wealthy. To illustrate this position by a review of the commencement,
progress, and decline of those nations with which history furnishes us examples,
with the causes that have contributed to hurry them to this their last stage,
would not only present to your view a melancholy monument of the weakness
of human institutions, but lead me beyond the bounds of the present enquiry.
Be assured however there is no fact better established by history, than this tendency or effort in all societies, to defeat the purpose of their own institution,
and terminate in despotism. If then we are not the unfaithful guardians of those
rights, which an all gracious providence hath bestowed upon us, should we not
attend to every circumstance that may contribute to preserve them? And will
it be questioned, that the extent of territory is one of those that will have no
influence on the subject? The governments that have been purely democratic,
to which only we should resort for satisfactory information upon this head, if

any ever were, are but few. In several it is true the people have had some share of power, as in that of Rome. But it cannot be questioned that in this the Nobles or aristocracy had the prevailing influence. The endless quarrels between the different branches or rather orders of the people, the Senate and plebians, is perhaps the real cause of the perpetual warfare and extensive conquests, made by this rapacious mistress of the world. When the people became incensed against the Senate, as they often had reason to be, the latter had always sufficient address, to give their passions other objects to act on, by turning them against foreign powers. With this view it seems to have been a political maxim with that branch, in whose hands the executive authority was also lodged, never to be at peace with all nations at the same time, and in this they succeeded tolerably well, for from the commencement to the final dissolution of the empire, the temple of Janus, always open in time of war, if we may credit the tradition of their best historians, was hardly ever closed. But so soon as the whole globe had acknowledged her authority, and bowed beneath the yoke, the immense fabric she had thus raised fell to pieces. External opposition that had raised it to the height it had attained, having ceased, its foundation was taken away. There was no principle within it to unite its parts together. From this it is to be presumed that if her government had been organized upon harmonious principles, and made the people happy under it, her dominion would never have extended over more than one-tenth the territory it did. But be this as it may, the government of Rome acknowledged distinct orders of people, in which indeed the aristocracy prevailed, and can of course furnish no example for us.[2] This may be said of Lacedemon and of Carthage, for according to the opinion of a profound historian and observer on the subject of government, that of Carthage was also divided and the greater portion of power taken from the people and placed in the hands of the aristocracy. If any ever were, Athens, Thebes, and Corinth, were for a time, pure democracies. But shall we draw our conclusion from their example, whose jurisdiction was more confined than that of some of our smallest states? In short, let us contemplate what forms, in what countries and time we please, where the rights of the people, and the spirit of liberty, were it any degree preserved, and we have the most solemn admonition to beware even making the attempt. The monarchy of Britain in which the executive power is armed with almost despotic authority, comprehends within it a territory smaller than that of this commonwealth, and yet it is believed its administration is happier than if it were more extensive. Even the king of France, sensible that his government will be happier for his subjects, and more faithful and beneficial for himself, has shewn a disposition to reestablish the provincial assemblies for this purpose, yet it cannot be denied that his powers are otherwise sufficiently great, or that any monarch was ever, in a greater degree, or more deservedly beloved by his people. But if these examples are not sufficient to warn us of the fatal consequences that will attend the vesting such powers in the Congress, let us turn our attention to those nearer at home, and which perhaps will make a deeper impression on our minds, and do we not behold the province of Maine separating from Massachusetts, Vermont from New York, Wyoming from Pennsylvania, and the district of Kentucky from Virginia, on this very principle, with others no less striking that might be enumerated.

It is true the improvement of government under this form, by representation, the discovery of which is attributed to modern times, might make some difference in this respect, but are there no bounds within which it should still be restrained? Shall it attempt things that seem from the concurrent testimony of all history to be the appropriate object of despotism? Maladies that are incurable after they have afflicted the body with all the pain and anguish incident, to a frail and feverish being, exhausted its efforts, and worn out its constitution, complete the work by terminating its existence. This government too, after having experienced the vicisitudes of fortune that might accompany its natural imperfections, of laws badly formed and indifferently executed, of anarchy disorder and confusion, after having worn out and broken the spirits of the people, would also have its end. But what form it would then assume is left for time to develope. The diseases of every government suggest its remedy. Other circumstances it is true give it a byas, but these have a principal influence in directing its course. Those of the federal system and which owed their birth and enormity to the want of strength in the federal head, had disposed the people to agree to an annihilation of their state governments, which yielded to the present one. Had this change been accomplished, by the designs of wicked and abandoned men, by the usurpations of a tyrant, or the seductions of art and intrigue, it is to be presumed, and the experience of other countries hath approved it, that the people would now return to that they had forsaken, with a degree of zeal and fervor proportioned to the sufferings they had borne. But if a long and patient experience had shewn its defects, a calm and dispassionate appeal had been made to their understandings, and a recollection of the great calamities, it had inflicted on them, demonstrated it was neither calculated, for the care of their liberties, their safety or common interests, they would make a new experiment and take a different course. From the causes above stated the incapacity of the legislative branch to form happy, wise, or uniform laws for the government of a territory so extensive, and of a people in pursuit of objects so opposite in their nature, had perhaps already often clogged its operations and suspended its course. This had gradually alienated the affections of the people and created in them a contempt for this branch of the government. The powers of the executive had of course been proportionably increased, for it is natural for the latter to supply the defects of the former. Accustomed to behold it in miniature, and to derive relief from its friendly interference, the people are at length prepared to have recourse to a Royal government, as the last resort the only safe assylum for the miserable and oppressed. And this perhaps would be the issue of the present government; and for these reasons I should dread its establishment over these states. For to however low and pitiable a condition we may have fallen; however deservedly we may have acquired the contempt and scorn of nations, yet I had rather submit in peace and quiet, to those reproaches which the proud and disdainful may throw upon us, than by commencing on a stage upon which the fortunes of all nations have been wrecked, however splendid and meteor like our transient exhibition might be, risk the enjoyment of those blessings we now possess.

But may not some middle course be struck, some plan be adopted to give the general government those rights of internal legislation necessary for its safety, and well being, in all cases, and yet leave to the states other powers they might exercise to advantage? If by this it is intended to comprehend the right of direct taxation and excise with the absolute control of the resources of the union, it will be easy to perceive its consequences. Those who are in any degree acquainted with the principles of government, or with those of the human heart well know that upon this point, the equal distribution of the resources of the union, between the two governments, will their balance depend. If you place the whole into the hands of one, it will require no casuistry, no great degree of depth in this science to determine which will preponderate. Acting on the bowels of the body will soon decay and die away. The pageant ornaments and trappings of power will not last long, for the reason and good sense of mankind turn with disgust upon the mockery of empty forms. Such an arrangement would therefore in my apprehension embark us on a more perilous and stormy sea, than even a complete annihilation of the state governments.

If then such a government as I have above described in either view presents an impracticable alternative, or such an one as we should not without a nearer and better view of it embrace, the other mode only remains or that which proposes the organization of a general government over the states forming a part of and acknowledged by the constitution of each, leaving at the same time a qualified government in each state for local objects. Let us examine this then since it is only the safe or even plausible course for us to take.

To organize a general government, that shall contain within it a particular one for each state, or in other words, to form a constitution for each state, which shall acknowledge that of the union, is no easy thing, for there never was an example of the kind before. The amphictionic council, Achæan, Belgic, or Helvetic confederacies were but leagues of independent states, somewhat similar to the present one. To mark the precise point at which the powers of the general government shall cease, and that from whence those of the states shall commence, to poise them in such manner as to prevent either destroying the other, will require the utmost force of human wisdom and ingenuity. No possible ground of variance or even interference should be left, for there would the conflict commence, that might perhaps prove fatal to both. As the very being or existence of the republican form in America, and of course the happiness and interests of the people depend on this point, the utmost clearness and perspicuity should be used to trace the boundary between them. The obvious line of separation is that of general and local interests. All those subjects that may fall within the former distinction, should be given to the confederacy, and those of the latter retained to the states. If the federal government has a right to exercise direct legislation within the states, their respective sovereignties are at an end, and a complete consolidation or incorporation of the whole into one, established in their stead. For in government it is, as in phisicks, a maxim, that two powers cannot occupy the same space at the same time. Let this therefore be the characteristic line of the division; internal legislation or the management of those concerns which are entirely local shall belong to the states, and that of those which have a foreign aspect, and in which they have a national concern, to the confederacy. In forming a constitution on these principles, the same rule should be observed, that has been in forming those of individual states; defining the powers given and qualifying the mode, in which they shall be exercised. All powers not ceded it is true belong to the people; but those given in a constitution are expressed in general terms, as that the Congress shall levy and collect duties; this involves in it the right of making laws for the purpose, for the means are included in the power; otherwise it is a nullity. The species of evidence and the mode of tryal are subordinate objects under it, and does it not follow that the Congress might regulate these at pleasure? How are we secured in the trial by jury? This most excellent mode of tryal which has been found, in those few countries where it has been adopted, the bulwark of their rights, and which is the terror of despotic governments, for it disarms them of half their power, is but a matter of police, of human invention; if then we gave general powers unless we qualified their exercise by securing this, might they not regulate it otherwise? I would not be understood to insinuate it would be the case, but that it were possible is improper. The spirit of the times might secure the people of America perhaps for a great length of time against it; but fundamental principles form a check, even when the spirit of the times hath changed, indeed they retard and controul it. As it is with the trial by jury so with the liberty of conscience; that of the press and many others. As to the powers themselves, the distinction being drawn, the enumeration would be of course. To those of the former Congress some few might be added, or from those of the constitution, some few taken away, for nominally there is not so great a difference between them as some people suppose. To the former for instance, let the absolute controul of commerce with the revenues arising from it be added. Let the right of apportionment be as in the constitution, for the ground on which the states have met on that point is certainly a happy compromise being that indeed which had been long recommended by Congress. Let them regulate the disciplining and training of the militia—the calling them forth and commanding them in service; for the militia of a country, is its only safe and proper defence. All countries are more or less exposed to danger, either from insurrection or invasion and the greater the authority of Congress over this respectable body of men, in whose hands every thing would be safe, the less necessity there would be, to have recourse to that bane of all societies, the destroyer of the rights of men, a standing army. But it may be urged the revenues from the impost would not be sufficient for national purposes, and that without the right of direct taxation, the government would be forced to have recourse, to the expedient of requisitions, the inefficacy of which had already been sufficiently experienced. The position in the first instance, as to the insufficiency of the revenues is doubtful; but the apprehension of the states neglecting requisitions under this, as they have done under the late government, still more so. When the United States became in effect a national government, by being incorporated with those of the states, possessed considerable revenues, had at their command a fleet and army, with the absolute controul of trade; I cannot but believe that their constitutional demands, or requisitions, would be complied with. Let the individual states also be restrained from exercising improper powers, making war, emitting paper bills of credit and the like. All restraints that were necessary for the wise administration of a good and virtuous government, would have my ready assent. It is not my intention to draft a form, a general idea is all I aim at, and in this perhaps I am tedious.

Having defined the powers, marked the line between, and secured as far as possible the harmony of the two governments, by making the former a part of the latter, it will be necessary to organize it upon such principles, as to secure the wisdom and happiness of its administration; for I presume it does not necessarily follow, because the constitutional acts of the government will be executed and become the laws of the land in each state that our researches should be at an end, and that we should conclude we had remedied all the defects of the present one. On the contrary our anxiety should be increased tenfold. From that our safety was to be attributed to its imbicility; but from this we should not be able to shelter ourselves under that protection. We should therefore be the more zealous, proportioned to the prize we have at stake, to distribute the powers and poize the government, so as to secure equal justice in all its acts, to every part of the confederacy; for wretched and forlon will the condition of that be, which shall not find itself equally secure under the protection, and in the enjoyment of its blessings, with every other part. From royalty itself, where the power is concentered in but one person, fluctuating in its systems and unsettled in its course, sometimes a ray of benevolence and even of justice is reflected on those whom it had marked out as the object of its resentment. Nature has cast into but few characters such malign and unfriendly dispositions, that their revenge cannot be satiated. But from a combination of states, acting systematically in pursuit of particular and local interests, wielding in their hands the powers of the government, and of course secure not only from censure but of the approbation and applause of those whom they served, however severely the attainment of the objects it contemplated, might bear upon the interests of the unfortunate minority, yet from their justice, it is to be feared, that neither moderation nor even mercy could be expected. But the present system is that we have to remedy and we should never loose sight of its defects. If the new government should be organized in the same manner with the old, consist of one branch only, each state appoint her own delegates and recall them at pleasure, I am satisfied it would in the administration in Congress, or passage of the acts, be found in the experiment in that respect, just such a government as the other. There would be the same negotiation, intrigue and management for the advantage of each state that now prevails. Its movements would be as slow and its decisions as unjust as they sometimes have been. In short it would still be a government of states in every respect and not a national one. How then shall we guard against, check and controul this intolerant and destructive state spirit? How infuse into all its departments a love, respect, and dread of the whole, for upon this every thing depends?

It has been long established by the most celebrated writers, but particularly illustrated and explained by the Prendent Montesquieu and Mr. Locke, that the division of the powers of a government over one state, or one people only, into three branches, the legislative; executive, and judiciary, is absolutely necessary for the preservation of liberty. This is now admitted by all who are not the friends of despotism, and I am persuaded it has already been demonstrated in the course of these observations, that such a division is, if possible, more necessary in a government to be organized over more than one. Taking this position then as established, I will proceed to an examination of the principles upon which this organization should be formed.

If the states as such or in their legislative character appoint any of the officers of this government, the effect will be the same, provided the rotative principle is preserved, which will I hope never be given up, that has already been experienced; for in the appointment is involved that of responsibility. It should therefore proceed from the people immediately, or by means of electors chosen for the purpose. This will make them amenable to the people only for their conduct, or to such constitutional tribunals where they are practicable, as they shall establish to take cognizance of offences. This we apprehend would contribute much to the establishment of a national government; each would move in the sphere the constitution had appointed for it, and be accountable to the people only for their conduct, the high and pure source, from whence they respectively derived their authorities.

The legislative branches are in all democratic governments, and of course would be so in this, the immediate representatives of the people. They should therefore be kept as dependent on them as possible, having in all respects the same interests with themselves. For offences in these branches the general government can provide no punishment, for there can be no tribunal under it, to take cognizance of them. Charges of corruption or prosecutions for it, or other offences, committed by those in these branches, should not be allowed from those in the others, for this might either unite them in mal-practices against their country, or create endless strife between them, and thereby destroy the balance of the government. A free people are the only proper judges of the merits of those who serve them, and they only should bring them to justice. This shews the necessity of frequent elections. The members of each should in my opinion return to the body of the people, those of the house of representatives at the expiration of every two years, and those of the senate of every four years, capable however always of re-election. Both these branches should if possible be filled on the principles of representation from all the states. For the house of representatives, the rule adopted in the constitution, is perhaps the proper one. Let twice that number, or a still greater ratio of numbers to that of representation, be the rule for the senate. The members of both branches should be incapable of appointment to other offices whilst in these, otherwise, a wide door will be left open for corruption. This is not an idle or visionary precaution, but in a great measure the pivot, upon which the upright and faithful administration of the government will depend. The experience of Britain hath demonstrated, how often the most valuable interests of the people, have been bartered away, by leading members of the house of commons for a seat in the house of peers, or some lucrative office in the government; how much greater then should our apprehension be, of danger in the present instance, when we recollect that the government is organized upon such principles as to acknowledge no responsibility to the states, and comprehends within it such an extent of territory, as to put it out of the power of those who inhabit its extremities, to have any knowledge of the conduct of their servants! The possibility of this kind of traffic should therefore be absolutely prohibited.

But the power of the legislature should be confined to those objects, which were intirely legislative in their nature, as the regulation of trade, requisitions for money, and the like. The soundest authorities and the melancholy experience of our state governments have shewn the propriety of this restraint, in a constitution over one state, and for reasons that are obvious the expedience, will be the more urgent, in the present instance. Its natural effort in all cases is, to grasp to itself all the powers delegated from the people, and to prostrate the other branches before it; stimulated on by the state spirit, which will in some degree still remain, the difficulty here will be proportionably increased. The ingenuity of man can devise no other, without an appeal to the people, which if possible should always be avoided, than that of giving the Executive, the other active branch an absolute negative on the laws; for otherwise its enterprizes must be successful. Many restraints might be designated by the constitution, but without effect. And from this at the same time that it preserved the balance of the government, no injury could be sustained. Against the encroachments of the Executive the fears and apprehensions of the whole continent would be awake, with a watchful jealousy they would observe its movements. But against the legislature (if we may reason by analogy of that branch in this) from those in other governments, no such apprehensions could be entertained. Its movements comparatively would be accompanied with the confidence of the people. Every incroachment upon its rights would be popular. In every contest between them it must of course yield the ground. In short unless the Executive had a negative on the laws of the legislature, it would soon exist only in name.

The right of impeachment and the mode of trial are of the first importance in this government. The former, if with the people or even the states themselves, would never be exerted or greatly abused; it should therefore belong to the house of representatives. And the latter should be vested in a court of that high confidence and respectability of character, as to partake of none of those passions that sway the bulk of mankind. Unconnected by office, and of course no way interested in the event; unacquainted with the crime except as it might appear before them by satisfactory testimony, they should hear calmly and judge dispassionately upon the merits of the cause. From their decision the guilty would receive a fair condemnation, or the innocent be restored again to the confidence of their country, and the people return satisfied that their passions had been awakened, and their fears alarmed without any just foundation. The sentence should be final, and not shifted off to another tribunal. A further prosecution may appear odious, and the just resentments of the people calm away, and totally subside. For these reasons the senate should form the court of impeachment.

But although the legislative branch shall be elected by the people, and amenable to them alone for their conduct, yet as the state sovereignties though qualified, will still remain, and of course the state spirit, in contradiction to a fœderal one, from necessity be more or less influential in its councils, we should turn our attention to the other branches of the government, as our firm resource. The Executive is that upon which, in many respects, we should rest our hopes, for an equal, a fœderal, and a wise administration. Every possible effort should therefore be used to expell from the hearts of those who fill it, a preference of one part of the community to another. The experience of other governments hath taught us, it is possible to devise checks, which from motives of policy and private interest, will even make bad men faithful public servants. The prospect of reward and the fear of punishment, as has already been observed, are the most powerful incentives to virtuous action. It should therefore be so organized, as to give every quarter indeed every man of the union, under the influence of these principles, as to those who fill it, an equal access to the human heart, whenever this equipoise is destroyed, and this high character taught to look up to this, or that state, or combination of states for the smiles or the frowns of government, from that moment will its oppression be felt, and a dreadful anarchy insue. And if you take from those whom the choice of their country hath called forth to this high station, the hope of further favour, and mark to them the extent of service, after the completion of which the door shall be forever closed upon them, in that degree will you deprive yourself of one of the principal instruments by which you are to preserve the equilibrium, and secure the public safety. Discharged forever from the service of the United States, will not the approbation of the union, cease to be the ruling passion, and an accommodation to state interests take its place and influence many of the public measures? For these reasons I could wish to see the right of impeachment, extended upon as liberal ground as possible, given for instance to the representatives of one third of the confederacy; and I could likewise wish to see the citizen at the head of this department, capable of re-election at the expiration of his service which should be at the end of every three or four years, so long as he should merit the confidence of his country.

The mode of election should also be a fundamental in the organization of this branch. If the command of this office was placed within the reach of court influence, the most alarming consequences were to be apprehended from it. If the ultimate decision should happen at the metropolis, it is easy to be perceived what an opportunity this would present for venality and corruption. It must be a great object particularly for either France or Britain to have the friend of their respective courts in this office, possessed of such extensive powers and which might dispense such important favours to them. The influence of the presiding magistrate himself, especially within the town in which he had for some time resided, and to whose citizens he had rendered many substantial services, and who of course would be averse to the introduction of a *novus homo* among them, would not be inconsiderable. In addition to which it is to be observed, that it forms a departure from a principle which should prevail through the whole, but particularly in the organization of this branch, a dependance of this officer, for every thing estimable among mankind, upon the people of America. By the people therefore should the appointment be made, not in person, but by the means of electors chosen for the purpose. To prevent the possibility of any interference, or byas on their free election, that of the electors by the people, should be on the same day in every state, and that of the President by the electors likewise on the same day and at some specified place in each, unless an invasion, or other extraordinary circumstance should prevent it; in which case perhaps the electors themselves, or the executive of the state might appoint some other. Whatever time might be employed in this mode of election is immaterial; it is of the first importance, and should never be dispensed with, that he be thus appointed.

But high power in the Executive branch require in every respect, a direct and immediate responsibility; for although it should be so organized as that whilst to those who fill it, and act with propriety in the discharge of its functions, the door should be left open for a continuance of public favour, yet the sword of justice should be held constantly suspended over the heads of those, who shall be convicted of having basely sacrificed the interests, or made attempts upon the liberties of their country. There should be no constitutional restraint, no equivocation of office, to shield a traitor from the justice of an injured people. No circumstance to blunt or turn aside the keen edge of their resentment. With the charge should the powers of his office cease. He should stand alone unsupported, and unprotected except by the integrity of his heart and the rectitude of his conduct. For these reasons the executive power should be vested altogether in one person; unrestrained by a constitutional council, its operations will be more easy and regular, and its responsibility the greater and more immediate. And for these reasons if there is a constitutional council it must be from its nature the most improper tribunal, that can be formed or conceived, for the tryal of the offences of the principal, since they must be either partakers of the crime, or some way or either a party interested in it.

With an Executive organized on these principles, being independent of the legislature, and in a very responsible situation, I should be well content to intrust great powers, because I should calculate with tolerable certainty upon an honest and a wise execution of them. The constitution perhaps suggests those, with some exceptions that are proper; whether it would be safe to give it the absolute controul of the fleet and army at all times, in peace and war, the ordering them out, and laying them by, without consent of the legislature, or even knowledge, is at least doubtful. In Great Britain this power may be committed to the King with propriety; but he is the Lord of hereditary dominions, and transmits the inheritance in his line forever. By betraying his trust he might lose his crown, and perhaps gain nothing, even if he established despotism. But with the President who perhaps depends on a quadriennial election the case is different. It is certainly a formidable power to place in the hands of any one public servant. I would however in no event interpose the opinion of the legislature, so as to controul the movements of these forces, but merely to affix the condition, or emergency, upon which his absolute power over them should commence. As I would repose the whole trust of this department in one officer, so he alone should be responsible for all its transactions. He might associate whom he pleased, of the wise men of America in his councils, but they should be of his own association. An allowance might be made him, to compensate them for their services, for which he should be accountable.

Controversies between independent nations are usually settled by the sword. It is to the misfortune of mankind that no tribunal has ever been established to adjust their interfering claims, and inforce its decrees. It has been the defect of all other confederacies, of whose institutions history has given us any account, that although attempts in some have been made in this respect to preserve the harmony, and lessen the calamities of mankind, yet the courts to whom their controversies have been submitted, the council or representative body of each, have not been organized on such principles as to insure justice in all their decisions. To this circumstance perhaps many of their calamities were to be attributed. The framers of the confederation in some degree also fell into this error for those only of a territorial kind were to be submitted to a fœderal court. Under that form its inconvenience has been often very sensibly felt, but under the present it would be insupportable. Great care should therefore be used, in the organization of this branch, to remedy this defect. The judiciary in this, as in all free governments, should be distinct from, and independent of the other branches, and equally permanent in its establishment. Performing its appropriate functions, the extent of its authority should be commensurate with theirs. As it forms the branch of a national government, so it should contemplate national objects only. Whatever cases might arise under the constitution, the laws of the legislature, and the acts of the Executive in conformity thereto, (however trifling or important the interests it affected might be) should have their final decision from this court. All cases affecting ambassadors, other public ministers and consuls—of admiralty and maritime jurisdiction—all controversies between different states—between the United States and a state—a state and the citizens of another state, citizens of the same state claiming lands under different states, should of course be submitted to its decision. In cases affecting ambassadors, other public ministers and consuls, and in which a state shall be a party, the Supreme Court should have original jurisdiction; in the other cases above mentioned appellate jurisdiction as to law only, and from the Supreme Courts of the respective states. The laws of the United States becoming under the constitution those of each state, their courts of course take cognizance of them, from whose decisions, the object of the union will be completely answered by an appeal to their court as to law only, and with great accommodation to the interests of the people. In the organization of this branch, the object should be to found it on the state establishments, and not independently of them, for in the latter case new and very extraordinary difficulties present themselves to view, among which the clashing of jurisdictions would perhaps be the least important. The judges should be appointed by the President, who would of course take them from among the meritorious of our citizens in the different quarters of the union.

Having shewn the defects of our present federal system, pointed out those remedies or amendments both as to its powers, and their distribution or organization, that have appeared to me advisable, I am naturally led in conformity to the plan I had laid down in the beginning of these observations, into a more minute comparison or examination, of the constitution now before you, by the standard or test of those principles I have endeavoured to establish. And this I will confess, is the most painful part of the present enquiry. But where there is a contrariety of sentiment, in any degree, there can be no other mode of investigation; and it is I am persuaded the fairer course, for if the principles themselves cannot be supported it necessarily results, that all reasoning or deductions from them fall to the ground.

It may be recollected that I have not objected to any of those powers which were necessary to add, to the energy, strength, resource, or respectability of the government, but have fought to divest it of those only which I conceived it could never exercise, were impracticable, and whilst they remained even if not brought forth into action, would lessen it in the confidence of the people, but if ever exerted prove the source of endless strife between the states and the general government, that must terminate in the ruin of either the one or the other, which I have considered, (perhaps improperly) as a great national calamity. Those to which I have particularly alluded are the right of direct taxation and of excise through all the states: and the more I have reflected on this subject the better satisfied I have been, that if the other powers were vested in it, and the government made as thereby it would be, strong, energetic and efficient, that the leaving those with the states would not only be happier for them, but more beneficial for it. For whether we examine it as an abstract proposition, or avail ourselves of those lights which the history of all times hath presented to our view, yet the demonstration, at least to my mind, seems satisfactory and conclusive, that under such a government, able and willing to compel the states to perform their duty, the want of which is the great defect of the present system, and which would thereby be completely remedied, that the same objects might be attained to better advantage through their intravention, than by any other mode or institution that could be adopted for the purpose. As this is perhaps the only objection which I have to the powers contained in the constitution, and is founded on principles I have already fully explained; it will be unnecessary to attempt a further illustration of it here. I shall therefore proceed, admitting the propriety of the general division into three branches, to an examination of the subordinate organization of the government, and first of the legislature.

Its division into two branches an house of representatives and senate has appeared to me to be perfectly right; and the mode prescribed for the election of the members of the former by the people not only practicable, but highly commendable. The right of originating money bills, and of impeachment, have also been properly assigned to this branch; the term of service and the principle of representation upon which its house will be formed appear likewise inexceptionable. In short this branch of the legislative is organized entirely to my wishes. I must however confess my mind has not as yet acknowledged in these aspects, the same prepossessions in favour of the senate. The great defect as has been already often observed in the present form, is that of its being a diplomatic corps, a government by and for states, and not in any view of it a national one. In changing it, the object should be to correct that defect in all cases whatever, so far as it might be practicable, which can only be done by taking the appointment of all its officers out of the hands of the states, in their legislative characters, and placing it in those of the people, or electors by them appointed for the purpose. This has been done with the members of the house of representatives, but departed from with those of the Senate. This branch will therefore be in every respect the representative of the states, dependent on and responsible to them for their conduct. In forming a right estimate of the consequences resulting from this property in the character of this body, and of the tone it may give to the measures of the government, we must examine its powers in every direction, and pursue its operation upon every subject. And first as to its share in the legislature or its influence upon all legislative acts.

The senate has an absolute negative upon all laws; from this it results that those not for the advantage of the states, or the prevailing faction in the government, to which they respectively belong will by those thus circumstanced be rejected; for is it to be presumed that because ten members from Virginia, eight from Massachusetts or Pennsylvania in the house of representatives, have passed a bill, whilst one from Rhode Island or Delaware only had rejected it, that these states will give up their equal suffrage in the senate? Is it not more presumable that their senators will look on at the nominal and unimportant superiority of those states, in the other house, laugh at their supposed triumph, and await coolly its submission to their board, where its fate will be inevitable?

Or is it to be supposed, that the right to originate money bills, a thing proper in itself, being the more democratic branch, in the house of representatives, will controul this disposition, especially when we recollect that they are both only representative branches, equally dependent on the passage of such a bill for their wages or salary, and that the members of the latter holding their offices for a shorter term, have perhaps not been able to introduce such a degree of œconomy and order into their finances. This is a check of great importance in the English constitution, and indeed the preservation of the democracy, but the construction and principles of the two governments are so radically different, that it will be easily perceived by the slightest observer, the same effects are not to be expected from it, at least not to the same extent in this, that are experienced in that. Making due allowance for those considerations that should be taken into view, I am therefore led to believe that the defective principles of the present government, through the means of the senate, in respect to form and representation, have been communicated to this branch of the constitution. Appointed by the states and of course responsible to them for their conduct, the senators will act for those to which they respectively belong; nor can we reasonably expect from their concession any great accommodation. Thus the state spirit, with an equality among the members of the union, will be preserved in this branch of the government, and if there was an absolute necessity for yielding the point of representation, yet none suggests itself, at least to me, for not remedying the defect in the form, which has been found so pernicious in the present one.

By the consent of two thirds of the senators *present*, treaties shall be formed; by that of a majority, ambassadors, other public ministers, and consuls, judges of the supreme court and other public officers not otherwise provided for by law, shall be appointed. The subjecting the decision of important questions to a dependance on the occasional presence or absence of any of the members, more especially as no quorum is established, appears to me improper. If the vote of two thirds of the body is in any instance necessary, for the security of the interests of any part of the union, why should the death or delinquency of a member deprive it of this safeguard, by submitting them to the controul of perhaps less than one fourth? It is further to be observed that whatever influence this branch may have in directing the measures of the executive, from the nature of its appointment, will be exerted to give it a narrow state byas, and that from this source alone, constructed as the two branches are, much injury is to be expected from this extraordinary coalition.

"The senate shall have the sole power to try all impeachments." The president is to act under their controul in the cases above stated, if in any instance a wanton violation by their direction or permission should be made, which though not probable is yet practicable, of the rights or interests of any part of the community, and after solemn debate in the house of representatives, this high officer should be brought by impeachment before this body to expiate his offence, what would be his fate, especially as he still held his office and might wield his powers in his defence? A king of England involved himself in great difficulties by an attempt to establish the validity of a general pardon, but had the constitution submitted the trial of state offenders to himself, there would have been no occasion for the contest. Admitting however the members of this body to be incapable of moral turpitude, may we not suppose, as might be the case in that of any individual state; in the operation of this government, that offences might be committed against one quarter of the community, and which before a dispassionate court would receive severe reprehension, that would be highly beneficial to the others? And in such a case could we expect from the representatives of these states a candid or impartial decision against the interests of their constituents?

The placing the executive power in the hands of one person, appears to be perfectly right. If this branch had been put into commission, the state spirit would have been communicated to it, and have tainted all its measures; in addition to this there would have been less responsibility. But the mode of election, does not in all respects appear, to merit such commendation. A departure from the strict representative line, by adding the equal vote of the senate to the number each state hath in the house of representatives, is made in the first instance; but it is still more exceptionable in other respects. If an election shall not be made, and in all probability this will often be the case, indeed the presumption is the contrary will seldom happen, a very extraordinary subsidiary mode is resorted to. Those having the five highest votes are to be ballotted for by the house of representatives, the vote to be taken by states, and one member from each giving the vote of the state. All cases that the constitution will admit of, should be considered as likely to happen some time or other. No person then I am persuaded who will make the calculation, can behold the facility by which the chair of the United States may be approached and achieved, even contrary to the wishes of the people, without equal anxiety and surprize. Let it be admitted that the temper of the times and the ardent spirit of liberty which now prevails, will guard it for the present from such easy access; but that person has profited but little, from the faithful admonition, which all history has given him, who shall conclude from thence, that this will always be the case. His right to remain in office after impeachment, with the influence though diminished, still attending it, appears to be highly improper. That of adjournment in case of impeachment, between the two branches, to such time as he shall think fit, is certainly too unqualified and extensive. The impropriety of the union of this branch with the senate has already been sufficiently dilated on; it will therefore be unnecessary to repeat the same arguments here. Contemplating however the consequences of this union, the expiration of his service, should in my opinion be accompanied with a temporary disqualification. The senators, would to save the commonwealth from injury, be able to give instruction to a new president, and it would perhaps be better, to change occasionally the acting party, of a combination that might otherwise be dangerous.

From the first clause respecting the judiciary it is obvious, that the Congress, although there shall be one Supreme Court only, may establish as many subordinate to it, as they shall think fit. The presumption is, they will establish so many as shall be necessary for the discharge of the functions of the department, to the advantage of the government, and benefit of the people. The extent therefore of the duties which become the exclusive object of a fœderal court, may give some insight into that establishment they might probably adopt; and when we observe that the cognizance of all cases arising under the constitution and the laws, either of a civil or criminal nature, in law or equity, with those other objects which it specifies, even between the citizens of the same state, are taken from those of each state and absolutely appropriated to the courts of the United States, we are led into a view of the very important interests it comprehends, and of the extensive scale upon which it operates. It will therefore be the duty of Congress to organize this branch, by the establishment of such subordinate courts, throughout the whole confederacy, in such manner as shall be found necessary to support the authority of the government, and carry justice home, so far as it may be practicable, to the doors of all its inhabitants. What mode may be best calculated to accomplish this end, belongs to that body to determine. Bound by no rule they may it is true (as in the commencement they probably would) avail themselves of those of each state; but this would be a measure of expedience only and not of right and may hereafter be changed as the fortunes of the government, and considerations of expedience may dictate. How far it might be proper to authorise the subjects of foreign powers to carry the citizens of any state into a fœderal court, and afterwards by appeal into the Supreme Court, is of questionable propriety. The principal argument in its favour appears to be that of securing the United States from the danger of controversies with such powers, under the partial decisions of those of the individual states. But if they knew such cases, were by a fundamental of our government submitted to them, it were reasonable to suppose, that all just cause of complaint, would be removed. The submission to a fœderal court of contests upon ordinary subjects, between citizens of the same state, or even of different states, or indeed upon any subject, that did not arise under territorial controversies between states, and which originally belonged to that court, appears to be highly improper and altogether unnecessary. The appeal as to fact is still more extraordinary and exceptionable. The verdict which has been found must of course be set aside, and the court subjected to the necessity of either trying the cause upon the evidence already given, with liberty to construe it at pleasure; of hearing it over again admitting other evidence, being judges of the fact themselves; or submitting it to another jury to find a second verdict, either of which modes appears to be highly exceptionable; for if the court become judges of fact under the old or a new trial, the right of trial by jury is dispensed with; and if a second jury shall be summoned, independent of the difficulty and hardship, attending the submission of controversies contracted at the extremities of the union, by people in some degree variant in their manners, customs, and prejudices, to a jury formed of those of any one town, the parties are necessarily exposed to the loss of time, (of importance especially to the lower classes of society) and the enormous expence inseparable from a tryal carried on at a great distance from home. What necessity there can be, so effectually to lay aside the state courts, (which though perhaps improperly organized at present are yet capable of improvement) and subject the good people of America to such new and unheard of difficulties, I must confess I am not able to comprehend, nor can I readily forsee the very important consequences into which it may lead.

A planter and lawyer, member of the Continental Congress, and future governor and president of the United States, James Monroe displayed the caution of a young man who did not want to offend Virginia's Federalists (see James Monroe entry in *Biographies*). This work was privately circulated and used to express Monroe's own reservations on the Constitution, especially his concerns for the loss of state power. He especially called for balanced government.

REFERENCES

Stuart Gerry Brown (ed.), *The Autobiography of James Monroe* (Syracuse: Syracuse University Press, 1959); James Monroe papers, Library of Congress; Storing, *Complete*, vol. 5.

NOTES

1. Probably 1781.
2. Monroe, like many other political thinkers, was obsessed with the fall of Rome.

George Mason, Speech in the Virginia State Ratification Convention, *June 4, 1788*

Mr. Chairman—Whether the Constitution be good or bad, the present clause clearly discovers, that it is a National Government, and no longer a confederation. I mean that clause which gives the first hint of the General Government laying direct taxes. The assumption of this power of laying direct taxes, does of itself, entirely change the confederation of the States into one consolidated Government. This power being at discretion, unconfined, and without any kind of controul, must carry every thing before it. The very idea of converting what was formerly a confederation, to a consolidated Government, is totally subversive of every principle which has hitherto governed us. This power is calculated to annihilate totally the State Governments. Will the people of this great community submit to be individually taxed by two different and distinct powers? Will they suffer themselves to be doubly harrassed? These two concurrent powers cannot exist long together; the one will destroy the other: The General Government being paramount to, and in every respect more powerful than, the State governments, the latter must give way to the former. Is it to be supposed that one National Government will suit so extensive a country, embracing so many climates, and containing inhabitants so very different in manners, habits, and customs? It is ascertained by history, that there never was a Government, over a very extensive country, without destroying the liberties of the people: History also, supported by the opinions of the best writers, shew us, that monarchy may suit a large territory, and despotic Governments ever so extensive a country; but that popular Governments can only exist in small territories. Is there a single example, on the face of the earth, to support a contrary opinion? Where is there one exception to this general rule? Was there ever an instance of a general National Government extending over so extensive a country, abounding in such a variety of climates, &c. where the people retained their liberty? I solemnly declare, that no man is a greater friend to a firm Union of the American States than I am: But, Sir, if this great end can be obtained without hazarding the rights of the people, why should we recur to such dangerous principles? Requisitions have been often refused, sometimes from an impossibility of complying with them; often from that great variety of circumstances which retard the collection of monies, and, perhaps, sometimes from a wilful design of procrastinating. But why shall we give up to the National Government this power, so dangerous in its nature, and for which its members will not have sufficient information?—Is it not well known, that what would be a proper tax in one State would be grievous in another? The Gentleman who hath favored us with an eulogium in favor of this system, must, after all the encomiums he has been pleased to bestow upon it, acknowledge, that our Federal Representatives must be unacquainted with the situation of their constituents: Sixty-five members cannot possibly know the situation and circumstances of all the inhabitants of this immense continent: When a certain sum comes to be taxed, and the mode of levying to be fixed, they will lay the tax on that article which will be most productive, and easiest in the collection, without consulting the real circumstances or convenience of a country, with which, in fact, they cannot be sufficiently acquainted. The mode of levying taxes is of the utmost consequence, and yet here it is to be determined by those who have neither knowledge of our situation, nor a common interest with us, nor a fellow feeling for us:—The subjects of taxation differ in three-fourths; nay, I might say with truth, in four-fifths of the States:—If we trust the National Government with an effectual way of raising the necessary sums,'tis sufficient; every thing we do further is trusting the happiness and rights of the people: Why then should we give up this dangerous power of individual taxation? Why leave the manner of laying taxes to those, who in the nature of things, cannot be acquainted with the situation of those on whom they are to impose them, when it can be done by those who are well acquainted with it? If instead of giving this oppressive power, we give them such an effectual alternative as will answer the purpose, without encountering the evil and danger that might arise from it, then I would chearfully acquiesce: And would it not be far more eligible? I candidly acknowledge the inefficacy of the confederation; but requisitions have been made, which were impossible to be complied with: Requisitions for more gold and silver than were in the United States: If we give the General Government the power of demanding their quotas of the States, with an alternative of laying direct taxes, in case of non compliance, then the mischief would be avoided; and the certainty of this conditional power would, in all human probability, prevent the application, and the sums necessary for the Union would be then laid by the States; by those who know how it can best be raised; by those who have a fellow-feeling for us. Give me leave to say, that the same sum raised one way with convenience and ease, would be very oppressive another way: Why then not leave this power to be exercised by those who know the mode most convenient for the inhabitants, and not by those who must necessarily apportion it in such manner as shall be oppressive? With respect to the representation so much applauded, I cannot think it such a full and free one as it is represented; but I must candidly acknowledge, that this defect results from the very nature of the Government. It would be impossible to have a full and adequate representation in the General Government; it would be too expensive and too unweildy: We are then under the necessity of having this a very inadequate representation: Is this general representation to be compared with the real, actual, substantial representation of the State Legislatures? It cannot bear a comparison. To make representation real and actual, the number of Representatives ought to be adequate; they ought to mix with the people, think as they think, feel as they feel, ought to be perfectly amenable to them, and thoroughly acquainted with their interest and condition: Now these great ingredients are, either not at all, or in so small a degree, to be found in our Federal Representatives, that we have no real, actual, substantial representation; but I acknowledge it results from the nature of the Government: The necessity of this inconvenience may appear a sufficient reason not to argue against it: But, Sir, it clearly shews, that we ought to give power with a sparing hand to a Government thus imperfectly constructed. To a Government, which, in the nature of things, cannot but be defective, no powers ought to be given, but such as are absolutely necessary: There is one thing in it which I conceive to be extremely dangerous. Gentlemen may talk of public virtue and confidence; we shall be told that the House of Representatives will consist of the most virtuous men on the Continent, and that in their hands we may trust our dearest rights. This, like all other assemblies, will be composed of some bad and some good men; and considering the natural lust of power so inherent in man, I fear the thirst of power will prevail to oppress the people:—What I conceive to be so dangerous, is the provision with respect to the number of Representatives: It does not expressly provide, that we shall have one for every 30,000, but that the number shall not exceed that proportion: The utmost that we can expect (and perhaps that is too much) is, that the present number shall be continued to us:—"The number of Representatives shall not exceed one for every 30,000." Now will not this be complied with, although the present number should never be increased; nay, although it should be decreased? Suppose Congress should say, that we should have one for every 200,000, will not the Constitution be complied with? For one for every 200,000 does not exceed one for every 30,000. There is a want of proportion that ought to be strictly guarded against: The worthy Gentleman tells us, we have no reason to fear; but I always fear for the rights of the people: I do not pretend to inspiration, but I think, it is apparent as the day, that the members will attend to local partial interests to prevent an augmentation of their number: I know not how they will be chosen, but whatever be the mode of choosing, our present number is but ten: And suppose our State is laid off in ten districts; those Gentlemen who shall be sent from those districts will lessen their own power and influence, in their respective districts, if they increase their number; for the greater the number of men among whom any given quantum of power is divided, the less the power of each individual. Thus they will have a local interest to prevent the increase of, and perhaps they will lessen their own number: This is evident on the face of the Constitution—so loose an expression ought to be guarded against; for Congress will be clearly within the requisition of the Constitution, although the number of Representatives should always continue what it is now, and the population of the country should increase to an immense number. Nay, they may reduce the number from 65, to one from each State, without violating the Constitution; and thus the number which is now too small, would then be infinitely too much so: But my principal objection is, that the confederation is converted to one general consolidated Government, which, from my best judgment of it (and which perhaps will be shewn in the course of this discussion, to be really well founded) is one of the worst curses that can possibly befal a nation. Does any man suppose, that one general National Government can exist in so extensive a country as this? I hope that a Government may be framed which may suit us, by drawing the line between the general and State Governments, and prevent that dangerous clashing of interest and power, which must, as it now stands, terminate in the destruction of one or the other. When we come to the Judiciary, we shall be more convinced, that this Government will terminate in the annihilation of the State Governments: The question then will be, whether a consolidated Government can preserve the freedom, and secure the great rights of the people.

If such amendments be introduced as shall exclude danger, I shall most gladly put my hand to it. When such amendments, as shall, from the best information, secure the great essential rights of the people, shall be agreed to by Gentlemen, I shall most heartily make the greatest concessions, and concur in any reasonable measure to obtain the desirable end of conciliation and unanimity. An indispensible amendment in this case, is, that Congress shall not exercise the power of raising direct taxes till the States shall have refused to comply with the requisitions of Congress. On this condition it may be granted, but I see no reason to grant it unconditionally; as the States can raise the taxes with more ease, and lay them on the inhabitants with more propriety, than it is possible for the General Government to do. If Congress hath this power without controul, the taxes will be laid by those who have no fellow-feeling or acquaintance with the people. This is my objection to the article now under consideration. It is a very great and important one. I therefore beg Gentlemen seriously to consider it. Should this power be restrained, I shall withdraw my objections to this part of the Constitution: But as it stands, it is an objection so strong in my mind, that its amendment is with me, a *sine qua non*, of its adoption. I wish for such amendments, and such only, as are necessary to secure the dearest rights of the people.

In this most important speech, George Mason worried about the lack of protection for individual rights in the Constitution (see George Mason entry in *Biographies*). He also believed that such a powerful federal government over so much land would leave the state governments and the minority of the people vulnerable to oppression. These concerns led to his drafting a bill of rights.

REFERENCES

Elliot, *Debates*, vol. 3; Storing, *Complete*, vol. 5.

Patrick Henry, Speech in the Virginia State Ratification Convention,
June 4, 1788

Mr. Chairman.—The public mind, as well as my own, is extremely uneasy at the proposed change of Government. Give me leave to form one of the number of those who wish to be thoroughly acquainted with the reasons of this perilous and uneasy situation—and why we are brought hither to decide on this great national question. I consider myself as the servant of the people of this Commonwealth, as a centinel over their rights, liberty, and happiness. I represent their feelings when I say, that they are exceedingly uneasy, being brought from that state of full security, which they enjoyed, to the present delusive appearance of things. A year ago the minds of our citizens were at perfect repose. Before the meeting of the late Federal Convention at Philadelphia, a general peace, and an universal tranquillity prevailed in this country;—but since that period they are exceedingly uneasy and disquieted. When I wished for an appointment to this Convention, my mind was extremely agitated for the situation of public affairs. I conceive the republic to be in extreme danger. If our situation be thus uneasy, whence has arisen this fearful jeopardy? It arises from this fatal system—it arises from a proposal to change our government:—A proposal that goes to the utter annihilation of the most solemn engagements of the States. A proposal of establishing 9 States into a confederacy, to the eventual exclusion of 4 States. It goes to the annihilation of those solemn treaties we have formed with foreign nations. The present circumstances of France—the good offices rendered us by that kingdom, require our most faithful and most punctual adherence to our treaty with her. We are in alliance with the Spaniards, the Dutch, the Prussians: Those treaties bound us as thirteen States, confederated together—Yet, here is a proposal to sever that confederacy. Is it possible that we shall abandon all our treaties and national engagements?—And for what? I expected to have heard the reasons of an event so unexpected to my mind, and many others. Was our civil polity, or public justice, endangered or sapped? Was the real existence of the country threatened—or was this preceded by a mournful progression of events? This proposal of altering our Federal Government is of a most alarming nature: Make the best of this new Government—say it is composed by any thing but inspiration—you ought to be extremely cautious, watchful, jealous of your liberty; for instead of securing your rights you may lose them forever. If a wrong step be now made, the republic may be lost forever. If this new Government will not come up to the expectation of the people, and they should be disappointed—their liberty will be lost, and tyranny must and will arise. I repeat it again, and I beg Gentlemen to consider, that a wrong step made now will plunge us into misery, and our Republic will be lost. It will be necessary for this Convention to have a faithful historical detail of the facts, that preceded the session of the Federal Convention, and the reasons that actuated its members in proposing an entire alteration of Government—and to demonstrate the dangers that awaited us: If they were of such awful magnitude, as to warrant a proposal so extremely perilous as this, I must assert, that this Convention has an absolute right to a thorough discovery of every circumstance relative to this great event. And here I would make this enquiry of those worthy characters who composed a part of the late Federal Convention. I am sure they were fully impressed with the necessity of forming a great consolidated Government, instead of a confederation. That this is a consolidated Government is demonstrably clear, and the danger of such a Government, is, to my mind, very striking. I have the highest veneration for those Gentlemen,—but, Sir, give me leave to demand, what right had they to say, *We, the People*. My political curiosity, exclusive of my anxious solicitude for the public welfare, leads me to ask, who authorised them to speak the language of, *We, the People*, instead of *We, the States?* States are the characteristics, and the soul of a confederation. If the States be not the agents of this compact, it must be one great consolidated National Government of the people of all the States. I have the highest respect for those Gentlemen who formed the Convention, and were some of them not here, I would express some testimonial of my esteem for them. America had on a former occasion put the utmost confidence in them: A confidence which was well placed: And I am sure, Sir, I would give up any thing to them; I would chearfully confide in them as my Representatives. But, Sir, on this great occasion, I would demand the cause of their conduct.—Even from that illustrious man, who saved us by his valor, I would have a reason for his conduct—that liberty which he has given us by his valor, tells me to ask this reason,—and sure I am, were he here, he would give us that reason[1]: But there are other Gentlemen here, who can give us this information. The people gave them no power to use their name. That they exceeded their power is perfectly clear. It is not mere curiosity that actuates me—I wish to hear the real actual existing danger, which should lead us to take those steps so dangerous in my conception. Disorders have arisen in other parts of America, but here, Sir, no dangers, no insurrection or tumult, has happened—every thing has been calm and tranquil. But notwithstanding this, we are wandering on the great ocean of human affairs. I see no landmark to guide us. We are running we know not whither. Difference in opinion has gone to a degree of inflammatory resentment in different parts of the country—which has been occasioned by this perilous innovation. The Federal Convention ought to have amended the old system—for this purpose they were solely delegated: The object of their mission extended to no other consideration. You must therefore forgive the solicitation of one unworthy member, to know what danger could have arisen under the present confederation, and what are the causes of this proposal to change our Government.

Patrick Henry, Revolutionary War patriot, governor, lawyer, planter, and Virginia's most famous Antifederalist, spoke often and at length in the state convention (see Patrick Henry entry in *Biographies*). This speech reveals his fears for personal freedom. Henry orated eloquently on how the Constitution proposed to create a consolidated government at the expense of the rights of the states.

REFERENCES

Elliot, *Debates*, vol. 3; William Wirt, *Patrick Henry: Life and Speeches* (New York: Charles Scribner's Sons, 1891), vol. 3.

NOTE

1. Henry is referring to George Washington.

William Grayson, Speech in the Virginia State Ratification Convention, *June 21, 1788*

Mr. Chairman, it seems to have been a rule with the gentlemen on the other side to argue from the excellency of human nature, in order to induce us to grant away (if I may be allowed the expression) the rights and liberties of our country. I make no doubt the same arguments were used on a variety of occasions. I suppose, sir, that this argument was used when Cromwell was invested with power. The same argument was used to gain our assent to the stamp act. I have no doubt it has been invariably the argument in all countries, when the concession of power has been in agitation. But power ought to have such checks and limitations as to prevent bad men from abusing it. It ought to be granted on a supposition that men will be bad; for it may be eventually so. With respect to the judiciary, my grand objection is, that it will interfere with the state judiciaries, in the same manner as the exercise of the power of direct taxation will interfere with the same power in the state governments; there being no superintending central power to keep in order these two contending jurisdictions. This is an objection which is unanswerable in its nature.

In England they have great courts, which have great and interfering powers. But the controlling power of Parliament, which is a *central focus*, corrects them. But here each party is to shift for itself. There is no arbiter or power to correct their interference. Recurrence can be only had to the sword. I shall endeavor to demonstrate the pernicious consequences of this interference. It was mentioned, as one reason why these great powers might harmonize, that the judges of the state courts might be federal judges. The idea was approbated, in my opinion, with a great deal of justice. They are the best check we have. They secure us from encroachments on our privileges. They are the principal defence of the states. How improper would it be to deprive the state of its only defensive armor! I hope the states will never part with it. There is something extremely disgraceful in the idea. How will it apply in the practice? The independent judges of Virginia are to be subordinate to the federal judiciary. Our judges in chancery are to be judges in the inferior federal tribunals. Something has been said of the independency of the federal judges. I will only observe that it is on as corrupt a basis as the art of man can place it. The *salaries of the judges* may be augmented. Augmentation of salary is the only method that can be taken to corrupt a judge.

It has been a thing desired by the people of England for many years, that the judges should be *independent*. This independency never was obtained till the second or third year of the reign of George III. It was omitted at the revolution by inattention. Their compensation is now fixed. and they hold their offices during good behavior. But I say that our federal judges are placed in a situation as liable to corruption as they could possibly be. How are judges to be operated upon? By the hopes of reward, and not the fear of a diminution of compensation. *Common decency* would prevent lessening the salary of a judge. Throughout the whole page of history, you will find the corruption of judges to have always arisen from that principle—the hope of reward. This is left open here. The flimsy argument brought by my friend, not as his own, but as supported by others, will not hold. It would be hoped that the judges should get too much rather than too little, and that they should be perfectly independent. What if you give six hundred or a thousand pounds annually to a judge? It is but a trifling object, when, by that little money, you purchase the most invaluable blessing that any country can enjoy.

There is to be one *Supreme Court*—for chancery, admiralty, common pleas, and exchequer, (which great cases are left in England to four great courts,) to which are added criminal jurisdiction, and all cases depending on the law of nations—a most extensive jurisdiction. This court has more power than any court under heaven. One set of judges ought not to have this power—and judges, particularly, who have temptation always before their eyes. The court thus organized are to execute laws made by thirteen nations, dissimilar in their customs, manners, laws, and interests. If we advert to the customs of these different sovereignties, we shall find them repugnant and dissimilar. Yet they are all forced to unite and concur in making these laws. They are to form them on one principle, and on one idea, whether the civil law, common law, or law of nations. The gentleman was driven, the other day, to the expedient of acknowledging the necessity of having thirteen different tax laws. This destroys the principle, that he who lays a tax should feel it and bear his proportion of it. This has not been answered: it will involve consequences so absurd, that, I presume, they will not attempt to make thirteen different codes. They will be obliged to make one code. How will they make one code, without being contradictory to some of the laws of the different states?

It is said there is to be *a court of equity*. There is no such thing in Pennsylvania, or in some other states in the Union. A nation, in making a law, ought not to make it repugnant to the spirit of the Constitution or the genius of the people. This rule cannot be observed in forming a general code. I wish to know how the people of Connecticut would agree with the lordly pride of your Virginia nobility. Its operation will be as repugnant and contradictory, in this case, as in the establishment of a court of equity. They may inflict punishments where the state governments will give rewards. This is not probable; but *still it is possible*. It would be a droll sight, to see a man on one side of the street punished for a breach of the federal law, and on the other side another man rewarded by the state legislature for the same act. Or suppose it were the same person that should be thus rewarded and punished at one time for the same act; it would be a droll sight, to see a man laughing on one side of his face, and crying on the other. I wish only to put this matter in a clear point of view; and I think that if thirteen states, different in every thing, shall have to make laws for the government of the whole, they cannot harmonize, or suit the genius of the people; there being no such thing as a spirit of laws, or a pervading principle, applying to every state individually. The only promise, in this respect, is, that there shall be a republican government in each state. But it does not say whether it is to be aristocratical or democratical.

My next objection to *the federal judiciary* is, that it is not expressed in a definite manner. The jurisdiction of all cases arising under the Constitution and the laws of the Union is of stupendous magnitude.

It is impossible for human nature to trace its extent. It is so vaguely and indefinitely expressed, that its latitude cannot be ascertained. Citizens or subjects of foreign states may sue citizens of the different states in the federal courts. It is extremely impolitic to place foreigners in a better situation than our own citizens. This was never the policy of other nations. It was the policy, in England, to put foreigners on a secure footing. The statute merchant and statute staple were favorable to them. But in no country are the laws more favorable to foreigners than to the citizens. If they be equally so, it is surely sufficient. Our own state merchants would be ruined by it, because they cannot recover debts so soon in the state courts as foreign merchants can recover of them in the federal courts. The consequence would be inevitable ruin to commerce. It will induce foreigners to decline becoming citizens. There is no reciprocity in it.

How will this apply to *British creditors*? I have ever been an advocate for paying the British creditors, both in Congress and elsewhere. But here we do injury to our own citizens. It is a maxim in law, that debts should be on the same original foundation they were on when contracted. I presume, when the contracts were made, the creditors had an idea of the state judiciaries only. The procrastination and delays of our courts were probably in contemplation by both parties. They could have no idea of the establishment of new tribunals to affect them. *Trial by jury* must have been in the contemplation of both parties, and the *venue* was in favor of the defendant. From these premises it is clearly discernible that it would be wrong to change the nature of the contracts. Whether they will make a law other than the state laws, I cannot determine.

But we are told that it is wise, politic, and preventive of controversies with foreign nations. The treaty of peace with Great Britain does not require that creditors should be put in a better situation than they were, but that there should be no hinderance to the collection of debts. It is therefore unwise and impolitic to give those creditors such an advantage over the debtors. But the citizens of different states are to sue each other in these courts. No reliance is to be put on the state judiciaries. The fear of unjust regulations and decisions in the states is urged as the reason of this jurisdiction. Paper money in Rhode Island has been instanced by gentlemen. There is one clause in the Constitution which prevents the issuing of paper money. If this clause should pass, (and it is unanimously wished by every one that it should not be objected to,) I apprehend an execution in Rhode Island would be as good and effective as in any state in the Union.

A state may sue a foreign state, or a foreign state may sue one of our states. This may form a *new*, American law of nations. Whence the idea could have originated, I cannot determine, unless from the idea that predominated in the

time of Henry IV. and Queen Elizabeth. They took it into their heads to consolidate all the states in the world into one great political body. Many ridiculous projects were imagined to reduce that absurd idea into practice; but they
were all given up at last. My honorable friend, whom I much respect, said that
the consent of the parties must be previously obtained. I agree that the consent of foreign nations must be had before they become parties; but it is not
so with our states. It is fixed in the Constitution that they shall become parties. This is not reciprocal. If the Congress cannot make a law against the Constitution, I apprehend they cannot make a law to abridge it. The judges are to
defend it. They can neither abridge nor extend it. There is no reciprocity in
this, that a foreign state should have a right to sue one of our states, whereas
a foreign state cannot be sued without its own consent. The idea to me is monstrous and extravagant. It cannot be reduced to practice.

Suppose one of our states objects to the decision; arms must be recurred to.
How can *a foreign state be compelled to submit to a decision?* Pennsylvania and
Connecticut had like, once, to have fallen together concerning their contested
boundaries. I was convinced that the mode provided in the Confederation, for
the decision of such disputes, would not answer. The success which attended
it, with respect to settling bounds, has proved to me, in some degree, that it
would not answer in any other case whatever. The same difficulty must attend
this mode in the execution. This high court has not a very extensive original
jurisdiction. It is not material. But its appellate jurisdiction is of immense magnitude; and what has it in view, unless to subvert the state governments? The
honorable gentleman who presides has introduced the high court of appeals.
I wish the federal appellate court was on the same foundation. If we investigate the subject, we shall find this jurisdiction perfectly unnecessary. It is said
that its object is to prevent subordinate tribunals from making unjust decisions,
to defraud creditors. I grant the suspicion is in some degree just. But would
not an appeal to the state courts of appeal, or supreme tribunals, correct the
decisions of inferior courts? Would not this put every thing right? Then there
would be no interference of jurisdiction.

But a gentleman (Mr. Marshall) says, we ought certainly to give this power
to Congress, because our state courts have more business than they can possibly do.[1] A gentleman was once asked to give up his estate because he had too
much; but he did not comply. Have we not established district courts, which
have for their object the full administration of justice? Our courts of chancery
might, by our legislature, be put in a good situation; so that there is nothing
in this observation.

But the same honorable gentleman says, that trial by jury is preserved by
implication. I think this was the idea. I beg leave to consider that, as well as
other observations of the honorable gentleman. After enumerating the subjects
of its jurisdiction, and confining its original cognizance to cases affecting ambassadors and other public ministers, and those in which a state shall be a party,
it expressly says, that, "in all other cases before mentioned, the Supreme Court
shall have appellate jurisdiction, both as to law and *fact*." I would beg the honorable gentleman to turn his attention to the word *appeal*, which I think comprehends chancery, admiralty, common law, and every thing. But this is with
such exceptions, and under such regulations, as Congress shall make. This, we

are told, will be an ample security. Congress may please to make these exceptions and regulations, but they may not, also. I lay it down as a principle, that trial by jury is given up to the discretion of Congress. If they take it away, will it be a breach of this Constitution? I apprehend not; for, as they have an absolute appellate jurisdiction of facts, they may alter them as they may think proper. It is possible that Congress may regulate it properly; but still it is at their discretion to do it or not. There has been so much said of the excellency of the trial by jury, that I need not enlarge upon it. The want of trial by jury in the Roman republic obliged them to establish the regulation of *patron* and *client*. I think this must be the case in every country where this trial does not exist. The poor people were obliged to be defended by their *patrons*.

It may be laid down as a rule that, where the governing power possesses an unlimited control over the *venue*, no man's life is in safety. How is it in this system? "The trial of all crimes shall be by jury, except in cases of impeachment; and such trial shall be held in the state where the said crimes shall have been committed." He has said that, when the power of a court is given, all its appendages and concomitants are given. Allowing this to be the case by implication, how is it? Does it apply to counties? No, sir. The idea is, that the states are to the general government as counties are to our state legislatures. What sort of a vicinage is given by Congress? The idea which I call a true vicinage is, that a man shall be tried by his neighbors. But the idea here is, that he may be tried in any part of the state. Were the *venue* to be established according to the federal districts, it would not come up to the true idea of vicinage. Delaware sends but one member: it would then extend to that whole state. This state sends ten members, and has ten districts; but this is far from the true idea of vicinage. The allusion another gentleman has made to this trial, as practised in England, is improper. It does not justify this regulation. The jury may come from any part of the state. They possess an absolute, uncontrollable power over the *venue*. The conclusion, then, is, that they can hang any one they please, by having a jury to suit their purpose. They might, on particular, extraordinary occasions, suspend the privilege. The Romans did it on creating a dictator. The British government does it when the *habeas corpus* is to be suspended—when the *salus populi* is affected. I never will consent to it unless it be properly defined.

Another gentleman has said that trial by jury has not been so sacred a thing among our ancestors, and that in England it may be destroyed by an act of Parliament. I believe the gentleman is mistaken. I believe it is secured by Magna Charta and the bill of rights. I believe no act of Parliament can affect it, if this principle be true,—that a law is not paramount to the constitution. I believe, whatever may be said of the mutability of the laws, and the defect of a written, fixed constitution, that it is generally thought, by Englishmen, that it is so sacred that no act of Parliament can affect it.

The interference of the federal judiciary and the state courts will involve the most serious and even ludicrous consequences. Both courts are to act on the same persons and things, and cannot possibly avoid interference. As to connection or coalition, it would be incestuous. How could they avoid it, on an execution from each court, either against the body or effects? How will it be with respect to mortgaged property? Suppose the same lands or slaves mortgaged to two different persons, and the mortgages foreclosed, one in the federal and another in the state court; will there be no interference in this case? It will be impossible to avoid interference in a million of cases. I would wish to know how it can be avoided; for it is an insuperable objection in my mind. I shall no longer fatigue the committee, but shall beg leave to make some observations another time.

William Grayson, a planter, lawyer, and member of the Continental Congress, later served in the United States Senate (see William Grayson entry in *Biographies*). He spoke often in the convention, and this speech reveals his worries about the powers of a federal judiciary over state courts. He compared the government created by the Constitution with the hated English government, as all remembered what that oppressive nation had done to the American people.

REFERENCES

Debates and Proceedings of the Convention of Virginia (Petersburg: Hunter and Prentis, 1788–1789); Elliot, *Debates*, vol. 3.

NOTE

1. Federalist John Marshall, future Chief Justice of the United States.

John Dawson, Speech in the Virginia State Ratification Convention,
June 24, 1788

Mr. Chairman,—When a nation is about to make a change in its political character, it behoves it to summon the experience of ages which have passed, to
collect the wisdom of the present day, to ascertain clearly those great principles of equal liberty, which secure the rights, the liberties, and properties of
the people. Such is the situation of the United States at this moment. We are
about to make such a change.

The Constitution proposed for the government of the United States, has
been a subject of general discussion; and while many able and honorable gentlemen within these walls, have, in the development of the various parts, delivered their sentiments with that freedom which will ever mark the citizens of
an independent State, and with that ability which will prove to the world their
eminent talents; I, Sir, although urged by my feelings, have forbore to say any
thing on my part, from a satisfactory impression of the inferiority of my talents, and from a wish to acquire every information which might assist my judgment in forming a decision on a question of such magnitude. But, Sir, as it
involves in its fate the interest of so extensive a country, every sentiment which
can be offered deserves its proportion of public attention. I shall therefore avoid
any apology for now rising although uncommon propriety might justify it, and
rather trust to the candour of those who hear me: Indeed I am induced to
come forward, not from any apprehension that my opinions will have weight,
but in order to discharge that duty which I owe to myself, and to those I have
the honor to represent.

The defects of the articles by which we are at present confederated, have
been echoed and re-echoed, not only from every quarter of this House, but
from every part of the continent. At the framing of those articles, a common
interest excited us to unite for the common good: But no sooner did this principle cease to operate, than the defects of the system were sensibly felt. Since
then the seeds of civil dissension have been gradually opening, and political
confusion has pervaded the States. During the short time of my political life,
having been fully impressed with the truth of these observations, when a proposition was made by Virginia to invite the sister States to a General Convention,
at Philadelphia, *to amend these defects*, I readily gave my assent; and when I
considered the very respectable characters who formed that body—when I reflected that they were, most of them, those sages and patriots, under whose
banners and by whose councils, it had been rescued from impending danger,

and placed among the nations of the earth—when I also turned my attention to that illustrious character, *to immortalize whose memory, Fame shall blow her trump* to the latest ages—I say, when I weighed all these considerations, I was almost persuaded to declare in favour of the proposed plan, and to exert my slender abilities in its favour. But, when I came to investigate it impartially, on the immutable principles of government, and to exercise that reason, with which the God of Nature hath endowed me, and which I will ever freely use, I was convinced of this important, though melancholy truth, "that the greatest men may err," and that their errors are sometimes of the greatest magnitude. I was persuaded that, although the proposed plan contains many things excellent, yet by the adoption of it, as it now stands, the liberties of America, in general; the property of Virginia in particular; would be endangered.

These being my sentiments; sentiments which I offer with the diffidence of a young politician, but with the firmness of a republican; which I am ready to change when I am convinced they are founded in error; but which I will support until that conviction—I should be a traitor to my country and unworthy that freedom, for which I trust I shall ever remain an advocate, was I to declare my entire approbation to the plan, as it now stands, or assent to its ratification without previous amendments.

During the deliberations of this Convention, several gentlemen of eminent talents, have exerted themselves to prove the necessity of the Union, by presenting to our view the relative situation of Virginia to the other States: The melancholy representation made to day, and frequently before, by an Honorable Gentleman (Governor *Randolph*) of our State reduced, in his estimation, to the lowest degree of degradation, must now haunt the recollection of any gentlemen in this Committee, how far he has drawn the picture to the life, or where it is too highly colored, rests with them to determine. To Gentlemen, however, Sir, of their abilities, the task was easy, and perhaps I may add unnecessary. It is a truth admitted on all sides, and I presume there is not a Gentleman, who hears me, who is not a friend to a Union of the Thirteen States.

But, Sir, an opinion is gone abroad (from whence it originated, or by whom it is supported, I will not venture to say) that the opponents to the paper on your table, are enemies to the Union; it may not therefore be improper for me to declare, that *I am* a warm friend to a firm, federal energetic Government; that I consider a confederation of the States, on republican principles, as a security to their mutual interest, and a disunion as injurious to the whole: But I shall lament exceedingly, when a confederation of independent States shall be converted into a consolidated Government; for when that event shall happen, I shall consider the history of American liberty as short as it has been brilliant, and we shall afford one more proof to the favorite maxim of tyrants, "that mankind cannot govern themselves."

An Honorable Gentleman (Col. *H. Lee*) came forward some days since, with all the powers of eloquence, and all the warmth of enthusiasm—after discanting on some military operations to the South, of which he was a spectator, and pronouncing sentence of condemnation on a Mr. *Shays*, to the North[1]—as a military character, he boldly throws the gauntlet and defies the warmest friend to the opposition to come forth, and say that the friends to the system on your table, are not also friends to republican liberty. Arguments, Sir, in this House, should ever be addressed to the reason, and should be applied to the system itself, and not to those who either support or oppose it. *I*, however, dare come forth, and tell that Honorable Gentleman, not with the military warmth of a young soldier, but with the firmness of a republican, that in my humble opinion, had the paper now on your table, and which is so ably supported, been presented to our view ten years ago (when the *American spirit* shone forth in the meridian of glory, and rendered us the wonder of an admiring world) it would have been considered as containing principles incompatible with republican liberty, and therefore doomed to infamy.

Having, Sir, made these loose observations, and having proved, I flatter myself, to this Honorable Convention, the motives from which my opposition to the proposed system originated; may I now be permitted to turn my attention, for a very few moments, to the system itself, and to point out some of the leading parts, most exceptionable in my estimation, and to which my original objections have not been removed, by the debate, but rather confirmed.

If we grant to Congress the power of direct taxation; if we yield to them the sword, and if we also invest them with the Judicial authority; two questions of the utmost importance, immediately present themselves to our inquiries—whether these powers will not be oppressive in their operations, and aided by other parts of the system, convert the Thirteen Confederate States into one consolidated government—and, whether any country, as extensive as North-America, and where climates, dispositions, and interests, are so essentially different, can be governed under one consolidated plan, except by the introduction of despotic principles—The warmest friends, Sir, to the Government, some of those who formed, signed, and have recommended it; some of those who have enthusiastically supported it in every quarter of this Continent; have answered my first query in the affirmative: They have admitted that it possesses few federal features and will ultimately end in a consolidated Government—a truth which in my opinion they would have denied in vain, for every article, every section, every clause, and almost every line, prove that it will have this tendency: And if this position has, during the course of the long and learned debates on this head, been established to the satisfaction of the Convention; I apprehend that the authority of all eminent writers on the subject, and the experience of all ages, cannot be controverted, and that it will be admitted that no government, formed on the principles of freedom, can pervade all North America.

This, Sir, is my great objection; an objection general in its nature, because it operates on the whole system; an objection which I early formed, which I flattered myself would have been removed, but which hath obliged me to say, has been confirmed by the observations which have been made by many learned Gentlemen, and which it would be tedious for me now to recapitulate.

That the Legislative, Executive, and Judicial powers, should be separate and distinct, in all free governments, is a political fact, so well established, that I presume I shall not be thought arrogant, when I affirm, that no country ever did, or ever can, long remain free, where they are blended. All the States have been in this sentiment, when they formed their State Constitutions, and therefore have guarded against the danger; and every school-boy in politics must be convinced of the propriety of the observation—and yet by the proposed plan, the Legislative and Executive powers are closely united; the Senate, who compose one part of the Legislature, are also as council to the President, the Supreme Head, and are concerned in passing laws, which they themselves are to execute.

The wisdom, Sir, of many nations, has induced them to enlarge the powers of their rulers, but there are very few instances of the relinquishment of power or the abridgement of authority, on the part of the governors. The very first clause of the eighth section of the first article, which gives to Congress the power "to lay and collect taxes, duties, imposts, excises, &c. &c." appears to me to be big with unnecessary danger, and to reduce human nature, to which I would willingly pay a compliment did not the experience of all ages rise up against me, to too great a test. The arguments, Sir, which have been urged by some Gentlemen, that the impost will defray all expenses, in my estimation, cannot be supported; and common sense will never assent to the assertions which have been made, that the government will not be an additional expence to this country. Will not the support of an army and navy—will not the establishment of a multiplicity of offices in the Legislative, Executive, and particularly the Judiciary departments, most of which will be of a national character, and must be supported with a superior degree of dignity and credit, be prodigious additions to the national expence? And, Sir, if the States are to retain, even the shadow of sovereignty, the expence thence arising must also be defrayed, and will be very considerable.

I come now, Sir, to speak of a clause, to which our attention has been frequently called, and on which many Gentlemen have already delivered their sentiments; a clause, in the estimation of some, of little consequence, and which rather serves as a pretext for scuffling for votes, but which, in my opinion, is one of the most important contained in the system, and to which there are many and weighty objections. I refer to the clause, empowering the President, by and with the consent of two thirds of the Senators present, to make treaties.—If, Sir, the dismemberment of empire—if the privation of the most essential national rights, and the very existence of a people, depend on this clause, surely, Sir, it merits the most thorough investigation; and if, on that investigation, it appears that those great rights are endangered, it highly behoves us to amend it in such manner as will prevent the evils which may arise from it as it now stands. My objections to it do not arise from a view of the particular situation of the western part of this State, although certainly we are bound, by every principle, to attend to the interest of our fellow-citizens in that quarter, but from an apprehension that the principle pervades all America, and that in its operation, it will be found highly injurious to the Southern States. It will, I presume, be readily admitted, that the dismemberment of empire is the highest act of sovereign authority, the exercise of which can be authorized only by absolute authority: Exclusive then, Sir, of any consideration which arises from the particular system of American politics, the guard established against the exercise of this power is by far too slender. The President with the concurrence of two-thirds of the Senate present, may make a treaty, by which any territory may be ceded or the navigation of any river surrendered; thereby granted to five States the exercise of a right acknowledged to be the highest act of sovereignty—to fifteen men, not the representatives of the country to be ceded, but, as has already happened, men whose interest and policy it may be to make such surrender. Admitting for a moment, that this point is as well guarded by the proposed plan, as by the old Articles of Confederation, to which however common sense can never assent, have we not already had cause to tremble, and ought we not to guard against the accomplishment of a scheme, to which nothing but an inattention to the general interest of America, and a selfish regard to the interest of particular States, could have given rise: Surely, Sir, we ought; and since we have already seen a diabolical attempt made to surrender the navigation of a river, the source of which is as yet unknown, and on which depends the importance of the southern part of America—since we have every reason to believe that the same principle which at first dictated this measure still exists and will forever operate—it is our duty; a duty we owe to ourselves; which we owe to the southern part of America, and which we owe to the natural rights of mankind, to guard against it in such manner as will forever prevent its accomplishment.[2] This, Sir, is not done by the clause, nor will it rest on that sure footing which I wish and which the importance of the subject demands, until the concurrence of three-fourths *of all the Senators*, shall be requisite to ratify a treaty respecting the cession of territory; the surrender of the navigation of rivers, or the use of the American seas.

That sacred palladium of liberty, the freedom of the press, the influence of which is so great that it is the opinion of the ablest writers, that no country can remain long in slavery where it is restrained, has not been expressed, nor are the liberties of the people ascertained and protected by any declaration of rights—that inestimable privilege, the most important which freemen can enjoy, the trial by jury in all civil cases has not been guarded by the system—and while they have been inattentive to these all important considerations, they have made provision for the introduction of standing armies in time of peace—These, Sir, ever have been used as the grand machines to suppress the liberties of the people, and will ever awaken the jealousy of republicans, so long as liberty is dear and tyranny odious to mankind.

Congress, Sir, have the power "to declare war," and also to raise and support armies, and if we suppose them to be a representation of the States, the *nexus imperii* of the British Constitution is here lost—there the King has the power of declaring war, and the Parliament that of raising money to support it. Governments ought not to depend on an army for their support, but ought to be so formed as to have the confidence, respect and affection of the citizens—Some degree of virtue, Sir, must exist, or freedom cannot live—A standing army will introduce idleness and extravagance, which will be followed by their sure concomitant vices—In a country extensive, like ours, the power of the sword is more sensibly felt, than in a small community—the advantages, Sir, of military science and discipline cannot be exerted unless a proper number of soldiers are united in one body, and actuated by one soul. The tyrant of a single town, or a small district, would soon discover that an hundred armed soldiers were a weak defence against ten thousand peasants or citizens: but ten thousand well disciplined soldiers will command, with despotic sway, millions of subjects, and will strike terror into the most numerous populace. It was this, Sir, which enabled the Prætorean bands of Rome, whose number scarcely amounted to ten thousand, after having violated the sanctity of the throne, by the attrocious murder of a most excellent Emperor, to dishonor the majesty of it, by proclaiming that the Roman Empire—the mistress of the world—was to be disposed of to the highest bidder, at public auction;—and to their licentious frenzy may be attributed the *first* cause of the decline and fall of that mighty Empire—We ought therefore strictly to guard against the establishment of an army, whose only occupation would be idleness, whose only effort the introduction of vice and dissipation, and who would, at some future day deprive us of our liberties, as a reward for past favors, by the introduction of some military despot.

I had it in contemplation, to have made some observations on the disposition of the judicial powers, but as my knowledge in that line is confined, and as the subject has been so ably handled by other Gentlemen, and the defects clearly developed, and as their arguments remain unanswered, I shall say nothing on that head;—the want of responsibility to the people from their Representatives, would furnish matter of ample discussion, but I pass it over in silence, only observing that it is a grand, and indeed a *daring* fault, and one which sanctions with security the most tyrannic edicts, of a despotic ruler. The ambiguous terms in which all rights are secured to the people, and the clear and comprehensive language used, when power is granted to Congress, also affords matter for suspicions and objections, but the able manner in which, my very worthy, my very eloquent, and truly patriotic friend and co-adjutor, whose name shall ever be hallowed in the temple of liberty, has handled this subject, would render any observations from me, tedious and unnecessary.[3]

Permit me then to conclude by reminding Gentlemen who appeal to history to prove the excellence of the proposed plan, that their mode of comparison is unjust—"Wealth and extent of territory, says the great Montesquieu, have a relation to Government, and the manners and customs of the people are closely connected with it." The same system of policy which might have been excellent in the Governments of antiquity, would not probably suit *us* at the present day—The question therefore which should be agitated, is not whether the proposed Constitution is better or worse than those which have from time to time existed, but whether it is calculated to secure our liberties and happiness at the present stage of the world.

For my own part, after an impartial investigation of it, and after a close attention, and candid consideration of the arguments which have been used, I am impressed with an opinion, that it is not—I am persuaded, that by adopting it, and then proposing amendments, that unfortunate traveller liberty is more endangered than the Union of the States will be by first proposing these amendments. I am so far an enthusiast in favor of liberty, that I never will trust the sacred deposit to other hands, nor will I exchange it for any earthly consideration—and I have such a fixed aversion to the bitter cup of slavery, that in my estimation a draught is not sweetened, whether administered by the hand of a Turk, a Briton, or an American.

Impressed then, Sir, with these sentiments, and governed by these principles, I shall decidedly give my vote in favor of previous amendments;—but, Sir, should the question be decided contrary to my wishes, the first wish of my heart is, that that decision may promote the happiness and prosperity of the country so dear to us all.

A planter and member of the Continental Congress who later served in the United States Congress, John Dawson emphasized that powerful central government was an opponent of the rights of the state governments (see John Dawson entry in *Biographies*). His "Fears for the Future" centered on worries that in a large republic personal liberties would be lost. Dawson also worried that Presidential treaty making could result in ceding western land to a foreign power. Dawson joined Henry and George Mason in calling for amending the Constitution with a bill of personal rights.

REFERENCE

Elliot, *Debates*, vol. 3.

NOTES

1. Refers to Shays' Rebellion in Massachusetts.
2. Refers to loss of navigation rights to the Mississippi River.
3. Refers to ally Patrick Henry.

John Tyler, Speech in the Virginia State Ratification Convention, *June 25, 1788*

I have seen their subsequent amendments, and, although they hold out something like the thing we wish, yet they have not entered pointedly and substantially into it. What have they said about direct taxation? They have said nothing on this subject. Is there any limitation of, or restriction on, the federal judicial power? I think not. So that gentlemen hold out the idea of amendments which will not alter one dangerous part of it. It contains many dangerous articles. No gentleman here can give such a construction of it as will give general satisfaction. Shall we be told that we shall be attacked by the Algerines, and that disunion will take place, unless we adopt it? Such language as this I did not expect here. Little did I think that matters would come to this, when we separated from the mother country. There, sir, every man is amenable to punishment. There is far less responsibility in this government. British tyranny would have been more tolerable. By our present government, every man is secure in his person, and the enjoyment of his property. There is no man who is not liable to be punished for misdeeds. I ask, What is it that disturbs men whose liberty is in the highest zenith? Human nature will always be the same. Men never were, nor ever will, be satisfied with their happiness.

They tell you that one letter's alteration will destroy it. I say that it is very far from being perfect. I ask, if it were put in immediate operation, whether the people could bear it—whether two bodies can tax the same species of property. The idea of two omnipotent powers is inconsistent. The natural tendency must be, either a revolt, or the destruction of the state governments, and a consolidation of them all into one general system. If we are to be consolidated, let it be on better grounds. So long as climate will have effect on men, so long will the different climates of the United States render us different. Therefore a consolidation is contrary to our nature, and can only be supported by an arbitrary government.

Previous and subsequent amendments are now the only dispute; and when gentlemen say that there is a greater probability of obtaining the one than the other, they accompany their assertions with no kind of argument. What is the reason that amendments cannot be got after ratification? Because we have granted power. Because the amendments you propose will diminish their power, and undo some clauses in that paper. This argument proves to me that they cannot be serious. It has been plainly proved to you that it is impracticable. Local advantages are given up, as well as the regulation of trade. When it is the case, will the little states agree to an alteration? When gentlemen insist on this, without producing any argument, they will find no credulity in me. Another convention ought to be had, whether the amendments be previous or subsequent. They say another convention is dangerous. How is this proved? It is only their assertion. Gentlemen tell us we shall be ruined without adoption. Is this reasonable? It does not appear so to me.

Much has been said on the subject of war by foreigners, and the Indians; but a great deal has been said in refutation of it. Give me leave to say that, from the situation of the powers of Europe at this time, no danger is to be apprehended from thence. Will the French go to war with you, if you do not pay them what you owe them? Will they thereby destroy that balance, to preserve which they have taken such immense trouble? But Great Britain will go to war with you, unless you comply with the treaty. Great Britain, which, to my sorrow, has monopolized our trade, is to go to war with us unless the law of treaties be binding. Is this reasonable? It is not the interest of Britain to quarrel with us. She will not hazard any measure which may tend to take our trade out of her hands. It is not the interest of Holland to see us destroyed or oppressed. It is the interest of every nation in Europe to keep up the balance of power, and therefore they will not suffer any nation to attack us, without immediately interfering.

But much is said of the propriety of our becoming a great and powerful nation. There is a great difference between offensive and defensive war. If we can defend ourselves, it is sufficient. Shall we sacrifice the peace and happiness of this country, to enable us to make wanton war?

My conduct throughout the revolution will justify me. I have invariably wished to oppose oppressions. It is true that I have now a paltry office. I am willing to give it up—away with it! It has no influence on my present conduct. I wish Congress to have the regulation of trade. I was of opinion that a partial regulation alone would not suffice. I was among those members who, a few years ago, proposed that regulation. I have lamented that I have put my hand to it, since this measure may have grown out of it. It was the hopes of our people to have their trade on a respectable footing. But it never entered into my head that we should quit liberty, and throw ourselves into the hands of an energetic government. Do you want men to be more free, or less free, than they are? Gentlemen have been called upon to show the causes of this measure. None have been shown. Gentlemen say we shall be ruined unless we adopt it. We must give up our opinions. We cannot judge for ourselves. I hope gentlemen, before this, have been satisfied that such language is improper. All states which have heretofore been lavish in the concession of power and relinquishment of privileges have lost their liberty. It has been often observed (and it cannot be too often observed) that liberty ought not to be given up without knowing the terms. The gentlemen themselves cannot agree in the construction of various clauses of it; and so long as this is the case, so long shall liberty be in danger.

Gentlemen say we are jealous. I am not jealous of this house. I could trust my life with them. If this Constitution were safer, I should not be afraid. But its defects warrant my suspicions and fears. We are not passing laws now, but laying the foundation on which laws are to be made. We ought, therefore, to be cautious how we decide. When I consider the Constitution in all its parts, I cannot but dread its operation. It contains a variety of powers too dangerous to be vested in any set of men whatsoever. Its power of direct taxation, the supremacy of the laws of the Union, and of treaties, are exceedingly dangerous. I have never heard any manner of calling the President to account for his conduct, nor even the members of the democratic branch of the government. We may turn out our ten members, but what can we do with the other fifty-five? The wisdom of Great Britain gave each state its own legislative assembly and judiciary, and a right to tax themselves. When they attempted to infringe that right, we declared war. This system violates that right. In the year 1781 the Assembly were obliged to pass a law, that forty members could pass laws. I have heard many members say that it was a great departure from the constitution, and that it would lead to aristocracy. If we could not trust forty, can we trust ten? Those who lay a tax ought to be amenable to the payment of a proportionate share of it. I see nothing in their subsequent amendments going to this point—that we shall have a right to tax ourselves.

But gentlemen say that this would destroy the Constitution. Of what avail, then, will their subsequent amendments be? Will gentlemen satisfy themselves that, when they adopt this Constitution, their country will be happy? Is not the country divided? Is it a happy government, which divides the people, and sets brother in opposition to brother? This measure has produced anarchy and confusion. We ought to have been unanimous, and gone side by side, as we went through the revolution. Instead of unanimity, it has produced a general diversity of opinions, which may terminate in the most unhappy consequences. We only wish to do away ambiguities, and establish our rights on clear and explicit terms. If this be done, we shall all be like one man—we shall unite and be happy. But if we adopt it in its present form, unanimity or concord can never take place. After adoption, we can never expect to see it amended; because they will consider requests and solicitations for amendments as in a high degree dictatorial. They will say, You have signed and sealed, and you cannot now retract.

When I review all these considerations, my heart is full, and can never be at peace till I see these defects removed. Our only consolation is the virtue of the present age. It is possible that, when they see the country divided, these politicians will reconcile the minds of their countrymen, by introducing such alterations as shall be deemed necessary. Were it not for this hope, I should be in despair. I shall say no more, but that I wish my name to be seen in the yeas and nays, that it may be known that my opposition arose from a full persuasion and conviction of its being dangerous to the liberties of my country.

The father of the later president of the United States, a lawyer, planter, and future governor of the state, John Tyler called for amendments to the Constitution before Virginians ratified it (see John Tyler entry in *Biographies*). He said that the Constitution had not adequately addressed the central government's excessive powers of taxation.

REFERENCES

Debates and Proceedings; Elliot, *Debates*, vol. 3.

Patrick Henry, Speech in the Virginia State Ratification Convention, *June 25, 1788*

Mr. Chairman, when we were told of the difficulty of obtaining previous amendments, I contended that they might be as easily obtained as subsequent amendments. We are told that nine states have adopted it. If so, when the government gets in motion, have they not a right to consider our amendments as well as if we adopted first? If we remonstrate, may they not consider and admit our amendments? But now, sir, when we have been favored with a view of their subsequent amendments, I am confirmed in what I apprehended; and that is, subsequent amendments will make our condition worse; for they are placed in such a point of view as will make this Convention ridiculous. I speak in plain, direct language. It is extorted from me. If this Convention will say, that the very right by which amendments are desired is not secured, then I say our rights are not secured. As we have the right of desiring amendments, why not exercise it? But gentlemen deny this right. It follows, of course, that, if this right be not secured, our other rights are not. The proposition of subsequent amendments is only to lull our apprehensions. We speak the language of contradiction and inconsistency, to say that rights are secured, and then say that they are not. Is not this placing this Convention in a contemptible light? Will not this produce contempt of us in Congress, and every other part of the world? Will gentlemen tell me that they are in earnest about these amendments?

I am convinced they mean nothing serious. What are the rights which they do not propose to secure—which they reject?—for I contend there are many essential and vital rights which are omitted. One is the power of direct taxation. Gentlemen will not even give this invaluable right a place among their subsequent amendments. And do gentlemen mean seriously that they will oppose us on this ground on the floor of Congress? If Virginia thinks it one of her dearest rights, she need not expect to have it amended. No, sir; it will be opposed. Taxes and excises are to be laid on us. The people are to be oppressed, and the state legislature prostrated. Very material amendments are omitted. With respect to your militia, we only request that, if Congress should refuse to find arms for them, this country may lay out their own money to purchase them. But what do the gentlemen on the other side say? As much as that they will oppose you in this point also; for, if my recollection has not failed me, they have discarded this also. And shall we be deprived of this privilege? We propose to have it, in case there shall be a necessity to claim it. And is this claim incompatible with the safety of this country—with the grandeur and strength of the United States? If gentlemen find peace and rest on their minds, when the relinquishment of our rights is declared to be necessary for the aggrandizement of the government, they are more contented than I am.

Another thing which they have not mentioned, is the power of *treaties.* Two thirds of the senators present can make treaties; and they are, when made, to be the supreme law of the land, and are to be paramount to the state constitutions. We wish to guard against the temporary suspension of our great national rights. We wish some qualification of this dangerous power. We wish to modify it. One amendment which has been wished for, in this respect, is, that no treaty should be made without the consent of a considerable majority of both houses. I might go on and enumerate many other great rights entirely neglected by their subsequent amendments; but I shall pass over them in silence. I am astonished at what my worthy friend (Mr. Innes) said—that we have no right of proposing previous amendments. That honorable gentleman is endowed with great eloquence—eloquence splendid, magnificent, and sufficient to shake the human mind! He has brought the whole force of America against this state. He has also strongly represented our comparative weakness, with respect to the powers of Europe. But when I review the actual state of things, I see that dangers from thence are merely ideal. His reasoning has no effect on me. He cannot shake my political faith. He admits our power over subsequent amendments, though not over previous amendments. Where is the distinction between them? If we have a right to depart from the letter of our commission in one instance, we have in the other; for subsequent amendments have no higher authority than previous. We shall be absolutely certain of escaping danger in the one case, but not in the other. I think the apprehension expressed by another honorable gentleman has no good foundation. He apprehended civil discord if we did not adopt. I am willing to concede that he loves his country. I will, for the sake of argument, allow that I am one of the meanest of those who love their country. But what does this amount to? The great and direct end of government is liberty. Secure our liberty and privileges, and the end of government is answered. If this be not effectually done, government is an evil. What amendments does he propose which secure our liberty? I ask pardon if I make a mistake, but it seems to me that his proposed subsequent amendments do not secure one single right. They say that your rights are secured in the paper on the table, so that these subsequent amendments are a mere supererogation. They are not necessary, because the objects intended to be secured by them are secured already. What is to become of the trial by jury? Had its security been made a part of the Constitution, it would have been sufficiently guarded. But as it is, in that proposition it is by no means explicitly secured. Is it not trifling to admit the necessity of securing it, and not do it in a positive, unequivocal manner? I wish I could place it in any other view than a trifling one. It is only intended to attack every project of introducing amendments. If they are serious, why do they not join us, and ask, in a manly, firm, and resolute manner, for these amendments? Their view is to defeat every attempt to amend. When they speak of their subsequent recommendations, they tell you that amendments must be got, and the next moment they say they are unnecessary!

I beg pardon of this house for having taken up more time than came to my share, and I thank them for the patience and polite attention with which I have been heard. If I shall be in the minority, I shall have those painful sensations which arise from a conviction of *being overpowered in a good cause*. Yet I will be a peaceable citizen. My head, my hand, and my heart, shall be at liberty to retrieve the loss of liberty, and remove the defects of that system in a constitutional way. I wish not to go to violence, but will wait with hopes that the spirit which predominated in the revolution is not yet gone, nor the cause of those who are attached to the revolution yet lost. I shall therefore patiently wait in expectation of seeing that government changed, so as to be compatible with the safety, liberty, and happiness, of the people.

Patrick Henry deserves the last word, as he continued his reasons for the need to amend the Constitution, especially to restrict excessive federal powers and to defend personal rights (see Patrick Henry entry in *Biographies*). In this speech, Henry again laid out his bill of rights for the individual. There was some lament in his voice, as he understood his compatriots had failed to force the state convention to adopt amendments.

REFERENCE

Elliot, *Debates*, vol. 3.

12
New York

June 17–July 26, 1788

Ratification #11, July 26, 1788

In favor 30–27

Robert Yates (?) ("Brutus"), I,
October 18, 1787

TO THE *CITIZENS* OF THE *STATE* OF *NEW-YORK*.

When the public is called to investigate and decide upon a question in which not only the present members of the community are deeply interested, but upon which the happiness and misery of generations yet unborn is in great measure suspended, the benevolent mind cannot help feeling itself peculiarly interested in the result.

In this situation, I trust the feeble efforts of an individual, to lead the minds of the people to a wise and prudent determination, cannot fail of being acceptable to the candid and dispassionate part of the community. Encouraged by this consideration, I have been induced to offer my thoughts upon the present important crisis of our public affairs.

Perhaps this country never saw so critical a period in their political concerns. We have felt the feebleness of the ties by which these United-States are held together, and the want of sufficient energy in our present confederation, to manage, in some instances, our general concerns. Various expedients have been proposed to remedy these evils, but none have succeeded. At length a Convention of the states has been assembled, they have formed a constitution which will now, probably, be submitted to the people to ratify or reject, who are the fountain of all power, to whom alone it of right belongs to make or unmake constitutions, or forms of government, at their pleasure. The most important question that was ever proposed to your decision, or to the decision of any people under heaven, is before you, and you are to decide upon it by men of your own election, chosen specially for this purpose. If the constitution, offered to your acceptance, be a wise one, calculated to preserve the invaluable blessings of liberty, to secure the inestimable rights of mankind, and promote human happiness, then, if you accept it, you will lay a lasting foundation of happiness for millions yet unborn; generations to come will rise up and call you blessed. You may rejoice in the prospects of this vast extended continent becoming filled with freemen, who will assert the dignity of human nature. You may solace yourselves with the idea, that society, in this favoured land, will fast advance to the highest point of perfection; the human mind will expand in knowledge and virtue, and the golden age be, in some measure, realised. But if, on the other hand, this form of government contains principles that will lead to the subversion of liberty—if it tends to establish a despotism, or, what is worse, a tyrannic aristocracy; then, if you adopt it, this only remaining assylum for liberty will be shut up, and posterity will execrate your memory.

Momentous then is the question you have to determine, and you are called upon by every motive which should influence a noble and virtuous mind, to examine it well, and to make up a wise judgment. It is insisted, indeed, that this constitution must be received, be it ever so imperfect. If it has its defects, it is said, they can be best amended when they are experienced. But remember, when the people once part with power, they can seldom or never resume it again but by force. Many instances can be produced in which the people have voluntarily increased the powers of their rulers; but few, if any, in which rulers have willingly abridged their authority. This is a sufficient reason to induce you to be careful, in the first instance, how you deposit the powers of government.

With these few introductory remarks, I shall proceed to a consideration of this constitution.

The first question that presents itself on the subject is, whether a confederated government be the best for the United States or not? Or in other words, whether the thirteen United States should be reduced to one great republic, governed by one legislature, and under the direction of one executive and judicial; or whether they should continue thirteen confederated republics, under the direction and controul of a supreme federal head for certain defined national purposes only?

This enquiry is important, because, although the government reported by the convention does not go to a perfect and entire consolidation, yet it approaches so near to it, that it must, if executed, certainly and infallibly terminate in it.

This government is to possess absolute and uncontroulable power, legislative, executive and judicial, with respect to every object to which it extends, for by the last clause of section 8th, article 1st, it is declared "that the Congress shall have power to make all laws which shall be necessary and proper for carrying into execution the foregoing powers, and all other powers vested by this constitution, in the government of the United States; or in any department or office thereof." And by the 6th article, it is declared "that this constitution, and the laws of the United States, which shall be made in pursuance thereof, and the treaties made, or which shall be made, under the authority of the United States, shall be the supreme law of the land; and the judges in every state shall be bound thereby, any thing in the constitution, or law of any state to the contrary notwithstanding." It appears from these articles that there is no need of any intervention of the state governments, between the Congress and the people, to execute any one power vested in the general government, and that the constitution and laws of every state are nullified and declared void, so far as they are or shall be inconsistent with this constitution, or the laws made in pursuance of it, or with treaties made under the authority of the United States.—The government then, so far as it extends, is a complete one, and not a confederation. It is as much one complete government as that of New-York or Massachusetts, has as absolute and perfect powers to make and execute all laws, to appoint officers, institute courts, declare offences, and annex penalties, with respect to every object to which it extends, as any other in the world. So far therefore as its powers reach, all ideas of confederation are given up and lost. It is true this government is limited to certain objects, or to speak more properly, some small degree of power is still left to the states, but a little attention to the powers vested in the general government, will convince every candid man, that if it is capable of being executed, all that is reserved for the individual states must very soon be annihilated, except so far as they are barely necessary to the organization of the general government. The powers of the general legislature extend to every case that is of the least importance—there is nothing valuable to human nature, nothing dear to freemen, but what is within its power. It has authority to make laws which will affect the lives, the liberty, and property of every man in the United States; nor can the constitution or laws of any state, in any way prevent or impede the full and complete execution of every power given. The legislative power is competent to lay taxes, duties, imposts, and excises;—there is no limitation to this power, unless it be said that the clause which directs the use to which those taxes, and duties shall be applied, may be said to be a limitation: but this is no restriction of the power at all, for by this clause they are to be applied to pay the debts and provide for the common defence and general welfare of the United States; but the legislature have authority to contract debts at their discretion; they are the sole judges of what is necessary to provide for the common defence, and they only are to determine what is for the general welfare; this power therefore is neither more nor less, than a power to lay and collect taxes, imposts, and excises, at their pleasure; not only the power to lay taxes unlimited, as to the amount they may require, but it is perfect and absolute to raise them in any mode they please. No state legislature, or any power in the state governments, have any more to do in carrying this into effect, than the authority of one state has to do with that of another. In the business therefore of laying and collecting taxes, the idea of confederation is totally lost, and that of one entire republic is embraced. It is proper here to remark, that the authority to lay and collect taxes is the most important of any power that can be granted; it connects with it almost all other powers, or at least will in process of time draw all other after it; it is the great mean of protection, security, and defence, in a good government, and the great engine of oppression and tyranny in a bad one. This cannot fail of being the case, if we consider the contracted limits which are set by this constitution, to the late governments, on this article of raising money. No state can emit paper money—lay any duties, or imposts, on imports, or exports, but by consent of the Congress; and then the net produce shall be for the benefit of the United States: the only mean therefore left, for any state to support its government and discharge its debts, is by direct taxation; and the United States have also power to lay and collect taxes, in any way they please. Every one who has thought on the subject, must be convinced that but small sums of money can be collected in any country, by direct taxes, when the fœderal government begins to exercise the right of taxation in all its parts, the legislatures of the several states will find it impossible to raise monies to support their governments. Without money they cannot be supported, and they must dwindle away, and, as before observed, their powers absorbed in that of the general government.

It might be here shewn, that the power in the federal legislative, to raise and support armies at pleasure, as well in peace as in war, and their controul over the militia, tend, not only to a consolidation of the government, but the destruction of liberty.—I shall not, however, dwell upon these, as a few observations upon the judicial power of this government, in addition to the preceding, will fully evince the truth of the position.

The judicial power of the United States is to be vested in a supreme court, and in such inferior courts as Congress may from time to time ordain and establish. The powers of these courts are very extensive; their jurisdiction comprehends all civil causes, except such as arise between citizens of the same state; and it extends to all cases in law and equity arising under the constitution. One inferior court must be established, I presume, in each state, at least, with the necessary executive officers appendant thereto. It is easy to see, that in the common course of things, these courts will eclipse the dignity, and take away from the respectability, of the state courts. These courts will be, in themselves, totally independent of the states, deriving their authority from the United States, and receiving from them fixed salaries; and in the course of human events it is to be expected, that they will swallow up all the powers of the courts in the respective states.

How far the clause in the 8th section of the 1st article may operate to do away all idea of confederated states, and to effect an entire consolidation of the whole into one general government, it is impossible to say. The powers given by this article are very general and comprehensive, and it may receive a construction to justify the passing almost any law. A power to make all laws, which shall be *necessary and proper*, for carrying into execution, all powers vested by the constitution in the government of the United States, or any department or officer thereof, is a power very comprehensive and definite, and may, for ought I know, be exercised in such manner as entirely to abolish the state legislatures. Suppose the legislature of a state should pass a law to raise money to support their government and pay the state debt, may the Congress repeal this law, because it may prevent the collection of a tax which they may think proper and necessary to lay, to provide for the general welfare of the United States? For all laws made, in pursuance of this constitution, are the supreme law of the land, and the judges in every state shall be bound thereby, any thing in the constitution or laws of the different states to the contrary notwithstanding.—By such a law, the government of a particular state might be overturned at one stroke, and thereby be deprived of every means of its support.

It is not meant, by stating this case, to insinuate that the constitution would warrant a law of this kind; or unnecessarily to alarm the fears of the people, by suggesting, that the federal legislature would be more likely to pass the limits assigned them by the constitution, than that of an individual state, further than they are less responsible to the people. But what is meant is, that the legislature of the United States are vested with the great and uncontroulable powers, of laying and collecting taxes, duties, imposts, and excises; of regulating trade, raising and supporting armies, organizing, arming, and disciplining the militia, instituting courts, and other general powers. And are by this clause invested with the power of making all laws, *proper and necessary*, for carrying all these into execution; and they may so exercise this power as entirely to annihilate all the state governments, and reduce this country to one single government. And if they may do it, it is pretty certain they will; for it will be found that the power retained by individual states, small as it is, will be a clog upon the wheels of the government of the United States; the latter therefore will be naturally inclined to remove it out of the way. Besides, it is a truth confirmed by the unerring experience of ages, that every man, and every body of men, invested with power, are ever disposed to increase it, and to acquire a superiority over every thing that stands in their way. This disposition, which is implanted in human nature, will operate in the federal legislature to lessen and ultimately to subvert the state authority, and having such advantages, will most certainly succeed, if the federal government succeeds at all. It must be very evident then, that what this constitution wants of being a complete consolidation of the several parts of the union into one complete government, possessed of perfect legislative, judicial, and executive powers, to all intents and purposes, it will necessarily acquire in its exercise and operation.

Let us now proceed to enquire, as I at first proposed, whether it be best the thirteen United States should be reduced to one great republic, or not? It is here taken for granted, that all agree in this, that whatever government we adopt, it ought to be a free one; that it should be so framed as to secure the liberty of the citizens of America, and such an one as to admit of a full, fair, and equal representation of the people. The question then will be, whether a government thus constituted, and founded on such principles, is practicable, and can be exercised over the whole United States, reduced into one state?

If respect is to be paid to the opinion of the greatest and wisest men who have ever thought or wrote on the science of government, we shall be constrained to conclude, that a free republic cannot succeed over a country of such immense extent, containing such a number of inhabitants, and these encreasing in such rapid progression as that of the whole United States. Among the many illustrious authorities which might be produced to this point, I shall content myself with quoting only two. The one is the baron de Montesquieu, spirit of laws, chap. xvi. vol. 1. "It is natural to a republic to have only a small territory, otherwise it cannot long subsist. In a large republic there are men of large fortunes, and consequently of less moderation; there are trusts too great to be placed in any single subject; he has interest of his own; he soon begins to think that he may be happy, great and glorious, by oppressing his fellow citizens; and that he may raise himself to grandeur on the ruins of his country. In a large republic, the public good is sacrificed to a thousand views; it is subordinate to exceptions, and depends on accidents. In a small one, the interest of the public is easier perceived, better understood, and more within the reach of every citizen; abuses are of less extent, and of course are less protected." Of the same opinion is the marquis Beccarari.

History furnishes no example of a free republic, any thing like the extent of the United States. The Grecian republics were of small extent; so also was that of the Romans. Both of these, it is true, in process of time, extended their conquests over large territories of country; and the consequence was, that their governments were changed from that of free governments to those of the most tyrannical that ever existed in the world.

Not only the opinion of the greatest men, and the experience of mankind, are against the idea of an extensive republic, but a variety of reasons may be drawn from the reason and nature of things, against it. In every government, the will of the sovereign is the law. In despotic governments, the supreme authority being lodged in one, his will is law, and can be as easily expressed to a large extensive territory as to a small one. In a pure democracy the people are the sovereign, and their will is declared by themselves; for this purpose they must all come together to deliberate, and decide. This kind of government cannot be exercised, therefore, over a country of any considerable extent; it must be confined to a single city, or at least limited to such bounds as that the people can conveniently assemble, be able to debate, understand the subject submitted to them, and declare their opinion concerning it.

In a free republic, although all laws are derived from the consent of the people, yet the people do not declare their consent by themselves in person, but by representatives, chosen by them, who are supposed to know the minds of their constituents, and to be possessed of integrity to declare this mind.

In every free government, the people must give their assent to the laws by which they are governed. This is the true criterion between a free government and an arbitrary one. The former are ruled by the will of the whole, expressed in any manner they may agree upon; the latter by the will of one, or a few. If the people are to give their assent to the laws, by persons chosen and appointed by them, the manner of the choice and the number chosen, must be such, as to possess, be disposed, and consequently qualified to declare the sentiments of the people; for if they do not know, or are not disposed to speak the sentiments of the people, the people do not govern, but the sovereignty is in a few. Now, in a large extended country, it is impossible to have a representation, possessing the sentiments, and of integrity, to declare the minds of the people, without having it so numerous and unwieldly, as to be subject in great measure to the inconveniency of a democratic government.

The territory of the United States is of vast extent; it now contains near three millions of souls, and is capable of containing much more than ten times that number. Is it practicable for a country, so large and so numerous as they will soon become, to elect a representation, that will speak their sentiments, without their becoming so numerous as to be incapable of transacting public business? It certainly is not.

In a republic, the manners, sentiments, and interests of the people should be similar. If this be not the case, there will be a constant clashing of opinions; and the representatives of one part will be continually striving against those of the other. This will retard the operations of government, and prevent such conclusions as will promote the public good. If we apply this remark to the condition of the United States, we shall be convinced that it forbids that we should be one government. The United States includes a variety of climates. The productions of the different parts of the union are very variant, and their interests, of consequence, diverse. Their manners and habits differ as much as their climates and productions; and their sentiments are by no means coincident. The laws and customs of the several states are, in many respects, very diverse, and in some opposite; each would be in favor of its own interests and customs, and, of consequence, a legislature, formed of representatives from the respective parts, would not only be too numerous to act with any care or decision, but would be composed of such heterogenous and discordant principles, as would constantly be contending with each other.

The laws cannot be executed in a republic, of an extent equal to that of the United States, with promptitude.

The magistrates in every government must be supported in the execution of the laws, either by an armed force, maintained at the public expence for that purpose; or by the people turning out to aid the magistrate upon his command, in case of resistance.

In despotic governments, as well as in all the monarchies of Europe, standing armies are kept up to execute the commands of the prince or the magistrate, and are employed for this purpose when occasion requires: But they have always proved the destruction of liberty, and is abhorrent to the spirit of a free republic. In England, where they depend upon the parliament for their annual support, they have always been complained of as oppressive and unconstitutional, and are seldom employed in executing of the laws; never except on extraordinary occasions, and then under the direction of a civil magistrate.

A free republic will never keep a standing army to execute its laws. It must depend upon the support of its citizens. But when a government is to receive its support from the aid of the citizens, it must be so constructed as to have the confidence, respect, and affection of the people. Men who, upon the call of the magistrate, offer themselves to execute the laws, are influenced to do it either by affection of the government, or from fear; where a standing army is at hand to punish offenders, every man is actuated by the latter principle, and therefore, when the magistrate calls, will obey: but, where this is not the case, the government must rest for its support upon the confidence and respect which the people have for their government and laws. The body of the people being attached, the government will always be sufficient to support and execute its laws, and to operate upon the fears of any faction which may be opposed to it, not only to prevent an opposition to the execution of the laws themselves, but also to compel the most of them to aid the magistrate; but the people will not be likely to have such confidence in their rulers, in a republic so extensive as the United States, as necessary for these purposes. The confidence which the people have in their rulers, in a free republic, arises from their knowing them, from their being responsible to them for their conduct, and from the power they have of displacing them when they misbehave: but in a republic of the extent of this continent, the people in general would be acquainted with very few of their rulers: the people at large would know little of their proceedings, and it would be extremely difficult to change them. The people in Georgia and New-Hampshire would not know one another's mind, and therefore could not act in concert to enable them to effect a general change of representatives. The different parts of so extensive a country could not possibly be made acquainted with the conduct of their representatives, nor be informed of the reasons upon which measures were founded. The consequence will be, they will have no confidence in their legislature, suspect them of ambitious views, be jealous of every measure they adopt, and will not support the laws they pass. Hence the government will be nerveless and inefficient, and no way will be left to render it otherwise, but by establishing an armed force to execute the laws at the point of the bayonet—a government of all others the most to be dreaded.

In a republic of such vast extent as the United-States, the legislature cannot attend to the various concerns and wants of its different parts. It cannot be sufficiently numerous to be acquainted with the local condition and wants of the different districts, and if it could, it is impossible it should have sufficient time to attend to and provide for all the variety of cases of this nature, that would be continually arising.

In so extensive a republic, the great officers of government would soon become above the controul of the people, and abuse their power to the purpose of aggrandizing themselves, and oppressing them. The trust committed to the executive offices, in a country of the extent of the United-States, must be various and of magnitude. The command of all the troops and navy of the republic, the appointment of officers, the power of pardoning offences, the collecting of all the public revenues, and the power of expending them, with a number of other powers, must be lodged and exercised in every state, in the hands of a few. When these are attended with great honor and emolument, as they always will be in large states, so as greatly to interest men to pursue them, and to be proper objects for ambitious and designing men, such men will be ever restless in their pursuit after them. They will use the power, when they have acquired it, to the purposes of gratifying their own interest and ambition, and it is scarcely possible, in a very large republic, to call them to account for their misconduct, or to prevent their abuse of power.

These are some of the reasons by which it appears, that a free republic cannot long subsist over a country of the great extent of these states. If then this new constitution is calculated to consolidate the thirteen states into one, as it evidently is, it ought not to be adopted.

Though I am of opinion, that it is a sufficient objection to this government, to reject it, that it creates the whole union into one government, under the form of a republic, yet if this objection was obviated, there are exceptions to it, which are so material and fundamental, that they ought to determine every man, who is a friend to the liberty and happiness of mankind, not to adopt it. I beg the candid and dispassionate attention of my countrymen while I state these objections—they are such as have obtruded themselves upon my mind upon a careful attention to the matter, and such as I sincerely believe are well founded. There are many objections, of small moment, of which I shall take no notice—perfection is not to be expected in any thing that is the production of man—and if I did not in my conscience believe that this scheme was defective in the fundamental principles—in the foundation upon which a free and equal government must rest—I would hold my peace.

Robert Yates, a lawyer, delegate to the Constitutional Convention, and later state supreme court justice, possessed a brilliant legal mind (see Robert Yates entry in *Biographies*). All thirteen of the "Brutus" essays, the last in February 1788, circulated widely in the press and as pamphlets, and deserve careful consideration. In the first, Yates insisted that the proposed Constitution violated the requirements for a free and independent government. He also feared for the civil rights of the people. Above all, Yates questioned whether a national government could be created in so large and diverse a country.

REFERENCES

New York *Journal*, October 18, 1787; Storing, *Complete*, vol. 2, is the best source for evidence of Yates's authorship of "Brutus," although the authorship remains controversial.

George Clinton (?) ("Cato"), V,
November 22, 1787

TO THE *CITIZENS* OF THE STATE O*F NEW-YORK*

In my last number I endeavored to prove that the language of the article relative to the establishment of the executive of this new government was vague and inexplicit, that the great powers of the President, connected with his duration in office would lead to oppression and ruin. That he would be governed by favorites and flatterers, or that a dangerous council would be collected from the great officers of state;—that the ten miles square, if the remarks of one of the wisest men, drawn from the experience of mankind, may be credited, would be the asylum of the base, idle, avaricious and ambitious, and that the court would possess a language and manners different from yours; that a vice-president is as unnecessary, as he is dangerous in his influence—that the president cannot represent you, because he is not of your own immediate choice, that if you adopt this government, you will incline to an arbitrary and odious aristocracy or monarchy—that the president possessed of the power, given him by this frame of government differs but very immaterially from the establishment of monarchy in Great-Britain, and I warned you to beware of the fallacious resemblance that is held out to you by the advocates of this new system between it and your own state governments.

And here I cannot help remarking, that inexplicitness seems to pervade this whole political fabric: certainty in political compacts which Mr. Coke *calls the mother and nurse of repose and quietness*, the want of which induced men to engage in political society, has ever been held by a wise and free people as essential to their security; as on the one hand it fixes barriers which the ambitious and tyrannically disposed magistrate dare not overleap, and on the other, becomes a wall of safety to the community—otherwise stipulations between the governors and governed are nugatory; and you might as well deposit the important powers of legislation and execution in one or a few and permit them to govern according to their disposition and will; but the world is too full of examples, which prove that *to live by one man's will became the cause of all men's misery.* Before the existence of express political compacts it was reasonably implied that the magistrate should govern with wisdom and justice, but mere implication was too feeble to restrain the unbridled ambition of a bad man, or afford security against negligence, cruelty, or any other defect of mind. It is alledged that the opinions and manners of the people of America, are capable to resist and prevent an extension of prerogative or oppression; but you must recollect that opinion and manners are mutable, and may not always be a permanent obstruction against the encroachments of government; that the progress of a commercial society begets luxury, the parent of inequality, the foe to virtue, and the enemy to restraint; and that ambition and voluptuousness aided by flattery, will teach magistrates, where limits are not explicitly fixed to have separate and distinct interests from the people, besides it will not be denied that government assimilates the manners and opinions of the community to it. Therefore, a general presumption that rulers will govern well is not a sufficient security.— You are then under a sacred obligation to provide for the safety of your posterity, and would you now basely desert their interests, when by a small share of prudence you may transmit to them a beautiful political patrimony, which will prevent the necessity of their travelling through seas of blood to obtain that, which your wisdom might have secured:—It is a duty you owe likewise to your own reputation, for you have a great name to lose; you are characterised as cautious, prudent and jealous in politics; whence is it therefore, that you are about to precipitate yourselves into a sea of uncertainty, and adopt a system so vague, and which has discarded so many of your valuable rights:—Is it because you do not believe that an American can be a tyrant? If this be the case you rest on a weak basis, Americans are like other men in similar situations, when the manners and opinions of the community are changed by the causes I mentioned before, and your political compact inexplicit, your posterity will find that great power connected with ambition, luxury, and flattery, will as readily produce a Caesar, Caligula, Nero, and Domitian in America, as the same causes did in the Roman empire.

But the next thing to be considered in conformity to my plan, is the first article of this new government, which comprises the erection of the house of representatives and senate, and prescribes their various powers and objects of legislation. The most general objections to the first article, are that biennial elections for representatives are a departure from the safe democratical principles of annual ones—that the number of representatives are too few; that the apportionment and principles of increase are unjust; that no attention has been paid to either the numbers or property in each state in forming the senate; that the mode in which they are appointed and their duration, will lead to the establishment of an aristocracy; that the senate and president are improperly connected, both as to appointments, and the making of treaties, which are to become the supreme law of the land; that the judicial in some measure, to wit, as to the trial of impeachments is placed in the senate a branch of the legislative, and some times a branch of the executive: that Congress have the improper power of making or altering the regulations prescribed by the different legislatures, respecting the time, place, and manner of holding elections for representatives; and the time and manner of choosing senators; that standing armies may be established, and appropriation of money made for their support, for two years; that the militia of the most remote state may be marched into those states situated at the opposite extreme of this continent; that the slave trade, is to all intents and purposes permanently established; and a slavish capitation, or poll-tax, may at any time be levied—these are some of the many evils that will attend the adoption of this government.

But with respect to the first objection, it may be remarked that a well digested democracy has this advantage over all others, to wit, that it affords to many the opportunity to be advanced to the supreme command, and the honors they thereby enjoy fills them with a desire of rendering themselves worthy of them; hence this desire becomes part of their education, is matured in manhood, and produces an ardent affection for their country, and it is the opinion of the great Sidney, and Montesquieu that this is in a great measure produced by annual election of magistrates.

If annual elections were to exist in this government, and learning and information to become more prevalent, you never will want men to execute whatever you could design—Sidney observes *that a well governed state is as fruitful to all good purposes as the seven headed serpent is said to have been in evil; when one head is cut off, many rise up in the place of it*. He remarks further, that *it was also thought, that free cities by frequent elections of magistrates became nurseries of great and able men, every man endeavouring to excel others, that he might be advanced to the honor he had no other title to, than what might arise from his merit, or reputation*, but the framers of this *perfect government*, as it is called, have departed from this democratical principle, and established bi-ennial elections, for the house of representatives, who are to be chosen by the people, and sextennial for the senate, who are to be chosen by the legislatures of the different states, and have given to the executive the unprecedented power of making temporary senators, in case of vacancies, by resignation or otherwise, and so far forth establishing a precedent for virtual representation (though in fact, their original appointment is virtual) thereby influencing the choice of the legislatures, or if they should not be so complaisant as to conform to his appointment—offence will be given to the executive and the temporary members, will appear ridiculous by rejection; this temporary member, during his time of appointment, will of course act by a power derived from the executive, and for, and under his immediate influence.

It is a very important objection to this government, that the representation consists of so few; too few to resist the influence of corruption, and the temptation to treachery, against which all governments ought to take precautions—how guarded you have been on this head, in your own state constitution, and yet the number of senators and representatives proposed for this vast continent, does not equal those of your own state; how great the disparity, if you compare them with the aggregate numbers in the United States. The history of representation in England, from which we have taken our model of legislation, is briefly this, before the institution of legislating by deputies, the whole free part of the community usually met for that purpose, when this became impossible, by the increase of numbers, the community was divided into districts, from each of which was sent such a number of deputies as was a complete representation of the various numbers and orders of citizens within them; but can it be asserted with truth, that six men can be a complete and full representation of the numbers and various orders of the people in this state? Another thing may be suggested against the small number of representatives is, that but few of you will have the chance of sharing even in this branch of the legislature; and that the choice will be confined to a very few; the more complete it is, the better will your interests be preserved, and the greater the opportunity you will have to participate in government, one of the principal securities of a free people; but this subject has been so ably and fully treated by a writer under the signature of Brutus, that I shall content myself with referring you to him thereon, reserving further observations on the other objections I have mentioned, for my future numbers.

Long-term governor and a political power in the state, George Clinton was a self-made lawyer who later served as vice president of the United States (see George Clinton entry in *Biographies*). He chaired the state ratification convention, and in this pamphlet he queried the excessive powers given to the president and to the federal Congress. Clinton feared that Congress's control over the time and place to hold elections would help to perpetuate an elite in the large and oppressive federal government.

REFERENCES

New York *Journal*, November 22, 1787; Storing, *Complete*, vol. 2 attributes "Brutus" to Clinton, but the authorship remains in dispute.

DeWitt Clinton, "Letters from a Countryman from Dutchess County," IV, V, *December 15, 1787–January 22, 1788*

IV
15 DECEMBER 1787

Dear Sir,

When I closed my third letter, I wished to be more explicit on some things which I had mentioned in that, as well as to make several observations on the new constitution, as it is called; but the conveyance waited and time would not admit of saying any further.

I will now resume the affair of calling a convention. When I said, that I could not see the propriety, or necessity, of the legislatures calling a convention, it was merely on the principle of calling one in consequence of the resolve or recommendation of the late convention, at Philadelphia: lest the people should infer, that the legislature, by recommending a state convention, considered the proceedings and resolve of the Philadelphia convention in some measure obligatory on them so to do. Which, as the latter rejected the authority of those by whom they were appointed (at least, that appears to me to have been the case with the delegate of this state, as well as with the delegates of several other states) and renounced all allegiance to the present United States, I cannot admit to be binding on the legislature, in any manner whatever, even had the late convention really offered a good constitution. But, as it is, I cannot help being of opinion, that the resolve or recommendation is an aggravation, if possible, of the crime and insult.—Should the legislature, when they meet, think that the calling of a convention will be the best means of restoring public tranquility, I shall acquiesce. But then, I wish them not to do it from a sense of any obligation which they are under to the act of their delegate, or that of the delegates of any other state, in the late convention; as the exorbitant act of that body, has, in my opinion, cancelled all obligation, on the part of this state, for considering their proceedings as binding. I should therefore be glad to see them very explicit on such a most *extraordinary* emergency; for surely such it must appear to all unprejudiced minds. It is to be hoped, that they will ascribe the effects to their true causes, which were an evident want of duty, and an inordinate desire for unlimited power, in some of the members who composed the convention; at the same time, pointing out to the people, in the plainest manner, the snare which is laid for them, and, that the adopting of it, will be their *last sovereign act*, unless it should be a violent resumption, by arms.

I imagine, that the faction were rather apprehensive of a reprimand, when they referred their plot to conventions of the people, "for their assent and ratification," in preference to the legislatures, by whom they had been appointed, and from whom they derived all the authority which they had to assemble for a very different purpose. Though, in their reference of it to conventions of the people; they have not been much more polite to those bodies, than they have to the legislatures, and that you must have observed; as it is not submitted to the former for their consideration, improvement, or rejection; but expressly "for their assent and ratification;" which seems to exclude all manner of choice! Was ever self-sufficiency more evident in man?

The legislatures are advised to call conventions of the people for *registering the revolt of their citizen and deputies, as the supreme law of the land!*—Could any thing be more humiliating to sovereign and independent states?—Would this junto have dared to offer such an indignity to any sovereign prince in Europe, had they been appointed by one?—I know that your answer must be in the negative. Why then thus presumptuously attempt to prostrate thirteen sovereignties?—But the answer is obvious, and therefore not requisite at this time.

If the legislature should not be pointedly clear on such an open attempt to dissolve the present confederacy, may we not, in a little time, expect a Shays, or, perhaps, a much more formidable insurgent in this state?

Have you considered the tendency of the 2d paragraph of the 6th article of the NEW EDICT?—It does not appear to me, that either the Centinel, Federal Farmer, or any other writer that I have seen, has sufficiently attended to that clause, and all the consequences which it may involve.[1] I am sensible, that the Centinel calls it a "sweeping clause", but, I imagine, not on account of what I am going to observe, or he would have been more explicit. These are the words:—"This constitution, and the laws of the United States which shall be made in pursuance thereof; and all treaties made, or which shall be made, under the authority of the United States, shall be the *supreme* law of the land, etc." You well know that I am not fond of disputing about words, unless they have an evident tendency to deceive or lead to error, in which case I think, they ought to be thoroughly canvassed, and well understood, especially in an affair of such vast importance as the present. The word 'supreme' is, I believe, generally received, in law and divinity, as an adjective of the superlative degree, and implies the highest in dignity or authority, etc. Now, if we analyze this clause, we shall see how it will appear.

The constitution is to be the *high-authority*—the laws made in pursuance of the constitution are to be the *highest authority*, and *all treaties made, or to be made are to be the highest authority*, and yet there is to be *but one highest authority!* However easy it may be for the contrivers of this, to reconcile it to their own views, I confess to you, that it appears to me something like creed-making.

If all the laws and treaties which may be made, in pursuance of this constitution (provided it be adopted) are to be of *as high authority*, as the constitution, I should be glad to know what security we can have for any one right, however sacred or essential, when there is no explicit proviso, that the laws and treaties which may be made, shall not be repugnant to the constitution?

It is true, that they are to be made in *pursuance* of the constitution; but, *pursuance* is a vague term, and, I presume, generally implies little more than "in consequence, etc."—I have always understood, that the laws derived all their just authority from the constitution, or social compact, as it is sometimes called; and that the latter receives its whole authority, in free governments, from the common consent of the people, and recognizes or acknowledges all their essential rights and liberties, as well as ascertains the reciprocal duties or relations between the governed and their governors, or, perhaps, more properly, their principal public servants, who undertake to manage or conduct the affairs of the community agreeable to certain fixed stipulations, which are mentioned in the original compact or constitution, and not otherwise, but at the risk of being disobeyed, or opposed, as the case may require.

If these ideas of a free government are just, ought there not to have been a positive distinction between the authority of the constitution and that of the laws, treaties, etc. The constitution, when once government is organized, will be mostly passive, but the laws, treaties, etc. of Congress, will be active and voluminous; whence it is easy to foresee what will become of the passive supremacy of it, when it happens to come in competition with two active supremacies, which are coeval and coequal with it, besides several others which will be added, you may rely: For there must be the supreme Lex Parliamentaria of a meagre, biennial representation of the people, and another of an encroaching lordly sexennial Senate, with the supreme prerogatives of a poor, greedy, quadrennial monarch, who must ever be ready to concur in any measures for fleecing the people, provided he is but allowed to participate of the spoil. And, to crown the whole, there must, of course, be a most supreme standing army for us to feed, cloathe and pay, if you will pardon the redundancy of the phrase.

Does it not appear to you, as if the framers of this clause had profited by the embarrassments which the British ministry frequently met with in their attempts to render acts of parliament, paramount to magna charta, or the great charter of the peoples essential rights, which is acknowledged, by the 43d. of Edward the 3d. not to be in the power of parliament to alter, change, or destroy; as all statutes made or to be made, against, or contrary to that constitution, or bill of rights, are, immediately, to be considered as null and void? I have many more observations to make on this political phenomenon, as well as its origination; but domestic affairs require my attention, and I must bid you adieu until another opportunity.

V

22 January 1788

Dear Sir,

Although an unavoidable impediment has prevented my corresponding with you, as often as I wished and intended, yet it has not, entirely, deprived me of all opportunity, of revolving the general convention and their proceedings in my mind. In doing which, I always endeavour to divest myself of every prepossession for, or against them, and their conduct, and, as impartially and candidly as I am capable, to view and consider the whole in every possible point of light, in which I can place it.—And, though it is readily granted, that the convention was composed of a number of very sensible men; yet, if we take the retrospect of the time, when it was first proposed, that there should be a general convention, and the design of it; and likewise reflect, that several of the gentlemen who composed the last convention, were also members of the first, as well as members of the different legislatures which deputed them, besides being delegates to Congress; by all which means they must have had frequent, and great opportunities of learning the sentiments of others with time to read and study the best authors on government, and make up their own minds; on the subject, previous to their last meeting. Shall we find, if we deduct a part of the constitution of this state, some part of the confederation, and the mode of election in Connecticut, etc. from what they have done, that all these combined circumstances, added to four months close application of great abilities and wisdom, which have been so often handied about, have produced any thing adequate to what might reasonably have been expected from such united advantages?—Nay, have they produced any thing but what they ought not to have produced? And, to say no worse of it, have they not descended below the dignity of their characters? Have they not said,—"Done in convention, by the unanimous consent of the states present, etc." shortly after which, we see, "New-York," and "Alexander Hamilton," annexed to it, as though the state were fully represented by that one deputy, when it had sent three deputies?[2]—And, either forgetting, or in hopes that others would forget, have they not afterwards said, "In convention, Monday September 17, 1787. Present, the states of New-Hampshire, Massachusetts, Connecticut," "Mr. Hamilton for New-York, etc.?" By what name ought this to be called? May not some of the wisdom of this world be truly called foolishness? I could very easily imagine, that a gentleman of far less understanding than "Alexander Hamilton," is said to be, would have had modesty enough to wait for further authority, before he set his name to an instrument of such immense importance to the state which entrusted him, and honored him with its interests and commands.

What was this but setting the state and his colleagues at open defiance, and, tacitly, telling the legislature and them, "I want none of your instructions, advice, nor assistance. I better know than you or they what ought to be done, and how to do it. Yes, I know what will suit you all, much better than any body else in the state. I know, that trial by jury, of the vicinage, is a foolish custom, besides frequently embarrassing the judges, it often disappoints the lawyers, and therefore, as I may never have it in my power again, I will now contribute all I can to the abolition of it." If it be true, that actions may speak plainer than words, which, I believe, is a maxim pretty well established, must not the foregoing, or something like it, have been the language or ideas held by that gentleman?

Can the conduct of a man be spoken too freely of, who, unauthorised, has attempted to transfer all power from the many, to the few? Has this state, or, have the United States, expended so much blood and treasure for the sake of exalting one, or the few, and depressing the many? If they have, or, if that was their view, then have they been guilty of an unpardonable offense against God and their country. But it cannot be—that never could have been *even in contemplation*, with the *honest patriots* of seventy-six.

The conduct of George Grenville, the Earl of Hillsborough, Lord Mansfield, the Earl of Bute, Lord North, the King and Parliament of Great Britain, as well as that of their adherents, the stamp-masters, etc. in America, has always been canvassed and treated with the utmost freedom, by the friends of this country. Whence then all this reserve and tenderness for a *junto* of our fellow citizens, who have cast off their allegiance to the United States, and endeavoured to rob us of our best inheritance?

Will it not be said, by the nations of Europe and posterity, that they acted with more spirit and enterprise in robbing us of it, than we have in defending it, though we pretended to know the value of it? Others may do as they please, but, for myself, I am determined to pursue them, with my pen, as long as I can wield it, unless they should make a solemn, public recantation.

Should the new constitution be sufficiently corrected *by a substantial* bill of rights, an equitable representation, chosen annually, or not eligible under two years, the senate chosen triennally, and not eligible in less than three years afterwards, which, apart from it, becoming a more general object to men of learning and genius, might also be a means of preventing monopolies by a few men or families—separating the legislative, judicial and executive departments entirely, and confining the national government to its proper objects; but, by no means admitting a standing army in time of peace, nor a select militia, which last, is a scheme that a certain head has, for some time, been teeming with, and is nothing else but an artful introduction to the other—Nor ought the militia, or any part of it, I think, to be marched out of the state, without the consent of the legislature, and then, not for more than a certain reasonable time, etc.—leaving the states sovereign and independent with respect to their internal police, and relinquishing every idea of drenching the bowels of Africa in gore, for the sake of enslaving its free-born innocent inhabitants, I imagine we might become a happy and respectable people. And, the conduct of the late general convention, by the violent effort which it has made to prostrate our invaluable liberties at the feet of power, fully evinces the absolute necessity of the most express stipulations, for all our essential rights.

But, should the constitution be adopted in its present form, without any amendment, I candidly think, that we should have been much happier, at least for a number of years, in our old connexion with Great-Britain, than with such an absurd heterogeneal kind of government as the convention have proposed for our implicit adoption. Indeed, at present, there are so many dissentients, and others daily becoming so, in all the states, and with arms in their hands, that I cannot see how it could well be organized, without a force superior to every opposition, and that must, of course, absorb all the resources of ways and means immediately, and would defeat many of its own purposes and promises.

Besides, where is the difference between the people's cutting one another's throats, for their own diversion, or cutting them for the pleasure and aggrandizement of one or a few?—If any, I should prefer the former; that is, for my own diversion, etc. I have no idea of being gladiator to any man or body of men whatever; nor marching 500 or 1000 miles to quell an insurrection of such emigrants as are proposed by the new constitution, to be introduced for one and twenty years. No, nor of butchering the natives, that a few great speculators and landholders may engross all the best soil for a song, and revive the old feudal system, which I know to be the wish of some of the advocates for the new government.

Is it not fortunate for this state, that the executive is not one of the aristocracy, or we might have been precipitated into measures, perhaps, which would have afforded us ample time for repentance?

If, at any time, I should trespass on your patience, I beg you will please to place it to the account of the general convention, and believe me to be, dear Sir,

> Your most obedient and
> very humble servant,
> A Countryman.

"Letters from a Countryman from Dutchess County" were published in the New York *Journal*, from November 1787 to February 1788. Nephew of Governor George Clinton, DeWitt was only eighteen in 1788 (see DeWitt Clinton entry in *Biographies*). In "Letters" IV and V he belies his age to defend state sovereignty and to attack excessive federal power. He insisted that the Federalists lied about the role of the states in the new government. Also an outspoken opponent of slavery, young Clinton foresaw a slave power conspiracy to control the direction of the country's growth. This lawyer went on to become a United States senator, governor, developer of the Erie Canal, and a presidential candidate.

REFERENCES

Clinton Papers, Columbia University; Jensen and Kaminski, *Documentary History*, vol. 13; New York *Journal*, December 1787–January 1788; Storing, *Complete*, vol. 6.

NOTES

1. Additional Antifederalist authors.
2. Abraham Yates and John Lansing had left the convention, refusing to sign the Constitution.

Hugh Hughes, "Letters from a Countryman," IV, *January 10, 1788*

IV
10 JANUARY 1788

Worthy Sir,

Since I wrote to you last, I have been giving the new constitution another reading, though, in truth, I got almost sick of it; and, I find by one clause, which I had not taken so much notice of before, that all laws, treaties, etc. made by this new government, is to be the supreme law of the land, the state constitutions, or any of their laws, to the contrary notwithstanding:—now besides, the powers it takes away, in so many words, from our state governments, and to be sure it takes so much, as to leave them, in my poor opinion, very little; its laws and treaties may take away more, and so alter and change what little is left, that no body among us, except the lawyers, will be able to know any thing about our own state constitution and laws—and, I do not believe, they themselves will understand them; I will warrant you, they will not like it the worse for that, for they will always give it such a meaning, as will best suit their own purposes. I find too, that all our state officers are to take an oath or affirmation to support this new constitution—now as they are bound by an oath to support our state constitution too—and as it is almost impossible to find out the meaning of the new constitution, and how much power would be taken away from the state governments in the first place, and altogether uncertain how much more may hereafter be taken away by laws and treaties which may be made under the new government, I cannot, for my share, see how an honest man will be able ever to take such an oath; for one day he may be bound by oath to observe a law made by his own government, and the next day out comes a law or treaty from the general government, by which he is obliged by oath to do the contrary; and if he doubts the right of the general government to make such a law or treaty, to be sure, he will be in a very disagreeable situation. Indeed, my good sir, it is a serious thing to trifle with an oath; and, I think, they ought to have mentioned clearly and plainly, how much power they meant to give to the new government, and how much they meant to leave with the states, before they required oaths of people; and, I believe, it is very certain, that if this general government takes place, they will never get an honest man to serve in either;—for no man but he that has a conscience that will stretch like a tripe, will swear to perform a duty that he cant understand.

I observe, that, by the new constitution, they have guaranteed to the respective states a republican form of government—now I conclude this was, because it was thought the best form and most pleasing to the people; but I cannot find, at the same time, that they have made any engagements, that this new government shall continue to be republican; and I see, they have contrived a way to change it into what they please, without giving themselves the trouble to consult the people about it: as they have taken away almost all powers from the state governments, I think this guarantee to them of a republican form of government will be of very little use, for what good can the mere form or shadow do, when the substance is lost?

Indeed, worthy sir, according to my weak judgment, this new constitution is a very bad one, and if ever it should be agreed to, I am afraid we shall have reason to rue it. It appears very strange to me, that some people who were lately fighting for liberty, should so soon turn tail, and now endeavour to establish a tyranny over their country: and I think, it is not uncharitable to conclude, that instead of contending with the old government for the sake of liberty, they were contending for power—which, no doubt, they will have plenty of, when the new constitution takes place: however, I hope, they will be disappointed, for I can assure you, there is not a man in our parts, but what thinks of it exactly as I do, and is determined at all hazards, to have nothing to do with it; for it would be vain and foolish, indeed, to spend so much blood and treasure to rid ourselves of one tyranny and set up a worse.

I am greatly indebted to you, for putting yourself to the trouble of sending me so many papers about this matter—and as they must be attended with some expence to you, I beg you will send me no more of them; for I have seen enough to convince me very fully, that the new constitution is a very bad one, and a hundredfold worse than our present government; and I do not perceive, that any of the writers in favour of it (although some of them use a vast many fine words, and shew a great deal of learning) are able to remove any of the objections which are made against it. Mr. Wilson, indeed, speaks very highly of it; but we have only his word for its goodness; and nothing is more natural than for a mother to speak well of her own bantling, however ordinary it may be. He seems, however, to be pretty honest in one thing—where he says, "It is the nature of man to pursue his own interest, in preference to the public good"—for they tell me he is a lawyer, and his interest then makes him for the new government, for it will be a noble thing for lawyers; besides, he appears to have an eye to some high place under it, since he speaks with great pleasure of the places of honour and emolument, being diverted to a new channel, by this change of system. As to Mr. Publius,[1] I have read a great many of his papers, and I really cannot find out what he would be at; he seems to me as if he was going to write a history, so I have concluded to wait and buy one of his books, when they come out. The only thing I can understand from him, as far as I have read, is, that it is better to be united than divided—that a great many people are stronger than a few—and that Scotland is better off since the union with England than before; and I think, he proves too, very clearly, that the fewer nations there are in the world, the fewer disputes will be about the law of nations—and the greater number that are joined in, one government, the abler will they be to raise ships and soldiers, and the less need for fighting; but I do not learn that any body denies these matters, or that they have any thing to do with the new constitution. Indeed I am at a loss to know, whether

Mr. Publius means to persuade us to return back to the old government, and make ourselves as happy as Scotland has by its union, or to accept of the new constitution, and get all the world to join with us, so as to make one large government—it would certainly, if what he says is true, be very convenient for Nova-Scotia and Canada, and, for ought I know, his advice will have great weight with them. I have also read several other of the pieces, which appear to be wrote by some other little authors, and by people of little consequence, though they seem to think themselves men of importance, and take upon them grand names, such as Curtius, Caesar, and the like. Now Mr. Caesar do not depend so much on reasoning as upon bullying—he abuses the people very much, and if he spoke in our neighbourhood as impudently as he writes in the newspapers, I question whether he would come off with whole bones: from the manner he talks of the people, he certainly cannot be one of them himself; I imagine he has lately come over from some old country, where they are all Lords and no common people—if so, it would be as well for him to go back again, as to meddle himself with our business, since he holds such a bad opinion of us. I have already gave you a great deal of trouble, honoured Sir, with my long letters—I shall therefore conclude, hoping if any thing new is stiring, that you would be kind enough, now and then, to drop me a line, and let me know how things are going in your city.

> I remain with great respect,
> Your assured friend and
> Humble servant,
> A Countryman.

A publicist and newspaperman, Hugh Hughes was a political lieutenant of the leading Antifederalists (see Hugh Hughes entry in *Biographies*). In the fourth "Letter from a Countryman," Hughes described the dangers to the states' trade interests from the national government's treaty-making authority. He also believed the Federalists would use the new government to control the economic direction of the new nation, and thus of the states.

REFERENCES

Jensen and Kaminski, *Documentary History*, vol. 13; New York *Journal*, January 10, 1788.

NOTE

1. Like so many other New York Antifederalists, Hughes is engaged in a written debate with the authors of the *Federalist Papers*.

Robert Yates and John Lansing, Jr., Letter to Governor George Clinton,
December 21, 1787

Albany, Dec. 21, 1787.

SIR, We do ourselves the honor to advise your excellency, that, in pursuance of concurrent resolutions of the honorable Senate and Assembly, we have, together with Mr. Hamilton, attended the Convention appointed for revising the Articles of Confederation, and reporting amendments to the same.

It is with the sincerest concern we observe, that in the prosecution of the important objects of our mission, we have been reduced to the disagreeable alternative of either exceeding the powers delegated to us, and giving our assent to measures which we conceived destructive of the political happiness of the citizens of the United States; or opposing our opinion to that of a body of respectable men, to whom those citizens had given the most unequivocal proofs of confidence. Thus circumstanced, under these impressions, to have hesitated would have been to be culpable. We therefore gave the principles of the Constitution, which has received the sanction of a majority of the Convention, our decided and unreserved dissent; but we must candidly confess, that we should have been equally opposed to any system, however modified, which had in object the consolidation of the United States into one Government.

We beg leave briefly to state some cogent reasons which, among others, influenced us to decide against a consolidation of the States. These are reducible into two heads.

1st. The limited and well defined powers under which we acted, and which could not, on any possible construction, embrace an idea of such magnitude as to assent to a general Constitution in subversion of that of the State.

2d. A conviction of the impracticability of establishing a general government, pervading every part of the United States, and extending essential benefits to all.

Our powers were explicit, and confined to the sole and express purpose of revising the articles of Confederation, and reporting such alterations and provisions therein, as should render the Federal Constitution adequate to the exigencies of Government, and the preservation of the Union.

From these expressions, we were led to believe that a system of consolidated government, could not, in the remotest degree, have been in contemplation of the Legislature of this State, for that so important a trust, as the adopting measures which tended to deprive the State government of its most essential rights of sovereignty, and to place it in a dependent situation, could not have been confided, by implication, and the circumstance, that the acts of the Convention were to receive a state approbation, in the last resort, forcibly corroborated the opinion, that our powers could not involve the subversion of a Constitution, which being immediately derived from the people, could only be abolished by their express consent, and not by a Legislature, possessing authority vested in them for its preservation. Nor could we suppose, that if it had been the intention of the legislature to abrogate the existing Confederation, they would, in such pointed terms, have directed the attention of their delegates to the revision and amendment of it, in total exclusion of every other idea.

Reasoning in this manner, we were of opinion, that the leading feature of every amendment ought to be the preservation of the individual States, in their uncontrolled constitutional rights; and that, in reserving these, a mode might have been devised, of granting to the Confederacy, the monies arising from a general system of revenue, the power of regulating commerce, and enforcing the observance of Foreign treaties, and other necessary matters of less moment.

Exclusive of our objections, originating from the want of power, we entertained an opinion that a general government, however guarded by declarations of rights or cautionary provisions, must unavoidably, in a short time, be productive of the destruction of the civil liberty of such citizens who could be effectually coerced by it; by reason of the extensive territory of the United States; the dispersed situation of its inhabitants, and the insuperable difficulty of controlling or counteracting the views of a set of men (however unconstitutional and oppressive their acts might be) possessed of all the powers of government, and who, from their remoteness from their constituents, and necessary permanency of office, could not be supposed to be uniformly actuated by an attention to their welfare and happiness; that however wise and energetic the principles of the general government might be, the extremities of the United States could not be kept in due submission and obedience to its laws at the distance of many hundred miles from the seat of government; that if the general Legislature was composed of so numerous a body of men as to represent the interest of all the inhabitants of the United States in the usual and true ideas of representation, the expence of supporting it would become intolerably burthensome, and that if a few only were invested with a power of legislation, the interests of a great majority of the inhabitants of the United States must necessarily be unknown, or if known even in the first stages of the operations of the new government, unattended to.

These reasons were in our opinion conclusive against any system of consolidated government: to that recommended by the Convention we suppose most of them forcibly apply.

It is not our intention to pursue this subject further than merely to explain our conduct in the discharge of the trust which the honorable legislature reposed in us—interested however, as we are in common with our fellow citizens in the result, we cannot forbear to declare that we have the strongest apprehensions that a government so organized as that recommended by the Convention, cannot afford that security to equal and permanent liberty, which we wished to make an invariable object of our pursuit.

We were not present at the completion of the new Constitution; but before we left the Convention, its principles were so well established as to convince us that no alteration was to be expected, to conform it to our ideas of expediency and safety. A persuasion that our further attendance would be fruitless and unavailing, rendered us less solicitious to return.

We have thus explained our motives for opposing the adoption of the National Constitution, which we conceived it our duty to communicate to your Excellency, to be submitted to the consideration of the honorable legislature.

We have the honor to be, with the greatest respect, your excellency's most obedient and very humble servants.

This letter was printed in the New York *Daily Advertiser* on January 14, 1788, and circulated widely throughout the country. John Lansing, Jr., a lawyer and member of the Continental Congress, served along with Robert Yates in the Constitutional Convention (see John Lansing entry in *Biographies*). Both men resigned from the convention and wrote this letter to explain to the governor why they had done so. Their letter is a wringing defense of personal liberty and a warning of the excessive powers given to the federal government. Both men wanted to revise the Articles of Confederation, and they opposed the proposed Constitution as creating an unworkable federal government, unable to govern such a large expanse of land.

REFERENCES

Elliot, *Debates*, vol. 1; New York *Daily Advertiser*; Storing, *Complete*, vol. 6.

John Williams to His Constituents, *January 29, 1788*

The new constitution is not yet taken up, various are the opinions upon this subject; if I can have my opinion carried it will be this, let it come to the people without either recommending or disapprobation; let the people judge for themselves—if the majority is for it, let it be adopted—if they are against it, let it be rejected, as all powers are, or ought to be, in the people; they, and they only, have the right to say whether the form of government shall be altered. For my own part, I must confess, under the present situation of affairs, something must be done, but whether the present system is the best will be the question. The powers given to the president are very great. The elections may be so altered as to destroy the liberty of the people. The direct taxation, and to be collected by officers of Congress, are powers which cannot be granted agreeable to our present constitution, nor will it be very convenient for Congress officers, and our state collectors, to be collecting both at one time, and as Congress may lay a poll tax, how will that agree with us. I need not tell you the injustices of it. If the new constitution is adopted, Congress hath all the impost and excise; this latter may be laid heavy on taverns and spirits, so that the emoluments from taverns, which are now converted to the use of the poor, must go to Congress; and what is yet worse, all the duties arising from any duties or excise, are to be appropriated to the use of Congress.

You will also observe that senators are for six years, and that small states have an equal number with large states, so that the advantage of having property in a maritime state, will be reduced to an equal value with the property where there is no navigation. If this is not taking our liberty, it is certainly diminishing our property, which is equal to it. What hath kept the taxes so low in this state—the reason is obvious, our impost duties. This is a privilege Providence hath endowed us with; our landed property will ever sell according to the conveniency of it; the lighter the tax, the higher the land; the nigher to market, the greater profits arising from our produce. Let our imposts and advantages be taken from us, shall we not be obliged to lay as heavy taxes as Connecticut, Boston, &c. What hath kept us from those burthens but the privileges, which we must lose if the present proposed constitution is adopted.

Williams, a physician and political officeholder, served in the state ratification convention, and later in the United States House (see John Williams entry in *Biographies*). His letter explains that he will fight in the state convention to control federal powers of taxation.

REFERENCE

Albany Federal Herald, February 25, 1788.

Melancton Smith ("A Plebian"),
April 1788

The advocates for the proposed new constitution, having been beaten off the field of argument, on its merits, have now taken new ground. They admit it is liable to well-founded objections—that a number of its articles ought to be amended; that if alterations do not take place, a door will be left open for an undue administration, and encroachments on the liberties of the people; and many of them go so far as to say, if it should continue for any considerable period, in its present form, it will lead to a subversion of our equal republican forms of government.—But still, although they admit this, they urge that it ought to be adopted, and that we should confide in procuring the necessary alterations after we have received it. Most of the leading characters, who advocate its reception, now profess their readiness to concur with those who oppose it, in bringing about the most material amendments contended for, provided they will first agree to accept the proffered system as it is. These concessions afford strong evidence, that the opposers of the constitution have reason on their side, and that they have not been influenced, in the part they have taken, by the mean and unworthy motives of selfish and private interests with which they have been illiberally charged.—As the favourers of the constitution, seem, if their professions are sincere, to be in a situation similar to that of Agrippa, when he cried out upon Paul's preaching—"almost thou persuadest me to be a christian," I cannot help indulging myself in expressing the same wish which St. Paul uttered on that occasion, "Would to God you were not only almost, but altogether such an one as I am." But also, as we hear no more of Agrippa's christianity after this interview with Paul, so it is much to be feared, that we shall hear nothing of amendments from most of the warm advocates for adopting the new government, after it gets into operation. When the government is once organized, and all the offices under it filled, the inducements which our great men will have to support it, will be much stronger than they are now to urge its reception. Many of them will then hold places of great honour and emolument, and others will be candidates for such places. It is much harder to relinquish honours or emoluments, which we have in possession, than to abandon the pursuit of them, while the attainment is held in a state of uncertainty.—The amendments contended for as necessary to be made, are of such a nature, as well tend to limit and abridge a number of the powers of the government. And is it probable, that those who enjoy these powers will be so likely to surrender them after they have them in possession, as to consent to have them restricted in the act of granting them? Common sense says—they will not.

When we consider the nature and operation of government, the idea of receiving a form radically defective, under the notion of making the necessary amendments, is evidently absurd.

Government is a compact entered into by mankind, in a state of society, for the promotion of their happiness. In forming this compact, common sense dictates, that no articles should be admitted that tend to defeat the end of its institution. If any such are proposed, they should be rejected. When the compact is once formed and put into operation, it is too late for individuals to object. The deed is executed—the conveyance is made—and the power of reassuming the right is gone, without the consent of the parties.—Besides, when a government is once in operation, it acquires strength by habit, and stability by exercise. If it is tolerably mild in its administration, the people sit down easy under it, be its principles and forms ever so repugnant to the maxims of liberty.—It steals, by insensible degrees, one right from the people after another, until it rivets its powers so as to put it beyond the ability of the community to restrict or limit it. The history of the world furnishes many instances of a people's increasing the powers of their rulers by persuasion, but I believe it would be difficult to produce one in which the rulers have been persuaded to relinquish their powers to the people. Wherever this has taken place, it has always been the effect of compulsion. These observations are so well-founded, that they are become a kind of axioms in politics; and the inference to be drawn from them is equally evident, which is this,—that, in forming a government, care should be taken not to confer powers which it will be necessary to take back: but if you err at all, let it be on the contrary side, because it is much easier, as well as safer, to enlarge the powers of your rulers, if they should prove not sufficiently extensive, than it is to abridge them if they should be too great.

It is agreed, the plan is defective—that some of the powers granted, are dangerous—others not well defined—and amendments are necessary. Why then not amend it? why not remove the cause of danger, and, if possible, even the apprehension of it? The instrument is yet in the hands of the people; it is not signed, sealed, and delivered, and they have power to give it any form they please.

But it is contended, adopt it first, and then amend it. I ask, why not amend, and then adopt it? Most certainly the latter mode of proceeding is more consistent with our ideas of prudence in the ordinary concerns of life. If men were about entering into a contract respecting their private concerns, it would be highly absurd in them to sign and seal an instrument containing stipulations which are contrary to their interests and wishes, under the expectation, that the parties, after its execution, would agree to make alterations agreeable to their desires.—They would insist upon the exceptionable clauses being altered before they would ratify the contract. And is a compact for the government of ourselves and our posterity of less moment than contracts between individuals? certainly not. But to this reasoning, which at first view would appear to admit of no reply, a variety of objections are made, and a number of reasons urged for adopting the system, and afterwards proposing amendments.—Such as have come under my observation, I shall state, and remark upon.

It is insisted, that the present situation of our country is such, as not to admit of a delay in forming a new government, or of time sufficient to deliberate and agree upon the amendments which are proper, without involving ourselves in a state of anarchy and confusion.

On this head, all the powers of rhetoric, and arts of description, are employed to paint the condition of this country, in the most hideous and frightful colours. We are told, that agriculture is without encouragement; trade is languishing; private faith and credit are disregarded, and public credit is prostrate; that the laws and magistrates are condemned and set at nought; that a spirit of licentiousness is rampant, and ready to break over every bound set to it by the government; that private embarrassments and distresses invade the house of every man of middling property, and insecurity threatens every man in affluent circumstances: in short, that we are in a state of the most grievous calamity at home, and that we are contemptible abroad, the scorn of foreign nations, and the ridicule of the world. From this high-wrought picture, one would suppose, that we were in a condition the most deplorable of any people upon earth. But suffer me, my countrymen, to call your attention to a serious and sober estimate of the situation in which you are placed, while I trace the embarrassments under which you labour, to their true sources. What is your condition? Does not every man sit under his own vine and under his own fig-tree, having none to make him afraid? Does not every one follow his calling without impediments and receive the reward of his well-earned industry? The farmer cultivates his land, and reaps the fruit which the bounty of heaven bestows on his honest toil. The mechanic is exercised in his art, and receives the reward of his labour. The merchant drives his commerce, and none can deprive him of the gain he honestly acquires; all classes and callings of men amongst us are protected in their various pursuits, and secured by the laws in the possession and enjoyment of the property obtained in those pursuits. The laws are as well executed as they ever were, in this or any other country. Neither the hand of private violence, nor the more to be dreaded hand of legal oppression, are reached out to distress us.

It is true, many individuals labour under embarrassments, but these are to be imputed to the unavoidable circumstances of things, rather than to any defect in our governments. We have just emerged from a long and expensive war. During its existence few people were in a situation to encrease their fortunes, but many to diminish them. Debts contracted before the war were left unpaid while it existed, and these were left a burden too heavy to be borne at the commencement of peace. Add to these, that when the war was over, too many of us, instead of reassuming our old habits of frugality and industry, by which alone every country must be placed in a prosperous condition, took up the profuse use of foreign commodities. The country was deluged with articles imported from abroad, and the cash of the country has been sent out to pay for them, and still left us labouring under the weight of a huge debt to persons abroad. These are the true sources to which we are to trace all the private difficulties of individuals: But will a new government relieve you from these? The advocates for it have not yet told you how it will do it—And I will venture to pronounce, that there is but one way in which it can be effected, and that is by industry and œconomy; limit your expences within your earnings; sell more than you buy, and every thing will be well on this score. Your present condition is such as is common to take place after the conclusion of a war. Those who can remember our situation after the termination of the war preceding the last, will recollect that our condition was similar to the present, but time and industry soon recovered us from it. Money was scarce, the produce of the country much lower than it has been since the peace, and many individuals were extremely embarrassed with debts; and this happened, although we did not experience the ravages, desolations, and loss of property, that were suffered during the late war.

With regard to our public and national concerns, what is there in our condition that threatens us with any immediate danger? We are at peace with all the world; no nation menaces us with war; Nor are we called upon by any cause of sufficient importance to attack any nation. The state governments answer the purposes of preserving the peace, and providing for present exigencies. Our condition as a nation is in no respect worse than it has been for several years past. Our public debt has been lessened in various ways, and the western territory, which has always been relied upon as a productive fund to discharge the national debt, has at length been brought to market, and a considerable part actually applied to its reduction. I mention these things to shew, that there is nothing special, in our present situation, as it respects our national affairs, that should induce us to accept the proffered system, without taking sufficient time to consider and amend it. I do not mean by this, to insinuate, that our government does not stand in need of a reform. It is admitted by all parties, that alterations are necessary in our federal constitution, but the circumstances of our case do by no means oblige us to precipitate this business, or require that we should adopt a system materially defective. We may safely take time to deliberate and amend, without in the mean time hazarding a condition, in any considerable degree, worse than the present.

But it is said, that if we postpone the ratification of this system until the necessary amendments are first incorporated, the consequence will be a civil war among the states. On this head weak minds are alarmed with being told, that the militia of Connecticut and Massachusetts on the one side, and of New-Jersey and Pennsylvania on the other, will attack us with hostile fury; and either destroy us from off the face of the earth, or at best divide us between the two states adjoining us on either side. The apprehension of danger is one of the most powerful incentives to human action, and is therefore generally excited on political questions: But still, a prudent man, though he foreseeth the evil and avoideth it, yet he will not be terrified by imaginary dangers. We ought therefore to enquire what ground there is to fear such an event?—There can be no reason to apprehend, that the other states will make war with us for not receiving the constitution proposed, until it is amended, but from one of the following causes: either that they will have just cause to do it, or that they have a disposition to do it. We will examine each of these:—That they will have no just cause to quarrel with us for not acceding, is evident, because we are under no obligation to do it, arising from any existing compact or previous stipulation. The confederation is the only compact now existing between the states: By the terms of it, it cannot be changed without the consent of every one of the parties to it. Nothing therefore can be more unreasonable than for part of the states to claim of the others, as matter of right, an accession to a system to which they have material objections. No war can therefore arise from this principle, but on the contrary, it is to be presumed, it will operate strongly the opposite way.—The states will reason on the subject in the following manner: On this momentuous question, every state has an indubitable right to judge for itself: This is secured to it by solemn compact, and if any of our sister states disagree with us upon the question, we ought to attend to their objections, and accommodate ourselves as far as possible to the amendments they propose.

As to the inclination of the states to make war with us, for declining to accede, until it is amended, this is highly improbable, not only because such a procedure would be most unjust and unreasonable in itself, but for various other reasons.

The idea of a civil war amongst the states is abhorrent to the principles and feelings of almost every man of every rank in the union. It is so obvious to every one of the least reflection, that in such an event we should hazard the loss of all things, without the hope of gaining any thing, that the man who should entertain a thought of this kind, would be justly deemed more fit to be shut up in Bedlam, than to be reasoned with. But the idea of one or more states attacking another, for insisting upon alterations in this system, before it is adopted, is more extravagant still; it is contradicting every principle of liberty which has been entertained by the states, violating the most solemn compact, and taking from the state the right of deliberation. Indeed to suppose, that a people, entertaining such refined ideas of the rights of human nature as to be induced to wage war with the most powerful nation on earth, upon a speculative point, and from the mere apprehension of danger only, should so far be lost to their own feelings and principles, as to deny to their brethren, who were associated with them in the arduous conflict, the right of free deliberation on a question of the first importance to their political happiness and safety, is equally an insult to the character of the people of America, and to common sense, and could only be suggested by a vicious heart and a corrupt mind.

The idea of being attacked by the other states, will appear visionary and chimerical, if we consider that tho' several of them have adopted the new constitution, yet the opposition to it has been numerous and formidable. The eastern states from whom we are told we have most to fear, should a civil war be blown up, would have full employ to keep in awe those who are opposed to it in their own governments. Massachusetts, after a long and dubious contest in their convention, has adopted it by an inconsiderable majority, and in the very act has marked it with a stigma in its present form. No man of candour, judging from their public proceedings, will undertake to say, on which side the majority of the people are. Connecticut, it is true, have acceded to it, by a large majority of their convention; but it is a fact well known, that a large proportion of the yeomanry of the country are against it:—And it is equally true, that a considerable part of those who voted for it in the convention, wish to see it altered. In both these states the body of the common people, who always do the fighting of a country, would be more likely to fight against than for it: Can it then be presumed, that a country, divided among themselves, upon a question where even the advocates for it, admit the system they contend for needs amendments, would make war upon a sister state, who only insist that should be done before they receive it, which it is granted ought to be done after, and where it is confessed no obligation lies upon them by compact to do it. Can it, I say, be imagined, that in such a case they would make war on a sister state? The idea is preposterous and chimerical.

It is further urged, we must adopt this plan because we have no chance of getting a better. This idea is inconsistent with the principles of those who advance it. They say, it must be altered, but it should be left until after it is put in operation. But if this objection is valid, the proposal of altering, after it is received, is mere delusion.

It is granted, that amendments ought to be made; that the exceptions taken to the constitution, are grounded on just principles, but it is still insisted, that alterations are not to be attempted until after it is received: But why not? Because it is said, there is no probability of agreeing in amendments previous to the adoption, but they may be easily made after it. I wish to be informed what there is in our situation or circumstances that renders it more probable that we shall agree in amendments better after, than before submitting to it? No good reason has as yet been given; it is evident none can be given: On the contrary, there are several considerations which induce a belief, that alterations may be obtained with more ease before, than after its reception, and if so, every one must agree, it is much the safest. The importance of preserving an union, and of establishing a government equal to the purpose of maintaining that union, is a sentiment deeply impressed on the mind of every citizen of America. It is now no longer doubted, that the confederation, in its present form, is inadequate to that end: Some reform in our government must take place. In this, all parties agree: It is therefore to be presumed, that this object will be pursued with ardour and perseverance, until it is attained by all parties. But when a government is adopted that promises to effect this, we are to expect the ardour of many, yea, of most people, will be abated;—their exertions will cease, or be languid, and they will sit down easy, although they may see, that the constitution which provides for this, does not sufficiently guard the rights of the people, or secure them against the encroachments of their rulers. The great end they had in view, the security of the union, they will consider effected, and this will divert their attention from that which is equally interesting, safety to their liberties. Besides, the human mind cannot continue intensely engaged for any great length of time upon one object. As after a storm, a calm generally succeeds, so after the minds of a people have been ardently employed upon a subject, especially upon that of government, we commonly find that they become cool and inattentive: Add to this, that those in the community who urge the adoption of this system, because they hope by it to be raised above the common level of their fellow citizens; because they expect to be among the number of the few who will be benefitted by it, will more easily be induced to consent to the amendments before it is received than afterwards. Before its reception, they will be inclined to be pliant and condescending; if they cannot obtain all they wish, they will consent to take less. They will yield part to obtain the rest. But when the plan is once agreed to, they will be tenacious of every power, they will strenuously contend to retain all they have got; this is natural to human nature, and it is consonant to the experience of mankind. For history affords us no examples of persons once possessed of power, resigning it willingly.

The reasonings made use of to persuade us, that no alterations can be agreed upon previous to the adoption of the system, are as curious as they are futile. It is alledged, that there was great diversity of sentiments in forming the proposed constitution; that it was the effect of mutual concessions and a spirit of accommodation, and from hence it is inferred, that farther changes cannot be hoped for. I should suppose that the contrary inference was the fair one. If the convention, who framed this plan, were possessed of such a spirit of moderation and condescension, as to be induced to yield to each other certain points, and to accommodate themselves to each other's opinions, and even prejudices, there is reason to expect, that this same spirit will continue and prevail in a future convention, and produce an union of sentiments on the points objected to. There is the more reason to hope for this, because the subject has received a full discussion, and the minds of the people much better known than they were when the convention sat. Previous to the meeting of the convention, the subject of a new form of government had been little thought of, and scarcely written upon at all. It is true, it was the general opinion, that some alterations were requisite in the federal system. This subject had been contemplated by almost every thinking man in the union. It had been the subject of many well-written essays, and was the anxious wish of every true friend to America. But it never was in the contemplation of one in a thousand of those who had reflected on the matter, to have an entire change in the nature of our federal government—to alter it from a confederation of states, to that of one entire government, which will swallow up that of the individual states. I will venture to say, that the idea of a government similar to the one proposed, never entered the mind of the legislatures who appointed the convention, and of but very few of the members who composed it, until they had assembled and heard it proposed in that body: much less had the people any conception of such a plan until after it was promulgated. While it was agitated, the debates of the convention were kept an impenetrable secret, and no opportunity was given for well informed men to offer their sentiments upon the subject. The system was therefore never publicly discussed, nor indeed could be, because it was not known to the people until after it was proposed. Since that, it has been the object of universal attention—it has been thought of by every reflecting man—been discussed in a public and private manner, in conversation and in print; its defects have been pointed out, and every objection to it stated; able advocates have written in its favour, and able opponents have written against it. And what is the result? It cannot be denied but that the general opinion is, that it contains material errors, and requires important amendments. This then being the general sentiment, both of the friends and foes of the system, can it be doubted, that another convention would concur in such amendments as would quiet the fears of the opposers, and effect a great degree of union on the subject?—An event most devoutly to be wished. But it is farther said, that there can be no prospect of procuring alterations before it is acceded to, because those who oppose it do not agree among themselves with respect to the amendments that are necessary. To this I reply, that this may be urged against attempting alterations after it is received, with as much force as before; and therefore, if it concludes any thing, it is, that we must receive any system of government proposed to us, because those who object to it do not entirely concur in their objections. But the assertion is not true to any considerable extent. There is a remarkable uniformity in the objections made to the constitution, on the most important points. It is also worthy of notice, that very few of the matters found fault with in it, are of a local nature, or such as affect any particular state; on the contrary, they are such as concern the principles of general liberty, in which the people of New-Hampshire, New-York, and Georgia are equally interested.

It would be easy to shew, that in the leading and most important objections that have been made to the plan, there has been, and is an entire concurrence of opinion among writers, and in public bodies throughout the United States.

I have not time fully to illustrate this by a minute narration of particulars; but to prove that this is the case, I shall adduce a number of important instances.

It has been objected to the new system, that it is calculated to, and will effect such a consolidation of the States, as to supplant and overturn the state governments. In this the minority of Pennsylvania, the opposition in Massachusetts, and all the writers of any ability or note in Philadelphia, New-York, and Boston concur. It may be added, that this appears to have been the opinion of the Massachusetts convention, and gave rise to that article in the amendments proposed, which confines the general government to the exercise only of powers expressly given.[1]

It has been said, that the representation in the general legislature is too small to secure liberty, or to answer the intention of representation. In this there is an union of sentiments in the opposers.

The constitution has been opposed, because it gives to the legislature an unlimited power of taxation, both with respect to direct and indirect taxes, a right to lay and collect taxes, duties, imposts, and excises of every kind and description, and to any amount. In this, there has been as general a concurrence of opinion as in the former.

The opposers to the constitution have said that it is dangerous, because the judicial power may extend to many cases which ought to be reserved to the decision of the State courts, and because the right of trial by jury is not secured in the judicial courts of the general government, in civil cases. All the opposers are agreed in this objection.

The power of the general legislature to alter and regulate the time, place, and manner of holding elections, has been stated as an argument against the adoption of the system. It has been urged, that this power will place in the hands of the general government, the authority, whenever they shall be disposed, and a favorable opportunity offers, to deprive the body of the people, in effect, of all share in the government. The opposers to the constitution universally agree in this objection, and of such force is it, that most of its ardent advocates admit its validity, and those who have made attempts to vindicate it, have been reduced to the necessity of using the most trifling arguments to justify it.

The mixture of legislative, judicial, and executive powers in the senate; the little degree of responsibility under which the great officers of government will be held; and the liberty granted by the system to establish and maintain a standing army, without any limitation or restriction, are also objected to the constitution; and in these, there is a great degree of unanimity of sentiment in the opposers.

From these remarks it appears, that the opponents to the system accord in the great and material points on which they wish amendments. For the truth of the assertion, I appeal to the protest of the minority of the convention of Pennsylvania, to all the publications against the constitution, and to the debates of the convention of Massachusetts. As a higher authority than these, I appeal to the amendments proposed by Massachusetts; these are to be considered as the sense of that body upon the defects of the system. And it is a fact, which I will venture to assert, that a large majority of that convention were of opinion, that a number of additional alterations ought to be made. Upon reading the articles which they propose as amendments, it will appear, that they object to indefinite powers in the legislature—to the power of laying direct taxes—to the authority of regulating elections—to the extent of the judicial powers, both as it respects the inferior courts and the appellate jurisdiction—to the smallness of the representation, &c.—It is admitted, that some writers have advanced objections that others have not noticed—that exceptions have been taken by some, that have not been insisted upon by others, and it is probable, that some of the opponents may approve what others will reject. But still these difference are on matters of small importance, and of such a nature as the persons who hold different opinions will not be tenacious of. Perfect uniformity of sentiment on so great a political subject is not to be expected. Every sensible man is impressed with this idea, and is therefore prepared to make concessions and accommodate on matters of small importance. It is sufficient that we agree in the great leading principles, which relate to the preservation of public liberty and private security. And on these I will venture to affirm we are as well agreed, as any people ever were on a question of this nature. I dare pronounce, that were the principal advocates for the proposed plan to write comments upon it, they would differ more in the sense they would give the constitution, than those who oppose it do, in the amendments they would wish. I am justified in this opinion, by the sentiments advanced by the different writers in favour of the constitution.

It is farther insisted, that six states have already adopted the constitution; that probably nine will agree to it; in which case it will be put in operation. That it is unreasonable to expect that those states which have acceded to it, will reconsider the subject in compliance with the wishes of a minority.

To perceive the force of this objection, it is proper to review the conduct and circumstances of the states which have acceded it. It cannot be controverted, that Connecticut and New-Jersey were very much influenced in their determinations on the question, by local considerations. The duty of impost laid by this state, has been a subject of complaint by those states. The new constitution transfers the power of imposing these duties from the state to the general government, and carries the proceeds to the use of the union, instead of that of those states. This is a very popular matter with the people of those states, and at the same time, is not advanced by the sensible opposers to the system in this state as an objection to it.—To excite in the minds of the people of these states an attachment to the new system, the amount of the revenue arising from our impost has been magnified to a much larger sum than it produces; it has been stated to amount to from sixty to eighty thousand pounds lawful money: and a gentleman of high eminence in Connecticut has lent the authority of his name to support it. It has been said, that Connecticut pays a third of this sum annually for impost, and Jersey nearly as much. It has farther been asserted, that the avails of the impost were applied to the separate use of the state of New-York. By these assertions the people have been grossly imposed upon, for neither of them are true.

The amount of the revenue from impost for two years past, has not exceeded fifty thousand pounds currency, per annum, and a draw-back of duties is allowed by law, upon all goods exported to either of the beforementioned states, in casks or packages unbroken.

The whole of this sum, and more, has been paid into the federal treasury for the support of the government of the union. All the states therefore have actually derived equal benefit with the state of New-York, from the impost. It may be said, I know, that this state has obtained credit for the amount, upon the requisitions of Congress: It is admitted; but still it is a fact, that other states, and especially those who complain, have paid no part of the monies required of them, and have scarcely made an effort to do it. The fact therefore is, that they have received as much advantage from the impost of this state, as we ourselves have. The proposed constitution directs to no mode, in which the deficiencies of states on former requisitions, are to be collected, but seems to hold out the idea, that we are to start anew, and all past payments be forgotten. It is natural to expect, that selfish motives will have too powerful an influence on men[']s minds, and that too often, they will shut the eyes of a people to their best and true interest. The people of those states have been persuaded to believe, that this new constitution will relieve them from the burden of taxes, by providing for all the exigencies of the union, by duties which can be raised only in the neighbouring states. When they come to be convinced, that this promise is a mere delusion, as they assuredly will, by finding the continental tax-gatherer knocking at their doors, if not before, they will be among the first to urge amendments, and perhaps the most violent to obtain them. But notwithstanding the local prejudices which operate upon the people of these states, a considerable part of them wish for amendments. It is not to be doubted, that a considerable majority of the people of Connecticut wish for them, and many in Jersey have the same desires, and their numbers are increasing: It cannot be disputed, that amendments would accord with the sentiments of a great majority in Massachusetts, or that they would be agreeable to the greater part of the people of Pennsylvania: There is no reason to doubt but that they would be agreeable to Delaware and Georgia—If then, the states who have already ratified the constitution, are desirous to have alterations made in it, what reason can be assigned why they should not cordially meet with overtures for that purpose from any state, and concur in appointing a convention to effect it? Mankind are easily induced to fall upon measures to obtain an object agreeable to them. In this case, the states would not only be moved by this universal principle of human nature, but by the strong and powerful motive of uniting all the states under a form of government agreeable to them.

I shall now dismiss the consideration of objections made to attempting alterations previous to the adoption of the plan, but before I close, I beg your indulgence, while I make some remarks on the splendid advantages, which the advocates for this system say are to be derived from it.—Hope and fear are two of the most active principles of our nature: We have considered how the latter is addressed on this occasion, and with how little reason: It will appear that the promises it makes, are as little to be relied upon, as its threatenings. We are amused with the fair prospects that are to open, when this government is put into operation—Agriculture is to flourish, and our fields to yield an hundred fold—Commerce is to expand her wings, and bear our productions to all the ports in the world—Money is to pour into our country through every channel—Arts and manufactures are to rear their heads, and every mecanic find full employ—Those who are in debt, are to find easy means to procure money to pay them—Public burdens and taxes are to be lightened, and yet all our public debts are soon to be discharged.—With such vain and delusive hopes are the minds of many honest and well meaning people fed, and by these means are they led inconsiderately to contend for a government, which is made to promise what it cannot perform; while their minds are diverted from contemplating its true nature, or considering whether it will not endanger their liberties, and work oppression.

Far be it from me to object to granting the general government the power of regulating trade, and of laying imposts and duties for that purpose, as well as for raising a revenue: But it is as far from me to flatter people with hopes of benefits to be derived from such a change in our government, which can never be realized. Some advantages may accrue from vesting in one general government, the right to regulate commerce, but it is a vain delusion to expect any thing like what is promised. The truth is, this country buys more than it sells: It imports more than it exports. There are too many merchants in proportion to the farmers and manufacturers. Until these defects are remedied, no government can relieve us. Common sense dictates, that if a man buys more than he sells, he will remain in debt; the same is true of a country.—And as long as this country imports more goods than she exports—the overplus must be paid for in money or not paid at all. These few remarks may convince us, that the radical remedy for the scarcity of cash is frugality and industry. Earn much and spend little, and you will be enabled to pay your debts, and have money in your pockets; and if you do not follow this advice, no government that can be framed, will relieve you.

As to the idea of being relieved from taxes by this government, it is an affront to common sense, to advance it. There is no complaint made against the present confederation more justly founded than this, that it is incompetent to provide the means to discharge our national debt, and to support the national government. Its inefficacy to these purposes, which was early seen and felt, was the first thing that suggested the necessity of changing the government; other things, it is true, were afterwards found to require alterations; but this was the most important, and accordingly we find, that while in some other things the powers of this government seem to be in some measure limited, on the subject of raising money, no bounds are set to it. It is authorised to raise money to any amount, and in any way it pleases. If then, the capital embarrassment in our present government arises from the want of money, and this constitution effectually authorises the raising of it, how are the taxes to be lessened by it? Certainly money can only be raised by taxes of some kind or other; it must be got either by additional impositions on trade, by excise, or by direct taxes, or what is more probable, by all together. In either way, it amounts to the same thing, and the position is clear, that as the necessities of the nation require more money than is now raised, the taxes must be enhanced. This you ought to know, and prepare yourself to submit to.—Besides, how is it possible that the taxes can be decreased when the expences of your government will be greatly advanced? It does not require any great skill in politics, or ability at calculation to shew, that the new government will cost more money to administer it, than the present. I shall not descend to an estimate of the cost of a federal town, the salaries of the president, vice-president, judges, and other great officers of state, nor calculate the amount of the pay the legislature will vote themselves, or the salaries that will be paid the innumerable revenue and subordinate officers. The bare mention of these things is sufficient to convince you, that the new government will be vastly more expensive than the old: And how is the money to answer these purposes to be obtained? It is obvious, it must be taken out of the pockets of the people, by taxes, in some mode or other.

Having remarked upon the arguments which have been advanced, to induce you to accede to this government, without amendments, and I trust refuted them, suffer me to close with an address dedicated by the affection of a brother, and the honest zeal of a lover of his country.

The present is the most important crisis at which you ever have arrived. You have before you a question big with consequences, unutterably important to yourselves, to your children, to generations yet unborn, to the cause of liberty and of mankind; every motive of religion and virtue, of private happiness and public good, of honour and dignity, should urge you to consider cooly and determine wisely.

Almost all the governments that have arisen among mankind, have sprung from force and violence. The records of history inform us of none that have been the result of cool and dispassionate reason and reflection: It is reserved for this favoured country to exhibit to mankind the first example.—This opportunity is now given us, and we are to exercise our rights in the choice of persons to represent us in convention, to deliberate and determine upon the constitution proposed: It will be to our everlasting disgrace to be indifferent on such a subject, for it is impossible, we can contemplate any thing that relates to the affairs of this life of half the importance.

You have heard that both sides on this great question, agree, that there are in it great defects; yet the one side tell you, choose such men as will adopt it, and then amend it—while the other say, amend previous to its adoption.—I have stated to you my reasons for the latter, and I think they are unanswerable.—Consider you the common people, the yeomanry of the country, for to such I principally address myself, you are to be the principal losers, if the constitution should prove oppressive. When a tyranny is established, there are always masters as well as slaves; the great and the well-born are generally the former, and the middling class the latter—Attempts have been made, and will be repeated, to alarm you with the fear of consequences; but reflect, there are consequences on both sides, and none can be apprehended more dreadful, than entailing on ourselves and posterity a government which will raise a few to the height of human greatness and wealth, while it will depress the many to the extreme of poverty and wretchedness. Consequences are under the controul of that all-wise and all-powerful being, whose providence directs the affairs of men: Our part is to act right, and we may then have confidence that the consequences will be favourable. The path in which you should walk is plain and open before you; be united as one man, and direct your choice to such men as have been uniform in their opposition to the proposed system in its present form, or without proper alterations: In men of this description you have reason to place confidence, while on the other hand, you have just cause to distrust those who urge the adoption of a bad constitution, under the delusive expectation of making amendments after it is acceded to. Your jealousy of such characters should be the more excited, when you consider that the advocates for the constitution have shifted their ground. When men are uniform in their opinions, it affords evidence that they are sincere: When they are shifting, it gives reason to believe, they do not change from conviction. It must be recollected, that when this plan was first announced to the public, its supporters cried it up as the most perfect production of human wisdom: It was represented either as having no defects, or if it had, they were so trifling and inconsiderable, that they served only, as the shades in a fine picture, to set off the piece to the greater advantage. One gentleman in Philadelphia went so far, in the ardour of his enthusiasm in its favour, as to pronounce, that the men who formed it were as really under the guidance of Divine Revelation, as was Moses, the Jewish lawgiver. Their language is now changed; the question has been discussed; the objections to the plan ably stated, and they are admitted to be unanswerable. The same men who held it almost perfect, now admit it is very imperfect; that it is necessary it should be amended. The only question between us, is simply this: Shall we accede to a bad constitution, under the uncertain prospect of getting it amended, after we have received it, or shall we amend it before we adopt it? Common sense will point out which is the most rational, which is the most secure line of conduct. May heaven inspire you with wisdom, union, moderation and firmness, and give you hearts to make a proper estimate of your invaluable privileges, and preserve them to you, to be transmitted to your posterity unimpaired, and may they be maintained in this our country, while Sun and Moon endure.

A Plebeian.

POSTSCRIPT

Since the foregoing pages have been put to the press, a pamphlet has appeared, entitled, "An address to the people of the state of New-York, on the subject of the new constitution, &c."[2] Upon a cursory examination of this performance (for I have not had leisure to give it more than a cursory examination) it appears to contain little more than declamation and observations that have been often repeated by the advocates of the new constitution.

An attentive reader will readily perceive, that almost every thing deserving the name of an argument in this publication, has received consideration, and, I trust, a satisfactory answer in the preceding remarks, so far as they apply to prove the necessity of an immediate adoption of the plan, without amendments.

I shall therefore only beg the patience of my readers, while I make a few very brief remarks on this piece.

The author introduces his observations with a short history of the revolution, and of the establishment of the present existing federal government. He draws a frightful picture of our condition under the present confederation. The whole of what he says on that head, stripped of its artificial colouring, amounts to this, that the existing system is rather recommendatory than coercive, or that Congress have not, in most cases, the power of enforcing their own resolves. This he calls "a new and wonderful system." However "wonderful" it may seem, it certainly is not "new." For most of the *federal governments* that have been in the world, have been of the same nature.—The United Netherlands are governed on the same plan. There are other governments also now existing, which are in a similar condition with our's, with regard to several particulars, on account of which this author denominates it "new and wonderful."—The king of Great-Britain "may make war, but has not power to raise money to carry it on." He may borrow money, but is without the means of repayment," &c. For these he is dependent on his parliament. But it is needless to add on this head, because it is admitted that the powers of the general government ought to be increased in several of the particulars this author instances. But these things are mentioned to shew, that the outcry made against the confederation, as being a system new, unheard of, and absurd, is really without foundation.

The author proceeds to depicture our present condition in the high-wrought strains common to his party.—I shall add nothing to what I have said on this subject in the former part of this pamphlet, but will only observe, that his imputing our being kept out of the possession of the western posts, and our want of peace with the Algerines, to the defects in our present government, is much easier said than proved. The British keep possession of these posts, because it subserves their interest, and probably will do so, until they perceive that we have gathered strength and resources sufficient to assert our rights with the sword. Let our government be what it will, this cannot be done without time and patience. In the present exhausted situation of the country, it would be madness in us, had we ever so perfect a government, to commence a war for the recovery of these posts.—With regard to the Algerines, there are but two ways in which their ravages can be prevented. The one is, by a successful war against them, and the other is by treaty. The powers of Congress under the confederation are completely competent either to declare war against them, or to form treaties. Money, it is true, is necessary to do both these. This only brings us to this conclusion, that the great defect in our present government, is the want of powers to provide money for the public exigencies. I am willing to grant *reasonable* powers on this score, but not unlimited ones; commercial treaties may be made under the present powers of Congress. I am persuaded we flatter ourselves with advantages which will result from them, that will never be realized. I know of no benefits that we receive from any that have yet been formed.

This author tells us, "it is not his design to investigate the merits of the plan, nor of the objections made to it." It is well he did not undertake it, for if he had, from the specimen he has given, the cause he assumes would not have probably gained much strength by it.

He however takes notice of two or three of the many objections brought against the plan.

"We are told, (says he) among other strange things, that the liberty of the press is left insecure by the proposed constitution, and yet that constitution says neither more nor less about it, than the constitution of the state of New-York does. We are told it deprives us of trial by jury, whereas the fact is, that it expressly secures it in certain cases, and takes it away in none, &c. it is absurd to construe the silence of this, or of our own constitution relative to a great number of our rights into a total extinction of them; silence and a blank paper neither grant nor take away anything."

It may be a strange thing to this author to hear the people of America anxious for the preservation of their rights, but those who understand the true principles of liberty, are no strangers to their importance. The man who supposes the constitution, in any part of it, is like a blank piece of paper, has very erroneous ideas of it. He may be assured every clause has a meaning, and many of them such extensive meaning, as would take a volume to unfold. The suggestion, that the liberty of the press is secure, because it is not in express words spoken of in the constitution, and that the trial by jury is not taken away, because it is not said in so many words and letters it is so, is puerile and unworthy of a man who pretends to reason. We contend, that by the indefinite powers granted to the general government, the liberty of the press may be restricted by duties, &c. and therefore the constitution ought to have stipulated for its freedom. The trial by jury, in all civil cases is left at the discretion of the general government, except in the supreme court on the appellate jurisdiction, and in this I affirm it is taken away, not by express words, but by fair and legitimate construction and inference; for the supreme court have expressly given them an appellate jurisdiction, in every case to which their powers extend (with two or three exceptions) both as to *law and fact*. The court are the judges; every man in the country, who has served as a juror, knows, that there is a distinction between the court and the jury, and that the lawyers in their pleading, make the distinction. If the court, upon appeals, are to determine both the law and the fact, there is no room for a jury, and the right of trial in this mode is taken away.

The author manifests equal levity in referring to the constitution of this state, to shew that it was useless to stipulate for the liberty of the press, or to insert a bill of rights in the constitution. With regard to the first, it is perhaps an imperfection in our constitution that the liberty of the press is not expressly reserved; but still there was not equal necessity of making this reservation in our State as in the general Constitution, for the common and statute law of England, and the laws of the colony are established, in which this privilege is fully defined and secured. It is true, a bill of rights is not prefixed to our constitution, as it is in that of some of the states; but still this author knows, that many essential rights are reserved in the body of it; and I will promise, that every opposer of this system will be satisfied, if the stipulations that they contend for are agreed to, whether they are prefixed, affixed, or inserted in the body of the constitution, and that they will not contend which way this is done, if it be but done. I shall add but one remark, and that is upon the hackneyed argument introduced by the author, drawn from the character and ability of the framers of the new constitution. The favourers of this system are not very prudent in bringing this forward. It provokes to an investigation of characters, which is an invidious task. I do not wish to detract from their merits, but I will venture to affirm, that twenty assemblies of equal number might be collected, equally respectable both in point of ability, integrity, and patriotism. Some of the characters which compose it I revere; others I consider as of small consequence, and a number are suspected of being great public defaulters, and to have been guilty of notorious peculation and fraud, with regard to public property in the hour of our distress. I will not descend to personalities, nor would I have said so much on the subject, had it not been in self defence. Let the constitution stand on its own merits. If it be good, it stands not in need of great men's names to support it. If it be bad, their names ought not to sanction it.

Melancton Smith, a merchant, lawyer, and member of the Continental Congress, was perhaps the state's most important Antifederalist writer (see Melancton Smith entry in *Biographies*). In "Plebian" he called for specific amendments to the Constitution, especially to protect individual rights. Smith was greatly concerned with the absence of the right to trial by a jury of one's peers, insisting that the authors of the Constitution seemed to lack concern for rights to a fair trial.

REFERENCES

Ford, *Pamphlets*; Melancton Smith, *An Address to the People of the State of New York* (New York: 1788); Storing, *Complete*, vol. 6.

NOTES

1. Here and elsewhere, Smith shows how much he uses the works of Antifederalists from other states.

2. Work of New York Federalist, John Jay.

John Williams, Speech in the New York State Ratification Convention, *June 21, 1788*

We are now, sir, said he, to investigate and decide upon a Constitution, in which not only the present members of the community are deeply interested, but upon which the happiness or misery of generations yet unborn is, in a great measure, suspended. I therefore hope for a wise and prudent determination. I believe that this country has never before seen such a critical period in political affairs. We have felt the feebleness of those ties by which the states are held together, and the want of that energy which is necessary to manage our general concerns. Various are the expedients which have been proposed to remedy these evils; but they have been proposed without effect; though I am persuaded that, if the Confederation had been attended to as its value justly merited, and proper attention paid to a few necessary amendments, it might have carried us on for a series of years, and probably have been in as great estimation with succeeding ages as it was in our long and painful war, notwithstanding the frightful picture that has been drawn of our situation, and the imputation of all our difficulties to the want of an energetic government. Indeed, sir, it appears to me that many of our present distresses flow from a source very different from the defects in the Confederation. Unhappily for us, immediately after our extrication from a cruel and unnatural war, luxury and dissipation overran the country, banishing all that economy, frugality, and industry, which had been exhibited during the war.

Sir, if we were to reassume all our old habits, we might expect to prosper. Let us, then, abandon all those foreign commodities which have hitherto deluged our country, which have loaded us with debt, and which, if continued, will forever involve us in difficulties. How many thousands are daily wearing the manufactures of Europe, when, by a little industry and frugality, they might wear those of their own country! One may venture to say, sir, that the greatest part of the goods are manufactured in Europe by persons who support themselves by our extravagance. And can we believe a government ever so well formed can relieve us from these evils? What dissipation is there from the immoderate use of spirits! Is it not notorious that men cannot be hired, in time of harvest, without giving them, on an average, a pint of rum per day? so that, on the lowest calculation, every twentieth part of the grain is expended on that article; and so, in proportion, all the farmer's produce. And what is worse, the disposition of eight tenths of the commonality is such, that, if they can get credit, they will purchase unnecessary articles, even to the amount of their crop, before it becomes merchantable. And therefore it is evident that the best government ever devised, without economy and frugality, will leave us in a situation no better than the present.

Sir, the enormous expense of the article of tea will amount, in two years, to our whole foreign debt. Much more might be said on the subject; but I fear I have trespassed on your patience already. The time of the committee would not have been so long taken up, had there not appeared a propriety in showing that all our present difficulties are not to be attributed to the defects in the Confederation; and, were the real truth known, part of its defects have been used as an instrument to make way for the proposed system; and whether or not it is calculated for greater emoluments and more placemen the committee will determine. However, from what has been said, and the mode agreed on for our proceedings, it appears probable that the system of government under consideration is preferred before the Confederation. This being the case, let us examine whether it be calculated to preserve the invaluable blessings of liberty, and secure the inestimable rights of mankind. If it be so, let us adopt it. But if it be found to contain principles that will lead to the subversion of liberty,— if it tends to establish a despotism, or, what is worse, a tyrannical aristocracy,— let us insist upon the necessary alterations and amendments.

Momentous is the question, and we are called upon by every motive to examine it well, and make up a wise and candid judgment.

In forming a constitution for a free country like this, the greatest care should be taken to define its powers, and guard against an abuse of authority. The constitution should be so formed as not to swallow up the state governments: the general government ought to be confined to certain national objects; and the states should retain such powers as concern their own internal police. We should consider whether or not this system is so formed, as, directly or indirectly, to annihilate the state governments. If so, care should be taken to check it in such a manner as to prevent this effect. Now, sir, with respect to the clause before us, I agree with the gentlemen from Albany and Duchess, who spoke yesterday. The number of representatives is, in my opinion, too small to resist corruption. Sir, how guarded is our state Constitution on this head! The number of the Senate and House of Representatives proposed in the Constitution does not surpass those of our state. How great the disparity, when compared with the aggregate number of the United States! The history of representation in England, from which we have taken our model, is briefly this: Before the institution of legislating by deputies, the whole free part of the community usually met for that purpose: when this became impracticable by increase of numbers, the people were divided into districts, from each of which was sent a number of deputies, for a complete representation of the various orders of the citizens within them. Can it be supposed that six men can be a complete representation of the various orders of the people of this state?

I conceive, too, that biennial elections are a departure from the true principles of democracy. A well-digested democracy has advantages over all other forms of government. It affords to many the opportunity of being advanced, and creates that desire of public promotion, and ardent affection for the public weal, which are so beneficial to our country. It was the opinion of the great Sidney and Montesquieu that annual elections are productive of this effect. But as there are more important defects in the proposed Constitution, I shall desist making any further observations at this time.

In order to convince gentlemen it is my sincere intention to accede to this system, when properly amended, I give it as my opinion that it will be best for gentlemen to confine themselves to certain points which are defective.

Before I conclude, I would only mention, that while, on one hand, I wish those endowed with a spirit of moderation through the whole debate, to give way to small matters, yet, on the other hand, not to be intimidated by imaginary dangers; for to say that a bad government must be established for fear of anarchy, is, in reality, saying that we must kill ourselves for fear of dying.

John Williams opened his Antifederalist assault on the Constitution with a call to clearly delineate the powers given to the federal government (see John Williams entry in *Biographies*). He worried that the Federalists had managed to cover up the central government's real threat to the rights of the states. These threats extended, he said, to rights of individuals. Williams also supported the call for amendments to the proposed Constitution creating a bill of individual rights.

REFERENCE

Elliot, *Debates*, vol. 2.

Melancton Smith, Speech in the New York State Ratification Convention, *June 23, 1788*

I did not intend to make any more observations on this article. Indeed, I have heard nothing to day, which has not been suggested before, except the polite reprimand I have received for my declamation. I should not have risen again, but to examine who proved himself the greatest declaimer. The gentleman wishes me to describe what I meant, by representing the feelings of the people. If I recollect right, I said the representative ought to understand, and govern his conduct by the true interest of the people.—I believe I stated this idea precisely. When he attempts to explain my ideas, he explains them away to nothing; and instead of answering, he distorts, and then sports with them. But he may rest assured, that in the present spirit of the Convention, to irritate is not the way to conciliate. The gentleman, by the false gloss he has given to my argument, makes me an enemy to the rich: This is not true. All I said, was, that mankind were influenced, in a great degree, by interests and prejudices:—That men, in different ranks of life, were exposed to different temptations—and that ambition was more peculiarly the passion of the rich and great. The gentleman supposes the poor have less sympathy with the sufferings of their fellow creatures; for that those who feel most distress themselves, have the least regard to the misfortunes of others:—Whether this be reasoning or declamation, let all who hear us determine. I observed that the rich were more exposed to those temptations, which rank and power hold out to view; that they were more luxurious and intemperate, because they had more fully the means of enjoyment; that they were more ambitious, because more in the hope of success. The gentleman says my principle is not true; for that a poor man will be as ambitious to be a constable, as a rich man to be a governor:—But he will not injure his country so much by the party he creates to support his ambition.

The next object of the gentleman's ridicule is my idea of an aristocracy; and he indeed has done me the honor, to rank me in the order. If then I am an aristocrat, and yet publicly caution my countrymen against the encroachments of the aristocrats, they will surely consider me as one of their most disinterested friends. My idea of aristocracy is not new:—It is embraced by many writers on government:—I would refer the gentleman for a definition of it to the honorable *John Adams*, one of our natural aristocrats. This writer will give him a description the most ample and satisfactory. But I by no means intended to carry my idea of it to such a ridiculous length as the gentleman would have me; nor will any of my expressions warrant the construction he imposes on them. My argument was, that in order to have a true and genuine representation, you must receive the middling class of people into your government—such as compose the body of this assembly. I observed, that a representation from the United States could not be so constituted, as to represent completely the feelings and interests of the people; but that we ought to come as near this object as possible. The gentlemen say, that the exactly proper number of representatives is so indeterminate and vague, that it is impossible for them to ascertain it with any precision. But surely, they are able to see the distinction between twenty and thirty. I acknowledged that a complete representation would make the legislature too numerous; and therefore, it is our duty to limit the powers, and form checks on the government, in proportion to the smallness of the number.

The honorable gentleman next animadverts on my apprehensions of corruption, and instances the present Congress, to prove an absurdity in my argument. But is this fair reasoning? There are many material checks to the operations of that body, which the future Congress will not have. In the first place, they are chosen annually:—What more powerful check! They are subject to recal: Nine states must agree to any important resolution, which will not be carried into execution, till it meets the approbation of the people in the state legislatures. Admitting what he says, that they have pledged their faith to support the acts of Congress: yet, if these be contrary to the essential interests of the people, they ought not to be acceded to for they are not bound to obey any law, which tends to destroy them.

It appears to me, that had economy been a motive for making the representation small; it might have operated more properly in leaving out some of the offices which this constitution requires. I am sensible that a great many of the common people, who do not reflect, imagine that a numerous representation involves a great expense:—But they are not aware of the real security it gives to an œconomical management in all the departments of government.

The gentleman further declared, that as far his acquaintance the general convention, and to rest satisfied, that the representation will increase in a sufficient degree, to answer the wishes of the most zealous advocates for liberty.

Melancton Smith debated Alexander Hamilton on whether the Constitution promoted an aristocracy (see Melancton Smith entry in *Biographies*). Smith's major argument concerned the election process, which he believed perpetuated the powers of the wealthy in deciding who held office. His solution was the creation of a large house of representatives so that people could feel personally represented by their leaders.

REFERENCE

Elliot, *Debates*, vol. 2.

Gilbert Livingston, Speech in the New York State Ratification Convention, *June 24, 1788*

He in the first place considered the importance of the senate, as a branch of the legislature, in three points of view.

First, they would possess legislative powers, co-extensive with those of the house of representatives, except with respect to originating revenue laws; which, however, they would have power to reject or amend, as in the case of other bills. Secondly, they would have an importance, even exceeding that of the representative house, as they would be composed of a smaller number, and possess more firmness and system. Thirdly, their consequence: and dignity would still farther transcend those of the other branch, from their longer continuance in office. These powers, Mr. *Livingston* contended, rendered the senate a dangerous body.

He went on, in the second place, to enumerate and animadvert on the powers, with which they were cloathed in their judicial capacity; and in their capacity of council to the president, and in the forming of treaties. In the last place, as if too much power could not be given to this body, they were made, he said, a council of appointment; by whom, ambassadors and other officers of state were to be appointed. These are the powers, continued he, which are vested in this small body of twenty-six men: In some cases, to be exercised by a bare quorum, which is fourteen; a majority of which number again, is eight. What are the checks provided to balance this great mass of powers? Our present Congress cannot serve longer than three years in six: They are at any time subject to recall. These and other checks were considered as necessary, at a period which I choose to honor with the name of virtuous. Sir, I venerate the spirit with which every thing was done, at the trying time in which the confederation was formed. America then, had a sufficiency of this virtue to resolve to resist, perhaps, the first nation in the universe, even unto bloodshed. What was her aim? equal liberty and safety. What ideas had she of this equal liberty? Read them in her articles of confederation. True it is, Sir, there are some powers wanted to make the glorious compact complete: But, Sir, let us be cautious, that we do not err more on the other hand, by giving power too profusely when perhaps it will be too late to recall it. Consider, Sir, the great influence which this body armed at all points will have. What will be the effect of this? Probably, a security of their re-election, as long as they please. Indeed, in my view, it will amount nearly to an appointment for life. What will be their situation in a federal town? Hallowed ground! Nothing so unclean as state laws to enter there; surrounded, as they will be, by an impenetrable wall of adamant and gold; the wealth of the whole country flowing into it—Their attention to their various business, will probably require their constant attendance.—In this Eden, will they reside, with their families, distant from the observation of the people. In such a situation, men are apt to forget their dependence—lose their sympathy, and contract selfish habits. Factions will be apt to be formed, if the body becomes permanent. The senators will associate only with men of their own class; and thus become strangers to the condition of the common people. They should not only return, and be obliged to live with the people, but return to their former rank of citizenship, both to revive their sense of dependence, and to gain a knowledge of the state of their country. This will afford opportunity to bring forward the genius and information of the states; and will be a stimulus to acquire political abilities. It will be a means of diffusing a more general knowledge of the measures and spirit of administration. These things will confirm the people's confidence in government. When they see those who have been high in office, residing among them, as private citizens, they will feel more forcibly, that the government is of their own choice. The members of this branch, having the idea impressed on their minds, that they are soon to return to the level, whence the suffrages of the people raised them; this good effect will follow: They will consider their interests as the same with those of their constituents; and that they legislate for themselves as well as others. They will not conceive themselves made to receive, enjoy and rule; nor the people solely to earn, pay and submit.

Mr. Chairman, I have endeavored, with as much perspicuity and candor as I am master of, shortly to state my objections to this clause—I would wish the committee to believe that they are not raised for the sake of opposition; but that I am very sincere in my sentiments in this important investigation. The senate, as they are now constituted, have little or no check on them. Indeed, Sir, too much is put into their hands. When we come to that part of the system which points out their powers, it will be the proper time to consider this subject more particularly.

I think, Sir, we must relinquish the idea of safety under this government, if the time for service is not further limited, and the power of recall given to the state legislatures. I am strengthened in my opinion, on this point, by an observation made yesterday by an honorable member from New-York, to this effect:—"That there should be no fear of corruption of the members in the house of representatives; especially, as they are, in two years, to return to the body of the people." I therefore move, that the committee adopt the following resolution as an amendment to this clause.

"*Resolved*, That no person shall be eligible as a senator for more than six years in any term of twelve years, and that it shall be in the power of the legislature of the several states, to recall their senators, or either of them, and to elect others in their stead, to serve for the remainder of the time for which such senator or senators so recalled were appointed."

Gilbert Livingston, from an old and powerful family, was an Albany lawyer and state legislator (see Gilbert Livingston entry in *Biographies*). In this speech, he spoke out against too much power given to the United States Senate. If leaders had the potential for corruption, Livingston claimed, then restrictions on government's powers were imperative. Also, Livingston wanted to make certain that amendments be made to the Constitution that were sure to pass.

REFERENCE

Elliot, *Debates*, vol. 2.

George Clinton, Speeches in the New York State Ratification Convention, *June 27, July 11, July 15, 1788*

JUNE 27, 1788

I wish to make a few remarks upon the clause under consideration, which I am influenced to do from attempts which have been made in the course of the debate to establish principles which appear to be not only to be new to mislead the mind.

I have before mentioned that I was apprehensive that we expressed from both sides of the Committee a desire to establish a strong energetic federal government and attachments to principles of republicanism, that while we agreed in the terms we differed essentially in the principles.

I think it proper on this occasion to declare that when I speak of a strong energetic federal government I mean such an one as is best calculated to preserve the peace and safety of the union and at the same time to secure the freedom and independence of the States. When I speak of a republican Government, I mean a government where the will of the people expressed by themselves as representatives is the law, and in the present compound government where part of the powers originate from the people in their moral capacity and part from the states in their political capacity, the will of the component parts expressed in the general government ought to be the law, and that the security of the States and the liberties of the people might depend in having this will fully and fairly expressed in the public councils.—These are the true principles of a free representative government—if they are not[,] the election of representatives is mere matter of form, and the government is not a government of the people, or states but of the few who exercise the powers of it—it may indeed be called a republic, for the idea is vague and indefinite and may include an arbitrary aristocracy—It has even been applied to the British Government by some writers.

I have been led to express these sentiments from observations which have been made on a former occasion and repeated on the present by an Honble Gentm. from N. York to wit, that the Senators ought to be subject to the recal of the legislatures of the States, because they would be too subject to the influence of local and State prejudices, and be thereby diverted from the pursuit of general interests—this, it is obvious is a doctrine contrary to common reason and the nature of things and every idea we can form of true representation and more especially when applied to the Legislatures of States which being a deliberative body cannot be supposed to be under the sudden impulses of passion and prejudice—nor can they ever fear want of information if their representatives in the general legislature do their duty.

The same Honble Gentm.[1] tempted to establish another principle, to wit, that the only true security the People can have against the undue exercise of powers in the government is derived from its being organized on Representative republican principles and a proper distribution and separation of the legislative judicial and executive branches of power. This at first review is specious and plausible for it must be universally admitted, that much security is derived from this power.

It is therefore the better calculated to lead the mind from the true point of inquiry, to wit, whether the powers of this government are well defined and limited to the proper objects. But, on this head, it will be only necessary to observe that the system itself establishes a different doctrine by express limitations in a variety of instances prohibiting the exercise of certain powers. For instance The suspension of the Writ of Habeus Corpus except in certain cases. The passing of bills of attainder and ex post facto laws. The creation of a nobility and a variety of other restrictions too tedious to mention.

If the principle advocated by the Honble Gentm. was true in almost any extent, it is obvious that these provisions would have been unnecessary and that after having provided for the organization of the government the distribution of its powers and a very few other objects, the whole system might have been comprised in the few following words, Congress shall have power to provide for the common defence and general welfare and to make all laws which in their judgment may be necessary and proper for these purposes.

The subject in debate is whether the power of levying internal taxes ought to be confided to Congress in the first instance, whether a matter so intimately connected with the internal police of the states,—a power which might so immediately operate on the property of individuals and so indefinite that it may effect the existence of the States ought in the first place to be confided in so feeble and imperfect a representation as that in the general government or whether it is not proper to reserve this power to the States except in cases where the delinquency may render their exercise of it in the genl. govt. necessary.

Great pains have been taken on one side to show that the States have concurrent jurisdiction with the genl. govt. In this instance, and this seems in some measure to be admitted by all. I confess however that with me it is not clearly established. At most it depends upon construction and this too arising from a maxim which has not been adhered to by the framers of the Constitution, that what power is not expressly granted to the genl. govt. is reserved—for if we recur to the system, we will find that in sundry instances there are prohibitions found against the exercise of powers, which would appear to be neither expressly or impliedly granted, particularly in a case I have before mentioned, the creation of a nobility. This alone would justify a doubt—but admit the principle.

Concurrent Jurisdictions are dangerous—they ought as far as possible to be avoided—they may and in all probability will endanger the peace and harmony of the union. They involve the political absurdity of imperium in imperio, so destructive to every idea of good govt.

The celebrated Lord Coke somewhere observes that certainty is the mother of quiet—It is unwise and dangerous therefore to suffer the fundamental compact to rest upon uncertain constructions, it will not fail to occasion discord between the genl. govt. and its members—and if it should we are told by the gentlemen who oppose the amendmt. that the latter will and must prevail and consequently the union will be dissolved. I submit it therefore to the Committee, whether it will not be wise to avoid so great an evil by rendering the meaning of the system in this and every other instance, where it may be doubtful, certain and unequivocal and by limitting its powers as far as may be consistent with the general safety to such objects only as will avoid a dangerous and improper interference of State and genl. authority.

It has been alledged by the Gentlemen opposed to the system that in many instances the genl. and state govt. will have discordant interests. This has been fully admitted by the Gentm. in favor of it in their speeches agt. the amendt. proposed for subjecting the Senators to the recal of the States—for one of the arguments offered against the amendt. was that by rendering them too dependent on the States, it would subject them to state or local views.

This govt. among other things is to form a more perfect union, yet it would appear that its operations might produce discord with its members. It is in my opinion however absurd in the last degree to propose that the states will combine agt. the genl. govt. as long as it is confined to proper objects and preserves the common interest—this would be to propose that the States will conspire to destroy themselves—and it has been added that the people from their attachments will even join them. I do not believe that either will happen unless provoked by an undue and wicked administration. And should this be the case if the people both in their moral and political capacities should consider the general government as an evil I heartily join the honble. gentl in his pious ejaculation and when speaking with respect to the existence of the states Government. God forbid that it should then continue to exist against the general will.

For my own part, I lay it down as a certain truth that unless the govt. is so constructed as to harmonize with the State Govts. and persue one common interest, that the system must fail and end in ruin. The best and surest support of a Republican Govt. is the confidence and attachment of the members of which it is composed—if they have clashing interests and interferring powers, this confidence and affection will cease and then if any government exists it must be supported by force and the coercion of the sword.

JULY 11, 1788

On a consideration of the objections which have been made to the Constitution proposed for our adoption, it will readily be discovered that most of them are founded upon or derive force from the idea, that the system is a departure from the principles of a Confederacy and embraces the essential powers of a general consolidated government; on the other hand, if we take a view of the arguments, which have been offered to refute these objections, it will appear that they are principally predicated on a denial of this position and attempt to establish the contrary doctrine. It is asserted that the rights of the states will remain uninvaded and that they will serve as effectual barriers to secure the liberties of the people against the undue encroachments of power—and it has even been admitted by one of the framers and ablest advocates of the system—that so extensive a territory as the United States, would not be governed, connected and preserved but by the supremacy of despotic power.

In order then to be able to form a proper judgment on this subject, it is necessary carefully to inquire how far this system partakes of or departs from the nature of a confederate republic; and what from the power it possesses and the objects it embraces, its probable operations will be.

The definition given of States and their rights by authors of the first authority is, that they are equally free and independent, as the individuals of which they are composed, naturally were—that they are to be considered as moral persons, having a will of their own and equal rights—that these rights are freedom, sovereignty, and independence. The celebrated Vattel treating on this subject, observes "that power or weakness does not in this respect produce any difference. A dwarf is as much a man as a giant; a small republic is as much a sovereign as the most powerful kingdom."

Hence it follows, that as the only inducement, which men can have to quit the condition, in which nature has placed them and enter into society is the preservation of their rights and liberties, so the only end of which states are induced to confederate, is mutual protection and the security of their equal rights,—and the idea of states confederating upon principles of inequality and destructive of their freedom and independence is as absurd and unreasonable as it would be to suppose that a man would take a draught of poison to preserve his life.

From these premises it is clearly deducible that the elements of every just league or confederacy, however diversified in the modification, ought to be. 1st. That as the States are the creative principle, the power of the confederacy, must originate from and operate upon them, and not upon the individuals, who composed them, and consequently be confined as far as possible to general extraneous concerns, reserving to the States the exclusive sovereignty and arrangement of their internal government and concerns.

2nd. That the states having equal rights to protect, ought to be equally represented.

3rd. That it is the will of the States, which is to be expressed in the federal council, as their interests arise and their safety may require, they ought to have the government of that will and therefore that the delegates who are to express that will, ought to be subject to their appointment and controul.

I presume that to the most superficial observer, it will appear that these principles are founded in the reason and nature of things. To enter into a train of reasoning to support them, would consequently be an unnecessary waste of time. I am persuaded they will not be controverted.

If then in the formation of a Confederacy, an adherence to these principles, is essential to the security of the rights of the confederating states, we shall find on an examination of this system, that except in appearance, it is a total departure from them and calculated in its operations, to destroy not to preserve their existence.

From the terms of the instrument it appears that the powers granted do not originate from the states in their political capacity but from the people at large—The style is "We the people of the United States" hence this government must be considered as an original compact, annulling the State Constitutions as far as its powers interfere with them and thus far destroying their distinct rights—The powers of this government operate not upon the States but immediately upon the people that compose them—They are not confined to the general and extraneous concerns of the States but extend to the most important internal affairs, to wit, the raising and levying of taxes direct and indirect—the regulation of bankruptcies, the establishing of rules for naturalization, the organizing and disciplining the militia, and the regulation of the Elections for Senators and Representatives in Congress.

The equality of Representation as States is also destroyed—The Legislative authority is divided into 2 branches, a house of Representatives and Senate.

In the house of Representatives the states cannot be said to have any share in the representation—as that branch is elected by the people in their moral capacity—but if the contrary should be alledged, yet the representation is unequal, the ratio of representation being in proportion to the number of inhabitants of which the States are respectively composed—In the Senate, indeed, they are equally represented, and in this instance it would appear to partake of the principles of a confederate government, but this feature of federalism is destroyed, as the mode of voting in the Senate is not by states but by voices, in the latter way the States may not be able to express their will for having two members who may vote differently on the same question, they may have two wills, a negative and a positive one. From whence it will appear that the only check which the states will possess in this or any other instance might be derived from their being electors of one Legislative branch of the general government.

From this concise view of the subject, it is evident, that the system is not constructed upon the principles of a federal republic, for wherever a federal feature appears in it it is united with the stronger impressions of consolidation, is neither raised upon an equality of rights or representation in the States.

The objects of a Confederacy being as before observed the preservation of the rights of the States and the States being the Creative principle, it is obvious that the Confederacy ought to depend upon the States for its existence but if we examine the present system, we will find that this principle is reversed and that the existence of the latter depends solely upon the former—and if we permit our sentiments on this occasion to be governed by the history of ages and the experience of mankind, as to the encroachments of power, when there is no constitutional or effectual bar to restrain them—we may safely venture to pronounce that it is not only possible but highly probable; that should the Constitution be adopted, it will ere long terminate in a consolidation of the United States into one general government.

It commences in a complete system of government—divided into Legislative, Executive, and Judicial Branches and totally independent of any other power for its continuance—it has a perfect control over the elections of its members—it possesses power over all the resources of the country with the absolute and uncontrolled command of the military services of the people while the States are left wholly destitute of any means of support, but what they hold at the will and pleasure of the general government—They are divested of the power of commanding the services of their own Citizens and reduced to the degraded situations of public corporations by being rendered liable to suits. But if any thing farther was necessary to their total annihilation, the powers vested in the judicial department, which is tendered totally independent both as to the terms and emolument of their offices (except as to an increase of salary) and whose decrees are uncontrollable and fully competent to that purpose since it possesses still more extensive power, than the legislative and if possible still more dangerous to the existence of the States—for besides comprehending within its jurisdiction all the variety of cases, to which the other branches of government extend, it is authorized to determine upon all cases in law and equity arising under the Constitution etc.—In every controversy therefore which may arise in cases where the States may be supposed to possess concurrent jurisdiction with the general government, as in the case of internal taxation, the decision of the supreme judicial upon equitable principles is to be final and by a fundamental principle of the government, these adjudications will be engrafted into the original compact. The more the powers of the general government are enlarged by these decisions the more extensive does the jurisdiction of the judges become. It is an old established maxim among lawyers that he is a good judge who enlarges the sphere of the jurisdiction of his Court—a maxim that has never failed to have been faithfully pursued—as instances we need only refer to the Courts of Kings Bench and Exchequer in England—but it will not require an extraordinary stretch of legal ingenuity in the judges to extend their power to every conceivable case and to collect into the sphere of their jurisdiction every judicial power which the States now possess.

The objects of this government as expressed in the preface to it, are "to form a more perfect union, establish justice, insure domestic tranquility, provide for the common defence, promote the general welfare, and secure the blessings of liberty"—These include every object for which government was established amongst man, and in every dispute about the powers granted, it is fair to infer that the means are commensurate with the end—and I believe we may venture to assert, that a good judge would not hesitate to draw this inference, especially when supported by the undefined powers granted by the 8th. section of the 1st. article and the construction that naturally arises from the prohibition against the creation of a nobility, a power which would otherwise appear to be neither expressly or impliedly granted.

I am sensible, it may be said, that the state governments are component parts of the general government and therefore that of necessity their existence must be preserved and that the Constitution has guaranteed to them a republican form but this, on the least reflection, will appear to be too feeble a security to be relied on, when they are divested of every resource for their own support and the terms too indefinite to afford any security to the liberties of the people, as it includes in it the idea of an arbitrary aristocracy as well as of a free government—The form may exist without the substance. It will be remembered that this was the case in Rome when under a despotism—The Senate existed as formerly—Consuls, Tribunes etc. were chosen by the people—but their powers were merely nominal, as they were ruled by the will of the reigning Tyrant—and the most arbitrary ministers and judges generally preserve the forms of law, while they disregard its precepts and pervert them to the purposes of oppression.

From these observations, it is evident, that the general government is not constructed upon federal principles, and that its operations will terminate in a dissolution of the States—That even if this should not be the case, they will be so enfeebled as not to afford that effectual security to the rights and liberties of the people, against the undue and extensive powers vested in the general government, as its advocates have led them to expect. This being the case, the objections which have been stated against the system, must appear to well founded—and it therefore becomes our indispensable duty to obviate them by suitable amendments calculated to abridge and limit the powers to general objects. The evils pointed out in the system are now within our power to remedy—but if we suffer ourselves to be influenced by specious reasoning unsupported by example to an unconditional adoption of an imperfect government, the opportunity will be forever lost, for history does not furnish a single instance of a government once established, voluntarily yielding up its powers to secure the rights and liberties of the people.

July 15, 1788

Altho I came to the Convention impressed with an idea that the system of Government proposed for our adoption was unsafe and dangerous to the liberties of the people and I conceive that the measures which were taken to introduce this change of govt. were equally exceptionable. Yet I was sensible that I was as all other men are liable to error and as I entertained a high opinion of the good sense, and patriotism of many of the gentlemen who advocated it, I came here with a firm determination to hear with coolness and candor the arguments which might be offered in its favor and to give them their due weight.

I have therefore avoided taking any considerable part in the debates lest as is too apt to be the case, I might become prejudiced in favor of my own reasoning—the little that I have said, it must appear has been rather to raise objections with a view of having them answered than to support any opinion on either side of the question—I have listened with candor and attention to every argument that has been offered in support of the system when under debate by paragraphs and as far as I have been capable, I have given them their due weight, and if they had been such as would have convinced me that my first opinion was wrong, I would have cheerfully acquiesced and used my utmost endeavours by the same arguments to spread conviction among my constituents and to reconcile them to the plan.

Unfortunately, however, this has not been the case—some explanations indeed have been made of articles doubtful in their nature, which I never thought very material—but I can with great truth and sincerity declare that notwithstanding every thing I have yet heard the principal objections agt. the system remain in my mind unimpaired and in full force.

Nothing has been offered to convince my judgment that the representation is not too feeble and imperfect considering the extensive and undefined powers that are committed to this government, or that there is a sufficient degree of security under this Constitution that the will of the people will be the law. And this it must be admitted is the only true definition of a free government. Nor is there sufficient security afforded for the existence of the states sovty. Which I consider the only stable security for the liberties of the people against the encroachments of power.

The system still appears to be radically defective in its organization—the most important legislative, judicial and executive powers being dangerously blended together in the President and Senate.—whereby responsibility is in a great measure destroyed.

The judicial department also appears to me equally defective—it is not however my intention at this time to enter into a detail of arguments to establish these points—it is not necessary to take up the time of the Committee in repeating arguments that have been already alledged by other gentlemen, especially as the amendments proposed which are calculated to cure these defects in some degree will naturally recal to the minds of gentlemen the reasons upon which they are founded.

In the cource of the debate some new doctrines have indeed been attempted to be established which if they could be supported would seem in a degree to obviate some of the objections that have been made to the system, to wit, that the only true security the people can have in a govt. is its being a representative govert. formed upon republican principles and a proper distribution of the Legislative, Judicial and Executive powers—

But it will be easily perceived that this doctrine is not only wrong in itself but even a departure from the principles pursued by the very framers of this Govert. because we will find that it contains several limitations such as the suspension of the Writ of Habeas Corpus, the passing of Bills of attainder and Ex post facto laws and the creation of a nobility—Whereas if the doctrine attempted to be established was true in almost any extent these provisions would have been utterly unnecessary—for after having provided for the organization of the government and the due distribution of its powers the whole system might have been comprised in these words—Congress shall have power to provide for the common defence and general welfare and to make all laws which in their judgment may be necessary and proper for these purposes or in the words of the powers that were given to the Roman Dictators To take care that the Republic receives no detriment.

The other principle I allude to will be found among the reasonings offered against the amendment rendering the Senate in a greater degree responsible to their Constituents than they now are. It will be remembered that it was alledged it would render them too dependent upon the will of the Legislatures of the States and that they might be influenced from pursuing the public good by the local views, passions and prejudices of their Constituents. I will only observe that these sentiments will not apply to a deliberative body and that it must appear that they are in every point of view contrary to the principles of a free representative government for if the representative is not to be subject to the will of his Constituents, lest he might be influenced to do wrong, but is in his representative capacity to express his own not their will, then it is evident that the will of a few must become their will, then it is evident that the will of a few must become the law, and this is the essence of Tyranny.

The Committee I trust will pardon me for this digression from the point in question. I shall now proceed to make some objections more particularly applicable to the question now before the Committee.

The motion on which the question arises is for postponing one previously made (the purport of which is to procure an unconditional adoption of the Constitution) and to introduce a different plan of adoption—The principal question that has been raised upon this subject, is whether the last mode will be such an adoption as that Congress can receive into the union.

This matter has been so fully and ably debated by Gentlemen on both sides of the House, that it would be vain in me to attempt to offer any new arguments, as it is fairly exhausted—That doubts may be raised and supported with a great degree of plausibility upon almost any political subject is certain—that in all questions of this kind, where the matter might depend upon the will of a public who are perhaps as frequently if not more so governed by motives of political expediency than other considerations, the issue must be attended with a degree of uncertainty—I have weighed with care and attention the arguments offered on both sides—I do not pretend to be capable of forming a perfect judgment upon the subject—but as far as my reasoning and reflection go, to me it appears that Congress may without a violation of the Constitution, receive the states on the terms of ratification proposed into the union—nay, I believe if they do not that their denial will not arise from the want of power. I believe I may venture to say that a refusal on this ground will be a more rigid adherence to compact and that too upon more refined constructive reasoning and metaphysical distinctions than ever a body of this kind adhered to before. I am persuaded there is not a State in the union, nay I question if there is in the world, who have not upon less interesting occasions made greater departure from the fundamental principles of the Government than this will be if it can be called a departure at all.—

I would ask whether in the establishment of this new Government, we find such a religious adherence to Compact—Has it not originated and grown into what it is from motives of political expediency? Has it not been submitted to upon this consideration alone? Have not all the measures that have introduced it and that are now bringing into action been in the force of compact, in direct violation of solemn plighted faith? Can this govt. ever be consistently with compact put into operation without the consent of every state in the union? Why then should we suppose upon this occasion that the states who have acceded to it contrary to original compact should hesitate to receive us when only justified in a refusal by refined and subtle distinctions? Would not this be indeed like swallowing a Camel and chocking with a gnat?

But by one Gentlmn. arguments have been alledged to show that it would not be the interest of the other states to receive us into the union—Let us examine the matter upon this ground. I will not take up the Honble. Gentmn's. reasoning with respect to the increase or decrease of influence it might occasion to the greater or smaller states.—these might have weight if the Govt. was fairly and firmly established and brought into operation—but I humbly conceive they can have none in the present situation of affairs. I beg Gentm. to reflect upon the real situation of the U.S. as to the Govt. Let them cooly and calmly reflect whether it is probable that they will be able to establish and support it—against the will of so large a proportion of the Community from one end of the Continent to the other unless essential amendments take place and in the meantime a suspension of the exercise of certain powers most obnoxious to the people?

It has been observed by an Honble. Gentm. that it has had 11 verdicts in its favor, the Convention at Philadelphia and 10 other states, and that therefore, we ought to acquiesce in it.—That Gentm. well knows it is essential to a verdict that the Jury be unanimous, and in this veiw it will be found to have but very few verdicts indeed, and if we apply the evidence that may be drawn from the arguments to which we allude it affords the strongest testimony the testimony of its warmest friends and advocates, that it is dangerously and radically defective, since they have recommended essential amends.

Have Gentmn. the smallest hope that the question will be carried on the motion—have they not the most convincing proofs to the contrary? Will not a negative be a rejection? Have they any reason to suppose it will promote the peace and harmony of the state? I entreat Gentlemen to reflect what will be the consequence if this proposal should be rejected and question taken upon the original motion.

We have been told of the necessity there is for a spirit of conciliation and unanimity upon this important point—the honble. Gentm. has in the most lively and pathetic manner pointed out the calamities that would ensue our rising divided upon this subject—I will not repreat what has been said upon this occasion—because I conceive that many of the observations that were thrown out by the Honble. Gentm. were highly indiscreet and improper—I wish they may never be repeated out of these walls—I verily believe they will tend to occasion the evils which I hope they were intended to prevent. Gentlemen ought to consider that the Country is divided upon this question that they have made up decidedly their sentiments and are warmly engaged in the support of them—that from the most conclusive testimony, a large majority of the people are opposed to the unconditional adoption of the system—some respect ought surely to be paid to their opinions; it cannot be reasonably supposed that they will yield to minority without the least concessions on the part of the latter—and if we reason rightly I believe we will be convinced that the danger will chiefly be in a deviation from the will of a majority.[2]

Mr. Chairman

altho' I have as I have before mentioned heard nothing in the Committee to change my opinion of the Constitution yet I shall be in favor of the present motion that I may have an opportunity of yielding my assent to the proposition made by the Honble. Gentm. from Dutchess.[3] I think it my duty at the same time to declare that I could only be induced to this from a strong attachment to the union—from a spirit of conciliation and an earnest desire to promote peace and harmony among the Citizens of the states to forward the interest and happiness of whom I am bound by ties uncommonly strong.

I shall conclude sir by just observing that I think the proposition is a reasonable one, that it contains nothing that can give offence or that can prevent its being accepted its object is barely to prevent the immediate operation of powers the most odious to our Constituents until they can be considered by the people of America to whose decision we declare our willingness to submit. There is nothing in the Proposition that can prevent the Government's going into full operation and having full effect as to all essential National Concerns— These conditions go only as to the Mode of changing the Government's Operations in the few instances mentioned in the Propositions.

I am convinced Sir, we have gone even beyond the will of our Constituents upon this occasion—but I have hopes that the reasons which have influenced us so to do will be satisfactory to them—

I will only add that the earnestness which has been discovered in this Committee to support most of the Clauses included among those termed conditional is with me an additional reason for holding them up in a conspicuous point of view as objects most wanting amendts.

In these speeches, Clinton focused on the excessive powers the Constitution gave to the central government (see George Clinton entry in *Biographies*). His experience in government had taught him that small and responsible government best represented the interests of the people. That is why Clinton also favored a written bill of personal rights to counter the powers of federal authority.

REFERENCES

Clinton's notes for these speeches may be found in the George Bancroft Papers, New York Public Library; Elliot, *Debates*, vol. 2; Storing, *Complete*, vol. 2.

NOTES

1. Here and elsewhere Clinton is referring to his arch-enemy Alexander Hamilton.
2. Again Clinton refers to Hamilton, only this time he attempts to counter threats from his bitter enemy.
3. Clinton's ally Melancton Smith.

John Lansing, Speech in the New York State Ratification Convention, *June 28, 1788*

This clause, Mr. Chairman, is, by every one, considered as one of the most important in the Constitution. The subject has been treated in a very diffusive manner. Among all the ingenious remarks that have been made, some are little more than repetitions; others are not very applicable or interesting. I shall beg leave to pass a few strictures on the paragraph; and, in my reply, shall confine myself to the arguments which have been advanced. The committee have been informed that it embraces a great variety of objects, and that it gives the general government a power to lay all kinds of *taxes,* that it confers a right of laying excises on all articles of American manufacture, of exacting an impost, in which the state governments cannot interfere, and of laying direct taxes without restriction. These powers reach every possible source of revenue. They will involve a variety of litigations, which can come only under the cognizance of the judiciary of the United States. Hence it must appear that these powers will affect, in an unlimited manner, the property of the citizens; that they will subject them, in a great degree, to the laws of the Union, and give an extensive jurisdiction to the federal courts. The objects of the amendment are, to prevent excises from being laid on the manufactures of the United States, and to provide that direct taxes shall not be imposed till requisitions have been made and proved fruitless.

All the reasoning of the gentlemen goes to prove that government ought to possess all the resources of a country. But so far as it respects government in general, it does not apply to this question. Giving the principle its full force, it does not prove that our federal government ought to have all the resources; because this government is but a part of a system, the whole of which should possess the means of support. It has been advanced repeatedly by the gentleman, that the powers of the United States should, like their objects, be national and general. It appears to him proper, therefore, that the nature of their resources should be correspondent. Sir, it has been declared that we can no longer place confidence in requisitions. A great deal of argument has been spent on this point. The gentlemen constantly consider the old mode of requisitions, and that proposed, in the same view. But not one of us has ever contended for requisitions in the form prescribed in the existing Confederation: hence the reasoning about the inefficacy of the ancient mode has no application to the one recommended; which rests on different principles, and has a sanction of which the other is totally destitute. In the one instance, it is necessary to execute the requisitions of Congress on the states collectively. There is no way of doing this but by coercing a whole community, which cannot be effected. But the amendment proposes to carry the laws of Congress to the doors of individuals. This circumstance will produce an entire change in the operation of requisitions, and will give them an efficiency which otherwise they could not have. In this view, it will appear that the gentleman's principles respecting the character and effects of requisitions can have no application in this dispute. Much pains has been taken to show that requisitions have not answered the public exigencies. All this has been fully admitted in former stages of the debate. It was said by a gentleman yesterday, that though considerable sums of money had been paid by the people, it was by way of bounties to the soldiers which was a coercion on individuals. If, then, this coercion had its effect, certainly its operation, upon the proposed plan, will be much more forcible. It has been said that, in sudden emergencies, all the resources of the country might be required; and that the supreme head ought to possess the power of providing for the public wants, in every degree. It is an undoubted fact, that, in all government, it is extremely difficult, on the spur of the occasion, to raise money by taxes. Nor is it necessary. In a commercial country, persons will always be found to advance money to the government, and to wait the regular operation of the revenue laws. It depends on the security of the taxes, and the certainty of being refunded. This amendment does not diminish the security or render the fund precarious. The certainty of repayment is as well established as if the government could levy the taxes originally on individuals.

Sir, have the states ever shown a disposition not to comply with the requisitions? We shall find that, in almost every instance, they have, so far forth as the passing a law of compliance, been carried into execution. To what, then, are the delinquencies to be attributed? They must be to the impoverished state of the country. If the state governments have been unable to compel the people to obey their laws, will Congress be able to coerce them? Will the federal taxes be better paid? But, sir, no reasonable man will be apprehensive of the non-compliance of the states, under the operation of the proposed plan. The right of enforcing the requisitions will furnish the strongest motive for the performance of the federal duty. With this powerful inducement, there is hardly a possibility of failure. It has been asked, Why give the individual states the preference? Why not suffer the general government to apply to the people in the first instance, without the formality of a requisition? This question has been repeatedly asked, and as often answered. It is because the state legislatures are more nearly connected with the people, and more acquainted with their situation and wants. They better know when to enforce or relax their laws; to embrace objects or relinquish them, according to change of circumstances: they have but a few varying interests to comprehend in general provisions. Congress do not possess these advantages; they cannot have so complete an acquaintance with the people; their laws, being necessarily uniform, cannot be calculated for the great diversity of objects which present themselves to government. It is possible that the men delegated may have interests different from those of the people. It is observed that we have had experience of different kinds of taxes, which have been executed by different officers,—for instance, county and state taxes,—and that there has been no clashing or interference. But, sir, in these cases, if any dispute arises, the parties appeal to a common tribunal; but if collectors are appointed by different governments, and authorized by different laws, the federal officer will appeal to a federal court; his adversary will appeal to the state court. Will not this create contests respecting jurisdiction? But the Constitution declares that the laws of the United States shall be supreme. There is no doubt, therefore, that they must prevail in every controversy; and every thing which has a tendency to obstruct the force of the general government must give way.

An honorable gentleman from New York has remarked that the idea of *danger to state governments* can only originate in a distempered fancy: he stated that they were necessary component parts of the system, and informed us how the President and senators were to be elected; his conclusion is, that the liberties of the people cannot be endangered. I shall only observe, that, however fanciful these apprehensions may appear to him, they have made serious impressions upon some of the greatest and best men.[1] Our fears arise from the experience of all ages and our knowledge of the dispositions of mankind. I believe the gentleman cannot point out an instance of the rights of a people remaining for a long period inviolate. The history of Europe has afforded remarkable examples of the loss of liberty by the usurpations of rulers. In the early periods of the government of the United Netherlands, the magistrates were elected by the people; but now they have become hereditary. The Venetians are, at this day, governed by an aristocracy. The senators, once the representatives of the people, were enabled, by gradual encroachments, at last to declare themselves perpetual. The office has since become hereditary, and the government entirely despotic. The gentleman has adduced one historical example, to prove that the members of a government, in the contests with the head, generally prevail. He observed that, in the struggles between the feudal sovereigns of Europe and their barons, the latter were usually victorious. If this were true, I believe the operations of such a system as the feudal will not warrant the general inference he draws. The feudal barons were obliged to assist the monarch, in his wars, with their persons and those of their vassals. This, in the early periods, was the sovereign's sole dependence. Not possessed of pecuniary revenues, or a standing military force, he was, whenever the barons withdrew their aid, or revolted against his authority, reduced to a very feeble situation. While he possessed not the means of carrying on his wars, independently of his nobles, his power was insignificant, and he was unsuccessful. But, sir, the moment he gained the command of revenues and an army, as soon as he obtained *the sword and the purse*, the current of success was turned; and his superiority over his barons was regularly augmented, and at last established. The barons, in their early wars, possessed other peculiar advantages: their number was small, they were actuated by one principle, and had one common object; it was to reduce still lower the feeble powers of the monarch: they were therefore easily brought to act in concert. Sir, wherever the revenues and the military force are, there will rest the power: the members or the head will prevail, as one or the other possesses these advantages. The gentleman, in his reasoning, has taken the wrong part of the example—that part which bears no resemblance to our system. Had he come down to a later period, he would indeed have seen the resemblance, and his historical facts would have directly militated against his argument. Sir, if you do not give the state governments a power to protect themselves, if you leave them no other check upon Congress than the power of appointing senators, they will certainly be overcome, like the barons of whom the gentleman has spoken. Neither our civil nor militia officers will afford many advantages of opposition against the national government: if they have any powers, it will ever be difficult to concentrate them, or give them a uniform direction. Their influence will hardly be felt, while the greater number of lucrative and honorable places, in the gift of the United States, will establish an influence which will prevail in every part of the continent.

It has been admitted by an honorable gentleman from New York, (Mr. Hamilton,) that the state governments are necessary to secure the liberties of the people. He has urged several forcible reasons why they ought to be preserved under the new system; and he has treated the idea of the general and state governments being hostile to each other as chimerical. I am, however, firmly persuaded that an hostility between them will exist. This was a received opinion in the late Convention at Philadelphia. That honorable gentleman was then fully convinced that it would exist, and argued, with much decision and great plausibility, that the state governments ought to be subverted, at least so far as to leave them only corporate rights, and that, even in that situation, they would endanger the existence of the general government. But the honorable gentleman's reflections have probably induced him to correct that sentiment.

John Lansing spoke often in the convention of his opposition to such a large and powerful federal government (see John Lansing entry in *Biographies*). In this particular speech, he called for amending the federal Constitution. He insisted that powers be specifically delegated because he wanted to curb any excessive authority given to federal officeholders. In this way, Lansing insisted, the rights of the state governments would find clear and explicit protection in the large new nation.

REFERENCES

Francis Childs, *Debates and Proceedings of the Convention of the State of New York* (Albany: State Printer, 1788); Elliot, *Debates*, vol. 2.

NOTE

1. Lansing is criticizing Alexander Hamilton.

Melancton Smith, Speech in the New York State Ratification Convention, *July 23, 1788*

On Wednesday the Convention finished the consideration of the amendments, and took up the proposition of adopting the Constitution with three conditions annexed. Mr. Jones moved to insert the words *in full confidence,* instead of the words *upon condition.* Mr. M. Smith rose and declared his determination to vote against a condition. He urged that however it might otherwise be presumed he was consistent in his principles and conduct. He was as thoroughly convinced then as he ever had been, that the Constitution was radically defective—amendments to it had always been the object of his pursuit, and until Virginia came in, he had reason to believe they might have been obtained previous to the operation of the Government. He was now satisfied they could not, and it was equally the dictate of reason and duty to quit his first ground, and advance so far as that they might be received into the Union. He should hereafter pursue his important and favorite object of amendments, with equal zeal as before, but in a practicable way; which was only in the mode prescribed by the Constitution. On the first suggestion of the plan then under consideration, he thought it might have answered the purpose; but from the reasonings of gentlemen in opposition to it, and whose opinions alone would deservedly have vast weight in the national councils, as well as from the sentiments of persons abroad, he was now persuaded the proposition would not be received, however doubtful it might appear, considered merely as an abstract and speculative question. The thing must now be abandoned as fallacious, for if persisted in, it would certainly prove in the event, only a dreadful deception to those who were serious for joining the Union. He then placed in a striking and affecting light, the situation of this State in case we should not be received by Congress. Convulsions in the Southern part, factions and discord in the rest. The strength of his own party, who were seriously anxious for amending the Government, would be dissipated; their union lost—their object probably defeated—and they would, to use the simple figurative language of scripture, be dispersed like sheep on a mountain. He therefore concluded that it was no more than a proper discharge of his public duty, as well as the most advisable way of obtaining the great end of his opposition, to vote against any proposition which would not be received as a ratification of the Constitution.

In this speech, the arch-Antifederalist Melancton Smith explains why he voted for ratification of the Constitution (see Melancton Smith entry in *Biographies*). He explained to his fellow delegates that there was no way to make a perfect government. But Smith's major reason for changing his position was because the state's Federalists had promised to support a bill of rights. With the knowledge that the Constitution already had received the requisite number of states needed for ratification, Smith's only hope for reform was in a bill of rights.

REFERENCE

Elliot, *Debates*, vol. 2.

John Lamb, Melancton Smith, and Charles Tillinghast, To the Counties within this State: New York, *November 4, 1788*

Gentlemen:

The circumstances and situation of things both before, and some time after our convention had met, warranted an universal opinion among all Federal Republicans, that it was proper to adopt the new constitution only on condition that those important alterations which were considered necessary to the protection of political and civil liberty, should be made: and this was founded not only on the defects of the Constitution, but on the anticipation that there would have been a majority in several of the State conventions of the same sentiments with our own; from whom we should have derived support. But in pursuing our opposition in this form, the sentiments and opinions of many in our Convention were changed; not, as we have reason to believe as to the principles of opposition, but as to the expediency of adopting under an alteration of circumstances, so that this State shall continue in the Union. At the same time, giving such constructions to some of its articles, and relying on the sentiments of a majority in the United States, with respect to an opinion of its defects, that the government would be restrained in the exercise of its most offensive and dangerous powers, until a new convention should have an opportunity of reconsidering and revising it, before it should have its full operation.

This alteration of sentiment with respect to a conditional adoption, and the mode of adopting it in its present manner, it is to be presumed, was caused by the reception of it by nine States successively; by which the government was capable to be put in operation; and likewise the immediate and subsequent adoption of it by Virginia, perhaps one of the most influential and important States in the Union. The confidence of those who were of these sentiments was excited, because many of the most important States, had acknowledged it by small majorities; and almost all, in such a way as was expressive of its defects: and hence they considered amendments as certain; subsequent as precedent.

Thus unsupported by any of the States in the prospect of a conditional adoption, and for these reasons, it became a political calculation with them, whether it was not most for the interests of this State, under all circumstances, to continue in the Union, and trust, for the reasons aforesaid, for amendments. Unhappily, this occasioned a diversity of opinion among our friends in the convention, who were for a conditional adoption only. However, the question, as you well know, was at last carried in the way it now stands. Altho' a division took place, both within and without the convention on this point, and for these reasons, yet we hope that a confidence remains on the minds of all, that each was governed by the principles of rectitude; and that the efforts and exertions of each other collectively, as well as individually, will be considered a duty in future; and made use of to obtain the great objects we have all had, and still have in view, to wit: the requisite amendments; by having a general convention called immediately, or as soon as possible after the organization of the new government.

With this design, we conceive it will be very necessary to advert to the ensuing election of members to represent this State in the assembly of the general government; and to endeavor to elect such characters as are in sentiment with us on the subject of amendments. Nor is the mode of election a matter of small importance, when it is considered that one mode may throw the balance in the hands of the advocates of an arbitrary government, while another may be favorable to equal liberty. The activity and duplicity of the principal of those who have contended for unequivocal adoption, and uncontrouled exercise of the new Constitution, notwithstanding their promises to assist in procuring a convention for the purposes already mentioned, have given us just causes of suspicion, that those promises were made with a view to deceive.

To facilitate a communication of sentiment and free discussion on this subject, with you and our friends in the other counties, and thereby further the great objects of our pursuit, and oppose with success the subtle practices of the adversaries of constitutional liberty, we have formed ourselves into a society for the purpose of procuring a general convention, agreeable to the circular letter of the late convention of this State; and we beg leave to recommend to your consideration the propriety of your joining together without delay for the like design.

We have only to add, that whatever diversity of sentiment may have taken place among the friends of equal liberty in our late convention, we are fully persuaded that they will unite their utmost exertions in the only mode which is now left. And should the present opportunity which is offered at the organization of the government, not be properly improved, it is highly probably such a favorable one will not be again presented; and the liberties of the people will then depend on the arbitrary decrees of their rulers.

In behalf of the Society, &c.

To Republican Committee of Ulster county.

In this notice to the county leaders, these Antifederalists announced their continued opposition to the Constitution, their repudiation of the state's Federalists, and their desire to amend the Constitution (see John Lamb, Melancton Smith, and Charles Tillinghast entries in *Biographies*).

REFERENCES

Leake, *Memoirs of John Lamb*; Minutes of the Federal Republican Society, John Lamb Papers, New York Historical Society.

13
North Carolina

July 21–August 4, 1788

Rejected, August 2, 1788

Against 183–83

November 16–21, 1789

Ratification #12, November 21, 1789

In favor 194–77

Willie Jones, "Proposal," North Carolina State Ratification Convention,
July 23, 1788

Mr. WILLIE JONES moved that the question upon the Constitution should be immediately put. He said that the Constitution had so long been the subject of the deliberation of every man in this country, and that the members of the Convention had had such ample opportunity to consider it, that he believed every one of them was prepared to give his vote then upon the question; that the situation of the public funds would not admit of lavishing the public money, but required the utmost economy and frugality; that, as there was a large representation from this state, an immediate decision would save the country a considerable sum of money. He thought it, therefore, prudent to put the question immediately. . . .

Mr. President, my reasons for proposing an immediate decision were, that I was prepared to give my vote, and believed that others were equally prepared as myself. If gentlemen differ from me in the propriety of this motion, I will submit. I agree with the gentleman that economical considerations are not of equal importance with the magnitude of the subject. He said that it would have been better, at once, for the electors to vote in their respective counties than to decide it here without discussion. Does he forget that the act of Assembly points out another mode?

Willie Jones, perhaps the richest and most powerful Antifederalist in the state, had served in the Continental Congress (see Willie Jones entry in *Biographies*). More a tactician than a theorist, Jones opened the convention offering an immediate vote and no debate. He lost this bid.

REFERENCES

Elliot, *Debates*, vol. 4 (Elliot collected most of the debates in North Carolina's first convention, and his second edition from 1836 remains the finest volume on North Carolina's Antifederalists). Another work on North Carolina that excerpts some of the Antifederalists' speeches is Louise Irby Trenholme, *The Ratification of the Federal Constitution in North Carolina* (New York: Columbia University Press, 1932).

Samuel Spencer, Speeches in the North Carolina State Ratification Convention, *July 28, 29, 1788*

July 28

Mr. Chairman, I rise to declare my disapprobation of this likewise. It is an essential article in our Constitution, that the legislative, the executive and the supreme judicial powers of government, ought to be forever separate and distinct from each other. The Senate in the proposed government of the United States, are possessed of the legislative authority in conjunction with the House of Representatives. They are likewise possessed of the sole power of trying all impeachments, which not being restrained to the officers of the United States, may be intended to include all the officers of the several states in the union. And by this clause they possess the chief of the executive power—they are in effect to form treaties, which are to be the law of the land, and they have obviously in effect the appointment of all the officers of the United States; the President may nominate, but they have a negative upon his nomination, till he has exhausted the number of those he wishes to be appointed: He will be obliged finally to acquiesce in the appointment of those which the Senate shall nominate, or else no appointment will take place. Hence it is easy to perceive, that the President, in order to do any business, or to answer any purpose in his department of his office, and to keep himself out of perpetual hot water, will be under a necessity to form a connection with that powerful body, and be contended to put himself at the head of the leading members who compose it. I do not expect at this day, that the outline and organization of this proposed government will be materially altered. But I cannot but be of opinion, that the government would have been infinitely better and more secure, if the President had been provided with a standing Council, composed of one Member from each of the states, the duration of whose office might have been the same as that of the President's office, or for any other period that might have been thought more proper. For it can hardly be supposed, that if two Senators can be sent from each state, who are fit to give counsel to the President, that one such cannot be found in each state, qualified for that purpose. Upon this plan, one half the expence of the Senate, as a standing Council to the President in the recess of Congress, would evidently be saved; each state would have equal weight in this Council, as it has now in the Senate: And what renders this plan the more eligible is, that two very important consequences would result from it, which cannot result from the present plan. The first is, that the whole executive department, being separate and distinct from that of the legislative and judicial, would be amenable to the justice of the land—the President and his Council, or either or any of them, might be impeached, tried and condemned for any misdemeanor in office. Whereas on the present plan proposed, the Senate who are to advise the President, and who in effect are possessed of the chief executive power, let their conduct be what it will, are not amenable to the public justice of their country; if they may be impeached, there is no tribunal invested with jurisdiction to try them. It is true that the proposed Constitution provides, that when the President is tried the Chief-Justice shall preside. But I take this to be very little more than a farce. What can the Senate try him for? For doing that which they have advised him to do, and which without their advice he would not have done. Except what he may do in a military capacity, when I presume he will be entitled to be tried by a court-martial of General officers, he can do nothing in the executive department without the advice of the Senate, unless it be to grant pardons, and adjourn the two Houses of Congress to some day to which they cannot agree to adjourn themselves, probably to some term that may be convenient to the leading Members of the Senate. I cannot conceive therefore, that the President can ever be tried by the Senate with any effect, or to any purpose, for any misdemeanor in his office, unless it should extend to high treason, or unless they should wish to fix the odium of any measure on him, in order to exculpate themselves; the latter of which I cannot suppose will ever happen.

Another important consequence of the plan I wish had taken place, is, that the office of the President being thereby unconnected with that of the legislative, as well as the judicial, he would enjoy that independence which is necessary to form the intended check upon the acts passed by the Legislature before they obtain the sanction of laws. But on the present plan, from the necessary connection of the President's office with that of the Senate, I have little ground to hope, that his firmness will long prevail against the overbearing power and influence of the Senate, so far as to answer the purpose of any considerable check upon the acts they may think proper to pass in conjunction with the House of Representatives. For he will soon find, that unless he inclines to compound with them, they can easily hinder and countroul him in the principal articles of his office. But if nothing else could be said in favour of the plan of a standing Council to the President, independent of the Senate, the dividing the power of the latter would be sufficient to recommend it; it being of the utmost importance toward the security of the government, and the liberties of the citizens under it. For I think it must be obvious to every unprejudiced mind, that the combining in the Senate, the power of legislation with a controuling share in the appointment of all the officers of the United States, except those chosen by the people, and the power of trying all impeachments that may be found against such officers, invests the Senate at once with such an enormity of power, and with such an overbearing and uncontroulable influence, as is incompatible with every idea of safety to the liberties of a free country, and is calculated to swallow up all other powers, and to render that body a despotic aristocracy.

JULY 29

Mr. Chairman, I hope to be excused for making some observations on what was said yesterday, by gentlemen in favour of these two clauses. The motion which was made that the committee should rise, precluded me from speaking then. The gentlemen have shewed much moderation and candour in conducting this business: But I still think that my observations are well founded, and that some amendments are necessary. The gentlemen said all matters not given up by this form of government, were retained by the respective states. I know that it ought to be so; it is the general doctrine, but it is necessary that it should be expressly declared in the Constitution, and not left to mere construction and opinion. I am authorised to say it was heretofore thought necessary. The Confederation says expressly, that all that was not given up by the United States, was retained by the respective states. If such a clause had been inserted in this Constitution, it would have superceded the necessity of a bill of rights. But that not being the case, it was necessary that a bill of rights, or something of that kind, should be a part of the Constitution. It was observed, that as the Constitution is to be a delegation of power from the several states to the United States, a bill of rights was unnecessary. But it will be noticed that this is a different case. The states do not act in their political capacities, but the government is proposed for individuals. The very caption of the Constitution shews that this is the case. The expression, "We the people of the United States," shews that this government is intended for individuals; there ought therefore to be a bill of rights. I am ready to acknowledge that the Congress ought to have the power of executing its laws. Heretofore, because all the laws of the Confederation were binding on the states in their political capacities, courts had nothing to do with them; but now the thing is entirely different. The laws of Congress will be binding on individuals, and those things which concern individuals will be brought properly before the courts. In the next place, all the officers are to take an oath to carry into execution this general government, and are bound to support every act of the government, of whatever nature it may be. This is a fourth reason for securing the rights of individuals. It was also observed, that the Federal Judiciary and the courts of the states under the federal authority, would have concurrent jurisdiction with respect to any subject that might arise under the Constitution. I am ready to say that I most heartily wish that whenever this government takes place, the two jurisdictions and the two governments, that is, the general and the several state governments, may go hand in hand, and that there may be no interference, but that every thing may be rightly conducted. But I will never concede that it is proper to divide the business between the two different courts. I have no doubt but there is wisdom enough in this state to decide the business in a proper manner, without the necessity of federal assistance to do our business. The worthy gentleman from Edenton, dwelt a considerable time on the observations on a bill of rights, contending that they were proper only in monarchies, which were founded on different principles from those of our government; and therefore, though they might be necessary for others, yet they were not necessary for us.[1] I still think that a bill of rights is necessary. This necessity arises from the nature of human societies. When individuals enter into society, they give up some rights to secure the rest. There are certain human rights that ought not to be given up, and which ought in some manner to be secured. With respect to these great essential rights, no latitude ought to be left. They are the most inestimable gifts of the great Creator, and therefore ought not be destroyed, but ought to be secured. They ought to be secured to individuals in consideration of the other rights which they give up to support society.

The trial by jury has been also spoken of. Every person who is acquainted with the nature of liberty, need not be informed of the importance of this trial. Juries are called the bulwarks of our rights and liberty; and no country can ever be enslaved as long as those cases which affect their lives and property, are to be decided in a great measure, by the consent of twelve honest, disinterested men, taken from the respectable body of yeomanry. It is highly improper that any clause which regards the security of the trial by jury should be any way doubtful. In the clause that has been read, it is ascertained that criminal cases are to be tried by jury, in the states wherein they are committed. It has been objected to that clause, that it is not sufficiently explicit. I think that it is not. It was observed, that one may be taken at a great distance. One reason of the resistance to the British government was, because they required that we should be carried to the country of Great-Britain, to be tried by juries of that country. But we insisted on being tried by juries of the vicinage in our own country. I think it therefore proper, that something explicit should be said with respect to the vicinage.

With regard to that part that the Supreme Court shall have appellate jurisdiction both as to law and fact, it has been observed, that though the Federal Court might decide without a jury, yet the court below, which tried it, might have a jury. I ask the gentleman what benefit would be received in the suit by having a jury trial in the court below, when the verdict is set aside in the Supreme Court. It was intended by this clause that the trial by jury should be suppressed in the superior and inferior courts. It has been said in defence of the omission concerning the trial by jury in civil cases, that one general regulation could not be made—that in several cases the Constitution of several states did not require a trial by jury; for instance, in cases of equity and admiralty, whereas in others it did; and that therefore it was proper to leave this subject at large. I am sure that for the security of liberty they ought to have been at the pains of drawing some line. I think that the respectable body who formed the Constitution, should have gone so far as to put matters on such a footing as that there should be no danger. They might have provided that all those cases which are now triable by a jury, should be tried in each state by a jury, according to the mode usually practised in such state. This would have been easily done if they had been at the trouble of writing five or six lines. Had it been done, we should have been entitled to say that our rights and liberties were not endangered. If we adopt this clause as it is, I think, notwithstanding what gentlemen have said, that there will be danger. There ought to be some amendments to it, to put this matter on a sure footing. There does not appear to me to be any kind of necessity that the Federal Court should have jurisdiction in the body of the country. I am ready to give up that in the cases expressly enumerated, an appellate jurisdiction, except in one or two instances, might be given. I wish them also to have jurisdiction in maritime affairs, and to try offences committed on the high seas. But in the body of a state, the jurisdiction of the courts in that state might extend to carry into execution the laws of Congress. It must be unnecessary for the Federal Courts to do it, and would create trouble and expence which might be avoided. In all cases where appeals are proper, I will agree that it is necessary there should be one Supreme Court. Were those things properly regulated, so that the Supreme Court might not be oppressive, I should have no objection to it.

A lawyer, planter, and leading state judge, Samuel Spencer addressed many topics on the Constitution (see Samuel Spencer entry in *Biographies*). In these speeches, he is concerned with the powers of the federal judiciary, the problem of local law being subservient to federal, and the excessive prerogatives of the United States Senate whose members could serve for life. Like many another Antifederalist, he called for a bill of rights to guarantee trial by jury.

REFERENCE

Elliot, *Debates*, vol. 4.

NOTE

1. Refers to James Iredell, Arch-Federalist.

Timothy Bloodworth, Remarks in the North Carolina State Ratification Convention, *July 29, 1788*

Mr. Chairman, I have listened with attention to the gentleman's arguments; but whether it be for want of sufficient attention, or from the grossness of my ideas, I cannot be satisfied with his defence of the omission, with respect to the trial by jury. He says that it would be impossible to fall on any satisfactory mode of regulating the trial by jury, because there are various customs relative to it in the different states. Is this a satisfactory cause for the omission? Why did it not provide that the trial by jury should be preserved in civil cases? It has said that the trial should be by jury in criminal cases; and yet this trial is different in its manner in criminal cases in the different states. If it has been possible to secure it in criminal cases, notwithstanding the diversity concerning it, why has it not been possible to secure it in civil cases? I wish this to be cleared up. By its not being provided for, it is expressly provided against. I still see the necessity of a bill of rights. Gentlemen use contradictory arguments on this subject, if I recollect right. Without the most express restrictions, Congress may trample on your rights. Every possible precaution should be taken when we grant powers. Rulers are always disposed to abuse them. I beg leave to call gentlemen's recollection to what happened under our Confederation. By it, nine states are required to make a treaty; yet seven states said that they could, with propriety, repeal part of the instructions given our secretary for foreign affairs, which prohibited him from making a treaty to give up the Mississippi to Spain, by which repeal the rest of his instructions enabled him to make such treaty. Seven states actually did repeal the prohibitory part of these instructions, and they insisted it was legal and proper. This was in fact a violation of the Confederation. If gentlemen thus put what construction they please upon words, how shall we be redressed, if Congress shall say that all that is not expressed is given up, and they assume a power which is expressly inconsistent with the rights of mankind? Where is the power to pretend to deny its legality? This has occurred to me, and I wish it to be explained. . . .

Mr. Chairman, when I was in Congress, the southern and northern interests divided at Susquehannah. I believe it is so now. The advantage to be gained by future population is no argument at all. Do we gain any thing when the other states have an equality of members in the Senate, notwithstanding the increase of members in the House of Representatives? This is no consequence at all. I am sorry to mention it, but I can produce an instance which will prove the facility of misconstruction.

They may trample on the rights of the people of North Carolina if there be not sufficient guards and checks. I only mentioned this to show that there may be misconstructions, and that, in so important a case as a constitution, every thing ought to be clear and intelligible, and no ground left for disputes. . . .

Mr. Chairman, I beg leave to ask if the payment of sums now due be *ex post facto.* Will it be an *ex post facto* law to compel the payment of money now due in silver coin? If suit be brought in the federal court against one of our citizens, for a sum of money, will paper money be received to satisfy the judgment? I inquire for information; my mind is not yet satisfied. It has been said that we are to send our own gentlemen to represent us, and that there is not the least doubt they will put that construction on it which will be most agreeable to the people they represent. But it behoves us to consider whether they can do so if they would, when they mix with the body of Congress. The Northern States are much more populous than the Southern ones. To the north of the Susquehannah there are thirty-six representatives, and to the south of it only twenty-nine. They will always outvote us. Sir, we ought to be particular in adopting a Constitution which may destroy our currency, when it is to be the supreme law of the land, and prohibits the emission of paper money. I am not, for my own part, for giving an indefinite power. Gentlemen of the best abilities differ in the construction of the Constitution. The members of Congress will differ too. Human nature is fallible. I am not for throwing ourselves out of the Union; but we ought to be cautious by proposing amendments. The majority in several great adopting states was very trifling. Several of them have proposed amendments, but not in the mode most satisfactory to my mind. I hope this Convention never will adopt it till the amendments are actually obtained.

A farmer, member of the Continental Congress, and eventually a United States Senator, Timothy Bloodworth made a number of important short speeches in the state convention (see Timothy Bloodworth entry in *Biographies*). Here he shows much concern over the right to trial by a jury of one's peers. In this speech, Bloodworth also expressed his fears that northern and southern interests were divided, and the new government could never contain the many disparate interests that made up the country.

REFERENCE

Elliot, *Debates*, vol. 4.

Matthew Locke, Remarks in the North Carolina State Ratification Convention, *July 29, 1788*

Mr. Chairman, I wish to throw some particular light upon the subject, according to my conceptions. I think the Constitution neither safe nor beneficial, as it grants powers unbounded with restrictions. One gentleman has said that it was necessary to give cognizance of causes to the federal court, because there was partiality in the judges of the states; that the state judges could not be depended upon in causes arising under the Constitution and laws of the Union. I agree that impartiality in judges is indispensable; but I think this alteration will not produce more impartiality than there is now in our courts, whatever evils it may bring forth. Must there not be judges in the federal courts, and those judges taken from some of the states? The same partiality, therefore, may be in them. For my part, I think it derogatory to the honor of this state to give this jurisdiction to the federal courts. It must be supposed that the same passions, dispositions, and failings of humanity which attend the state judges, will be equally the lot of the federal judges. To justify giving this cognizance to those courts, it must be supposed that all justice and equity are given up at once in the states. Such reasoning is very strange to me. I fear greatly for this state, and for other states. I find there has a considerable stress been laid upon the injustice of laws made heretofore. Great reflections are thrown on South Carolina for passing *pine-barren* and *instalment* laws, and on this state for making paper money. I wish those gentlemen who made those observations would consider the necessity which compelled us in a great measure to make such money. I never thought the law which authorized it a good law. If the evil could have been avoided, it would have been a very bad law; but necessity, sir, justified it in some degree. I believe I have gained as little by it as any in this house. If we are to judge of the future by what we have seen, we shall find as much or more injustice in Congress than in our legislature. Necessity compelled them to pass the law, in order to save vast numbers of people from ruin. I hope to be excused in observing that it would have been hard for our late Continental army to lay down their arms, with which they had valiantly and successfully fought for their country, without receiving or being promised and assured of some compensation for their past services. What a situation would this country have been in, if they had had the power over the *purse* and *sword!* If they had the powers given up by this Constitution, what a wretched situation would this country have been in! Congress was unable to pay them, but passed many resolutions and laws in their favor, particularly one that each state should make up the depreciation of the pay of the Continental line, who were distressed for the want of an adequate compensation for their services. This state could not pay her proportion in specie. To have laid a tax for that purpose would have been oppressive. What was to be done? The only expedient was to pass a law to make paper money, and make it a tender. The Continental line was satisfied, and approved of the measure, it being done at their instance in some degree. Notwithstanding it was supposed to be highly beneficial to the state, it is found to bein injourious to it. Saving expense is a very great object, but this incurred much expense. This subject has for many years embroiled the state; but the situation of the country, and the distress of the people are so great, that the public measures must be accomodated to their circumstances with peculiar delicacy and caution, or another insurrection may be the consequence. As to what the gentlemen said of the trial by jury, it surprises me much to hear gentlemen of such great abilities speak such language. It is clearly insecure, nor can ingenuity and subtle arguments prove the contrary. I trust this country is too sensible of the value of liberty, and her citizens have bought it too dearly, to give it up hastily.

A farmer, member of the Continental Congress, and later a representative to the United States House, Matthew Locke preferred that the state legislature deal with money policies rather than the federal Congress (see Matthew Locke entry in *Biographies*). As a representative of the state's poorer western farmers, he believed the Constitution favored the wealty eastern seaboard states. Locke also suggested that if North Carolina remained out of the Union it had nothing to fear from the proposed federal government.

REFERENCE

Elliot, *Debates*, vol. 4.

William Lenoir, Speech in the North Carolina State Ratification Convention, *July 30, 1788*

Mr. Chairman, I conceive that I shall not be out of order to make some observations on this last part of the system, and take some retrospective view of some other parts of it. I think it not proper for our adoption, as I consider that it endangers our liberties. When we consider this system collectively, we must be surprised to think that any set of men, who were delegated to amend the Confederation, should propose to annihilate it; for that and this system are utterly different, and cannot exist together. It has been said that the fullest confidence should be put in those characters who formed this Constitution. We will admit them, in private and public transactions, to be good characters. But, sir, it appears to me, and every other member of this committee, that they exceeded their powers. Those gentlemen had no sort of power to form a new constitution altogether; neither had the citizens of this country such an idea in their view. I cannot undertake to say what principles actuated them. I must conceive they were mistaken in their politics, and that this system does not secure the unalienable rights of freemen. It has some aristocratical and some monarchical features, and perhaps some of them intended the establishment of one of these governments. Whatever might be their intent, according to my views, it will lead to the most dangerous aristocracy that ever was thought of—an aristocracy established on a constitutional bottom! I conceive (and I believe most of this committee will likewise) that this is so dangerous, that I should like as well to have no constitution at all. Their powers are almost unlimited.

A constitution ought to be understood by every one. The most humble and trifling characters in the country have a right to know what foundation they stand upon. I confess I do not see the end of the powers here proposed, nor the reasons for granting them. The principal end of a constitution is to set forth what must be given up for the community at large, and to secure those rights which ought never to be infringed. The proposed plan secures no right; or, if it does, it is in so vague and undeterminate a manner, that we do not understand it. My constituents instructed me to oppose the adoption of this Constitution. The principal reasons are as follow: The right of representation is not fairly and explicitly preserved to the people, it being easy to evade that privilege as provided in this system, and the terms of election being too long. If our General Assembly be corrupt, at the end of the year we can make new men of them by sending others in their stead. It is not so here. If there be any reason to think that human nature is corrupt, and that there is a disposition in men to aspire to power, they may embrace an opportunity, during their long continuance in office, by means of their powers to take away the rights of the people. The senators are chosen for six years, and two thirds of them, with the President, have most extensive powers. They may enter into a dangerous combination. And they may be continually reelected. The President may be as good a man as any in existence, but he is but a man. He may be corrupt. He has an opportunity of forming plans dangerous to the community at large. I shall not enter into the *minutiæ* of this system, but I conceive, whatever may have been the intention of its framers, that it leads to a most dangerous aristocracy. It appears to me that, instead of securing the sovereignty of the states, it is calculated to melt them down into one solid empire. If the citizens of this state like a consolidated government, I hope they will have virtue enough to secure their rights. I am sorry to make use of the expression, but it appears to me to be a scheme to reduce this government to an aristocracy. It guaranties a republican form of government to the states; when all these powers are in Congress, it will only be a form. It will be past recovery, when Congress has the power of the purse and the sword. The power of the sword is in explicit terms given to it. The power of direct taxation gives the purse. They may prohibit the trial by jury, which is a most sacred and valuable right. There is nothing contained in this Constitution to bar them from it. The federal courts have also appellate cognizance of law and fact; the sole cause of which is to deprive the people of that trial, which it is optional in them to grant or not. We find no provision against infringement on the rights of conscience. Ecclesiastical courts may be established, which will be destructive to our citizens. They may make any establishment they think proper. They have also an exclusive legislation in their ten miles square, to which may be added their power over the militia, who may be carried thither and kept there for life. Should any one grumble at their acts, he would be deemed a traitor, and perhaps taken up and carried to the exclusive legislation, and there tried without a jury. We are told there is no cause to fear. When we consider the great powers of Congress, there is great cause of alarm. They can disarm the militia. If they were armed, they would be a resource against great oppressions. The laws of a great empire are difficult to be executed. If the laws of the Union were oppressive, they could not carry them into effect, if the people were possessed of proper means of defence.

It was cried out that we were in a most desperate situation, and that Congress could not discharge any of their most sacred contracts. I believe it to be the case. But why give more power than is necessary? The men who went to the Federal Convention went for the express purpose of amending the government, by giving it such additional powers as were necessary. If we should accede to this system, it may be thought proper, by a few designing persons, to destroy it, in a future age, in the same manner that the old system is laid aside. The Confederation was binding on all the states. It could not be destroyed but with the consent of all the states. There was an express article to that purpose. The men who were deputed to the Convention, instead of amending the old, as they were solely empowered and directed to do, proposed a new system. If the best characters departed so far from their authority, what may not be apprehended from others, who may be agents in the new government?

It is natural for men to aspire to power—it is the nature of mankind to be tyrannical; therefore it is necessary for us to secure our rights and liberties as far as we can. But it is asked why we should suspect men who are to be chosen by ourselves, while it is their interest to act justly, and while men have self-interest at heart. I think the reasons which I have given are sufficient to answer that question. We ought to consider the depravity of human nature, the predominant thirst of power which is in the breast of every one, the temptations our rulers may have, and the unlimited confidence placed in them by this system. These are the foundation of my fears. They would be so long in the general government that they would forget the grievances of the people of the states.

But it is said we shall be ruined if separated from the other states, which will be the case if we do not adopt. If so, I would put less confidence in those states. The states are all bound together by the Confederation, and the rest cannot break from us without violating the most solemn compact. If they break that, they will this.

But it is urged that we ought to adopt, because so many other states have. In those states which have patronized and ratified it, many great men have opposed it. The motives of those states I know not. It is the goodness of the Constitution we are to examine. We are to exercise our own judgments, and act independently. And as I conceive we are not out of the Union, I hope this Constitution will not be adopted till amendments are made. Amendments are wished for by the other states. It was urged here that the President should have power to grant reprieves and pardons. This power is necessary with proper restrictions. But the President may be at the head of a combination against the rights of the people, and may reprieve or pardon the whole. It is answered to this, that he cannot pardon in cases of impeachment. What is the punishment in such cases? Only removal from office and future disqualification. It does not touch life or property. He has power to do away punishment in every other case. It is too unlimited, in my opinion. It may be exercised to the public good, but may also be perverted to a different purpose. Should we get those who will attend to our interest, we should be safe under any Constitution, or without any. If we send men of a different disposition, we shall be in danger. Let us give them only such powers as are necessary for the good of the community.

The President has other great powers. He has the nomination of all officers, and a qualified negative on the laws He may delay the wheels of government. He may drive the Senate to concur with his proposal. He has other extensive powers. There is no assurance of the liberty of the press. They may make it treason to write against the most arbitrary proceedings. They have power to control our elections as much as they please. It may be very oppressive on this state, and all the Southern States.

Much has been said of taxation, and the inequality of it on the states. But nothing has been said of the mode of furnishing men. In what proportion are the states to furnish men? Is it in proportion to the whites and blacks? I presume it is. This state has one hundred thousand blacks. By this Constitution, fifty negroes are equal to thirty whites. This state, therefore, besides the proportion she must raise for her white people, must furnish an additional number for her blacks, in proportion as thirty is to fifty. Suppose there be a state to the northward that has sixty thousand persons; this state must furnish as many men for the blacks as that whole state, exclusive of those she must furnish for her whites. Slaves, instead of strengthening, weaken the state; the regulation, therefore, will greatly injure it, and the other Southern States. There is another clause which I do not, perhaps, understand. The power of taxation seems to me not to extend to the lands of the people of the United States; for the rule of taxation is the number of the whites and three fifths of the blacks. Should it be the case that they have no power of taxing this object, must not direct taxation be hard upon the greater part of this state? I am not confident that it is so, but it appears to me that they cannot lay taxes on this object. This will oppress the poor people who have large families of whites, and no slaves to assist them in cultivating the soil, although the taxes are to be laid in proportion to three fifths of the negroes, and all the whites. Another disadvantage to this state will arise from it. This state has made a contract with its citizens. The public securities and certificates I allude to. These may be negotiated to men who live in other states. Should that be the case, these gentlemen will have demands against this state on that account. The Constitution points out the mode of recovery; it must be in the federal court only, because controversies between a state and the citizens of another state are cognizable only in the federal courts. They cannot be paid but in gold and silver. Actual specie will be recovered in that court. This would be an intolerable grievance without remedy.

I wish not to be so understood as to be so averse to this system, as that I should object to all parts of it, or attempt to reflect on the reputation of those gentlemen who formed it; though it appears to me that I would not have agreed to any proposal but the amendment of the Confederation. If there were any security for the liberty of the people, I would, for my own part, agree to it. But in this case, as millions yet unborn are concerned, and deeply interested in our decision, I would have the most positive and pointed security. I shall therefore hope that, before this house will proceed to adopt this Constitution, they will propose such amendments to it as will make it complete; and when amendments are adopted, perhaps I will be as ready to accede to it as any man. One thing will make it aristocratical. Its powers are very indefinite. There was a very necessary clause in the Confederation, which is omitted in this system. That was a clause declaring that every power, &c., not given to Congress, was reserved to the states. The omission of this clause makes the power so much greater. Men will naturally put the fullest construction on the power given them. Therefore lay all restraint on them, and form a plan to be understood by every gentleman of this committee, and every individual of the community.

William Lenoir, a popular political leader, rejected the right of the Philadelphia convention to revise the Articles of Confederation in such a radical fashion (see William Lenoir entry in *Biographies*). He also worried that, with a government so large and so far away, the Federalists would be able to control the flow of political information to the states. The reserved powers in the Constitution, Lenoir said, placed the nation in the hands of a dictator.

REFERENCE

Elliot, *Debates*, vol. 4.

Rev. David Caldwell, Remarks in the North Carolina State Ratification Convention, *July 30, 1788*

Mr. *Caldwell* thought that some danger might arise. He imagined it might be objected to in a political as well as in a religious view. In the first place, he said there was an invitation for Jews, and Pagans of every kind, to come among us. At some future period, said he, this might endanger the character of the United States. Moreover, even those who do not regard religion, acknowledge that the Christian religion is best calculated of all religions to make good members of society, on account of its morality. I think then, added he, that in a political view, those gentlemen who formed this Constitution, should not have given this invitation to Jews and Heathens. All those who have any religion are against the emigration of those people from the eastern hemisphere.

A famous minister and teacher, David Caldwell said that he feared for religious freedom under the proposed Constitution (see David Caldwell entry in *Biographies*). Alas, Caldwell went beyond tolerance to claim that infidels would control the new government. That led him to oppose immigrants other than Protestants from entering the United States.

REFERENCE

Elliot, *Debates*, vol. 4.

Willie Jones, Speech in the North Carolina State Ratification Convention, *July 31, 1788*

Mr. Chairman, the gentleman last up has mentioned the resolution of Congress now lying before us, and the act of Assembly under which we met here, which says that we should deliberate and determine on the Constitution. What is to be inferred from that? Are we to ratify it at all events? Have we not an equal right to reject? We do not determine by neither rejecting nor adopting. It is objected we shall be out of the Union. So I wish to be. We are left at liberty to come in at any time. It is said we shall suffer a great loss for want of a share of the impost. I have no doubt we shall have it when we come in, as much as if we adopted now. I have a resolution in my pocket, which I intend to introduce if this resolution is carried, recommending it to the legislature to lay an impost, for the use of Congress, on goods imported into this state, similar to that which may be laid by Congress on goods imported into the adopting states. This shows the committee what is my intention, and on what footing we are to be. This being the case, I will forfeit my life that we shall come in for a share. It is said that all the offices of Congress will be filled, and we shall have no share in appointing the officers. This is an objection of very little importance. Gentlemen need not be in such haste. If left eighteen months or two years without offices, it is no great cause of alarm. The gentleman further said that we could send no representatives, but must send ambassadors to Congress, as a foreign power. I assert the contrary; and that, whenever a convention of the states is called, North Carolina will be called upon like the rest. I do not know what these gentlemen would desire.

I am very sensible that there is a great majority against the Constitution. If we take the question as they propose they know it would be rejected, and bring on us all the dreadful consequences which they feelingly foretell, but which can never in the least alarm me. I have endeavored to fall in with their opinions, but could not. We have a right, in plain terms, to refuse it if we think proper. I have, in my proposition, adopted, word for word, the Virginia amendments, with one or two additional ones. We run no risk of being excluded from the Union when we think proper to come in. Virginia, our next neighbor, will not oppose our admission. We have a common cause with her. She wishes the same alterations. We are of the greatest importance to her. She will have great weight in Congress; and there is no doubt but she will do every thing she can to bring us into the Union. South Carolina and Georgia are deeply interested in our being admitted. The Creek nation would overturn these two states without our aid. They cannot exist without North Carolina. There is no doubt we shall obtain our amendments, and come into the Union when we please. Massachusetts, New Hampshire, and other states, have proposed amendments. New York will do also, if she ratifies. There will be a majority of the states, and the most respectable, important, and extensive states also, desirous of amendments, and favorable to our admission.

As great names have been mentioned, I beg leave to mention the authority of Mr. Jefferson, whose great abilities and respectability are well known. When the Convention sat in Richmond, in Virginia, Mr. Madison received a letter from him. In that letter he said he wished nine states would adopt it, not because it deserved ratification, but to preserve the Union. But he wished that the other four states would reject it, that there might be a certainty of obtaining amendments. Congress may go on, and take no notice of our amendments; but I am confident they will do nothing of importance till a convention he called. If I recollect rightly, amendments may be ratified either by conventions or the legislatures of the states. In either case, it may take up about eighteen months. For my part, I would rather be eighteen years out of the Union than adopt it in its present defective form.

Willie Jones sums up the threat in the Constitution to individual rights (see Willie Jones entry in *Biographies*). He called for the outright rejection of the Constitution rather than amending it, because he believed that the process of making a constitution had to be started anew. Like others in North Carolina, Jones did not mind remaining outside of the new nation.

REFERENCE

Elliot, *Debates*, vol. 4.

Thomas Person, Letter to John Lamb,
August 6, 1788

Your favour of the 19th. May last, was only received the 23rd. of July & then Open, the third day after our Convention had Assembled, whose Conclusions on the extraordinary Change of Government, proposed for Our Acceptance I transmit to you with pleasure, firmly persuaded that our proceedings which were temperate & Calm as well as the Result of our political Contest in the cause of republican Liberty, will be highly pleasing to you & our friends in your State & thro' the Union—

It is my decided opinion (& no man is better Acquainted with the publick mind) that nine tenth of the people of this State are opposed to the adoption of the New System, without very Considerable Amendments, & I might without incurring any great hazard to err, assure you, that a very Considerable Number conceive an Idea of a Genl. Government, in this extensive Country, impracticable & Dangerous.—But this is a Subject on which I feel myself more disposed to concur with better Judges than to Dogmatically decide & only State it as a doctrine gaining ground in this part of the World—Our Convention met at Hillsborough on the day appointed & on the 22nd. resolved itself into a Committee of the Whole house, & continued their discussions from day to day (Sundays excepted) until the 1st. Inst. on which we called the decisive question when there appeared, for non-concurrance 184—& 83 for Adopting—but recommending numerous amendmts., which were repugnant to their Eloquence & reasoning in debate; a Circumstance something surprising, but that proves nevertheless, that even its advocates think the plan radically bad, by these exertions to render it Virtually better.

However, I can assure you if the total rejection had been proposed, even in terms of Reprobation, the motion would have succeeded, but we conceived it more decent & moderate to refer it in the mode you will see prefixed to our bill of Rights & Amendments, in Confidence that the Union & prosperity of America may yet be preserved by temperance & Wisdom, in defiance of precipitation & some Arts which I suspect tho' I cannot enumerate or trace them—There is so little Security left now for obtaining Amendments, especially if your State is adoptive, that it probably may be wise in those States, or the Minorities in them, to oppose all representation until Amendments are obtain'd or to send into the New Congress only such men of unequivocal Charectors as will oppose every operation of the System until it is render'd consistant with the preservation of our Liberties too precious to be Sacreficed to *Authority, name, ambition,* or *design,*—Your proposition for opening a Correspondence

I embrace with great charfulness, it meets wth. my Cordial approbation as well as my Friends, urged only by Motives for the prosperity of the Union—And I have only to lament that such measures were not persued earlier, as they would in my opinion have prevented or abated the mischief which the public cause has already received—I take the freedom to request, that you may forward the proceedings of your Convention, & any thing else you may think conducive to the public weal; our Assembly will meet the 1st. monday in Novr. next at Fayettville where we would easily as well as Charfully receive any thing wch. you might think interesting to the good people of this State.—I have the Honour to be with profound respect to you Sir & Thro you to the Federal republican Committee Yr. & Their Assd. Frd. & Hbl. Servt.

Thomas Person, a surveyor and planter, served in the state senate before and after the Constitution (see Thomas Person entry in *Biographies*). In this letter to General John Lamb of New York, Person explained why North Carolina's first state convention had rejected the Constitution, and he urged committees be set up across state lines to form a political alliance against the new Constitution.

REFERENCES

William K. Boyd, "North Carolina and the Federal Convention," *Historical Papers*, Trinity College Historical Society, series XIV; Original in John Lamb papers, New York Historical Society.

14
Conclusion and Afterword

Aedanus Burke, "Questions to Samuel Bryan," *November 1789*

In what State and in what year was the measure proposed? What were the causes which led to the measure? by what men, or body of men or party? Or was it for the purpose of investing Congress with any additional and what powers then deemed necessary? Tell particularly.

What was the State of navigation, trade, and the General, and particular State police of the Union about the latter end of the year 1786? Or at that time was there in the States in general, and in any, and what particular State, what is commonly called *Anarchy?* or a spirit in the people of Licentiousness? or of enmity to their magistrates, or opposition or dislike to order and Government? Was the embarrassments of the U.S. at that period & since the peace owing to this kind of spirit? or to other & what causes? Tell particularly.

To what cause necessity or pretext, was it owing, that after the peace, the commerce and navigation of the U.S. was ruined? Why their credit abroad & confidence at home lost? To what cause is it to be ascribed their issuing paper money? Or what States did issue such money? The terms of redeeming it in each State, the consequence of such paper emissions—its intrinsic value.

Was there in 1786 or at any time before that period any influential men, or any, and what party, and in what States, whose views, interests or sentiments were unfavorable, or otherwise to the popular Govt. or favorable to a regal one? Or if so from what motives? Or was there any party and who were they inclined to avail themselves of the popularity of a certain *personage* to bring about any, and what revolution in the Government?

When the different States appointed delegates to the Convention, what was the general opinion of the people of Pennsylvania or its neighbouring States concerning the powers & duty which those delegates were about to execute? Or was it in contemplation of the people, or of any and what part that the republican system of Govt. should be overturned, or materially altered? What was the opinion of the people, their attachment, or dislike to the Confederation? If it was deemed practicable were it amended by conferring more authority in affairs relating to commerce? or what other affairs?

What is your opinion, whether confederate Republics can manage the affairs of the Confederacy, in the mode of the old Confederation; or by putting the powers of the Confederacy into high departments, & parcelling it out after the form of a regal Govt. as at present?

What are the special words of the act of Pennsylvania & neighbouring States, by which authority is given to their respective delegates for the Convention?

At what time did the General Convention meet, & in what part of Philadelphia? And in what manner public or private, was the business or debates conducted? Or if the Convention was split into any and what parties? Or if a certain personage took any and what active part, in framing the system? The history and proceedings of this Convention is particularly requested.

Did the Cincinnati meet at the time the Convention sat or not? What part was taken by that Society then or afterwards.

What were the public opinion & expectations of the Convention's proceedings while they sat? Or did the public or any party, expect any system of govt. like that which was offered, or not?

When the new system the result of their deliberations, was offered to the Public, what was the effect produced on the minds of the public upon the subject? Or did the people split into any and what faction or party in consequence.

What part or side was taken by the following classes of citizens of Pennsylvania & elsewhere vizt.

Cincinnati[1]	Mechanics	
Civil Officers	Seafaring men	
Monied men	Creditors	
Merchants	Debtors	
Lawyers	Middle Country	
Divines	Sea Coast	} Inhabitants
Men of Letters	Back Country	
Whigs	Foreigners—	
Tories		
Women		

Which of all these were instrumental, and to what extent, and from what views or motives for or against the system?

What was then temper & disposition of the two parties against each other? What party names—or if any beside federalist and Antifedl.? Who invented the latter names? What effect had it?

Among those who were in opposition to the new-system, was there any preconcert, correspondence or mutual understanding to act with unanimity? Or if not thro' what cause was it neglected or omitted?

Among the federalists was there any such preconcert, or system of mutual aid, in any and what States, and what men or party combined to adopt the New Constitution? And what was the nature of such combination?

Was there any attempt and what to prevent an investigation of its merits? Or was there sufficient given for that purpose? or take the opinion of the people on it? or any attempt made by the antifederalists to gain time & for what purpose, or to prevent publications on the subject?

Or did the federalists use any and what means to prevent any such publications from going forth? or to intercept letters or communications. What use was made of the Post-Office, and by whose means or agency was it done?

What were the principal publications for and against the New-System? Who the reputed authors?

How soon after the system was offered to the public that the Legislatures and States of Pennsylvania, Jersey, Delaware &c. took it up, and passed it—the history of this business in Pennsylvania.

If any arts used to accelerate its adoption? or to elect, or reject for State Convention, such as were friendly, or otherwise to the system? When Convention met, what the temper of the parties? In discussing the system, whether violent, insolent, or otherwise?

Who were the leading and influential men in Pennsylvania in favor of it? Their names? Who in Jersey? Who in Delaware and Maryland? Their views and character.

In those States who were the Leading and influential Antifederalists? and from what parts of the States?

In State Convention of Pennsylvania or Legislature, was there a secession of some of the members? How many and for what cause? Were they not made prisoners and forced back again to form a house? by whom and in what manner—the history of this business—

Was the Constitution adopted in Pennsylvania in consequence of such force put on the seceding members? Was it resented by the public? If not why? How palliated or justified by the federalists? Conduct of minority after adoption? Their protest or address how received by their constituents?

Through this whole business, what was the spirit of the populace of the City, or low Country? or were the Anti's in any fear or danger of writing or speaking against the Constitution? Or was there any Mob to crush or punish opposition or was it practicable to raise a mob—the history of this business.

If any and what arts used by the federalists to mislead or deceive the people to adopt it? or to suppress the publications or objections of the other party?

If any rumours, or false reports spread to defame, or ascribe any and what improper motives to the opposition of the Anti's—what were the arts used?

If any and what impediments in the Printing offices—the conduct and character of the Printers in general in this business? Were there any Printers and who & where, who opposed the Constitution? Or were Printers under any and what fear or restraint to publish against the New-System? Or did the Printers act independently or otherwise?

How far was the Press instrumental in bringing about the Revolution in Govt.? Or could this be brought about without availing themselves as they did of the partiality of the Printers?

Were any Printers, and who abused, or oppressed or had subscriptions withdrawn for publishing against the system? The treatment to Coll. Oswald, Greenleaf and what other Printers?[2]

Aedanus Burke planned to write a history of the Antifederalist defeat (see Aedanus Burke entry in *Biographies*). This letter, in the form of questions, and Pennsylvanian Samuel Bryan's reply, best sums up the many grievances and worries the Antifederalists had against the Constitution.

REFERENCES

A draft of Burke's queries is in the John Nicholson Papers, Pennsylvania Historical and Museum Commission; the best analysis of this remarkable correspondence is Saul Cornell (ed.), "'Reflections on the Late Remarkable Revolution in Government': Aedanus Burke and Samuel Bryan's Unpublished History of the Ratification of the Constitution," *Pennsylvania Magazine of History and Biography* 112 (1998): 103–130; Jensen and Kaminski, *Documentary History*, vol. 2.

NOTES

1. Society of former Revolutionary War officers.
2. Eleazor Oswald and Thomas Greenleaf, Antifederalist editors (see *Biographies*).

Samuel Bryan, Letter to Aedanus Burke, *December 5, 1789*

Previous to the appointment of the Convention there seemed to be in Pennsylvania a general Wish for a more efficient Confederation. The public Debt was unpaid & unfunded. We were deluged with foreign Goods, which it was evident might have paid large Sums to the Continental Treasury, if Duties could have been generally laid & collected, & at the same Time the levying such Duties would have checked the extravagant Consumption. Whilst Congress could only recommend Measures & the States individually could refuse to execute them it was obvious that we were in Danger of falling to Pieces. The opposition of Rhode Island to the five per Cent had made a deep Impression upon Peoples Minds. A Desire of strengthening the Hands of Congress was very general; but no particular Scheme seemed to be digested, except that most Men seemed to wish Congress possessed of Power to levy Duties on imported Goods. At this Time the Convention was proposed & Members were elected for Pennsylvania about the Beginning of the Year 1787;—I do not remember the particular Time. Very little Bustle was made & little or no Opposition. What has been called the anticonstitutional or Aristocratic Party then governed our Councils and the Representatives in Convention were chosen almost wholly of that Party & entirely from the City of Philadelphia. The Convention met without much Expectation of any thing very important being done by them till towards the Close, altho some Intimations were made, before hand, by some foolish Members (as they were thought) of the Society of Cincinnatus that Nothing less than a Monarchy was to be erected & that the people of Massachusetts were driven into Rebellion for the very purpose of smoothing the Way to this Step by their Suppression. Little Regard however was paid to these Speeches till towards the Close of the Session of the Convention, when Surmises were spread from other Quarters that Something injurious to the Liberties of the People was about to be produced. These Surmises were again contradicted in some Degree;—and the Convention rose with favourable Prospects.

I am not able to give a particular State of Trade in Pennsylvania in 1786. But in General it was in a very unfavourable Situation. Our Navigation was almost wholly in the Hands of Foreigners, chiefly English; and a great Part of the Negotiation & Sale of Merchandize was in the same hands. The numerous Classes of Tradesmen who depend on Commerce & particularly those who depend on Navigation were distressed. There was no Anarchy nor any considerable Degree of Licentiousness in Pennsylvania. Party Spirit was high; but much more violent on Paper than any where else. The Tories, with the Spirit of Chagrin & Resentment which flowed from their Disappointments & what they called persecution (chiefly arising from the Test law) had taken Side with the Anticonstitutional or aristocratic party in Opposition to the Constitutionalists who had before held the Reins of Government. But on the whole we were much more peaceable & orderly than our Neighbours, who read our Newspapers, believed us to be. And Pennsylvania, all along, besides supporting her own Government, had given the most effectual Aid to the United States, particularly in Money.

The Ruin of the Commerce & Navigation of the United States was owing to a Concurrence of Causes. Some of the Northern Fisheries had been long nourished by Bounties from Great Britain before the War; and those Bounties were now withdrawn. We had a Deluge of Money at the Close of the War, which raised the Prices of our own Commodities at home and the vast Diminution of Industry increased this Mischief. Trade during the War had fallen into the Hands of successful, but ignorant, adventurers who did not understand Commerce. The English Manufacturers, at the End of the War, were vastly overloaded with those kinds of Goods, which were calculated only for the American Markets, and they crowded them upon us by the Hand of their own Clerks & Agents, in such immense Quantities, that it was impossible for us ever to pay for them. These Goods were either sold for small prices or trusted out without Discretion & never paid for. But the Exclusion of our Ships from so many of the British & French Ports & the Want of Mediterranean Passes have contributed to the Destruction of our Navigation more than all other Causes.

As to the Paper Money of Pennsylvania which has been issued since the War, it was made in 1785 for the purpose of establishing Funds for payment of the Interest to public Creditors & to lend to such as were under the Necessity of borrowing, at a Time when there were very few private Lenders. I am not well acquainted with the Detail of its Funds, Quantities & Times of Redemption. It has too much fluctuated in its Credit & has been as low as 33⅓ p Cent Discount. In Jersey the same Motives for issuing Paper money prevailed & its Fate had been similar. I understand it is now at two third of its nominal Value.

When the federal Constitution was proposed to the people, the Desire of increasing the powers of Congress was great & this Object had a mighty Influence in its Favor. The popularity of Genl. W. & Doctor Franklin had still more. The people in the Towns who depended, in any Measure, on Trade, expected great Relief from it. The Gentlemen of the late Army, & the Tools of Aristocracy were loud in its Support;—and as the chief Opposition to it was believed to arise from such as belonged to the Constitutional Party, the whole Body of the old Tories, a numerous & wealthy Sett of Men, joined in its Support. There is too much Reason to believe that some Men among us had deeper Views than they chose to declare & wished a Government even less popular than the one proposed; but in Pennsylvania they have been very reserved on this Head. The Opposition was very powerful & their Language was for adopting the Constitution & procuring Amendments afterwards.

I have anticipated this Question.

The Writer of this had confined his Views of Alteration to be made in the old Confederation to a mere Enlargement of the Powers of Congress, particularly as to maritime Affairs. He thinks the Experiment ought at least to have been tried, whether we could not have succeeded under a Confederation of independent States, before we proceeded to consolidate all power in one general Government.

Copies of the Acts of Assembly, which are public, will furnish the best Answer to this Question.

The Convention sat in the State house & debated in private. It has nevertheless been said &, I suppose, is beyond a Doubt that the Members were much divided & that the present Form of Constitution was agreed to as a Compromise, when they had almost despaired of agreeing upon any one.

The Cincinnati met shortly before the Convention. Some speeches of Individuals in private Companies were reported to the Effect before mentioned.

This is anticipated.

When the System was published some Writers in the Newspapers stated many Objections to it. The Party in opposition were the old Constitutional Whiggs for the most part. Numbers of these however &, especially in the Towns, joined in supporting the new federal Constitution.

The Cincinnati were in Support of it.

The Civil officers were threatened in News paper publications, if they should oppose, & were mostly in favor it.

Monied Men & particularly the Stockholders in the Bank were in favor of it.

The Merchants in favor of it.

Lawyers;—the greatest part in favor of it.

Divines of all Denominations, with very few Exceptions, in favor of it. They had suffered by Paper Money.

Men of Letters, many of them, were opposed to it.

Whigs;—the Majority of them opposed to it.

Tories;—almost all for it.

The Women;—all admire Genl. W.

Mechanics;—such as depend on Commerce & Navigation in favor. The others divided according to their former Attachments to the Revolution & Constitution of Pennsylvania or their Prejudices against them.

Seafaring Men followed the Mercantile Interest & were strenuous in favor of it.

Creditors were influenced in favor of it by their Aversion to Paper money;—yet some were opposed to it.

Debtors are often Creditors in their Turn & the Paper money had great Effect on Men's Minds. The Public Creditors were much divided, according to their former Predilections & Attachments.

The Counties nearest the Navigation were in favor of it generally;—those more remote in Opposition. The Farmers were perhaps more numerous in Opposition than any other Sett of Men. Most Townsmen were for it.

The Foreigners were chiefly connected with the Mercantile people & were in favor of it. Even the foreign Seamen were made useful to the Support of it in Philadelphia.

The Party Names, before the Convention sat, were Whigs & Tories, which

Names were wearing out;—and Constitutionalist & those who called themselves Republicans & who were also called Aristocratics & Anticonstitutional-
ists. In this last class were included most of the Merchants, most of the monied
Men, most of the Gentlemen in the late Army & many of the Mob in the
Towns.

The Name of Federalists or Federal Men grew up at New York & in the
Eastern States, some Time before the Calling of the Convention, to denominate such as were attached to the general Support of the United States, in Opposition to those who preferred local & particular Advantages, such as those
who opposed the five per Cent Duty or who with held their Quotas of Contribution to the general Treasury of the United States. This Name was taken
possession of by those who were in favor of the new federal Government as
they called it & the opposers were called Antifederalists.

Those in Opposition seem to have had no Preconcert, nor any Suspicion of
what was coming forward. The same Objections were made in different Parts
of the Continent, almost at the same Time, merely as they were obviously dictated by the Subject. Local Ideas seem to have entered very little into the Objections.

The Evidence of a preconcerted System, in those who are called Federalists,
appears rather from the Effect than from any certain Knowledge before hand.
The thing however must have been easy to them from their Situation in the
great Towns & many of them being wealthy Men & Merchants, who have continual Correspondence with each other.

The Printers were certainly most of them more willing to publish for, then
against the new Constitution. They depended more upon the People in the
Towns than in the Country. The Towns people withdrew their Subscriptions
from those who printed Papers against, and violent Threats were thrown out
against the Antis & Attempts were made to injure them in their Business.

Letters were frequently intercepted, & some of them selected & published
by the Federalists. Private Conversation was listened to by Eves-droppers. Pamphlets & Newspapers were stopt & destroyed. This was the more easily done
as most of the Towns, even down to the smallest villages, were in possession
of the Federalists. I can say Nothing about the Post Office.

The Writer of this has very imperfect Knowledge on this Subject.

In Pennsylvania the Business of the Ratification was extremely hurried. The
Assembly voted, if I remember right, to call a Convention for its Ratification
before they were officially notified of its being recommended by Congress; and
the Election was hurried through before it was generally known what was
doing. Many even in the Counties not very remote were totally uninformed of
any Election being intended before it was finished I have not Materials to be
more particular.

In the State Convention the Behavior of the Federalists was highly insolent
& contemptuous. Out of Doors, even in Philadelphia, their Behavior was more
moderate after the Election for Members of Congress than before. The Election had discovered a Degree of Strength in the Antis which they did not expect & which Nothing but Surprize & the Accident of extreme bad Weather
which was unfavorable to the collecting of people scattered thro the Country

could have got the better of. There was one Instance of Violence a short Time before which was not generally countenanced.

I have not Time to enumerate the Persons were active in supporting the Measures.

Nor of those against.

There was a Secession from the Legislature for the Purpose of preventing Measures from being precipitated. Some of those seceding were made prisoners insulted & dragged back, by the Sergeant at Arms & a Mob of Assistants.

The publications of the Day will be the best Answer to this Question.

The Minds of People in Philadelphia were highly inflamed against the Opposers & some of them were unquestionably over awed;—some of them injured. Nothing perhaps checked this Spirit of Outrage so much as similar Instances in Cumberland County & Huntingdon County & others & a Discovery of the real Strength of Opposition.

The usual Arts of Party were used, besides those which have been enumerated.

The Adoption of the Constitution by North Carolina was frequently asserted & published in pretended Letters. Other Letters were fabricated & published; but they have slipt my Memory.

In General it may be said that Col. Oswald was almost the only Printer who published in Opposition in Philadelphia & that he has been injured in Consequence. I cannot be more particular.

The printing presses were notoriously the great Instruments of the American Revolution.

I cannot be very particular on this head.

REFERENCES

Bryan Papers, Historical Society of Pennsylvania; Jensen and Kaminski, *Documentary History*, vol. 2.

NOTE

1. George Washington and Benjamin Franklin.

Benjamin Austin, Jr., *Constitutional Republicanism in Opposition to Fallacious Federalism* (1803), 7–8

Harmony, peace, and moderation depend on the body of *republican citizens*, acting upon one consolidated principle in support of the constitution and the laws of the government. An union of republicans and monarchists can never be expected; union with those who advocate unnecessary taxes, and those who are opposed to them, is chimerical; . . . The union sought after, depends on the candid deliberation of the well-disposed citizens, whose happiness is involved in the permanency of a wise and economical administration.

He acknowledges to have written with freedom: but the controversy of the present day, as connected with the future happiness of our common country, demands an unequivocal investigation of public men and measures.

He has been particular in some of his numbers (published originally in newspapers) to appeal to good sense, and unbiased judgment, of the YOUNG MEN.

The author stands on the basis of the constitution; and while he maintains an attitude, which is justifiable by this compact, the billingsgate effusion of a desperate faction will be unnoticed. If any man will meet him with his NAME, he is willing to investigate the subject, becoming a gentleman and citizen. After this explicit declaration, whoever replies in abusive language, in an ANONYMOUS DISGUISE, will be treated as such character ought ever to be, with silent contempt.

In this book, Benjamin Austin, Jr., an ally of Samuel Adams and a staunch Massachusetts Republican in the Jeffersonian era, explains his continued Antifederalist grievances against the Federalists (see Benjamin Austin entry in *Biographies*). He was particularly worried about the Federalists' ability to impose a tax that would harm Massachusetts's foreign trade. Austin also continues to reveal the concerns many Antifederalists had over anonymous attacks on their values and integrity.

REFERENCE

Benjamin Austin, Jr., *Constitutional Republicanism in Opposition to Fallacious Federalism* (Boston: Adams and Rhoades, 1803).

Mercy Otis Warren, *History of the Rise, Progress, and Termination of the American Revolution*, III (1805), chap. 31, 357–365

It was thought by fome, who had been recently informed of the fecret tranfactions of the convention at Philadelphia, that the greateft happinefs of the greateft number was not the principal object of their contemplations, when they ordered their doors to be locked, their members inhibited from all communications abroad, and when propofals were made that their journals fhould be burnt, left their confultations and debates fhould be viewed by the fcrutinizing eye of a free people.[1] Thefe extraordinary movements appeared to them the refult of the paffions of a few. It is certain, that truth, whether moral, philofophical, or political, fhrinks not from the eye of inveftigration.

The ideas of royalty, or any thing that wore the appearance of regal forms and inftitutions, were generally difgufting to Americans, and particularly fo to many characters who early came forward, and continued to the end of the conflict, ftedfaft in oppofition to the crown of Britain. They thought that after America had encountered the power, and obtained a releafe from foreign bondage, and had recently overcome domeftic difficulties and difcontents, and even quieted the fpirit of infurrection in their own ftates; that the republican fyftem for which they had fought, fhould not be hazarded by vefting any man or body of men with powers that might militate with the principles, which had been cherifhed with fond enthufiafm, by a large majority of the inhabitants throughout the union.

Republicanifm, the idol of fome men, and independence, the glory of all, were thought by many to be in danger of dwindling into theory; the firft had been defaced for a time, by a degree of anarchy, and fears were now awakened that the laft might be annihilated by views of private ambition.

The people were generally diffatisfied with the high pretenfions of the officers of the army, whofe equality of condition previous to the war, was, with few exceptions, on the fame grade with themfelves. The affumption of an appropriate rank was difgufting, in a fet of men, who had moft of them been taken from mechanic employments, or the fober occupations of agriculture. Thus jealoufies were diffufed, with regard to the officers of the old army, the Cincinnati, and feveral other claffes of men, whom they fufpected as cherifhing hopes and expectations of erecting a government too fplendid for the tafte and profeffions of Americans. They faw a number of young gentlemen coming forward, ardent and fanguine in the fupport of the principles of monarchy and ariftocracy. They faw a number of profeffional characters too ready to relinquifh former opinions, and adopt new ones more congenial to the policy of courts, than to the maxims of a free people. They faw fome apoftate whigs in public employments, and fymptoms of declenfion in others, which threatened the annihilation of the darling opinion, that the whole fovereignty in the re-publican fyftem is in the people: "that the people "have a right to amend and alter, or annul "their conftitution and frame a new one, when-"ever they fhall think it will better promote "their own welfare and happinefs to do it."

This brought forward objections to the propofed conftitution of govern-ment, then under confideration. Thefe objections were not the refult of igno-rance; they were made by men of the firft abilities in every ftate; men who were fenfible of the neceffity of ftrong and energetic inftitutions, and a ftrict fubor-dination and obedience to law. Thefe judicious men were folicitous that every thing fhould be clearly defined; they were jealous of each ambiguity in law or government, or the fmalleft circumftance that might have a tendency to cur-tail the republican fyftem, or render ineffectual the facrifices they had made, for the fecurity of civil and religious liberty to themfelves; they alfo wifhed for the tranfmiffion of the enjoyment of the equal rights of man to their lateft pof-terity. They were of opinion, that every article that admitted of doubtful con-ftruction, fhould be amended, before it became the fupreme law of the land. They were now apprehenfive of being precipitated, without due confideration, into the adoption of a fyftem that might bind them and their pofterity in the chains of defpotifm, while they held up the ideas of a free and equal partici-pation of the privileges of pure and genuine republicanifm.

Warm debates in favor of further confideration, and much energetic argu-ment took place, between gentlemen of the firft abilities, in feveral of the ftate conventions. The fyftem was however ratified in hafte by a fufficient number of ftates to carry it into operation, and amendments left to the wifdom, juftice, and decifion of future generations, according as exigencies might require.[2] This was not fufficient to diffipate the apprehenfions of gentlemen who had been uniform and upright in their intentions, and immoveably fixed in the princi-ples of the revolution, and had never turned their eyes from the point in pur-fuit, until the independence of America was acknowledged by the principal monarchs in Europe.

But while the fyftem was under difcuffion, ftrong objections were brought forward in the conventions of the feveral ftates. Thofe gentlemen who were oppofed to the adoption of the new conftitution *in toto*, obferved, that there was no bill of rights to guard againft future innovations. They complained that the trial by jury in civil caufes was not fecured; they obferved, that fome of the warmeft partifans, who had been difpofed to adopt without examination, had ftarted at the difcovery, that this effential right was curtailed; that the pow-ers of the executive and judiciary were dangeroufly blended: that the appellate jurifdiction of the fupreme federal court, fubjected the inhabitants of the United States, by a litigious procefs that militated with the rights formerly claimed by the individual ftates, to be drawn from one end of the continent to the other, for trial. They wifhed for a rotation in office, or fome fufficient bar againft the perpetuity of it, in the fame hands for life; they thought it nec-effary there fhould be this check to the overbearing influence of office, and that every man fhould be rendered ineligible at certain periods, to keep the mind in equilibrio, and teach him the feelings of the governed, and better qualify him to govern in his turn. It was alfo obferved by them, that all fources of revenue formerly poffeffed by the individual ftates were now under the control of congrefs.

Subfequent meafures were not yet realized; banks, monopolies, and a funding fyftem, were projects that had never been thought of, in the early ftages of an infant republic, and had they been fuggefted before the prefent period, would have ftartled both the foldier and the peafant. The fober principled ftatefmen, and the judicious band of worthies, who originated the fyftem of freedom, digefted it in the cabinet, and conducted the public councils, which led to the independence of America, with a firm, difinterefted magnanimity, and an energy feldom found in the courts of princes would have revolted at thofe ideas. Nor were they lefs alarmed at the contemplation of a prefident with princely powers, a fextennial fenate, biennial elections of reprefentatives, and a federal city, "whofe cloud-capt towers" might fcreen the ftate culprit from the hand of juftice, while its exclufive jurifdiction might, in fome future day, protect the riot of ftanding armies encamped within its limits. Thefe were profpects viewed by them with the utmoft abhorrence.

Indeed the opinions of the gentlemen who formed the general convention, differed very widely, on many of the articles of the new conftitution, before it was fent abroad for the difcuffion of the people at large. Some of them feceded, and retired without figning at all, others complied from a conviction of the neceffity of accommodation and conceffion, left they fhould be obliged to feparate without any efficient meafures, that would produce the falutary purpofes for which many characters of the firft abilities had been convened. The philofophic doctor Franklin obferved, when he lent his fignature to the adoption of the new conftitution, "that its complexion was doubtful; "that it might laft for ages, involve one quar-"ter of the globe, and probably terminate in "defpotifm."[3] He figned the inftrument for the confolidation of the government of the United States with tears, and apologized for doing it at all, from the doubts and apprehenfions he felt, that his countrymen might not be able to do better, even if they called a new convention.

Many of the intelligent yeomanry and of the great bulk of independent landholders, who had tafted the fweets of mediocrity, equality, and liberty, read every unconditional ratification of the new fyftem in filent anguifh, folded the folemn page with a figh, and wept over the names of the native fons of America, who had fold their lives to leave the legacy of freedom to their children. On this appearance of a confolidated government, which they thought required fuch important amendments, they feared that a dereliction of fome of their choiceft privileges might be fealed, without duly confidering the fatal confequences of too much precipitation. "The right of taxation, and the "command of the military," fays an ingenious writer, "is the completion of defpotifm." The laft of thefe was configned to the hands of the prefident, and the firft they feared would be too much under his influence. The obfervers of human conduct were not infenfible, that too much power vefted in the hands of any individual, was liable to abufes, either from his own paffions, or the fuggeftions of others, of lefs upright and immaculate intentions than himfelf.

Of thirteen ftate conventions, to which the conftitution was fubmitted, thofe

of Connecticut, New Jerfey, Pennfylvania, Delaware, Maryland, and Georgia,
ratified it unconditionally, and thofe of New Hampfhire, Maffachufetts, New
York, Virginia, and South Carolina, in full confidence of amendments, which
they thought neceffary, and propofed to the firft congrefs; the other two, of
Rhode Ifland and North Carolina, rejected it. Thus, it is evident that a majority of the ftates were convinced that the conftitution, as at firft propofed, endangered their liberties; that to the oppofition in the federal and ftate
conventions, are the public indebted for the amendments and amelioration of
the conftitution, which have united all parties in the vigorous fupport of it;
and that in a land of freedom, fovereignty, and independence, the great and
important affairs of ftate will be finally fubject to reafon, juftice, and found policy.

In this brilliant early history of the Revolutionary period, Mercy Otis Warren
of Massachusetts wrote of the opposition of the revolutionary generation to
the Constitution (see Mercy Otis Warren entry in *Biographies*). Although she
finished her account of the Constitution struggle with some hope for national
reconciliation, in the continued spirit of her opposition she described eloquently why so many loyal defenders of liberty had taken issue with the Constitution. Her warnings about excessive government, the rights of individuals,
and the future of the states sum up the Antifederalists' concerns as well as their
contributions to the ongoing discourse over the nature of governance in this
country.

REFERENCE

Mercy Otis Warren, *Rise and Progress of the American Revolution* (Boston: Adams and
Rhoades, 1805), vol. 3.

NOTES

1. This convention was compofed of fome gentlemen of the firft character and abilities; of fome men of fhining talents and doubtful character: fome of them were uniform republicans, others decided monarchifts, with a few neutrals, ready to join the
ftrongeft party. It was not ftrange there was much clafhing and debate, where fuch dif-
fentient opinions exifted: but after fome modification and conceffion, a conftitution was
formed, which when the amendments took place immediately on its adoption, the government of the United States ftood on a bafis which rendered the people refpectable
abroad and fafe at home.

2. Many amendments were made foon after the adoption of the conftitution.

3. See doctor Franklin's fpeech, on his figning the articles of the new conftitution
of government, which was to be laid before the people.

Index

Boldface characters are used to distinguish between the page numbers of the Biographies volume (**B**) and the Major Writings volume (**MW**). For example, page **B**xv is in the Biographies preface.

About the Author

JON L. WAKELYN is Professor of History at Kent State University. He is the author or editor of ten books, including *The Politics of a Literary Man*, *Southern Pamphlets on Secession*, *Leaders of th Americal Civil War*, *Southern and Unionist Pamphlets of the Civil War*, and *Confederates against the Confederacy*.